William Jorsen

Radford College

SALT WATER & PRINTER'S INK

SALT WATER
&
PRINTER'S INK

NORFOLK AND ITS NEWSPAPERS, 1865-1965

by

Lenoir Chambers

and

Joseph E. Shank

with a final chapter by

Harold Sugg

THE UNIVERSITY OF NORTH CAROLINA PRESS

CHAPEL HILL

PREFACE

A RECORD OF NEWSPAPERS AND THEIR PUBLISHERS AND EDITORS IS NECESsarily a record of the places where the newspapers were published and of the people who read them. Newspapers are an organic part of the life around them. They influence it and are influenced by it. As it changes, they change. A story of newspapers cannot help being a story of cities and regions, and in some degree of the nation. And if the newspapers' view of this life has the limitations of journalism, it also has the virtues of the sharp and instant focus that historians seek when they turn to the daily press for what people knew and thought at a given moment.

The origin of this book is to be found in the rounding out on November 21, 1965, of the hundredth year since *The Norfolk Virginian* began publication. The *Virginian* was the first native, independent newspaper to be established in Norfolk after the Civil War had killed or mortally wounded all prewar newspapers. Its very existence stimulated the establishment of other newspapers and so led the way down the lines of newspapers to the present *Virginian-Pilot* in the morning and *Ledger-Star* in the evening.

The dozen newspapers in these lines from 1865 to 1965 invoked a wide variety of personalities, often sparkling, rarely dull. The degree of talent as well as integrity among them is high, and the talent sometimes reaches brilliance. The courage is remarkable. It had to be: no cowards lived long in this contest for survival. The slow break away from old traditions, the broadening tolerance, and the gradual advance toward full participation in national life mark decade after decade. This is both an American and a human spectacle.

As business, this century of newspaper publication in Norfolk shows vividly how easy it was to start a newspaper in the poverty of the late 1860's and the 1870's and even later, but how difficult it was for the creators of those newspapers to lead them into the eras when newspapers were growing larger, more machinery was required, costs were higher, and effective management was vital. The early beginners were rarely business men, and when competition increased they rarely survived. In time the newspaper manager was found to be as essential as the newspaper editor. In time the newspaper without competence in the counting room died. In a city where newspapers once were numerous, the record of this hundred years shows why they grew into the few that were better.

Thus the Norfolk newspaper story over these hundred years is more revealing than the life of a single city might suggest. Not that Norfolk was ever a merely conventional city. Its very location made it different from the inland regions and most of the larger American cities, and its severe early experiences hardened many of the differences. It was born of the sea. The Atlantic is its front yard and western Europe is a neighbor. It was a cosmopolitan community when it was a village. Often it was forced to be self-reliant; often it was independent in its thinking. Always it was affected immediately and often disastrously by war. But if Norfolk possesses, and over the decades has exhibited, aspects that sometimes can be called unique, the newspaper record in many essentials has aspects of universality.

The sources of this record are, in very large degree, the files of the newspapers that came together to form the present newspapers: the *Virginian*, the *Journal*, the *Landmark*, the *Pilot*, the *Virginian-Pilot*, the *Virginian-Pilot and the Norfolk Landmark*, which later was abbreviated to the *Virginian-Pilot* again, all morning newspapers; and the *Public Ledger*, the *Dispatch*, the *Portsmouth Star*, the *Ledger-Dispatch*, the *Ledger-Dispatch and the Portsmouth Star*, and the *Ledger-Star*, all evening newspapers.

In 1958 Frank Batten, publisher of the present newspapers, engaged the recently retired *Ledger-Dispatch* news editor, Joseph E. Shank, to examine the files page by page and to record information relating to the newspapers themselves and to events that were significant in their broader history.

This was an enormous task. For most of the subsequent years, Mr. Shank carried it forward with intelligence and persistence. He reduced the vast wordage of all these newspapers to approximately a million words of notes in narrative style. They form a rare collection among newspaper records in America. In addition, Mr. Shank interviewed persons who had been connected earlier with the newspapers, or members of their families, and obtained written recollections from retired editors, reporters, and others. He is grateful to them all for valuable information.

In 1963 Mr. Batten engaged me, then recently retired from the editorship of the *Virginian-Pilot* (earlier editor of the *Ledger-Dispatch*) to write the history. Investigation of historical sources in Norfolk, in Virginia, and elsewhere, and other preliminary work were necessary. Minute books of stockholders' and directors' meetings of several of the newspapers were made available. But all this was auxiliary. The story emerges primarily from the newspaper-eye views of the times and of life itself, as it was recorded in the files.

Mr. Batten and Paul S. Huber, Jr., president of Norfolk-Portsmouth Newspapers, Inc., the publishing corporation, have contributed, freely and without restriction, information and documents of various kinds. The history as a project came under the responsibility of Harold G. Sugg, assistant publisher. He has devoted much time to the publishing arrangements and has been helpful in many other respects, including the writing of the final chapter. Appropriately that chapter is wholly his work rather than mine.

I am indebted to Robert Mason, editor of the *Virginian-Pilot*, in particular for assistance in the tangles of the *Virginian-Pilot's* reporting of the original flights of the Wright brothers, and to William H. Fitzpatrick, editor of the *Ledger-Star*, for sound counsel. Charles L. Kaufman, corporation counsel and a member of the board of directors, clarified certain corporation details. Mrs. Samuel L. Slover has given valuable information about her husband's career.

I have made use many times of records in the newspapers' library where Miss Bess Whitworth, the librarian, and her staff put themselves to much trouble in searching out details. Members of the staff of the Norfolk Public Library under Arthur M. Kirkby, its librarian, especially in the Sargeant Room (local history) in the Kirn Memorial Library under Mrs. Virginia Pinkerton, were unfailingly sympathetic to numerous requests for aid.

I am grateful to other librarians, including Mrs. Elizabeth G. Freeman of the Petersburg Public Library; Richard F. Lancaster of the Virginia Room of the Roanoke Public Library; Miss Lottie E. Driver of the Newport News Public Library; Mrs. Sarah W. Flannery, Co-ordinator for the Humanities, and Kenneth C. Barnes, Periodical and Newspaper Department, of the Boston Public Library; Stanley F. Dunnetski, Newspaper Service, Chicago Public Library; and the librarian of the Cincinnati *Enquirer*.

Mrs. Robert L. Thompson, of Raleigh, North Carolina, was especially and generously helpful in producing information about her kinsman, Charles Pinckney Sapp, the young *Virginian-Pilot* editor. Dean Norval Neil Luxon, of the Journalism School of the University of North Carolina, and John Hohenberg, of the faculty of the Columbia University Graduate School of Journalism and secretary of the Advisory Board on the Pulitzer Prizes, furnished me useful information. B. W. Baker, of Portsmouth, and John B. Jenkins, Jr., of Norfolk, helped me at moments when I was puzzled, and Armistead Bayne, of Norfolk, aided frequently. James E. Mays, Ronald J. Primm, and Robert L. Yingling of the newspapers' staff assembled with zest and considerable labor the pictures and illustrative material. Most of the illustrations are from the ancient cameras of the late Charles Borjes, who was a *Virginian-Pilot* institution, and H. D. Vollmer, retired but still a contributing columnist for the *Ledger-Star*. I am indebted to my first reader, Mrs. Peggy Patrick, for typing and retyping badly mutilated copy with cheerfulness.

And to scores of authors of newspaper histories I give thanks, after reading their books again or for the first time, for their showing me what I should attempt to do in writing this chapter in the history of American newspapers.

Norfolk   LENOIR CHAMBERS
December, 1966

CONTENTS

ILLUSTRATIONS

A GENEALOGY OF THE VIRGINIAN-PILOT AND THE LEDGER-STAR

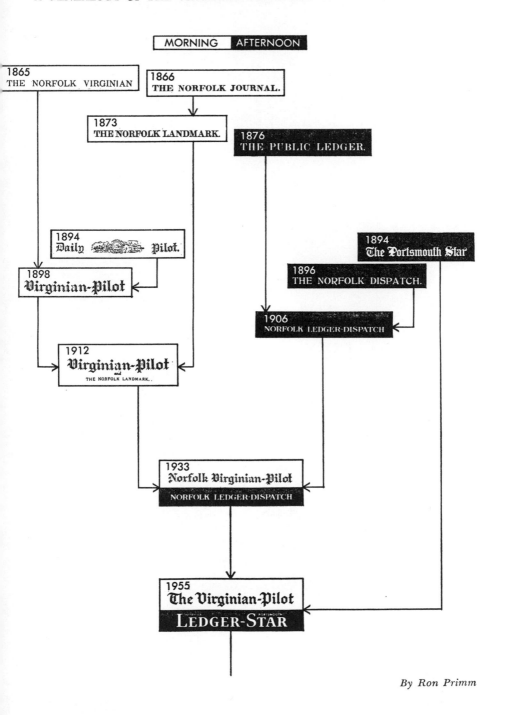

By Ron Primm

SALT WATER & PRINTER'S INK

THE LONG RECORD OF NORFOLK NEWSPAPERS, STARTING WITH THE WEEKLY *Virginia Gazette Or, Norfolk Intelligencer* in 1774, is cut in two as though by an ax by the American Civil War. The newspapers that were published before the Civil War belonged to an age that died with the war and in so doing carried the last of its newspapers with it. The newspapers that came into existence after the Civil War belonged to an era that was new and separate and different.

Since the end of the prewar era and the death of all newspapers born of the military occupation, one hundred years have now passed. The record of the newspapers that began with this hundred years leads directly to the newspapers published now. It leads from 1865 to the 1960's, from the new life that emerged slowly after the great American tragedy to the life of all America today and to the nature and character of modern American journalism.

The earliest of the Norfolk newspapers of the post-Civil War century was the first of the ancestors of the present newspapers; *The Norfolk Virginian*, born on the morning of Tuesday, November 21, 1865.

It was a bleak time to be born. Lee had surrendered only seven months earlier. Jefferson Davis was a heavily guarded prisoner in a Fort Monroe casemate almost in sight across Hampton Roads. Union soldiers who had ruled Norfolk in a military occupation rarely matched in American history still walked the streets. No one knew whether Virginia would be a state of the Union again, or under what conditions, or when. No one could confidently define, in the constitutional sense, what Virginia was at the moment. But one thing Norfolk did know: it knew the meaning of defeat.

Now, in this autumn of 1865, Norfolk—with its 15,000 population, two-thirds white, one-third Negro—lay in economic depression and social and political confusion. The Negroes were exuberant, and their exuberance and the prospect of their voting seemed to the old leadership even more ominous for the future than their reveling in the freedom of idleness did for the present. For most people of Norfolk the loss of civil government, the subjection to military rule with its inevitable bitterness, clashes, and tragedies, the isolation from natural travel and trade and contacts and associations, the inescapable poverty—all these in addition to the deaths on the battlefield and the humiliation of surrender—had reduced the city to physical distress and spiritual gloom.

When he took command of the region late in 1863, Major General Benjamin F. Butler called Norfolk "the filthiest place I ever saw where there were human inhabitants of a civilized order. . . . I found the streets, wharves, and squares . . . in a most filthy, ruinous, and disordered state, so much so that life and limb are not safe upon them to the wayfarer. . . . I found the fire department entirely disorganized and its material out of repairs and useless. The city was unlighted for months . . . it was impossible to properly guard or police it."[1]

Nor did Mrs. Butler, living in the command headquarters in Fort Monroe, discover a more pleasant scene. To her son in Massachusetts she wrote late in 1863:

> We are not very lively. . . . The walls of the Fortress shut us in like a prison. . . . Day before yesterday we [Mrs. Butler and her daughter, Blanche] were over to Norfolk, and came home worried to death. Norfolk is an old town, the buildings mostly of brick, and pavements uneven and broken, we were sadly jolted and shook riding over them. We went through the town and out to see the fortifications, then crossed the ferry to Portsmouth, and went all through the Gosport Navy Yard. The rebels tried to destroy it, but the docks were so splendidly built of stone and solid masonry, the buildings of brick and iron, that they could neither burn nor blast them altogether, but they injured a great deal that will take a long time to repair. . . .[2]

That was two years before the birth of the *Virginian*. Only six months before it was born the young Washington reporter and war correspondent, Whitelaw Reid from Ohio—later proprietor and editor of the New York *Tribune*, minister to France, ambassador to the

1. Benjamin F. Butler, *Private and Official Correspondence of Major-General Benjamin F. Butler During the Period of the Civil War* (Norwood, Massachusetts, 1917), III, 452.
2. *Ibid.*, p. 194.

Court of St. James's in London, and Republican candidate for Vice President in 1892—set out on a trip through the Southern states. When he arrived at Norfolk in May of 1865 the military met him with carriages, and

> . . . we were whirled rapidly past the tumble-down warehouses, through streets of stores from which every former proprietor had gone . . . past elegant residences of prominent Rebels, in whose parlors sat the wives of Yankee officers. . . . Norfolk ought to do, and will do a fine business—whenever it has any country to do business for. It must always be the great shipping point for the Virginia and North Carolina coast. . . . But, thus far, there is scarcely any business, save what the army has brought, and what the impoverished inhabitants who remain are themselves able to support. Sutlers have sat in the high places until they have amassed fortunes; but the merchants whose deserted store rooms they are occupying are paroled and ruined rebel officers. . . . And the very number of able-bodied men in the country has been sadly reduced.[3]

The war and the military occupation that brought this woe had killed or mortally wounded all daily newspapers that were being published in April of 1861. Gone was the *Norfolk & Portsmouth Herald* that began as a biweekly in 1794 and as a daily in 1840. Gone was the *Daily Courier* that was established in 1844 and, in the obscure transactions of the occupation period, was "succeeded" by a newspaper of another name. Gone was the *Daily Southern Argus* that in 1848 raised the Democratic flag in a Whig town under the slogan, "Southern Views and Southern Rights." It died in 1861.

Gone too was the *American Beacon,* founded in 1815 as a daily newspaper and therefore the earliest of the daily newspapers of Norfolk. It disappeared in times of such confusion that it is difficult now to mark the precise moment of its death. And across the Elizabeth River, in Portsmouth, gone was the *Daily Transcript,* born in 1849, a victim of the first year of the war.

The only prewar newspaper that did survive the war and the occupation, the *Day Book,* was suspended for three years during the war by military authorities and was so badly damaged in the process that complete recovery after the war proved impossible. The break between prewar and postwar is not the less definite and historic because the *Day Book* dragged on until January, 1881.

To fill the vacuum created by the death of the prewar newspapers,

---

3. Whitelaw Reid, *After the War: A Southern Tour—May 1, 1865, to May 1, 1866* (New York, 1866) pp. 18-20.

and to make their own governmental administration easier, the Union military commanders established or encouraged and nourished the occupation press. In less than a month after Major General John E. Wool landed six thousand troops at Ocean View and marched on May 10, 1862, into unresisting Norfolk, the Norfolk *Union* began to appear. In 1863, the *Old Dominion* was born of Union sympathizers in Portsmouth and shortly moved across the Elizabeth River to Norfolk. Before the year ran out the *Daily Times* was established. All these published military orders, printed a little local news, and circulated governmental propaganda.

Early in 1864, a few weeks after Major General Benjamin F. Butler took command of the Department of Virginia and North Carolina —wearing a bad reputation in Confederate judgment after his command of the New Orleans occupation—he established the best of the occupation newspapers, the *New Regime*. An officer of his staff, Captain John Clark, directed its operation. Clark had been an editor and one of the proprietors of the Boston *Courier* and was a capable newspaperman. After Butler moved away early in 1865, the *New Regime* ceased publication, but Clark and his associates established in June, 1865, the Norfolk *Post*.

The *Post* was a lively newspaper for a few months. But no such newspaper could hope for success in the Norfolk that was emerging as the military control began to fade. The time had arrived for postwar Norfolk to produce out of its own life, and out of the life around it, its own newspapers. The *Virginian* was the first response to that need and that challenge.

The *Virginian* was created by a group of printers and editors from Petersburg operating under the title of G. A. Sykes & Co., in which Gustavus Adolphus Sykes and Anthony M. Keiley were the partners, and J. Richard Lewellen was an associate. (E. B. Branch, who was associated with Sykes and Keiley in Petersburg operations, may have had an interest too.) They knew printing and press work and possessed some equipment and supplies, although after four years of war their inventory could not have been large. But they were not novices. They had learned what it meant to publish a newspaper in Virginia in 1865.

Sykes and Lewellen were native Virginians, the latter with Mexican War experience and a long Civil War record that had advanced him to lieutenant colonel in Mahone's Brigade. Keiley came out of New Jersey when two years old, attended the University of Virginia, and turned immediately to newspaper work and politics. He too was a Confederate officer and had been wounded and captured. He joined Sykes and Branch in establishing the Petersburg *Daily News* less than five weeks after Appomattox.

There Keiley defended the South in his editorial columns and criticized Northern radicals. Military authorities locked the doors of the *Daily News* and carried the editor off to Richmond to cool his heels—and his head—in Castle Thunder prison. In three days they let him out without trial, on parole. The *Daily News* was dead, but Sykes, Branch, and Keiley quickly produced the Petersburg *Index*. It had softer tones and an untarnished publisher, W. L. Williams. Their own roles as proprietors were not acknowledged for a year. They knew that Petersburg wanted a newspaper that, in their own words, reflected the true sentiments of the people.

And then, looking around with a sharp eye, they knew that Norfolk and Portsmouth, lacking such a newspaper, wished and needed one too. They launched the *Virginian*. Sykes and Keiley remained in Petersburg with the *Index*. Lewellen moved to Norfolk as business manager of the *Virginian*.

Keiley was editor and wrote editorials, perhaps aided by a young protege, William E. Cameron, who in time would be one of the notable figures in the *Virginian*'s history—and the state's. But an editor was needed on the spot to be in daily and hourly charge, to contribute familiarity with the Norfolk and lower Tidewater scene, and to present visible and personal evidence of local rootage. The *Virginian* found its man. "We have secured," the Prospectus of G. A. Sykes & Co. announced, "the services of James Barron Hope, Esq., as Associate Editor, a gentleman whose elegant pen and thorough knowledge of, and devotion to, the interests of Virginia, need no commendation at our hands."

Hope was then thirty-six years old and a descendant of the Barron family that had been connected since the Revolution with American naval operations. He was born in the Gosport Navy Yard in Portsmouth while his grandfather, Commodore James Barron (the younger), was its commandant. After early schooling in Germantown, Pennsylvania, when the Commodore was commandant of the Philadelphia Navy Yard, and in Hampton, Virginia, where his parents lived (Wilton Hope and Jane Barron Hope), he graduated from the College of William and Mary in 1847.

As the civilian secretary of his uncle, Captain Samuel Barron of the United States Navy, young Hope saw something of naval life while cruising in the West Indies. Then he studied law. And then, in

April, 1849, he fought, on the beach near Fort Monroe, one of the celebrated duels of the times. His opponent, J. Pembroke Jones, was an ensign in the United States Navy and eventually would be a Confederate naval officer of distinction among the ironclads. At the first shots both duelists fell severely wounded. Hampton Roads blazed with excitement.

After both men recovered, their difficulty (in the words of the *Virginian* of a later day) was "most honorably adjusted."

By 1857 Hope was Commonwealth's Attorney in Hampton and simultaneously the poet for the 250th anniversary celebration of the Jamestown settlement. He had written poems for the *Southern Literary Messenger* and other magazines under the pen name of "The Late Henry Ellen, Esq." Many of them were included in his first volume of verse, published in 1857. A year later he was the poet at the dedication of Crawford's statue of George Washington that stands today in Capitol Square in Richmond and the Phi Beta Kappa poet at graduation exercises at the College of William and Mary. These public poems, of which he wrote others later, were long and serious efforts, much admired in their day.

In the early months of the war Hope was the secretary of Commodore French Forrest, commandant of the Gosport Navy Yard where he had been born. He wrote occasionally for the Norfolk *Day Book.* Later as an army captain he was with Joseph E. Johnston at the surrender in North Carolina that came after Appomattox.

When the *Virginian* engaged him as associate editor, Hope was better known as a literary personality, a tall, slender figure, much admired for his sensitive spirit and his courteous instincts and manners. He had yet to prove his newspaper ability in the competition of the market place, but few people doubted that he was able. For a new newspaper in Norfolk, especially one established by men from out of town, Hope was a valuable asset. The proprietors knew it. They put his name at the top of the editorial page—the only name that was there.

These men were all looking toward the future, where their careers would be made, not—save in moments of memory—to the past. Lewellen and Hope were Norfolk newspaper figures for many years. Keiley went far: to the Richmond newspaper field and the mayoralty of the capital; to state politics and Democratic state chairman; to appointments from President Cleveland as minister to Rome and to Vienna, only to encounter technical objections in those capitals that turned him back, and eventually to an international court in Cairo that dealt with Turkish problems in the Middle East. They gave much to the *Virginian* in character, professional capacity, and a variety of talents. The one thing they could not give was capital. In this respect, too, they were representative of the new day.

Much of the spirit of the founders glows in the Prospectus, printed in early issues of the *Virginian* and signed "G. A. Sykes & Co." "We design," the new owners proclaimed, "that the VIRGINIAN shall be especially devoted to the advancement and prosperity of Norfolk and her sister city [Portsmouth], and the large section of Virginia whose interests are common with theirs." Then to the first manifestation of frankness both for readers at home and upstate:

> Under a uniform system of partial legislation—under the unfounded jealousy of other cities, but, far more than all else, under the apathy, indifference and want of energy of her own people, Norfolk has gradually dwindled from the first to the last place among the great Atlantic ports, until in domestic trade, in foreign commerce, and in the wealth and enterprise devoted to both, she is of less importance today than she was forty years ago.

This plain talk demanded immediate amplification. The Prospectus developed the *Virginian*'s convictions and purposes thus:

> We shall labor to convince our fellow-citizens throughout the Commonwealth, that Virginia can never be a wealthy and powerful state until she fosters commerce. We shall endeavor to prove to the people of other cities in the state, that the prosperity of Norfolk is their prosperity, her interests theirs, her decline their loss.
>
> But, chiefly we shall endeavor to convince the capitalists, the merchants, the professional men, the mechanics and artizans of Norfolk and Portsmouth, that it lies with them to say whether, with all their unsurpassed advantages, with two lines of railroad penetrating the richest regions of this and neighboring states, with a continuous communication with the Mississippi, with a noble river penetrating the heart of Virginia and whose navigation to its very falls is rarely suspended, with canals connecting them with the most fertile portion of North Carolina, with a harbor confessedly, in its spaciousness, in its safety, its ease of access and its uniform accessibility without an equal on the North Atlantic coast, these cities shall continue to be a mere dependency of Baltimore, instead of taking rank, as they deserve, with the foremost marts of the continent.
>
> To display these advantages, to stimulate immigration, to attract capital, and to awaken the energy and enterprise of our

fellow-citizens, are objects to which we shall devote whatever of zeal, ability, experience and all the resources and capital we can command.

"The partial legislation," the "unfounded jealousy of other cities," and the references to cities as a source of help, all reflected awareness of historic economic struggles and of political realities. The port with its shipping and its spirit of trade, its outward look and its more cosmopolitan population, the Norfolk "with salt in her veins and seaweed in her hair" (as a much later *Virginian-Pilot* editor, Louis I. Jaffé, once described her), had been significantly different from upstate and rural Virginia in activity and thought since the Seventeenth Century and often economically at odds with it. In early struggles for railroad routing and connections and state support, the fall line cities and the rural life surrounding them sometimes had combined against the city by the sea. In moments of bitterness the cry had been raised in Norfolk that it should unite with North Carolina. Much history, much frustration, then and later, is suggested by the Prospectus.

With the flag of economic development thus raised, the *Virginian*'s owners and editors turned to what they called "now the prominent topics of political controversy." They pledged "cordial support to the magnanimous policy" of President Johnson. As to the Civil War and its aftermath:

> We accept . . . , frankly and fully, the results of this war. We admit that slavery is destroyed—not by proclamation, for there is no power or source of law—but by the final fiat of arms, and we concede our duty to conform our legislation to this great change.
>
> Since it has been determined by force of arms that Virginia must live *in* the Union we hold it to be the duty of all to see that she is *of* the Union. We hold that military rule is foreign to the genius of our government and the spirit of our people, and utterly incompatible with liberty, and that its exercise is justified alone by temporary and exceptional conditions and circumstances, which it is the highest duty of good citizenship to remove as speedily as possible.
>
> We hold test oaths to be unconstitutional, tyrannical, subversive of the sanctity of a civil oath, a fatal and facile engine of oppression.
>
> We contend that forty centuries of experiment, in every possible situation, have failed to furnish one argument or fact evincing the capacity of the negro for equal participation with white men in a republican form of government.

Finally, we conceive it to be our duty as citizens to cultivate friendly political relations with the citizens of all portions of our common Union . . . .

On its editorial page on this first day the *Virginian* emphasized with more of a literary flourish (probably the mark of Hope) some of these ideas and some others it embraced and would seek to live by: "We have seen many of our theories of state sovereignty sent to the tomb of all the Capulets. We have seen our entire system of labor subverted in an hour by the fiat of arms. . . . We appealed to the arbitration of battle, and when the fight was done, we sheathed our swords, and said, like King Francis (not without some comfort in the thought), we have not lost our honor. . . . We accepted the result all the more cheerfully because we were familiar with the views and opinions which had been discussed and argued before the war."

Then to what the *Virginian* wanted to stress most:

"But we were not prepared, nor are we now prepared to entertain the idea of negro suffrage.

"Those who advocate this measure are apparently ignorant of the fact that the elective franchise is a *political, not a natural right—that it is a question of public policy, not of individual conception."*

The heavy coloration of troubled times permeated these words. The Thirteenth Amendment was not yet part of the Constitution, though it would be in a month; the Fourteenth and Fifteenth Amendments would not be ratified until 1868 and 1870. Andrew Johnson seemed to most Virginians a far better hope than Thaddeus Stevens. The state had a civil government of sorts, headed by Governor Francis Harrison Pierpont. He had risen to office in West Virginia after the breakoff in 1861 of twenty-four counties, and he exercised theoretical control over those parts of Virginia which Federal arms reached, and ultimately all of it, though the real power remained in the hands of military authorities.

Nearly all conditions of life would grow worse before they began to grow better. The *Virginian*'s choice, however, was clear. "If," the first editorial on its first day of publication declared, "we stand firmly by the honor, interests and rights of the gallant, generous people of our State with intelligent zeal, with unfaltering devotion, with an honest sincerity, born of the conviction and the fact that their cause is ours—has been and shall be—we forecast with confidence the establishment of the VIRGINIAN among institutions of Norfolk."

The first reader who picked up the first *Virginian* held in his hands a four-page newspaper with six columns to the page. The pages were an inch and a half shorter than the pages of a century later and about a half-inch broader. The columns were broader by more than a half-inch. At the top of the front page was a masthead severe in its simplicity, with no sign of a curlicue. The words, "The Norfolk Virginian," in hand-drawn letters of a size close to sixty-point and of a type design much like Bodoni, caught the eye first.

The type in the body of the columns was smaller than that used a century later: seven-point then against nine-point now. Most headlines were only a little larger than the body type. They were confined to one-column width, had few banks—or additional lines—and generally none at all. In striking contrast to modern front pages, this front page lacked fresh, recently developed news and tended more to long, magazine-type articles, sometimes with paragraphs a column long. The effect was that of a sweep of gray across the page.

This was largely because the *Virginian*, like most newspapers of its day, was printed on a flatbed press, not a rotary one. Two of its pages, the front page and the back page, were printed simultaneously on one sheet of paper. Then the sheet of paper was turned over, and the pages two and three were printed simultaneously on the opposite side. Proper folding produced pages in consecutive order. Generally there was a distinct interval, which might last for hours, between the printing of pages one and four and of pages two and three.

For advertisements the initial charges were seventy-five cents for "one square," which meant ten lines or less, one column wide, and forty cents for each repetition. This was for daily or "transient" advertising. "For terms of advertising per quarter, apply at this office," the *Virginian* advised. "All advertisements," it warned, "are collectable in advance."

A subscription for a year cost $8.00, payable in advance; for six months, $5.00; for any period less than six months, $1.00 a month. Subscribers in Norfolk and Portsmouth "will have the paper left by Carriers at TWENTY CENTS per week." Single copies were five cents. There was no Sunday issue until 1874, and when the *Virginian* began publishing on Sunday it ceased to publish a Monday edition.

Norfolk's city limits extended then from the Elizabeth River waterfront south of the original Main Street axis of the first town to a northern boundary along part of present Princess Anne Road. The western boundary followed the waterfront from Town Point into The Hague (so named later) and then ran from the Botetourt-Mowbray Arch area northeastward to the eventual Princess Anne Road line between Cedar Grove and Elmwood Cemeteries, and thence eastward to the Hebrew cemetery. There the boundary turned abruptly southward along a line in the Newton's Creek of that day, east of Chapel and Landing Streets, until it reached the Elizabeth River near the later Norfolk & Western Railway station and warehouses.

These 1.3 square miles were cut up by inlets, creeks, and marshes. Decades and millions of dollars would be necessary to drain off, fill in, build up, cover and pave these ancient proofs of Norfolk's intimate relationship with the sea. The low, sluggish water was often the dump for a community that had no engineered sewerage system and was hard put, in its flat lowland, to discover or provide clean water for daily living. The war and the occupation accentuated all these problems.

But this was, even in all its 1865 dilapidation, a city with distinctive structures; the City Hall with its columns and dome at the head of Back Creek, later the Court House and then the MacArthur Memorial; the Custom House with its high steps on Main Street near the foot of Granby Street; St. Paul's Episcopal Church, the dean of houses of worship, with roots long before the American Revolution; Norfolk Academy's classical lines on Bank Street that later became the Juvenile and Domestic Relations Court; the Atlantic and the National Hotels on Main Street; the cluster of churches in the Cumberland-Bank-Charlotte-Freemason neighborhood; and the residences on and near Granby and on Main, Bute, Charlotte, Freemason, and Cumberland Streets.

Business had concentrated largely on Main Street and immediately adjacent streets, principally to the south. Its center of activity was near the juncture of Main and Market Square.

Close to the center of this area stood the first quarters of the *Virginian,* a narrow, three-story building on the south side of Main Street between Commerce Street and Roanoke Avenue, nearly opposite Atlantic Street. There it remained for three years. For part of that time at least it would appear that the mechanical work of the newspaper was done in a building on the east side of Commerce Street, in the rear of the "counting house." Nearly all of its normal sources of news were within easy walking distance.

Four other daily newspapers were being published in Norfolk when the *Virginian* first appeared: the *Day Book,* the *Old Dominion,* the *Daily Times,* and the *Post.* But the fifth newspaper had advantages which the other four lacked. It had the combination of Virginia background, Confederate respectability, and professional competence.

It lacked capital, and it was competing in a community already over-staffed with newspapers. The region had only so much to offer in circulation or advertising revenue, and a five-way division flattened out the possibilities. The *Virginian* had to struggle desperately from the start, and the hard times of its early months shook its owners and editors.

THE NEW NEWSPAPER FOUND MUCH TO REPORT AND DISCUSS. COMMODORE Matthew Fontaine Maury, the much respected Virginian with Annapolis training who had pioneered in the geography of the oceans before returning to his native state for the war, was refugeeing in Mexico. Emperor Maximilian appointed him commissioner of immigration.

With this news the *Virginian* published a long appeal by the former Tennessee governor, Isham G. Harris, on opportunities for Virginians in Mexico, where he was. In January it published a column and a half from Maury himself. The Confederate colony in Mexico City thought Maximilian's position was assured, and it assumed his blessing of the immigration campaign would heighten its appeal. The *Virginian* admired Maury as a man and as "the great nautical philosopher." It thought his appeal "the most condensed, and at the same time the most comprehensive view of Mexico ever laid before the American public."

"But," the newspaper continued, "we most earnestly enter our protest against its main suggestion. . . . There never was a time in the history of Virginia when the presence of population was so vital a necessity as now. It becomes our bounden duty to stay right here, and with head and heart and hand and mind and soul and body devote ourselves to the upbuilding of the Old Dominion."

Another Civil War echo disturbed the *Virginian*. A report came in—from Houston, Texas, which had it from a Virginia clergyman—that the widow of Stonewall Jackson was destitute. This filled the *Virginian* "with pain, surprise and incredulity . . . we deem it our duty most respectfully to suggest to the Virginia legislature . . . the propriety, not to say necessity, of making an inquiry into the facts of the case. Impoverished as we are, a sum by popular subscription could be raised tomorrow in Virginia amply large enough to secure the disconsolate relict of the great soldier against the possibility of want . . . ."

A much broader result of the war disturbed the *Virginian* more. In December of 1865 it discussed a New York *Tribune* report that sixty-five thousand former slaves had drifted into Williamsburg and the nearby counties of York, Warwick, and James City. The freedmen were reported "eking out a scanty and precarious existence by fishing in summer and oystering in winter."

The *Virginian* saw this as a disturbing economic problem. "Every interest in the state demands labor," it declared. "Systematic labor will receive at once a fair compensation, but the fact that our improved lands are going out of cultivation shows, in a most melancholy and forcible manner, how far the demand is in excess of the supply. The negro . . . should be made to comprehend his new duties, and rendered tributary to the wants of the country."

Three months later, in March of 1866, the *Virginian* returned to this subject. Efforts to encourage former slaves to migrate to Liberia were having little success. Another effort to induce surplus Negro population to settle in Florida was doing no better. But "can they subsist where they are?" the newspaper asked. "The region upon which they are settled from Williamsburg to Hampton is vastly overcrowded . . . . The lands about them have gone out of cultivation . . . it is perfectly apparent that if they remain where they are, they must sink into the most abject poverty; for the source from which they received such abundant supply of ready money is permanently dry. . . ."

"But," the *Virginian* continued, "there is another class of people entitled to some consideration at the hands of the government. The impoverished and ruined inhabitants of that fertile region, which once was blooming like a garden, deserve a moment's serious thought . . . the entire tract of country from Yorktown to Old Point presents a grim contrast to what it was five years ago. . . . The face of the country has been seared and blistered by war. . . . The desolation is complete. . . ."

In reporting news from Richmond the *Virginian* was running about three days late, the mark of the passage of the mails from Richmond to Norfolk. It was even later when reprinting from more distant cities. In December, 1865, it had published with delight a statement from the acting postmaster general that mail service was "to commence January 1." But on January 10 a Suffolk letter writer complained that it had taken seventeen days for a letter to go the eighteen miles from Suffolk to Norfolk, and added: "At present, our postmaster receives and sends his mail from and to Norfolk by private arrangement, which is the best we can do." And on March 22, the *Virginian* said that "we now receive mail from Richmond only every other day." It suggested that if James River boat operators would not provide daily mail service, an arrangement should be made with the Norfolk & Petersburg Railroad—a slightly longer route but a more assured form of transportation.

There were other complaints that winter and spring of 1866, and other signs of recovery too, all characteristic of the times. St. Paul's Episcopal Church, "nearly 130 years old, having been erected in 1739," reopened in February after being "closed for so long a time" and would "perhaps survive the ravages of time and the devastations of war another hundred years or more."

The Twentieth New York Infantry, long in Portsmouth, marched out and sailed away on January 29. "There are no troops now in Portsmouth," sang the *Virginian*. But the Twelfth United States Infantry remained in Norfolk, and Brevet Major General A. T. Torbert ("Commander of the Post" with headquarters on Granby Street) symbolized Federal authority. The Macon house in Portsmouth "which has been used as a barracks or headquarters, has been turned over to the proprietor, but we understand," the *Virginian* continued, "the building has been much abused and is in very bad condition."

It was not the only thing the *Virginian* thought was in bad condition. Portsmouth streets, it announced in February, "are in filthy condition and require immediate cleansing." In Norfolk, the editor had said a little earlier, "the streets are filthy, and so are the lots—cesspools of corruption." The newspaper was sharp with the Select Council (one of the city's two legislative bodies, the other being the Common Council) for its refusal to provide four assistant inspectors requested by the Board of Health to help clean the city. "The Select Council," it said, "assumed a responsibility which is without warrant. They are not professional men. . . . . If the victims of cholera or yellow fever fill our cemeteries, upon them will rest the responsibilities."

Nor did the *Virginian* like the manner in which the Norfolk-Portsmouth ferries were being operated. Military authorities had turned the property back to Portsmouth and Norfolk County, joint owners. But stopping the ferry operation at night at nine o'clock seemed to the newspaper "a backward movement" and "against the spirit of the times. We apprehend," it added, that "the ferry is in dead hands."

The editors didn't like the police situation in Norfolk either. "We practically have no police. If we are not robbed in our houses we run the risk of being garroted upon the streets." (A hundred years later they might have said "yoked.") "To rank as a city," the *Virginian* added, "there are two reforms we must have—a corporation court judge and an efficient police force." The latter, it warned, would have to be well paid.

Policemen were not the only lack. "Water, Water All Around and Not a Drop for Manufacturing Purposes," ran a *Virginian* headline. It dropped the water problem briefly to recite the virtues of Fort Norfolk on its western flank as a site for a naval base for ironclad vessels which Washington was believed to be looking for, though nothing came of that idea. But it returned to the subject when an engineer reported that tapping Lake Drummond in Dismal Swamp for drinking water was worth the effort. The "juniper water" to be had there, the engineer thought, was "remarkable for its sanitary qualities when unadulterated with whiskey." Norfolk had no city water supply system. People relied on wells and cisterns.

Most of these subjects of news and editorial comment were normal material for newspapers, and the *Virginian* treated them normally and with the frankness it had promised in its Prospectus. But it was also a spokesman for a defeated people, now in distress, who were not happy about the rising political power in Congress. Nothing that winter and spring surpassed the *Virginian*'s interest in events in Washington that would mark the course of the future for Virginia.

The *Virginian* had seen President Johnson as the hope of the South against "radical machinations in Congress" emanating from a faction "with the knavery of cowards and the cowardice of knaves." These Congressmen—the *Virginian* was thinking of Sumner and Stevens and their followers—"finding from official information that the rebels were disarmed, and utterly helpless and harmless, and had been following the plow for eight months, determined that this was a most fortunate as well as perfectly safe opportunity to indulge that petty instinct of tyranny which leads the meanly wicked to torture the helpless."

"To the assault they are making on civil liberty and natural right," the *Virginian* said in December, 1865, "the strongest barrier is the simple dignity of these conquered provinces." To this theme the newspaper returned again and again. It noted with satisfaction that the eight Virginians elected to Congress but rejected by Congress had returned quietly to their homes. Then it declared: "Let the people imitate, as we believe they have inspired, this dignified example. . . . The day of deliverance will come. This great Commonwealth, older by generations than the Union, will assuredly survive Thaddeus Stevens and Charles Sumner. She will live when the American people will blush at their memory—but blush still more at the folly and fanaticism which gave them power. Meanwhile, let us plant and water and God will give the increase."

In this spirit the *Virginian* said in February that President Johnson, then deep in his struggle with Congress, "deserves the support of every right-thinking man." Before the month was out, it had to say that "the rupture between the President and Congress is now complete." It needed four columns that day to report the political storms in Washington. When Johnson vetoed the civil rights bill in March, the *Virginian* published, with evident relish, the full text of the veto message on page one though it ran to three columns. The only other news on that page was General Lee's testimony before the Senate subcommittee investigating whether any of "the so-called Confederate States of America" were entitled to be represented in Congress.

But Congress overrode the President's veto of the civil rights bill, and a Negro parade in Norfolk on April 16 to celebrate the event led to the killing of two white persons and a Negro. Though Federal troops restored order temporarily, armed bands of white men killed several Negroes that night, and lesser disorders continued. It was Norfolk's worst violence in the Reconstruction period.

The *Virginian* reported both sides of the national debate on Reconstruction. It published not only Ohio Senator Ben Wade's savage attack on the President in March but a *Chicago Tribune* editorial which declared "the power in the rebel states can never pass into the hands of loyal anti-slavery men until the change is effected by the colored voter. If any state is not prepared for this, let it wait. . . . The ballot is essential to liberty." Yet the *Virginian* undoubtedly agreed with General Lee's statement: "My own opinion is that, at this time, they [Negroes] cannot vote intelligently. . . . What the future may prove . . . I cannot say."

Throughout these early months the *Virginian*, a new newspaper competing with four others, could hardly have produced much in profits. It changed from six columns per page to seven in January, 1866, six weeks after it began publication, thereby gaining four columns for news or advertisements, although all columns now were narrower. In March it announced that after receiving "the enormous bill . . . for one month's consumption of gas, amounting to $136.80, we have been experimenting." It experimented with twenty-one kerosene lamps as replacements for seventeen gas burners. "The kerosene mode answers our purpose . . . . Our expense for a month has been $30.60 . . . . This is the mode we have adopted to avoid the high rate for gas." The words brought the Norfolk Gas Light Company to its feet with a column and a half of defense, but the *Virginian* hung on to its kerosene lamps.

Two and a half years later, in September of 1868, Hope told an anniversary reception that in the year ending in September, 1867, the newspaper grossed $36,500 and in the year ending in September, 1868, it grossed $40,000. For its first ten months to September, 1866, its gross receipts must have been much lower. No records remain to show profits or losses or to permit comparisons with other newspapers. But by April of 1866 the whole newspaper situation in Norfolk was facing radical changes which not only altered the *Virginian*'s ownership and editorial structures but those of every other newspaper in Norfolk.

3 · THE *JOURNAL* ENCOUNTERS
MICHAEL GLENNAN

THESE BROAD CHANGES BEGAN ON APRIL 21, 1866. JAMES BARRON HOPE announced that day in a farewell to *Virginian* readers that he had retired as associate editor; the newspaper's proprietors had sold an interest to Lewellen, the business manager; and William E. Cameron, local editor of the Petersburg *Index*, was coming to Norfolk as editor of the *Virginian*.

Before Lewellen purchased an interest (Hope continued), the proprietors of the *Virginian* offered that interest to Hope and Holt Wilson, local editor. Hope wrote that "this offer we were compelled, reluctantly, to decline." He spoke warmly of Lewellen, "the new partner in the paper;" and he invoked "the kind regards of the community for the accomplished gentleman [Cameron] who succeeds me."

A month later Hope went to the *Day Book* as editor and Holt Wilson went as local editor. The *Day Book* was then a morning newspaper expressing Democratic views.

The partners in G. A. Sykes & Co. may have been disappointed in financial returns in Norfolk, though they had given the *Virginian* only five months to show its worth. They may have had their eyes on the Richmond newspaper field, where some of them went later. Hope and Wilson probably declined the purchase of an interest before it was offered to Lewellen because they could not produce the money (although it would not have taken much). But Keiley had now cut all editorial ties with the *Virginian*, and, since Sykes had never been an active factor in daily operations, the crack in the original founding group was large. The *Virginian* was becoming more of a Norfolk newspaper.

Cameron was born in Petersburg in 1842 and went to local schools and to the Horner Military School in North Carolina. He studied briefly at Washington University in St. Louis, clerked on a Mississippi steamboat, and won an appointment to West Point. But the war caught him before he could go. He acted as drillmaster for Missouri troops, marched into the field with them, and was captured. Escaping the first night, he returned to Virginia and joined the Twelfth Virginia Infantry in Mahone's Brigade. From the time Lee assumed command of the Army of Northern Virginia to the end of the war Cameron participated in every engagement of that army except Sharpsburg, and he missed that battle only because he had been wounded in the preceding Second Manassas operation. He rose from private to captain and to regimental and brigade adjutant general.

When Cameron came to Norfolk as editor of the *Virginian* he was twenty-three years old. He faced a challenge in trying to fill Hope's shoes, but Cameron had capacity. He would prove it as editor and later as champion of a public issue that engulfed the state, and eventually as governor of Virginia. Forty years after first coming to Norfolk he would come back as editor of the *Virginian-Pilot.*

The changes of April and May set off other changes. Shortly thereafter, the firm of J. R. Lewellen & Co. was organized to take control of the *Virginian*. Associated with Lewellen were Solomon Hodges and his brother, Edward H. Hodges, J. C. Adkisson, and Theodorick B. Ruffin. The Hodges brothers and Adkisson were printers with the *Virginian*. Ruffin was a printer too but better known as a local news editor. Lewellen was now forty-five years old, but his partners were much younger: Ruffin, thirty-two; Adkisson, twenty-six; Solomon Hodges, twenty-five, and Edward apparently younger. They had practical printing knowledge but negligible capital and no publishing experience. The enterprise seemed to hang on Lewellen.

Lewellen was active, vigorous, and experienced, and he might have won the hard fight that faced the *Virginian*. But he had hardly taken command of the newspaper through the new firm that bore his name when another and a more attractive opportunity tempted him. He leaped at it. Within a few months, before the *Virginian* celebrated its first birthday on November 21, 1866, he disposed of his interest there in order to be general manager of a new newspaper called the *Norfolk Journal*, and superintendent of the book and job printing establishment associated with it.

Lewellen sold out to his partners, the two Hodges, Adkisson, and Ruffin. By November, 1866, they had established the firm of S. Hodges & Co. and were the owners of the newspaper. Seventeen years later Michael Glennan, owner and editor then, said that the new owners bought the *Virginian* "on a capital of $55.00, the total amount of spare change in their pockets, and the terms of the agreement were that the entire purchase money should be paid in two years, in equal weekly installments, and a failure to meet any one of the payments would be considered a forfeiture, and the payments looked upon as so much rent."

S. Hodges & Co. discovered quickly that the *Virginian* did not even have an editor. Cameron had purchased the Petersburg *Index* with G. A. Sykes that November and after seven months in Norfolk returned to his old home to publish it. He was not a man to run away from a battle—military, journalistic, or political—merely because the going was hard. But there was much about the *Virginian* at the moment to discourage nearly anyone, and perhaps there was much about the *Index* to encourage him to join Sykes in publishing it. Yet his departure must have been a blow.

In twelve months the *Virginian* had passed from G. A. Sykes & Co. to J. R. Lewellen & Co. and now to S. Hodges & Co. It had lost its Petersburg founders. It had lost Lewellen, its first business manager and subsequent leader. It had lost Hope, its associate editor, and Wilson, its local editor. It had lost Joseph G. Fiveash, its circulation "agent," who went with Lewellen to the *Journal*. It had lost Cameron, its second editor. It had no commanding personality at the helm, and its financial reserve had not yet been born.

Worse yet, the *Virginian* was facing what seemed to be the most formidable opposition it had yet encountered. The Norfolk *Journal* appeared on the morning of December 4, 1866. It was a standard-sized, four-page newspaper, much like the *Virginian* in style and make-up, as would be expected: Lewellen had designed both. Like the *Virginian*, the *Journal* used (at the start) pages one and four for background material that could be set in type and printed early. Most of the fresh news was on pages two and three. The heads over stories, reports, and articles showed the same severe conservatism. Even the poetry that often graced the top of the first column of page four of the *Virginian* was matched by poetry just as sentimental in the same spot in the *Journal*.

The *Journal*'s masthead announced that it was published by the Norfolk Printing House Company, although that corporation was not identified in full for six weeks. Nor did the *Journal* carry the name of manager or editor. But it printed a column advertisement of the printing facilities acquired through purchase of two shops in Norfolk, and this advertisement carried the name of J. Richard Lewellen as "Superintendent" of the company. The *Journal* was published in

quarters on Roanoke Avenue in a row of buildings owned by Burruss & Rogers.

The new projects resulted from the initiative of Colonel William
Lamb more than anyone else. This militant Norfolkian was the
grandson of William B. Lamb, who was mayor for three terms early
in the nineteenth century, and the son of William W. Lamb, who
as mayor for three terms in the middle of the century had been forced
to surrender the city to General Wool in 1862. The youngest of the
three Lambs was thirty years old. He was best known as commander
of Confederate troops in the defense of Fort Fisher, chief barrier to
the Federal capture of Wilmington, North Carolina, then the last important port in Confederate hands. In the bitter fighting there in
January of 1865 Colonel Lamb was wounded, but he came out of it
a hero in most Confederate eyes.

Before the war Lamb had been a proprietor of the *Daily Southern
Argus*, the secessionist newspaper in Norfolk. In 1866 he was a commission merchant. In time he would follow his father and grandfather
into the mayoralty. Whatever he did—and he would do much over
the next thirty years in his city and state—he was a distinctive personality, able, individualistic, disputatious, and aggressive.

The leading editorial of the *Journal's* first issue told much about
the spirit in which the newspaper was established. It promised to
champion "the development of the interests of Norfolk as a commercial port connected by rail with an interior country of vast resources."
It stressed canal connections with North Carolina. But the *Journal*,
this editorial proclaimed, "will eschew politics—estimating this subject to be, at present, utterly unprofitable; but it will give a comprehensive synopsis of the legislative proceedings of the State and of the
Congress of the United States." What it had in mind, as it said subsequently, was that "we must first get back into the Union."

The *Journal* announced also that it had "been brought into business by leading business men of the city." That was the point which
the *Virginian* stressed in welcoming its new rival. The *Journal*, said
the *Virginian*, is "the enterprise of a number of Norfolk merchants"
and is "devoted mainly to the business interests of the community."

Eventually but, oddly enough, not until January 25, 1867, the
Journal added more details about the Norfolk Printing House Company. Included was its purchase of "the good will and materials" of
the *Daily Old Dominion*, Norfolk *Times*, and *Journal of Commerce*,
thus clearing the ground of weak but possibly annoying newspaper
growth. The *Daily Old Dominion* was the Portsmouth-born, Norfolk-

developed newspaper established in 1863 to preach Republican doctrine. The *Times* was of the same vintage and flavor. The *Journal of Commerce* was a weekly that published its first number in mid-1866.

The policy of eschewing politics rested on the inability of Virginia citizens at the moment to be masters of their fate. That was being decided in Washington, not in Virginia. But the politics of the Reconstruction period were of such importance and public interest that the *Journal's* purpose to remain aloof was unrealistic. For all their inability to control events then, Virginians could not "eschew" politics. In time the *Journal* found it could not either.

There was no doubt about the high standing in Norfolk and the influence and power of the subscribers to the stock of the new company. This formidable group included two bank presidents, Gilbert C. Walker of the Exchange National Bank, shortly to be governor of Virginia, and John B. Whitehead of the Franklin Savings Bank; the commission merchants, C. W. Grandy & Sons and Alexander Bell, in addition to Colonel Lamb; the ship builder, William A. Graves; the carriage maker, A. Wrenn; the druggists, Ludlow & Martin; the book sellers, Vickery & Co.; the president of the Albemarle & Chesapeake Canal, Marshall Parks; the capitalist, George Newton; the merchant, J. M. Walters; the liquor house of Sangster & Co.; the surgeon, Dr. M. Fitzgibbons; the collector of internal revenue, Simon Stone; the attorney and later judge, George Blow; and the member of the House of Delegates and former proprietor of the *Argus*, Abram F. Leonard.

The subscribers included also Lewellen, called "publisher," and Holt Wilson and William Sharp, each called "editor." Wilson had been local editor (city editor in later terminology) of the *Virginian*. Sharp had been local editor of the *Old Dominion*, and for a short time he and Leonard edited it. The *Journal's* reticence obscured details, but in a year or so, and certainly by 1868, Wilson went to the Petersburg *Express* and William R. Galt became the *Journal's* editor. He remained in that post during critical stages of the Reconstruction period. About 1871, and clearly by 1872, Major Baker P. Lee had become the *Journal's* editor.

Galt's father had been postmaster in Norfolk during Andrew Jackson's presidency. One of his brothers was Alexander Galt, a sculptor whose work could be found in many localities, north and south. He himself studied at the College of William and Mary and won a master's degree at the University of Virginia in 1841 when twenty-three years old. He taught school for many years in Norfolk. In the opinion of the later established Norfolk *Landmark*, Galt "presided over the early studies and training of more of our citizens than any other man perhaps . . . a man of great learning and vigorous intellect . . . a man of the sturdiest character, brave and high minded." H e appears to have continued his school teaching while he was the *Journal*'s editor. Major Lee's tenure, as we shall see, was brief.

S. Hodges & Co. must have watched all these events with acute interest. The printer-partners were deep in difficulty, but they set about putting their house in order as though all were well. For editor they turned to their news room, pulled out J. Marshall Hanna, and crowned him with the title, meantime getting out the paper as best they could.

The least known of the editors of the *Virginian*, or of any newspaper which succeeded it, Hanna was destined to remain in office only a few months. His picture suggests a Custer-like personality. He wore his hair almost to his shoulders, after the fashion in war and peace of a few of the Southern gallants, and he had a look of boldness and even of brashness. He knew his way around among the newspaper shops of the times.

In Norfolk, Hanna was promoted to meet an emergency in a newspaper organization which, in the half desperate, almost unbelievable moment of its birth, seemed to be transitional itself. But these partners were made of tough fibre. They were not afraid to add to their gamble of buying the *Virginian* the gamble of going over into a Portsmouth school, and tapping twenty-two-year-old Michael Glennan on the shoulder, and telling him that he was general manager of the newspaper—January 17, 1867. It was a personnel decision of historic importance, although anyone could have been excused for not realizing it at the moment.

The youthful Glennan was born in 1844 in Maynooth, County Kildare, Ireland, and came to the United States at the age of four. The family went first to Boston, then to New York, before reaching Norfolk. In 1857 William Lamb gave the boy work in the mailing room of the *Argus*, and he spent four years there, from thirteen to seventeen, at $4.00 a week. The experience must have made a deep impression on him, but in 1861 the coming of the war made more.

Michael was lame from what generally was described as "rheumatism," but he did not lack energy, zeal, or courage. When he carried a message at top speed to Brigadier General William B. Taliaferro, the early Confederate commander in Norfolk, telling him that Federal troops were advancing on the Navy Yard in Portsmouth, the General liked the boy so much that he made him an orderly. His ailment was thought to be a barrier later, and he had difficulty gaining acceptance from a Virginia unit.   But the Thirty-seventh North Carolina Infantry took him on for quartermaster work.   He was at Fort Fisher under Lamb in 1865 and was made prisoner there; and, after parole, he surrendered again under Johnston.

Back at home, the young man turned to teaching—three pupils, he said later, one of whom paid him.   But he was very much on his toes, eager, alert, determined, self-confident, and a born entrepreneur. Some of the printer-partners may have known him in the *Argus* days and may have sensed these qualities.   He could not know much about newspaper management, but he had the spark, and for most of the next thirty years he would be the dominant personality in the *Virginian*'s command.   Even now, in the newspaper's poverty and discouragement, one of his first steps was to pluck James Barron Hope from the *Day Book* and install him as editor of the *Virginian*—a stroke of excellent judgment and great value.

It was a new day.   The last of the wartime newspapers had died. The prewar *Day Book*, under the management of the veteran, John R. Hathaway, was struggling to survive.   But the *Virginian* and the *Journal* represented the postwar spirit—the *Journal* reflecting the commercial life of the town and well armed for the struggle ahead, the *Virginian* reflecting the older newspaper spirit harnessed now to the energy and ambition of youth, scrapping for existence, bolder by necessity, under Glennan and Hope and the printer-partners.

THE *Virginian*'s CHANGES BROUGHT COMMENT FROM OTHER NEWSPAPERS, and its response was public notice that Hanna, the new editor, was a peppery personality. "We are much obliged to the press of Virginia and out of it for their favorable opinion of us," the response began, but it turned quickly to this stinger: "We don't object to the unfavorable flings and innuendoes that have been cast upon us. That is part of the business of the press, especially that part of the Virginia press who have no ideas of their own. We would especially commend this paragraph to the editors of the Richmond Dispatch, the Lynchburg Virginian and the Petersburg Index [edited now by Cameron, late of the *Virginian*], all of whose articles seem now to be worn, tired and threadbare of a subject for discussion."

Other aspects of the times worried the *Virginian*, notably prize-fighting and the presence of women in governmental employment. "Twice now within a few months," it recorded in November, 1866, "the soil of Virginia has been desecrated and trodden into a compost of blood and mire by the brutal principals and patrons of the 'prize ring,' who come over from New York and Baltimore and Washington."

"These bruisers," it summed up, "should be taught that immunity from the law consists in playing where they practice; in fighting out on more ignoble ground than Virginia soil the base principles of the 'prize fight,' which have no foothold here, and which form no part of a Virginia education."

Six months later, in June, 1867, the *Virginian* carried a report headed thus:

HORRORS OF THE PRIZE RING

A Desperate Encounter, Barney Aaron the Victor
Brutalizing Sights, Incidents &C

The report told of the sixty-eight rounds which Aaron and Sam Collyer (who "had numerous friends here and much money staked upon his success") fought beside Aquia Creek, down the Potomac River from Washington. Round sixty-seven ended "by a clinch, the men falling through the ropes, Collyer underneath and Aaron's hand in close proximity to Collyer's eye." In round sixty-eight "Aaron was carried to the middle of the ring by his seconds," but Collyer couldn't make it. "When it was discovered that Collyer's eye was completely out of its socket, it was put back by his second, but his sight was completely gone. . . . Thus ended this brutal encounter, the last, we hope, that will ever disgrace the soil of any land."

The Aaron-Collyer fight was "the topic of our streets," the *Virginian* had to confess. Its bulletin board "was besieged and when our extra was published, it went like wild fire."

The presence of "several hundred women" employed in governmental departments in Washington was "a startling disclosure." So must have been the statement that the "printing bureau of the treasury department" was "in the hands of profligates and prostitutes." It turned out that "most of the women employed at Washington obtain their places through the influence of members of Congress" where now the Republican Radicals, not admired in Norfolk newspaper offices, were in command. The *Virginian* liked nothing about this touch of modernity.

Closer at hand the *Journal* taught the *Virginian* a lesson in handling news. Its issue of January 9, 1867, carried on its front page, where fresh news was rare, this head over a long story:

TERRIBLE CALAMITY
The Atlantic Hotel in Flames

THE BUILDING ENTIRELY CONSUMED
The Engines Without Water

NOT HOSE ENOUGH TO REACH THE DOCK
Other Buildings Taking Fire

GENERAL CONFLAGRATION FEARED
Immense Loss of Valuable Property

THE FIRE SPREADING
Building on Bank Street Afire

First National Bank in Peril

No Lives Known to be Lost

(The Atlantic Hotel of that day was on the north side of Main Street, between Bank and Atlantic—earlier Gray—Streets, nearly opposite Roanoke Avenue.)

The utilization of the front page for a big, running news story of the day represented change. So, for the Norfolk press, did the twelve banks in the head. The hand-wringing of the story's lead was not far from the style of the period: "We begin to write with a heavy heart and unsteady hand, for ere we close this account we fear it will become our painful duty to record one of the most terrible calamities that has visited our city in many a year." Nor did the second paragraph vary much from the leisurely approach characteristic of much reporting of the 1860's:

> At 1 a.m. the fire bells sounded the alarm, but there was no apparent cause for it in any part of the city and few persons stirred abroad. Our duty led us forth and we were informed that the Atlantic Hotel was on fire. The steam engine was in front of the building and many persons were inside. There was not the first appearance of fire beyond the building, smoke not even issuing therefrom. We entered and were informed that the interior of the dining room was ablaze. In approaching the saloon with others, our party was driven back by the dense smoke which came forth when the door was opened. The smoke began to spread through the building.

The slow development of the fire gave the hotel's occupants time to escape without drama, and the anonymous reporter concerned himself only slightly with them. But, once under way, he carried his readers with increasing speed through the spread of the fire, the "feeble stream of water flowing," the ladders that were "put" and "the assurance they seemed to bring," the exhaustion of water in the cisterns and "in the well," "the fear" that "now took possession of us all that the beautiful structure, the pride of our city, must fall. . . ."

On through the night the reporter fought in the spirit of his breed for his facts, fought against mounting developments, fought against time:

> 3:30 a.m. The entire hotel front is one sheet of flame. The spectacle presented is one of appalling grandeur. . .
>
> 3:45 a.m. The old Argus office is on fire. The flames have crossed the street [Main Street]. . . .
>
> 4 a.m. The city is as light as noon day . . . Roanoke Avenue is full of people hurrying to some safe place with their goods and chattels. The streets are running in rivulets with Mr. Borum's best liquors. . . .

4:45 a.m. The beautiful little bank building of R. H. Chamberlaine is now enveloped in flames. The First National Bank, which adjoins it, on the corner of Bank and Main Street, is in danger. As we close the walls of the Atlantic Hotel are falling with thundering crashes and the fire is spreading. . . .

5 a.m. We are just from the scene. We think the National Bank is safe. The United Fire Company has at length found water, and is throwing a gallant stream upon the flames with telling effect. The property destroyed is well insured.

Give that reporter a good mark! He saw the human details. He reported by the hours, the half-hours, the quarter-hours. He broke the old patterns of news writing and taught new lessons of human interest. After him it would not be so easy to bury the big, exciting news under the sedate manners of the past.

The *Virginian* carried the fire story on page three, where its most important local news appeared. The longest news story on its front page that day was clipped from the Madrid *Times*. It reported a fight between a Spaniard and a cobra. The *Journal*, for its big moment, could display flexibility the more easily because that day the *Virginian* carried nearly twice as much advertising.

In another area the *Virginian* scored a triumph of its own. Late in the autumn of 1867 General Butler came to Norfolk (he was interested then in draining part of the Dismal Swamp), and a hackman named Adams gained fame by refusing to let the General ride in his conveyance. "B. F. B. has had a striking instance that Norfolk still remains true to herself, and that there are men to be found in this city who will not bow the knee to the gilded calf," the *Virginian* proclaimed.

But that was only a start. Every publicly reported action of Butler in those years when he was in Congress was likely to draw slashing comment from Norfolk newspapers. Rarely was his name mentioned without his being called "Spoons Butler" in memory of the tales about the disappearance of family silver in New Orleans when he was in command there. His presence in Norfolk inspired someone on the *Virginian*, probably Hope, to write this variation of the standard denunciations:

The Spoons, Forks and other articles of Silver Ware in the city of Norfolk held a meeting on Sunday evening, in which the Committee on Public Safety reported the following preamble and resolutions as expressive of the objects of the Convention: WHEREAS, we are reliably informed that the immortal hero, B. F. B., has arrived in Norfolk, with his eyes ingeniously adjusted to look two ways at once; and

WHEREAS, it is reasonable to suppose that he meditates disturbing our domestic tranquility, and breaking up our family relations; and

WHEREAS, under these circumstances it becomes our duty to provide for our own safety and that of our families; therefore be it . . . .

Resolved, That the best way in which this danger should be avoided is taught in the campaigns of B. F. B. himself.

Resolved, That acting on hints thus furnished, we recommend immediate flight and concealment. . . .

At this moment a brand-new Spoon, that glittered like a moonbeam, ran into the hall and cried out, "I saw a cross-eyed man coming this way." A sudden clatter shook the room. Ladles, Spoons, Forks, Tea-trays, Salvers, Urns, Butter Knives, Dishes, and a thousand other particles sprang to their feet in the wildest confusion, and bolted for the door.

During the night an extraordinary series of plumps into neighboring cisterns were remarked on by the watchmen, and it is supposed that the entire supply of domestic silver in Norfolk has betaken itself to those old familiar haunts as a wise precaution against our *"distinguished visitor."*

The tenseness of the newspaper competition in Norfolk, heightened by the bitterness of the times—for Virginia was deep in the Reconstruction period—showed up in the late 1860's in sharp comment between the editors. When the Norfolk *Republican* appeared in February, 1867, the *Virginian* greeted it in these words: "It burst upon us full of bitter sentiments and agrarian principles, and only lacks the device of a fretful porcupine to make it the most complete embodiment of aggressive petulance and premeditated mischief. It combines the truculence of the bully with the ethics of the brigand, and teaches the philosophy of confusion worse confounded with unreserved audacity. We lament this in the most unaffected manner."

Annoyed by the *Day Book's* assertion (the *Virginian* called it "the evening sheet") that the unclaimed letter list published in the *Virginian* was not inserted by authority of law and consequently was not paid for, the *Virginian* turned on the *Day Book* with the counter that "this statement manifested either the writer's gross ignorance of the subject, or, that for purposes of his own, he wilfully and deliberately published what he knew to be false."

These exchanges in March, 1867, were mild compared with exchanges in September. The *Day Book* called then upon the *Journal* "to enliven the area by giving its readers some of those charming articles it produced while flourishing under the former names of New Regime, Norfolk Post and Old Dominion during the Federal occupation of Norfolk. . . . Come, neighbor, overhaul your back files and give your readers an insight into the manner in which you then spoke of Southern women who were so unfortunate as to be dragged through the streets by savage negro soldiers."

The reference to the *New Regime*, the Norfolk *Post*, and the *Old Dominion* grew out of the purchase of the "good will and materials" of newspapers of the occupation period by the Norfolk Printing House Company when it set about establishing the *Journal* in December, 1866. But to charge the *Journal* of September, 1867, with blood-kinship with those newspapers of the Butler era was, by the prevailing code, a grave matter.

The *Journal* so regarded it. It printed the *Day Book*'s words with the formal announcement that "the above is from the Norfolk Day Book of Saturday, September 28." Then it fired its first salvo: "We pronounce the editor, John R. Hathaway, an infamous liar and slanderer."

With that for a start, the *Journal* declared that "his black heart has conceived the infamy which is exhibited in the above venomous and mendacious article . . . he knew the fact that it [the *Journal*] has no connection with those papers whatever, and that he was lying. . . . The managers of the *Journal* as well as some of the stockholders were engaged in fighting the battles of the Confederacy while this hunchback wretch remained at home, voluntarily took the oath, and acted as a foreman of Ben Butler until he picked him out of the position as a creature not to be trusted." Then to the climax: "The entire article is nothing more nor less than the attempt of the villainous assassin, and we pronounce its author a mean, low, grovelling and despicable wretch, who should be shunned by all honorable men.

"All in substance that we have here stated has already been said to him personally, and the miserable craven had no spirit to resent it."

In spite of the nature of the charges and the ferocity of the language the heavens did not fall, and all newspapers continued to appear.

A year and a half later (March, 1869) the *Virginian* and the *Journal* got into a tangle of an unusual kind. In their comments on each other, which flared out of their different political views in that critical election year in Virginia, the *Journal* referred to *Virginian* editorials as the views of the editor, Hope—to "he" and "him" and "his"—instead of as the views of the *Virginian*. This irritated the *Virginian*'s owners, from whom emerged a paragraph: "Let us hear no more of 'he' and 'him' and 'his.' The *Virginian* is an institution, and the plainest requirements of good taste enforce our demands."

But the *Journal* retorted: "Beg pardon, neighbor, but the 'institution' which we recognize in the *Virginian* is its accomplished editor." This stirred the *Virginian* again. "A paragraph appeared in the Norfolk Journal yesterday which reflected upon this paper, and which we will not further notice than to say that it was untrue, ungenerous, unjust and ungentlemanly, and no such trash should ever emanate from an honest contemporary."

The next day the *Virginian* withdrew this paragraph, which it said had been used without the knowledge of the editor, and then wound up the matter with this statement:

> The public will perceive that the Journal, while it apparently pays a compliment to the editor of this paper, at the same time throws an insult and sneer at the proprietors. . . .
> For nearly two years and a half the present proprietors of this paper have labored night and day with untiring and unceasing toil to make the Virginian a permanent institution. Poor, and without one cent of capital to back us, we commenced our struggle; and it was one that only those who have felt adversity can appreciate . . . a struggle which, thanks to God and the support of a kind, generous and sympathetic public, we were able to go through with, and in the end find our labors crowned with success. It was a struggle, too, in which others had given up in despair, but in which we came forth victors. . . . By our toil we made the Virginian an institution. . .
>
> In asserting this we are conscious that we detract nothing from the well known reputation and worth of our editor, Captain Hope . . . and we take occasion here to publicly express to him our thanks.
>
> With this explanation we leave the public to judge of the attack insidiously made on the proprietors of this paper by the writer in the Journal.
>
> S. Hodges & Co.

A good deal about the printer-partners and Glennan, their business manager, emerges from this statement. They knew that their editor—older, versatile, much admired—was more widely known than any of them. But they also knew that through their industry they themselves had accomplished much and that the *Virginian* was more important than any one man who was contributing toward its growth.

Another flare-up between newspapers came near the end of the Reconstruction period. After the critical election of 1869 which made

Gilbert C. Walker governor and led to Virginia's restoration in the Union, the *Day Book* reported that members of the *Virginian*'s organization had scratched Walker's name when they voted in the election. This touched a sore spot. The *Virginian* had trouble finding a position and holding it in that election (as we shall see). The report moved Glennan to action which he described in a formal statement July 14:

> To the Public:
>
> In company with Captain W. W. Old, I, as one of the proprietors of the Norfolk Virginian, called at the office of the Day Book yesterday, and finding Mr. Hathaway [proprietor and editor] present, asked him if he believed to be true the assertion made in his paper of that morning to the effect that "the owners, managers and employees of the Virginian scratched Mr. Walker's name at the late election," and on receiving a hesitating reply I pronounced the article maliciously false and himself a malicious liar . . . the persistent attacks of the Day Book on the proprietors and interests of this paper arise from no patriotic or sincere motives, but simply show a low, jealous and contemptible disposition to damage its business prosperity —which fact must be manifest to the entire community. . . .
>
> M. Glennan

Throughout this period both the *Virginian* and the *Journal* often treated the *Day Book* with contempt. Their own differences they could take in stride without forgetting the courtesies. In February, 1868, fire swept through the row of buildings on Roanoke Avenue owned by Burruss & Rogers and damaged the *Journal*'s printing plant. Publication had to be suspended for a week. "Early next week our friends will be able to resume publication," the *Virginian* announced. "Until then they invoke the indulgence of the community."

When the *Journal* reappeared, from "a new and spacious office over the book store of Messrs. Wilson and Walke" on Roanoke Avenue, the *Virginian* was "gratified to hail the reappearance of our able contemporary. . . . We hope our friends across the street may find this temporary vexation a substantial advantage in the end."

The *Virginian* had begun to prosper a little during the late 1860's, bad though those years were politically, and was feeling better about life in general except the new ideas, like voting by Negroes, which came up in the Reconstruction years. Early in the Hodges-Glennan regime it cut the price of single copies from five to three cents and hoisted a slogan to its editorial masthead: "It is better to fight for the good than to rail at the ill." That did not last long. When Hope came in as editor, his name went to the top of the page.

In September, 1867 (possibly having learned from the *Journal's* handling of the Atlantic Hotel fire), the *Virginian* began to place more local news—"city intelligence and discussions of local topics" was its term—on the front page. The third page was still the main news page, and the fourth was for "poems, trifles of various sorts, and telegraphic dispatches" which now were "reported for the Virginian by Western Union Line" and were getting more space, though not good position. The *Virginian* promised at least two columns of reading matter out of seven columns on each page, it was planning a weekly edition, and by 1870 (March) it was setting up a literary department.

Here the *Virginian* would "endeavor to give its readers some just idea of the current literature of the day. . . . Weak and false criticisms have produced among the masses of the South an acquiescence in the arrogant assertion that the North is the only exponent of culture, refinement and creative power in this country. The oracles of New England . . . tell us that the soil so lately 'cursed by slavery' can support neither literature nor arts. These learned pundits forget that both Greece and Rome, under this 'curse,' produced works that have endured to this day. . . ."

These were plainly the words of Hope. Just as plainly it was Glennan who proclaimed that the *Virginian* had the largest circulation in the city and was "the official paper of the city—publishing all the laws and ordinances emanating from the city government." The *Journal* disputed both claims whenever it thought it worthwhile, but neither produced figures.

Glennan was on the way up the command ladder. By November, 1867, before he had been manager a year, he acquired an interest in the *Virginian*—from which partner or partners is not clear; none of them dropped out. More significantly, when Solomon Hodges retired three years later because of poor health, he sold his interest to the remaining partners: Glennan, Ruffin, Edward H. Hodges, and Adkisson, and they changed (February 19, 1870) the name of the firm. It was now Glennan, Ruffin & Co. Glennan had probably taken the lead two years earlier in urging the *Virginian* to move into new and larger quarters.

The shift came in August, 1868. The *Virginian* moved then into a building put up for it by W. B. Rogers at 56 and 58 Roanoke Avenue. This was "two doors from Main Street," only a few steps from the original quarters and close to the heart of the business and financial district.

Here the *Virginian* remained through 1878. In those ten years it made some changes in interior arrangements, but for most of the time the first floor was given over to the business offices, advertising, and the mailing room. The news and editorial rooms and the job printing quarters were on the second floor. The composing room—where the printers and makeup men worked—was on the third floor. The press room and the steam engine which furnished power for the plant were on the ground floor in the rear of the business office.

These new quarters made it easier for the *Virginian* to publish in October, 1868, six pages daily for a four-day trade convention—the two extra pages were a supplement for the convention—which was designed "to make Norfolk the shipping point for much of the South and Southwest." The *Virginian* said two thousand delegates attended this convention.

Other signs indicated that newspapers in Virginia were growing up. The *Virginian* concurred strongly in the contention of the Richmond *Enquirer* that a state press association should be formed. The *Enquirer* had pleaded: "Let us establish some fixed rates for advertising. Let us try to stop the system of puffing—which is lying. And let us try to stop the publication of advertisements as selected reading matter. And let us resolve to receive no free tickets and no presents of any sort."

The *Virginian* followed up quickly (September 22 and 25, 1869):

> These are all admirable suggestions, and we find reason every day to lament that they are not uniformly adopted by the press of the state. . . . The contemplated convention should secure from the Associated Press greater consideration than it now receives, and should be prepared to submit a plan for the regulation of this matter to the central office. . . . [three days later] the Associated Press neglects the Norfolk newspapers. We frequently receive news which had appeared in the New York newspapers, and which our scissors could secure just as well or better than the wires send it.

A state press association came in time, but there were no quick solutions to all these problems. Nor did such problems, troublesome though they were to newspapers, compare in importance, difficulty, or emotionalism with the dominating issue of Norfolk and Virginia, and to a large extent, of the country: The problems of Reconstruction and the one-by-one return of the states to the Union. For Virginia this period ran to 1870. For newspapers it was a testing time of hardly less strain than war itself.

5 · BACK IN THE MAIN STREAM

THE COLLAPSE OF PRESIDENT JOHNSON'S RECONSTRUCTION PLAN AND THE development of the much sterner congressional plan led in March of 1867 to new military control. Virginia emerged as Military District Number 1 with Major General John M. Schofield as commander of the district.

Both the *Virginian* and the *Journal* discussed these developments in quiet tones. They were not happy—"we are in a sad and deplorable plight," the *Journal* said—but they expected nothing pleasant then. General Schofield they regarded as a man of intelligent and moderate views. The *Journal*, though it called the new regime one "which all lovers of liberty throughout the civilized world must deplore," thought "its rigors may be tempered by the temper of the executive. . . . . He is regarded as a conservative . . . his sentiments seem to rebel against the debasement of the Old Dominion." In April of 1867 the *Virginian* went much further:

> The great boon of political freedom has suddenly been granted to 4,000,000 blacks, for generations previous held in bondage, and therefore deprived of that intelligence absolutely necessary for the wise and proper exercise of this once exalted and valued privilege. . . . Master and slave now stand upon the same platform of common rights. Let us, therefore, not stand aloof from the colored man . . . but rather extend to him a helping hand. Let us convince him . . . that we are and must be friends. . . . Let us see that the freedmen do not pass under the control of designing fanatics to be used for their own selfish aggrandizement and purpose of plunder. . . . Let us teach them that it is truth rather than force that makes us truly free. See that they do not make the fatal mistake of confounding license with liberty.

The next day (this was shortly after the *Day Book* had scolded the *Journal* for its policy of eschewing politics) the *Virginian* examined further the responsibility of newspapers and citizens:

> Several of our contemporaries come to us filled with vague remonstrances against what they call "dirt eating." As well as we can understand these journals, they mean to insist on a "masterly inactivity," and in point of fact to cover their retreat from positions which the common sense of the Southern people have pronounced to be untenable. We deprecate the controversy; but we cannot help saying to our friends they are in error. We live in the midst of a great revolution and inaction is simply impossible. . . . It is not only impossible, but unwise. . . . The fold-your-arms policy is simply unmanly. . . .
> What shall we do then? The answer is easily given. When the time comes for us to register, let every man come forward and prepare for the day of election . . . he who would be free must strike the blow, and the only blow we can strike is at the polls.

The *Journal* did not go this far, but it had, of necessity, abandoned its policy of eschewing politics. It did note that "while under military rule, the press is liable to be muzzled or suppressed whenever the military commander of the district may determine that the public service requires such an exercise of authority." It called attention to a recent warning to the Richmond *Times* and to the suppression of a newspaper in Mobile, Alabama. These, the *Journal* said, were reasons "why all of us should be anxious to relieve ourselves of military government. . . . We have the reality upon us. Let us busy ourselves about it, and not about what is apprehended would be or will be, if we were back in the Union."

In June of 1867 Schofield called for a new registration and the election of delegates to a state constitutional convention. This would be the first time Negroes could vote, and the interest among them and among all people was intense.

Citizens who had taken an oath to support the United States Constitution (a congressman or an army officer, for instance) and thereafter had joined or had aided the Confederate military forces were not eligible to vote; but these were a small proportion of the whole— about ten thousand in Virginia, by most estimates. Membership in the Confederate forces not preceded by an oath to support the United States Constitution did not bar participation in this election. Potential white voters outnumbered potential Negro voters by perhaps forty-five thousand. To the disgust, often the anger, of the *Virginian* a substantial proportion of white men would have nothing to do with Reconstruction processes, including this election of delegates.

Sensing that these abstainers would throw control the other way, and bitter at that prospect, the *Virginian* wrote sharply the day before the voting under the head: "So You Won't Vote for Yankees, Eh?" Radical Republicans in Norfolk had nominated Henry Bowden, a native white lawyer, and Dr. Thomas C. Bayne, a former slave who had practiced dentistry in Boston before moving back to Norfolk. Conservatives, calling themselves the People's Party in this election, had named Dr. W. W. Wing, a former postmaster, and Gilbert C. Walker, president of the Exchange National Bank and one of the subscribers to *Journal* stock. Both of these had moved into Norfolk from the northern side of the Potomac. The *Virginian* warned:

> You'll see what will be the result of refusing to vote for conservatives, because, forsooth, they happened to be born north of a certain degree of latitude. You will put into your convention men who were indeed born in Virginia—such men, we mean, as Mr. Bowden . . . or Dr. Bayne. You will fill your councils and town offices with radicals of all colors, and when your property and your business and your judiciary and your public schools are under the control of these native-born (!) Virginians, then you will scream and shriek and howl about what you would have done; but it will be of no use, your repentance will be too late. Up and arouse yourselves. . . . Vote for Walker and Wing and save old Norfolk from ruin.

It *was* of no use. Bowden and Bayne beat Wing and Walker. Although state registration had shown 120,101 whites to 105,832 Negroes, the Radical Republican Party elected 72 delegates (of whom 25 were Negroes) to 33 Conservative delegates. Across the state the Negro vote was more than 17,000 above the white vote. Some 40,000 potential white voters did not vote.

The *Virginian* looked that fact squarely in the face. Because "there is no use grieving over spilled milk, we shall indulge in none of the regrets which we feel at the apathy of our people. . . . Let us organize for the momentous issue which is yet to be submitted to us. When the new constitution is presented to us for ratification, it will be a poisoned chalice from the hands of political Borgias, and we should be prepared in time with an antidote. Organization will supply it."

But the *Journal* had more to get off its chest. Calling on white people to organize a statewide conservative party—a prophetic proposal this was—to stop the Republican movement, it declared that "we must throw aside all past issues as dead. We must receive into our embrace all who will go with us, without reference to former opinions or where they happened to be born. . . . The white people will have it within their power, if they exercise it, to defeat the constitution framed by the convention should it not be such as to justify ratification."

But the constitutional convention that met in December of 1867 had the votes, the determination, and the leadership to lay down its own program. It elected John C. Underwood as president, and the document that emerged in April, 1868, was known thereafter as the Underwood constitution.

Underwood had come to Virginia before the war from New York state. He was a delegate to the Republican National Convention of 1856, and after that left Virginia—almost, it could be said, was driven out because of his abolitionist views. During the war he was an auditor in the Treasury Department in Washington, and after the war he grew active in Republican affairs in Virginia. Ultimately Underwood was a United States judge in Virginia, much disliked by old-line Virginians, who thought his handling of judicial duties was atrocious.

Other things were happening in that December of 1867. President Johnson's message to Congress so impressed the *Virginian*, especially his call for an end to the military districts established by Congress, that it published eight columns of his words. But the message did not impress the House of Representatives. It was moving toward impeachment of the President.

When Virginia conservatives met in Richmond in the same December, with Hope one of the Norfolk delegates, they appealed for all men of whatever party or birth to work for constitutionalism and restoration of the Union, and for governmental control by white people. A new party was being born, calling itself Conservative, consisting of Democrats, Whigs, and moderate Republicans. It sought a new name to obscure old differences. A. H. H. Stuart, of Staunton, who had been Secretary of the Interior in Fillmore's cabinet, presided at this meeting. He was a rising political influence in Virginia.

While the Norfolk newspapers waited gloomily for the details of the Underwood constitution, they were diverted and puzzled by General Schofield's removal of Governor Pierpont and his appointment of Henry H. Wells as successor. Wells had come out of Michigan, where he was a member of the state legislature, and had been a Union cavalryman in the war. Later he was provost-marshal of Alexandria and practiced law there. Pierpont was no favorite along Roanoke

Avenue, but the editors liked Wells even less. What really excited them was the report that General Butler, then in Congress and a prosecutor in the Johnson impeachment proceedings, was the force behind Pierpont's removal. Butler and Pierpont had been enemies from war days.

The report set off the *Virginian's* denunciatory guns. "The illustrious Son of Thunder," it declared, looking straight at Butler, "made friends with Grant as Herodias danced before Herod, for a consideration, which was the official head of Pierpont." But Wells did not escape. "When we reflect upon the long list of governors of Virginia," the *Virginian* said, "and then come down to Pierpont and Wells, it is very much like looking at an inverted pyramid. . . . Prince of Scalawags! Immortal Wells! King of Carpetbaggers, we salute thee!"

Inside the Underwood convention the discussion of disfranchisement provisions and the so-called ironclad oath of office defined issues that led the *Virginian* to cry out in anguish that the new constitution would be "the most abominable contrivance for ruining white people in order to benefit negroes."

The disfranchisement clause would prevent voting by men who had aided rebellion, militarily or in any other way, whether previously they had taken an oath to support the Federal constitution or not. The test oath applied to officeholders of all degrees, from governor to a local school board member. Each would have to swear that he had never voluntarily given aid, comfort, or encouragement to persons engaged in armed hostility against the United States; that he had "neither sought nor accepted . . . any office whatever under any authority, or pretended authority, in hostility to the United States;" and that he had "not yielded a voluntary support to any pretended government, authority, power or constitution within the United States, hostile or inimical thereto."

The oath brought Schofield to his feet in protest. He addressed the convention itself on the practical impossibility of administering the affairs of the state without the assistance in public office of numerous men who would be eliminated by the oath. In certain counties, he said, he had found perhaps two capable men who could take the oath when he needed thirty capable men for public offices. But the convention refused to suspend the rules in order to consider modification of the oath. On April 17, 1868, it approved the constitution as a whole, fifty-one to twenty-six.

A week later minority delegates drew up a statement of their objections. The *Virginian* printed (in small type) six columns of these objections, then published the statement in pamphlet form, and sold nearly five thousand copies. Aside from disfranchisement and oath requirements, the attack centered on congressional redistricting, which was said to give Negroes a majority in five of the eight districts; on provisions for equal civil and political rights and public privileges; on the secret ballot in place of the traditional voting by voice; on county government plans, called cumbersome and expensive, and public school costs, which were held to be exorbitant. Mixing of the races in public schools was left to the General Assembly. The public school provisions as a whole were regarded in later years as a strong stimulus for education and one of the best parts of the Underwood constitution. The terms of the test oath, said the minority, meant that not one white man in a thousand could take it.

The oath moved General Grant to action. In May, 1868, when near the Republican nomination for President, he sent to the House of Representatives a communication from Major General E. R. S. Canby, then the commander of Military District Number 1 after Schofield was ordered to other duties. Canby asserted bluntly that "some action by Congress will be needed to remove" the oath. "Its effect" would be "to deprive the government still further of the services of intelligent and well-disposed men whose technical disqualification is their only fault."

Grant's action forced the newspapers in Norfolk to make new appraisals of him. Shortly after the war he won appreciation from the *Virginian*. Later he seemed to be siding with Radical Republicans. Now he seemed aware of the practical difficulties of government in Virginia. But the House of Representatives paid no serious attention to Grant's complaint. To Virginians it seemed that they would have to provide their own salvation.

The Ku Klux Klan flared up in Tennessee in that spring of 1868. "But a week ago," the *Virginian* said in March, "it was the subject of a joke and laughter. In the twinkling of an eye it has expanded into huge proportions . . . full of power and passion." But it was not to the Ku Klux Klan that conservative Virginians began to turn: it was to political maneuver.

Grant's election brought little surprise. Congress delayed setting a date for voting in Virginia on the new constitution, and that issue and the election of a governor passed over into 1869. President Johnson's proclamation of amnesty at Christmas brought a note of cheer. But the pleasantest event of 1868, in the eyes of Norfolk newspapers, had come in August when Massachusetts Democrats defeated Butler's bid for renomination for Congress. The *Virginian's* judgment:

> We are happy to announce that Gen. B. F. Butler, especially execrated by the people of Norfolk as the Prince of the Rogues and Arch-duke of Bummers, has been thrown overboard in his congressional district.
>
> He has been voted a political Jonah, and over he went, pudge jumb!! with the mournful certainty that no whale of the vasty deep of oblivion would furnish charitable jaws to spew him up again on the shores of active political life.
>
> We hail this as a great triumph. . . . Above all, it shows that the Yankees of his district spit upon a bully, a liar, a coward and a spoon finder. . . . He is beginning to get what he deserves. . . .

Inside Virginia the political maneuvering took the form, first, of a series of letters to newspapers signed Senex, the pen name, it became known later, of the Conservative Party leader, A. H. H. Stuart. He presented a bold argument. Negro suffrage, he submitted, was inevitable. Nothing could stop it; Virginia could not alter it. The strategic course, therefore, was to accept Negro suffrage and look elsewhere for counters to the evils that most Virginians thought Negro suffrage would bring. Could anything be gained by such a course?

Yes, Stuart contended. Greater evils were the disfranchisement and oath provisions of the Underwood constitution. They were the vital targets. Accept Negro suffrage, which was a certainty in any event. Fight to remove the objectionable clauses from the proposed constitution. If they could be stripped away, then the white majority in time could gain control of government.

The Senex letters split Conservative ranks down the middle. In Norfolk the *Virginian* regarded Negro suffrage as the worst of all evils, but it opposed every form of Republicanism. The *Journal* had held since its birth that getting back into the Union was the primary need. It liked the line suggested by Senex. The two newspapers clashed repeatedly.

March of 1869 brought another striking development. Norfolk's Gilbert C. Walker, thirty-seven years old and a moderate Republican, announced for the governorship, for which the Conservative Party already had nominated R. E. Withers, editor of the Lynchburg *News*. An upstate New Yorker, Walker had attended Williams and Hamilton Colleges, and had practiced law in Chicago and been a Douglas Democrat. When the war came on, he turned Republican, won a colonel's commission, and eventually moved to Norfolk as a civilian.

In 1869 Walker was a stockholder (the *Journal* reported he owned $50,000 worth of stock) in the Atlantic Iron Works Company which, because of its plant west of Norfolk, gave the name of Atlantic City to an area that later was annexed by Norfolk. In a dark economic period he organized the Exchange National Bank. In 1868 he went to Liverpool in the effort to stimulate transatlantic business for Norfolk. His political debut, when he ran for delegate in the constitutional convention of 1867-68, was not successful, but it established him as an opponent of Radical Republicanism. His tall figure, handsome head, and affable manner had brought him favorable public attention. He was not the only Northerner who moved to Norfolk in those years and won a place on merit, but he was perhaps the most conspicuous.

The Walker candidacy made the *Virginian* squirm. It recognized his personal merit, but it could not disregard his Republicanism. "Our townsman, Colonel Walker, has opened the canvass in this state by a speech of which we published an extract March 27," it said. "The tone and temper of his address serve to make the contrast between himself and Wells still more conspicuous than before, and were we without an organization [the Conservative Party] and candidate [Withers] of our own, we do not hesitate to say that we should infinitely prefer him over his carpetbagger competitor."

But though the *Virginian* did have "an organization and candidate" of its own, political maneuvering was changing the one and eliminating the other. Conservatives argued among themselves that if both Withers and Walker ran, the conservative vote would divide and Wells would win. The *Virginian* would have none of that argument. "If the people can elect Colonel Walker as a Republican opposed to the Underwood constitution," it argued, "we can with greater certainty elect Colonel Withers. . . . To attain this end why forfeit our pledges and stultify ourselves?"

To this sort of argument the *Journal* retorted that "the political course of the Norfolk *Virginian* has involved that paper in a mesh of difficulties and inconsistencies from which all its writhings and twistings fail to free it . . . it evinces too much false pride, or too much obstinacy. . . ." For Stuart and the Conservative Party leaders would not be stopped. Under the slogan of "Universal Suffrage and Universal Amnesty," they forced the resignation of Withers and his fellow candidates. That left the field clear for a direct clash between Wells, the candidate of Radical Republicans, and Walker, the candidate of moderate Republicans plus the greater part of the Virginia Conservatives, who in turn included the greater part of the Virginia Democrats.

But not the *Virginian.* Just before the Conservative state convention of April, 1869, that would determine the course, the *Virginian* went further than it had ever gone on any public issue:

> We stand fast in opposition to the obnoxious equality, school, tax, jury and gerrymandering provisions of the Underwood constitution; and as long as the freedom of the press remains, we shall protest against Republicanism. . . . Tell us to join the Republican party in any form—tell us to endorse negro suffrage—tell us to bend the pregnant hinges of the knee to presidential or congressional dictation—and we reiterate the sentiment for which we have been taken to task: "Better that every man, woman and child in Virginia were shot." Now if the Conservative convention attempts to pledge us to any of these things we bolt.

Only great strain could move a newspaper of the character of the *Virginian* to such lengths. But its tactics were impractical. The deeper it dug its defenses, the more lonely it found itself. Politically it was not realistic; verbally it was far gone in emotionalism. The very ground it stood on was shifting.

In May, President Grant gave his approval to—and thereby in the political sense justified—the Conservative program. Congress approved Grant's recommendation that separate votes could be cast on the disfranchising provision and on the test oath provision, both of which now would be excluded from the Underwood constitution if voters so decided. The goal of the Conservative Party was coming closer.

Walker's opening campaign speech in Norfolk called Negro suffrage an irrevocable fact—"one that no effort on our part can wipe out." But provisions of the Underwood constitution would disfranchise 95 per cent of the white men, he thought, and to prevent this he would devote all his power. White men who refused to vote on the issues would, in effect, vote for the unexpurgated constitution. "We agree with this much," the *Virginian* grimly commented.

When a Conservative statement, summing up just before the election, declared that "not to vote with our friends is to give half support to our enemies," the *Virginian* itself summed up: "Being without a candidate of our own, we prefer Mr. Walker to his carpetbag opponent, but first, last and all the time we implore our friends to vote down the Underwood constitution. . . . Cast your ballots against the two clauses [disfranchisement and test oath] and then against the entire instrument." On the eve of the voting the *Virginian*, though still fighting for its views, conceded that an expurgated constitution would be adopted.

So the July vote itself ran. Walker carried the state over Wells by 119,535 to 101,204, though Wells carried Norfolk by 2,094 to 2,014. Voters in the state beat the test oath by 124,360 to 84,410 and the disfranchisement provision by 124,715 to 83,458. Otherwise they voted for the Underwood constitution by 210,585 to 6,136. Norfolk voters split almost equally on the oath and disfranchisement provisions, but upheld them. On the constitution otherwise only 170 Norfolk voters said nay.

In better temper after the voting, the *Virginian* cried out: "Farewell to carpetbaggers! Mister Wells has come to grief. He has nothing left but to pack his bag and creep out of the state which he has so long disgraced and outraged."

Two months later, in September, 1869, the Grant administration prodded Wells into resigning, and Walker was named provisional governor until the term of office to which he had been elected began in January, 1870. The *Virginian*, still lacking a Richmond correspondent or other means of immediately covering Walker's inauguration as provisional governor, fell back on its old reliance: reprinting the Richmond *Dispatch*'s reports a day later. But it had its own views about the new governor:

> It is known to him and this community that we stood by Colonel Withers to the last; and that we supported Colonel Walker, as we earnestly did, on personal and not political grounds.
>
> We shall give him our best aid in the management of the affairs of state; and we belong to those who, having read his speeches carefully, do not expect from him anything but a "true Republican" administration. Differing widely in Federal politics, we can understand that his action in state affairs will be wise and judicious. . . .
>
> We shall not look at his actions with a partisan microscope but with the naked eye of candor.
>
> We would willingly pause here; but, unhappily the Governor of Virginia in these evil times has Federal relations which we cannot ignore. The time was when the states dictated to the Federal authority, but that time has passed; and Governor Walker finds himself installed in office during a period of transition in which local liberty and central power stand arrayed on their last battlefield, with all the might in favor of the central power.

His own sagacity will tell him that it is here that his chief danger lies.

Walker appointed Cameron, the editor, as his secretary, and the *Virginian* thought that "in this appointment we have the best guarantee that the administration, which we hope some day to see standing on its own legs, will be catholic and wise—a combination of the old, to which we stick, and the new, of which Captain Cameron was so able and active an exponent." But three months of secretarial work were enough for Cameron, and the *Virginian* agreed that "his quick and eager temper is better suited to the active duties of the press than to the routine office."

In October, 1869, the General Assembly quickly ratified the Fourteenth and Fifteenth Amendments, the first by 36 to 4 in the Senate and 126 to 6 in the House of Delegates, and the second by 40 to 2 in the Senate and unanimously in the House. Ratification was essential to restoration in the Union, but the approach to unanimity on all votes for amendments which many Virginians did not like was impressive evidence of how much Virginians wished to return to the Union.

That done, the General Assembly sent a committee to Washington to confer with the administration on Virginia's restoration. Politicians there were puzzled and at first hesitant. They had not encountered anything like the Conservative coalition that elected Walker. What did it mean when Republicans produced the winning candidate and Democrats (whatever they called themselves at the moment) produced much of the winning vote? How long would this Conservative Party stand up as such? To what extent could national political leaders count on it? Who would control Virginia politically if it broke up?

It *had* been an unusual setup. It *was* confusing to see a Republican candidate, out of New York and Chicago, with a Union colonel's commission and a Virginia residence not yet five years old, getting such strong Confederate support so soon after Appomattox. But the arrangements satisfied Virginia and Washington majorities, primarily because Walker's election represented a middle-of-the-road movement between the extremes of Radicalism and Bourbonism, both of which Virginia avoided, and emphatically because this seemed the shortest, quickest route to restoration in the Union.

Restoration came finally on January 27, 1870, to the immense delight of the *Journal* and to the more restrained approval of the *Virginian*. The latter was not so strongly attached to "the old, to which we stick," that it did not wish to escape from military rule. Throughout Virginia, where affection for the old Union was strong—had not earlier Virginians played leading roles in establishing it?—the satisfaction was wide and deep. Nowhere was that satisfaction expressed more ardently than in the *Journal*:

> With honor untarnished and escutcheon undimmed the grand old Commonwealth emerges from the smoke of the conflict, victorious at last over foes without and foes within, and once again takes position among the sisterhood of states . . . We who girded our armor early in this conflict may be pardoned perhaps a little enthusiasm in the moment of triumph. When we look back upon the sneers which we encountered, the taunts with which we were greeted, it is a little difficult not to repress some feeling of elation at our success. . . .

But the road from surrender to restoration had been marked by much tragedy. Nothing better illustrated the temper of the times among men of intelligence and of old codes of behavior, or the violence of language and action which could erupt when old and new political forces were clashing, than the duel in 1869 between two newspapermen, William E. Cameron and Robert W. Hughes.

Cameron was still editor of the Petersburg *Index*. Hughes, a leading advocate of Wells in the election of that year and a champion of old-line Republicans, was writing editorials for the Richmond *State Journal*. Born in Powhatan County and reared in Abingdon, he practiced law in Richmond and wrote much for newspapers there. His political views were positive; his sharpness and power in expressing them were marks of a keen mind. Later Hughes ran for governor and lost to James L. Kemper, a one-time Confederate general. After Underwood's death he was named his successor as United States judge of the Eastern District of Virginia. He lived many years in Norfolk, wrote biographies of considerable merit, and always was a vigorous and pungent personality. In June, 1869, a month before the election, he was all partisan and all fighter. So was Cameron.

On June 14 the *Virginian* reprinted a "report of a proposed affair of honor" from the Richmond *Dispatch* of June 12. The Petersburg *Index* had published editorial comment which began thus:

> There is an article in Friday evening's State Journal which in its very violence and virulence betrays its parentage. Hell has no fury like a woman scorned perhaps, but humanity knows no hatred so bitter, so reckless, so unrelenting, as that which the traitor feels toward those whom he has betrayed. None but a renegade Virginian, smarting under the sense of his own

shameless treachery, and brimming with enmity to all that is
better and truer than himself—an Arnold seeking to clothe his
baseness by slander of the cause he has sold—would have penned
such language in regard to Virginia gentlemen as what which
we quote.

Then the *Index* published this quotation from the *State Journal*:

If names could typify the meaning of words, the *mene, mene
tekel upharsin,* which a bloody and destructive history has pronounced upon the sectional party that has so long ruled and
ruined in Virginia, is especially expressed in such names as Bocock, Douglas and Aylett. These are but types that have gone
forth to re-invoke the people to courses of treason. It is well
for the causes of loyalty, reconstruction and state regeneration
that a class of parricides so notorious, with the mark of Cain
on their foreheads, and the guilt of Cain upon their consciences,
have gone out as the champions of a discontented, remonstrant
and incorrigible sectionalism. They know that the ascendency
of national ideas and loyal sentiments must consign them to
fixed and branded obscurity, and in the spirit of Beelzebub,
"Better to rule in hell than to serve in heaven," they are ready
to drag down the Commonwealth into a deeper damnation than
that in which she already writhes and perishes.[1]

Having thus laid out the words which he found objectionable,
Cameron expressed in the *Index* his opinion of the man who wrote
them, the newspaper in which they appeared, and the judgment that
produced them. He wrote:

There is one journalist in this state who is at the same time
sufficiently capable as a writer and utterly degraded enough in
character to have indited these lines. He is one of those who
lent truculence and almost inhuman bitterness to the Richmond
Examiner during the war—the man upon whom John M. Daniel
chiefly relied for his strongest appeals to the worst passions of
our people. [Daniel was editor of the Richmond *Examiner.*]
He sat at the feet of John B. Floyd, a disciple who forgot all
that was good in the lessons of his master, but seized upon the
bad with the instinct of natural depravity, cultivating and developing it to a depth which Peter in his denial never knew.

1. The men referred to are apparently Thomas Stanley Bocock, 1815-91, who
was delegate to the Virginia General Assembly, representative in the United States
Congress, speaker in the Confederate States Congress, and delegate to the Democratic National Conventions of 1868, 1876, and 1880; Beverly Browne Douglas, 1822-
78, who was senator in the Virginia General Assembly, 1852-65, delegate to the
Democratic National Convention in 1868, and representative in the United States
Congress; and Patrick Henry Aylett, 1825-70, who was a lawyer, politician, and
contributor to the Richmond *Examiner.*

THE NORFOLK VIRGINIAN.

VOLUME I.　　　　　NORFOLK, VA., THURSDAY, NOVEMBER 23, 1865.　　　　　NUMBER 3.

The third issue of *The Norfolk Virginian*, dated November 23, 1865, is the earliest copy extant.

James Barron Hope, founder and editor of *The Norfolk Landmark*.

Michael Glennan managed *The Norfolk Virginian*, 1876-98.

Paul S. Huber, president of Norfolk Newspapers, Inc., 1933.

Louis I. Jaffé, editor of the Norfolk *Virginian-Pilot*, 1919-50.

[Floyd was governor of Virginia, 1849-52; secretary of war in Buchanan's cabinet, 1857-61; a general in the Confederate military forces until his death in 1863].

His first act after the war was to connect himself with the dirtiest of all the poisonous sheets which disgraced Virginia since 1864—the Richmond Republic—and his undeniable versatility as a writer was there employed to brand as infamous all that he had advocated for six years previous. Since then he has played a part which is, thank God, a stranger to Virginia journalism. His venal pen has been sold to the highest bidder to bolster any and every cause whose directors were willing to buy his brains. He has said that his articles were merchandise, and that if sufficiently remunerated he would feel justified in advocating polygamy. And the time came when his former friends, finding how valueless were the views which the public knew were bought and sold like herrings in the market place, ceased to remember his talent in the presence of his want of principle.

He is now contributing editorially to the Richmond State Journal, which has lost thereby four-fifths of its previous claims to respectability. The people of Virginia want no stronger evidence of unreliability in a public print than to know that its sentiments flow from the purchased pen of Robert W. Hughes.

What followed was, in view of the two men thus arrayed and of the code by which they lived, inevitable. The Richmond *Dispatch* reported, and the *Virginian* reprinted, that Ernest Wiltz, local editor of the *State Journal*, rode from Richmond to Petersburg with a note from Hughes to Cameron described as "in the nature of a peremptory challenge" and requesting Cameron to "name a friend."

Cameron assumed responsibility for what had appeared in the *Index*, declined the full and public retraction that was demanded, and named Ernest Lagarde, local editor of the Petersburg *Daily Express*, to act for him. A "hostile meeting" was agreed upon.

It was difficult—in this instance, impossible—to keep such an affair, involving two such well-known men, hidden from law enforcement officials, especially after the cause of the affair had been spread before the public for anyone to read. Richmond's Mayor George Chahoon had Wiltz arrested and put under bond to keep the peace. But Petersburg officials could not find Cameron and Lagarde.

The seconds arranged a meeting at the village of Chester, near Richmond. The principals, accompanied by friends (General Mahone was one of those with Cameron), were approaching the spot when a Chesterfield County constable and a justice of the peace suddenly appeared. The Cameron and Hughes parties fled. Cameron got away.

The others were caught. The justice of the peace put all of them under bonds to keep the peace.

Still undeterred, the two parties regrouped and planned once more to meet. Forfeiture of bonds would follow a meeting in Virginia, but not in another state. The seconds chose ground on the bank of the Dismal Swamp Canal, just across the North Carolina border from Norfolk, near what was called The Line House.

The two groups found it necessary to travel to the chosen ground by a freight train. Rigid in obedience to the code, they arranged to have two passenger cars attached to the freight train. In one sat Cameron and his friends. In the other sat Hughes and his friends. They debouched at Deep Creek near Norfolk. Two hacks were waiting at the station. In separate conveyances they rode to the field of honor.

This time no agent of the law had succeeded in pursuit. At the command to fire, Cameron fired and missed—fired without aim, by the written account. Hughes took more careful aim, fired deliberately, and got his man. His bullet hit Cameron in the left side of the chest. It was a flesh wound, "not penetrating to the cavity of the chest or entering the muscles of the region."

Hughes demanded a second round of fire. Cameron agreed. But Cameron's surgeon said he had been hit too hard and forbade his patient to continue the duel. Cameron's friends drew up a statement and submitted it to Hughes and his friends. Hughes accepted it. It read: "Mr. Cameron received a flesh wound immediately over the lower lobe of the left lung, which disabled him entirely, according to the statement of his physician. Mr. Hughes, having demanded a second fire, was informed by us that Mr. Cameron was unable to receive another fire. Mr. Hughes, having received satisfaction, the meeting is therefore adjourned."

Cameron received surgical treatment on the spot and was placed in his hack. Both parties returned to Deep Creek, caught a return freight train at 9:30 p.m. and arrived at Petersburg at 7:00 a.m. the next day. It was the Sabbath morning.

Years later (as reported in the Norfolk *Ledger-Dispatch*, September 29, 1959) when Cameron was governor of Virginia and Hughes was United States judge, they met by chance in a Richmond hotel bar. Cameron walked toward Hughes, touched his arm, and said, "Judge, let me buy you a drink."

"That would be a pleasure," Hughes replied.

Arm in arm, they walked to the bar.

DUELS WERE NEWS OF IMPORTANCE AND HIGH READABILITY, AND THE NEWS-papers of Virginia printed as much about the Cameron-Hughes duel as they could learn. Public opinion against duels was hardening, as law enforcement actions and constitutional provisions show. But the feeling did not prevent men—a small minority of the total population —who had inherited certain concepts of social behavior, or others who sought to adopt and exemplify these concepts, from following the dictates of the code. The time was less than five years after the war, and violence could manifest itself in many ways. For instance:

The murder of H. Rives Pollard, the Richmond editor, in November, 1868, not only was compounded of passion and personal vengeance but also involved newspaper personalities and therefore excited the press all the more. Pollard was editor then of a weekly called *Southern Opinion*. While he was with the Richmond *Examiner* in January, 1866, he had been one of the principals in a celebrated gun battle in the rotunda of the State Capitol against Nathaniel Tyler and William D. Coleman, both of the Richmond *Enquirer*. Nobody was hit. The House of Delegates, which had been in session a few feet away, tried and formally reprimanded Pollard. This wild affray was reported for the New York *Times* by E. P. Brooks in a humorous and sarcastic style that Pollard thought insulting enough to require him to cowhide Brooks in the lobby of the Spotswood Hotel—all of which the *Virginian* reported in voluminous detail by clipping the Richmond *Dispatch*'s stories.

Pollard's associate editor in 1868 was J. Marshall Hanna, recently editor of the *Virginian*. He wrote the report in *Southern Opinion* that led to the murder, but he was represented as writing under orders from Pollard and was not held responsible for what followed.

Hanna's detailed story appeared later as a reprint on the *Vir-*

ginian's front page. It told of the romance of Mary Grant, "a favorite of the Richmond social set," and Horace Ford, a young man of Goochland County who had "ventured out for a swim in the sea of gay life and love." They were engaged to be married—"he plighted his troth and accepted her tiny hand" was the language of *Southern Opinion*.

Later Ford told friends he was leaving for Texas and did not mention his affianced. Then, the story ran, Mary determined to follow him. But actually, *Southern Opinion* explained, the two went to New York, and "there is a very sorry family history connected with the case, which it is not our province to reveal."

Southern Opinion had revealed enough for Mary's brother, James Grant. Armed with a shotgun and two pistols, he stationed himself in a building facing Pollard's Main Street newspaper office. When Pollard approached his office, Grant, from his concealed position, fired one blast of his gun, and Pollard fell dead.

The whole state gasped at this affair. The *Virginian's* account ran to more than two columns on page one. "We have no harsh judgment to pronounce upon the deceased," the *Virginian* reflected on the editorial page, but it did not like Pollard's kind of journalism.

> . . . we do say [it continued] that in temper and judgment he evidently lacked the coolness of the one and the soundness of the other necessary to a fit discharge of the responsible duties of a public journalist. Of his cruel assassination, we have little to remark at present, for this will at once become the subject of a judicial investigation . . . but we trust this dreadful event will put an end now and forever to that peculiar style of sensational writing upon which Mr. Pollard had deliberately modeled his editorial career.
>
> There is a broad line of demarkation between the criticism of men who are in public position or aspirants for office, and the invasion of the domestic circle or delineation of the habits of private persons. . . .

Two days later the *Virginian* had additional reflections: "We . . . place on record, in the plainest and most unmistakable terms, our abhorrence of the cowardly manner in which the editor of the Southern Opinion was put to death. We do not remember, within our experience, any such event, nor have we seen any person who does recall a similar occurrence in Virginia. Men have been shot down in the streets of our cities; they have fallen in duels, but until now we have lacked the deliberate act of the assassin. The example set in this case is wicked and cowardly. . . ."

The Northern press thought so too, and the *Virginian* had to deal with the New York *Times.* That newspaper "announced the other day with great gravity that Southern civilization is symbolized by the pistol, and left the impression upon its readers that 'murder' was recognized by our people as an 'art', and practiced with a sort of dilletanteism awful to behold. All this grew out of the assassination of Mr. Pollard. That one fact, in the judgment of the critic, authorized his flattering conclusion."

Thereupon the *Virginian* rebuked critics in a region where, if the *Illustrated Police News* was an authority, criminality flourished, though "we will not imitate the writer in the Times and say that the columns of the Police News furnish a just exhibit of the morals of that great section." But the *Virginian* did agree with Henry Ward Beecher "in his declaration that the vice of New England is the hardest and most cruel in the world."

In the trial in March, 1869, Grant's counsel told the jury that it had two duties: "to determine whether or not Grant had killed Pollard, and, if he did, to ask themselves if he was not right." Nobody doubted that Grant had killed Pollard, and, as the verdict showed, no real doubt existed in the minds of the jurors of the answer to the second question. They acquitted Grant.

The *Virginian* wound up the case by declaring the original article—the one Hanna wrote for Pollard—was "scurrilous . . . full of falsehood and slanderous accusations." But the acquittal "must clearly be regarded by no means as an approval of a dangerous and too frequent practice in this country—that of seeking the redress of grievances by taking the law into one's own hands—but rather it is an indication of the feeling with which an entire community indignantly protests against anything like 'blackmailing'...."

No such solemnities marked another affair of the times. In May of 1869 the *Virginian* reported that William H. Brooks, Sr., a mayor of Norfolk by military appointment during the Union army occupation, had received "a severe castigation with a cowhide at the hands of Miss Ellen Carter, of irreproachable character."

Miss Carter had heard that the former mayor had used scandalous language about her. She had no male protectors at hand, but she did not need any. She went to the current mayor's office to find out what redress she could get from the law. The answer was unsatisfactory. Thereupon she bought a "keen rawhide" for twenty-five cents and stationed herself along the path which the former mayor would take.

When he came by, Miss Carter rushed into action with the rawhide flying. Four times, five times, she slashed His ex-Honor across the face. He attacked her with a cudgel. They clinched. He fell to the ground. The rawhide cut his cheek again and again. He scrambled up and fled. All that was left were his oaths to be avenged. But they hardly mattered so long as Miss Carter retained her rawhide.

For wide interest the newspapers of the times, with the *Virginian* especially vigorous, found it difficult—or thought they did—to beat a hanging. Norfolk itself had few hangings. As late as 1887, when the *Virginian* printed a historical review of celebrated hangings, it could find only four in the city in sixty-six years. The first of these, far back in 1821, was the execution of two Spaniards, Santiago Castilano and Emanuel Garcia, who had been convicted of killing Peter La Gaudette, a Frenchman. These two hangings were frequently recalled when hanging was being considered as a method of execution, a public entertainment or, from the hangman's point of view, a skill and even an art.

In its 1887 review the *Virginian* reported, not overlooking many details, that the hangman was nervous and bungled the fitting of the noose on Garcia's neck. He failed to put the knot under the left ear. Castilano protested but to no avail; Garcia "strangled to death amid the most agonizing tortures fearful to behold." Castilano, on the other hand, asked and received the privilege of "adjusting the rope around his own neck, which he did with the utmost coolness . . . and he died without a struggle."

But if Norfolk offered few hangings for public display, other localities in Virginia and North Carolina did. When a former soldier in the Union army, originally of Massachusetts, was hanged in Portsmouth in October, 1868, for rape, much of the debate related to whether his accomplice should have been hanged too. Governor Wells commuted his sentence to life imprisonment. Because the accomplice was a Negro, the issue went far enough to interest the New York *Herald*. It noted that "the white man was taken and the Negro was left," and it reflected on political possibilities in such circumstances and asked, "In view of this extraordinary case who should say the Negro had no rights which the white man is bound to respect?"

Two years later Isle of Wight County hanged four Negro men for killing a white man. The *Virginian* printed more than three columns about it on page one. The proceedings were so badly fouled up that the *Virginian*'s account denounced the hangman as "a brutal monster" who had "dishonored his occupation" by horrors "which made strong men shudder and turn pale." New York, Richmond, and Petersburg newspapers had reporters on the scene.

Nearby Suffolk presented a hanging in 1873 that drew much more newspaper attention. There James Brown, a Negro, was hanged for killing two women whom he wished to rob. The crime was on June 1, and the execution on July 11—swift justice.

So great was the interest that extra coaches had to be attached to the train from Norfolk. Ten newspapers had reporters on the scene: the Norfolk *Virginian*, the Norfolk *Journal*, the New York *Herald*, the New York *World*, the Richmond *Dispatch*, the Richmond *Whig*, the Richmond *Courier*, the Petersburg *Index*, the Rockingham *Register*, and the Portsmouth *Enterprise*. The *Virginian's* front-page story the next day had a head with these droplines:

THE GALLOWS
A Terrible Crime Avenged
James Brown Executed
A Man Without Friends
His Remarks on the Scaffold
He Exculpates His Wife
Selling His Body
His Neck Broken
Immense Gathering
Good Order Prevails
Incidents

This was a formidable head for a report that began in this leisurely manner: "Yesterday was a somewhat remarkable day in Suffolk, and there were more visitors in that ancient village than at any time within the memory of the oldest inhabitant. All were intent on witnessing the execution of James Brown. . . ." This time efficiency prevailed on the scaffold, and the event, not the details with which it was carried out, had to preach whatever sermon there was.

In 1879 the *Virginian* sent a reporter to Hillsborough, North Carolina, nearly two hundred miles away, to cover the hanging of three men, and required two columns to report the details. The next day (May 18) it congratulated itself on "the enterprise" which had been "exhibited yesterday in a marked manner by its full account of the triple execution in North Carolina. It was an enterprise not shown by any other paper in the two states." Within the next two months the *Virginian* sent reporters to cover five other hangings in Virginia and North Carolina. One of these, in Warrenton, was the first in Virginia from which a new statute barred the general public and limited witnesses to court officials and about twenty-five other witnesses.

In 1880 when the official hangman of London came to the United States—the Norfolk newspapers called him Marwood, without first name or initials, as befitted a celebrity—his methods received careful consideration. Marwood was particular about his rope. He insisted on a length of eight or nine feet. Thus equipped, he argued, he could execute a wretch less painfully than an executioner with a guillotine, an ax, or a shorter rope. He inspected gallows in the United States and pronounced them semibarbarous. In Norfolk his views received the close attention that any expert's would. When he died in 1883 his career was reviewed with the respect due to one who had executed more than a hundred criminals in a dozen years.

Norfolk newspapers regarded the first electric chair execution in the United States, in 1890, as important news. Virginia used the gallows much longer, and apparently with increasing skill. Of a double hanging in Danville in 1892, the Norfolk *Public Ledger* (established in 1876) reported that "a better execution was never witnessed, both dying without a struggle."

But hangings nearly always had backgrounds of notable violence, or involved people who possessed or gained notoriety, or had aroused public passion. Such incitements were added to the curiosity which made executions public entertainments in more sedate civilizations in western Europe as well as in many American states. Lynchings did not reach their peak until the 1890's. Mob actions earlier were more likely to emerge from mass displays and demonstrations, like the parade of Negroes in April, 1866, to celebrate the passage of the civil rights bill of that year. Four years later, in November, 1870, a riot in Norfolk, growing out of a political meeting, included violent disorders and strikingly different reports of how they began and who was responsible.

Secretary of the Navy George M. Robeson had come to the city to urge the reelection of the Radical Republican congressman, James H. Platt. At a meeting in the courthouse yard former Mayor Francis DeCordy, former Governor Wells, and Professor John M. Langston of Howard University spoke too. Present also for the purpose of "dividing the time," in the language of the *Virginian*, was William E. Cameron. He had been invited by Platt.

Secretary Robeson's speech was marked by disorders between blacks whom primarily he was addressing and whites who hovered on the outskirts of the crowd. He got through with it, but, according to a friendly account, he narrowly escaped being hit in the face with a bundle of nails tied up in rags. But when Professor Langston came forward as the next speaker—the *Virginian* identified him as "a negro by the name of Lancaster"—Cameron and his friends protested that it was their turn. Later, replied Republican spokesmen. Now, insisted the Cameron men. Not until Langston finishes, they were told.

And with that the clashes between Conservatives and Radicals, already bad, flared up in a series of fights, beatings, shootings, and the killing of one or more participants and the wounding of many more.

When the newspapers began to report these events, their news stories were strikingly contradictory, and, in the spirit of contemporary political writing, they were emotional, partisan, and denunciatory. In these respects the chief antagonists were the *Virginian* and the Richmond *State Journal*, whose account the *Virginian* described as a "mendacious history of the Norfolk riot." After contemplating these reports Federal Judge John C. Underwood, of constitution-making fame, and hardly an impartial witness himself, wrote his own account for the Washington *Chronicle*. It began thus: "We had a grand torchlight procession and one of the most able and scholarly speeches from Secretary Robeson that I ever heard," but it had to end like this: "I am sorry, however, to be compelled to add that after the secretary had finished and Professor Langston had begun to speak, the chivalry began to hoot, throw eggs, fire pistols into the crowd, wounding several, and finally breaking up the meeting."

To its credit—and perhaps because it knew interesting reading matter when it encountered it—the *Virginian*, after publishing its own report, reprinted on later days not only the "mendacious" report of the Richmond *State Journal* but the dissenting opinion of Judge Underwood.

IN THE YEARS THAT LED TO VIRGINIA'S RESTORATION TO THE UNION AND far beyond, the dominant public need and the fighting issue for the newspapers of Norfolk, second only to Reconstruction issues, was railway development. When the city came out of the war, it had no operating railroad connections whatever. Military forces had ripped up the rails and burned the bridges of both the Norfolk & Petersburg Railroad, which the young engineer William Mahone had built in the 1850's, and the Seaboard & Roanoke, which ran southwestward into North Carolina to the Roanoke River near Weldon.

 Waterborne transportation connected Norfolk through the Albemarle and Chesapeake Canal, and in lesser degree through the Dismal Swamp Canal, with coastal North Carolina; through the James River with Richmond; through Chesapeake Bay with Washington and Baltimore; through lesser bays, rivers, and inlets with the neighboring towns, like Hampton; and through Hampton Roads and out the Virginia Capes with the Atlantic Ocean. These were unparalleled resources in Virginia, but for their full development long-line connections south and north, and above all westward—as men thought then— were essential for the port.

In the first flush of railroad building and the scramble for state aid before the war, Norfolk had encountered heavy opposition from the fall line cities of Alexandria, Richmond, and Petersburg. They exercised large political influence. The state itself was deeply committed to canal construction on a grand scale toward the Kanawha and Ohio Rivers.

The *Virginian* reprinted in December, 1869, a New York *Tribune* estimate that $50,000,000 more would be needed to build a canal connecting the James and the Kanawha, for which Virginia had already spent $10,000,000. The figures were disputed but not the certainty of large sums needed for such an enterprise. The lack of east-west connections had dropped Norfolk far behind more northerly ports before the war. Now, after the war, the economic, financial, and political struggle began again.

The Seaboard & Roanoke needed more than six months for repairs before trains could run, the Norfolk & Petersburg nearer ten months. But neither line could carry trains deeper into regions where many raw materials were produced. Each was only a first step toward the Far South or the Mississippi Valley, the Middle West, the Pacific Coast. Hence the excitement in Norfolk in 1867 when the Norfolk & Great Western Railroad was designed—on paper—to run westward near the North Carolina border to Danville and on to Bristol and thence, in a dream of empire, to San Francisco.

Stock in this railroad was on sale in July of that year. In Norfolk, Colonel William Lamb, Gilbert C. Walker (before he was elected governor), and General George Blow directed the sale. In upstate counties land was being sold along the line on which the railroad would pass. The *Virginian* grew enthusiastic. Its first arguments were built on the immigration possibilities that fascinated Tidewater Virginia during these years.

"Are we to see" this steady tide of immigrants "flow forever past our doors toward the Northwest or into the middle states to increase their opulence and power," the *Virginian* asked, "while we, with our broad fields and noble rivers and rich valleys and mountains of mineral wealth languish for population? . . . we feel perfectly assured that the most practical scheme yet presented on a comprehensive scale to the public is that of the Norfolk & Great Western Railroad. Population means wealth and power. It is the one thing which we lack to place us in the front rank of the American states. . . ."

When a Pennsylvania engineer asserted that "Norfolk was destined by providence to be the largest city on the Atlantic coast," he found himself overnight a Norfolk hero. At a mass meeting in Norfolk in September of 1867 General Blow declared that "the proposed route is the very best in an easterly and westerly direction to attract to our city the products of the great west." The meeting adopted resolutions supporting the Great Western, which, it was told, was no rival of the more northerly east-west route that people were also talking about, along the Norfolk & Petersburg and connections yet to be attained farther west.

When progress toward the Great Western seemed slow, the *Virginian* pointed out a year later, in August of 1868, that "men from England and Scotland have visited the state with a view to purchase cheap lands. Let no man suppose that the scheme has been abandoned." Six months later in January of 1869, when the *Virginian* got hold of a physical survey of Virginia by Commodore Matthew Fontaine Maury, then a member of the Virginia Military Institute faculty, it pointed with pride to his encouraging words. "The grand geographical fact that Norfolk on the Atlantic corresponds with San Francisco on the Pacific in commercial value is illustrated in a thousand ways," the *Virginian* concluded.

Even when the golden spike was driven in the Union Pacific Railroad, the *Virginian* (in May, 1869) expressed "well-founded doubt as to the practicality of the line to do what was claimed for it . . . we fancy the more we hear of it, the deeper will become the now general conviction that this scheme has been from the beginning the most stupendous 'job' that ever disgraced any country in the world."

And when the firm of Link & Company was reported to be investing $7,000,000 in the Great Western, and settling "good people" on 500,000 acres along the route, the cheers rose again. But when the Link boom burst in August, 1869, the Richmond *Enquirer* (no friend of the Great Western) said the Great Western would have to get along "in the old way, and will not have 1,000 laborers at work in 60 days and will not be finished by January 1, 1872—unless they can catch Link and make him pay."

There was rarely any rapport between Norfolk and Richmond in those years. To the opposition of Richmond and upstate interests in other east-west and north-south lines was added the interest of larger railroads to the North, principally the Baltimore & Ohio, which had its own route through the mountains and its own connections with the growing Middle West, and the Pennsylvania, which had far-flung lines and would never welcome new rivals. Norfolk often felt isolated and alone and therefore would grasp more eagerly at straws in the wind.

This the city did again when, in April, 1870, Colonel Thomas S. Flournoy, president of the Norfolk & Great Western, said construction would start August 1 if public support developed. In June, Norfolk merchants and other citizens called by resolution for a referendum to sanction the city's purchase of $1,000,000 of Great Western bonds. Colonel Lamb presided at the meeting which adopted the resolution, and Michael Glennan, of the *Virginian*, acted as secretary.

A fight immediately developed. One Norfolk citizen, W. H. Turner, tried at the meeting to set aside the bond-buying proposal. Norfolk already had a bonded debt of $1,711,000 and a floating debt of $325,000, he pointed out. City bonds were selling at fifty to fifty-five cents on the dollar, and interest had not been paid for twelve months.

Colonel Lamb retorted that the men who were building the Southern Pacific were interested in the Great Western, and the opportunity was too large for Norfolk to miss. He expected to see Norfolk become the eastern terminus of the Southern Pacific. When the resolution won approval, the Corporation Court set the referendum for July 19.

The *Virginian* plunged into the campaign. It published insistent editorials calling for approval of the bond purchase. It ran a series of ten articles—signed "Civis," who was not publicly identified—ranging from New York's experience with the Erie Canal and Baltimore's interest in the Baltimore & Ohio Railroad to Norfolk's unrealized railroad opportunities in the past and its inadequate connections now. It printed a statement from Flournoy and Mahone of the consolidated line built on the Norfolk & Petersburg that there was no conflict between the two. It delighted in Flournoy's announcement that the Great Western would have its principal offices and shops in Norfolk.

But all this did not prevent the bond plan from being beaten at the polls. It won a majority of the votes but lacked forty-six of reaching the required three-fifths majority. "The negro vote, plus the fact that two-thirds of the registered voters did not go to the polls, KILLED NORFOLK'S CHANCES FOR THIS TRUNK LINE RAILROAD," the *Virginian* asserted. Twelve years would have to pass before a new railroad company, the Atlantic & Danville, was organized in the 1880's to build a railroad where the first link of the unrealistic Great Western was planned.

In another direction Norfolk's struggle for railroads to the West brought richer fruits and, in the long run, immense benefits. Before the war the Norfolk & Petersburg had been a valuable line so far as it extended, bringing to Norfolk the products of southern Virginia and, through transfer at Petersburg, the products of western Virginia. As soon as he returned from the war, Mahone sought to regain the presidency of the railroad, then in Federal hands. When he succeeded, he set about restoring the line to operating condition. He had trains running by February, 1866.

This energy attracted the favorable attention of the Southside Railroad, which extended 123 miles westward from Petersburg to Lynchburg. Before 1866 ran out Mahone had gained the presidency of this railroad, and his eyes were on the Virginia & Tennessee Railroad, which extended 204 miles farther westward from Lynchburg to Bristol on the Tennessee border. If consolidated the three lines would run more than 400 miles from Norfolk across Virginia, but not only that: they would reach out toward the Ohio River. A fourth railroad, the unconstructed but planned Virginia & Kentucky, could carry the line to a connection with the Ohio at Louisville.

These were high stakes, and they excited men's minds. But the Virginia & Tennessee balked at joining the other lines. A wave of opposition developed from other railroads in Virginia and from Maryland and Pennsylvania railroads, now reaching southward to tap Virginia potentials. Mahone's ambitions and his hard-driving methods created personal enemies. The state had nearly $3,000,000 invested in the Norfolk & Petersburg and the Southside, and altogether it had some $18,000,000 invested in railroads, canals, and such public works. The larger interests charged that consolidation would create a monster that would endanger the state's, as well as private, investments.

The old upstate feeling was rampant. "What is Norfolk in the present line—what will she be in the proposed consolidation?" the Lynchburg *Virginian* demanded. "Merely the *shipping point* which Lynchburg *now* is for freight seeking a rapid transit to a foreign market. The proposition then is (and it is nothing more or less) to shift that point from Lynchburg to Norfolk—Norfolk which at the present time has about as much to do with an airline to foreign trade and commercial centres as B. Butler has with the kingdom of Heaven."

In this hard fight Mahone, embracing politics with ardor, turned to the General Assembly. Governor Pierpont was on his side, and early in 1867 the House of Delegates approved a bill authorizing the Norfolk & Petersburg, the Southside, and the Virginia & Tennessee to unite by action of their private stockholders. The new company, if brought thus into being, would be called the Atlantic, Mississippi & Ohio. It would be required to construct within five years the Virginia & Kentucky Railroad from Bristol as far as Cumberland Gap, where Kentucky interests would carry the line on to Louisville.

The A. M. & O. would also have authority to buy the stock holdings of Virginia in the four companies and bonds held by the state against these companies, but unless it bought all such stocks and bonds by May 1, 1868, the charter of the general company would be null and void—a provision that opened the way to bitter fighting.

In April, 1867, the Virginia Senate approved the consolidation plan, and the dream approached reality. The old animosities held up action for months, but in November Mahone was elected president of the A. M. & O. with its authorized capitalization of $25,000,000 and with the unprecedented salary for himself of $25,000—as big as the President of the United States's, his critics gasped. They accused Mahone of many kinds of grandiloquence. Much earlier he had married Otelia Butler. Now, said his enemies, he thought as he contemplated the A. M. & O. with pride that the letters stood for "All Mine and Otelia's."

Troubles rose. The railroad could not buy all state-held stocks and bonds by May 1, 1868, and the charter lapsed. The three railroads were united only in Mahone's presidency of each. The General Assembly would have to approve consolidation again. Both sides squared off for what, twenty-five years later, the Richmond *Dispatch* called "the most terrific railroad fight ever known in the history of Virginia." All the newspapers helped to wage this war: The Richmond *Whig* (which Mahone controlled), the Richmond *State Journal*, the Petersburg *Index*, the Bristol *News*, the Norfolk *Day Book*, and the *Virginian* favoring the consolidation, and the Richmond *Enquirer*, the Richmond *Dispatch*, the Lynchburg *News*, the Lynchburg *Virginian*, and the Norfolk *Journal* opposing, most of them on all counts but the *Journal* because of details of the consolidation rather than the principle of consolidation.

The railroad fight involved the governorship. Pierpont was still for consolidation. But when Mahone heard that Wells, Republican candidate to succeed Pierpont, opposed consolidation and favored selling the state's railroad holdings, he went for Wells' political scalp. He helped the Conservatives to induce Withers to withdraw as candidate for governor in 1869, rallied support for Walker, who, with his Norfolk background, was a strong consolidation man, and managed much of Walker's campaign. Mahone was even charged with responsibility—probably with justification too—for maneuvers within the Republican convention of that year which put a Negro on the Wells ticket as candidate for lieutenant governor in order to discredit the ticket among white voters.

Not all Norfolk sentiment supported consolidation. When the issue came before the directors of the Board of Trade, a fight developed there, largely because Colonel Lamb disapproved of the Mahone leadership. Consolidation carried, though only by 11 to 6. But the *Virginian* never wavered. It followed the Board of Trade's action by patiently explaining (after setting forth other aspects of the plan):

> From Bristol there exists a gap of 150 miles (95 in Virginia, 55 in Kentucky) to form an uninterrupted connection with

Louisville on the Ohio River. When that link is completed a car started in Norfolk may run upon an unbroken road to San Francisco on the Pacific, and a train coming eastward from Louisville or St. Louis will enter Virginia at Cumberland Gap and run upon a line which is nowhere tapped by any competing work of similar gauge. Our friends in Kentucky are becoming impatient at our delay in undertaking construction of this link. They pledge that if Virginia will go to Cumberland Gap, Kentucky will be ready to meet her there. The link cannot be made without first consolidating the three roads that lead from Norfolk to Bristol.

Finally, on June 7, 1870, shortly after Virginia had rejoined the Union, the consolidation bill won legislative approval. The news sent Norfolk into a celebration that included a salute of 111 guns (one for every vote in the two legislative houses) and brought out the long lines of tar barrels in downtown Norfolk that turned night into day for a parade, public speaking, and a wave of exultation.

The Seaboard & Roanoke, the other railroad reliance of Norfolk for nearly two decades after the Civil War (from its terminal in Portsmouth), tapped a large agricultural region in eastern North Carolina. It brought in so much cotton that Norfolk rose close to the top among American cotton ports, and its connections led into central North Carolina for the rising industrialism of the Piedmont. Thus it was a powerful factor in making Norfolk North Carolina's chief port. It stimulated the personal and social relations of Norfolk and North Carolina that originated in the Seventeenth Century and were strong three hundred years later. Long before that time the Seaboard & Roanoke had become one of the foundation pillars on which the Seaboard Air Line Railroad had been erected.

In the dark years of struggle and frustration no other voice in Norfolk—and hardly any other factor of any shape or form—had been so persistent, so unwavering, so convinced of the virtue of appropriate railroad development, and so determined to get it for Norfolk as the *Virginian*. The *Journal* was, by the nature of its ownership and the minds of its editors, more restrained and more cautious. On the *Virginian* the rising Glennan influence stood for growth. The newspaper was demonstrating that spirit in these years.

AS EARLY AS 1865 THE NORFOLK *Post*—THE NEWSPAPER OF "THE BOSTON men who remained over from Ben Butler's New Regime"—had adjured its readers to "just imagine, ye advocates of pumps and cisterns, the contents of such inconvenient receptacles." The *Post* declared that it saw taken from the old well on the corner of Main and Nebraska Streets "four copies of the old Index, any quantity of tin-pots and kettles, several infantile genus canine, one old tabby, and boots and shoes accordingly." Many Norfolk people, having drunk from wells and cisterns all their lives, wanted no change now. But it was a season for new ideas, and in October, 1865, the voters by a three to one decision authorized the borrowing of half a million dollars for a city water system. The source of the water was not yet determined.

But it was also a season when the status of Norfolk in the money markets was low. The city could not borrow the money. It resumed the old system of drinking from wells and cisterns, debating at home and in the city councils about what to do, and arguing the merits of juniper water from Lake Drummond in Dismal Swamp against other sources close at hand, like the lakes near Moore's Bridges in Princess Anne County, and still other sources farther away, like the Blackwater River and other streams to the west of the city.

The succeeding years, 1866, 1867, and 1868, saw a series of investigations, recommendations, and struggles to arrive at a decision. By August of 1868 the city councils were satisfied that "a full supply of pure and wholesome water can be obtained from the Dismal Swamp." They asked voters to authorize expenditures for this purpose.

But the *Virginian* did not trust the men who would administer the money. The city government was controlled then by Republicans. "We are placed at the mercy of the councils and rendered liable to the frauds and oppressions of a 'ring' should the measure be adopted," the *Virginian* argued. "Now who is willing to trust these powers to commissioners appointed by the councils of Norfolk?"

The voters supported this view. In September they turned down the program, and a good thing, too, the *Virginian* declared. Voters felt, the newspapers explained, that "to sanction the scheme would be to commit fat mutton to the keeping of wolves, cheese to the custody of rats, and for this reason mainly the plan was rejected. . . . The people desire a plan which will give them the control and supervision of the work. . . ."

Then came, in the summer of 1869, a great drought. Norfolk's search for "a plentiful supply of pure and wholesome water," the *Virginian* reported, "assumed importance with the heated term, the cessation of our cisterns, and an impending water famine." By September the famine was so serious that the Washington steamer was bringing in one hundred casks of water for Norfolk to drink. All the familiar saws about Lake Drummond and the Princess Anne lakes were heard again. Rains broke the drought in October, but merely postponed the ultimate decisions in engineering and finance.

It was 1872 before the councils decided to tap Deep Creek, into which water from Dismal Swamp flowed. Only when they had awarded a contract did they discover that this plan infringed on the rights of the Dismal Swamp Canal Company, which protested hard and successfully.

The *Virginian* was upset. It had published a long editorial, carefully argued and well sustained, in June of 1871, which went back to 1856 for a start and reviewed numerous arguments down to date, chiefly to approve Lake Drummond's juniper water. To support the case the *Virginian* quoted an engineer who said that "the United States ships for half a century before the war have been supplied for long voyages with juniper water from the Dismal Swamp. This water was preferred in the navy to any in the United States. . . . Age removes its color. . . ." But by January of 1872, contemplating the Dismal Swamp Canal's injunction, the *Virginian* was reflecting sadly: "It seems that the process of getting water in this city is to be attended with all the traditional bother of getting blood out of a turnip."

One difficulty was the city's low credit standing. A $300,000 bond issue, designed for water improvements, found few takers although offered at 8 per cent interest and a discount of 15 per cent. The Richmond *Dispatch* published a fatherly editorial soundly rebuking Norfolk's financial practices, and the *Virginian* reprinted the editorial on January 5. It said:

We regret to hear that Norfolk is not meeting the interest on her public debt. Norfolk is making a great mistake. Assuredly she is able to pay her interest. She has prospered since the war—not as rapidly as she wished—none of us have, but she has prospered. The country around her yields hundreds of dollars to the tens that were made by tilling the soil previous to the war. Such examples of immense shipments of produce from the wharves of Norfolk were never seen before. . . . It is a trade that is peculiar to this age of steam, and is a great blessing to the country, as it places the vegetables and fruits of the gentle Southern clime fresh and healthy upon the colder Northern latitudes weeks before the same are matured there.

We should infer that Norfolk is better off now than she ever was before . . . Assuredly, now is the time to establish her credit as well as build up her commerce. . . .

The Richmond *Whig* joined in this advice but more sharply. In the controversy over the state debt that was emerging as the dominating issue of the times, the *Whig* favored adjustment of the debt while the Norfolk newspapers favored funding of the debt, as did newspapers in Fredericksburg. "Norfolk was the model after which the state funding bill was fashioned," the *Whig* asserted, "and how much are the bonds and coupons of Norfolk and Fredericksburg worth? Will they pay taxes? Are these good people animated by the spirit of the fox in the fable who had lost his tail? Do they wish to reduce the Commonwealth to their tail-less condition?"

The *Virginian* commented on both of the Richmond judgments. Of the *Dispatch's* editorial it said: "We might as well understand at once that money is character. We should resume payments in currency and alleviate the anxiety of our creditors." To the *Whig's* remarks it added this postscript: "What our creditors want is money, and until they see how they are to get it, we may expect our condition to be discussed just in the temper in which the Whig has spoken."

Six months later (July 31, 1872) the *Virginian* was able to publish a news story with this headline:

WATERWORKS. Source of Supply on North Side
Pure and Healthy Water to be Obtained
Moore's Bridges and Vicinity Adequate for the Purpose

The story told of the decision to tap the water at Moore's Bridges, including Lawson's Pond and Bradford's Lake near Lynnhaven Bay. These sources were regarded as ample for supplying the needed 500,000 gallons daily. They were close enough to Norfolk to make the operation comparatively inexpensive.

The *Virginian* approved. It had favored Lake Drummond directly, or the Deep Creek plan, for several reasons, one of them being "to make Portsmouth and the Navy Yard tributary to the support of our enterprise." But "we shall give the commissioners our aid in carrying out that which they have adopted . . . we have stood from the beginning on the broad platform of pure water, in abundant supply, at the least cost."

The new water came in slowly. It was not until the middle 1870's that it was in wide use. But the principle had been established. Although water problems would plague Norfolk again and again they would be the problems of a growing community that had at least the foundation on which it could expand.

Drainage was a tough problem too, for a city built, as Norfolk was, on low, flat ground cut up by numerous bodies of water. The *Journal*, looking at Back Creek as it extended from Bank Street westward to Granby and beyond to the Elizabeth River (where City Hall Avenue now is), called it in July of 1871 a "great, pestiferous, noisome, odorous, odious, and unsightly marsh."

As summer came in a year later the *Virginian* demanded (May, 1872) that the city government do something about the "marshes between Bank and Granby Streets and the Stone Bridge [where Granby Street crossed the marsh] and the harbor." The *Virginian* even proposed, as a temporary expedient, a plan that involved dredging and utilization of the tide to get rid of "the offensive matter carried down into the marshes where, through lack of outflow, it is evaporated and blown over the city by the summer winds."

But neither that plan nor any other was put into effect until 1881. Then private vigor rather than official action wrestled successfully with the problem. A Norfolk businessman with the true entrepreneur spirit, A. A. McCullough, began filling in the marsh on both sides and pressing the water into a narrow channel. He produced with made-land some sixty acres with sound value for warehouses, businesses of many kinds, and even residences. Three years later, with the arrival of the first sewerage system, the city replaced the leftover canal with an underground culvert, filled it in, and thus created City Hall Avenue. The newspapers cheered these achievements.

They cheered horse cars, too. In August, 1869, the Norfolk City Railroad opened its books for subscriptions from the public to establish its lines. Incorporators had taken fifteen hundred shares. Would the public take the other five hundred? The *Virginian* encouraged the sale. Horse cars were profitable in Wilmington, North Carolina, it argued. Why not in Norfolk?

By the following August five cars arrived at Norfolk. They were "magnificent vehicles," the *Virginian* reported, "built of the best materials . . . beautifully decorated . . . to seat 20 persons . . . the chances of accident are greatly reduced . . . a patent box for the reception of tickets prevents delay." (A much later and less reverential report said the drivers sat on "secondhand piano stools.")

Furthermore, "the draught animals to draw these cars have been selected with great care . . . picked out of an immense number on account of their strength, symmetry and endurance . . . their equal pace and steady behavior." The *Virginian* hoped to see "our esteemed townsman, Virginius Freeman, the superintendent . . . called on before long to increase his cars from five to fifty."

The cars ran from the Main and Granby corner northward on Granby to Charlotte Street, then west to the Bute-Botetourt neighborhood. There a turntable permitted the cars to go back to Main and Granby. On Main the cars moved eastward to Church Street and then northward to Princess Anne Road. There another turntable sent them back toward Main Street.

Operations began August 13, 1870, with great éclat. The cars were crowded, some people riding, wrote a reporter, "just for the novelty of the thing." But the strength, symmetry, and endurance of the horses proved insufficient. In March, 1872, "young sprightly mules" were being substituted for "broken down horses," although under horses the cars were "one of the features of Norfolk," said the *Virginian*, "and we know of nothing which has ever been so conducive to the public comfort."

What happened to the young, sprightly mules is not clear, but when a mysterious disease among horses swept the Atlantic seaboard in October, 1872 (later diagnosed as "epizootic influenza"), it was the illness of horses, not of mules, that in early November shut down this transportation in Norfolk. The *Virginian* met this crisis by suggesting the organization of ox teams. But after a few weeks the horses (nothing reported about mules) were back at work. In May of 1882 two-horse teams began to draw larger cars. They carried on the tradition until trolley cars arrived in October, 1894.

Public schools came before the Civil War, the city charter being changed in 1850 to provide them and schools being established by 1857—very early for the South. A tax of $4.00 for each male adult able to pay was the principal support. The war broke down these schools and left them in disarray. But by October of 1867 the *Virginian* could report a pupil attendance of 625, up from 525 the previous year, and some experiments with night schools were being made.

The financial support in Norfolk was so shaky that the *Virginian* reported in January of 1867 the resignation of a school principal "in consequence of the difficulties he labored under in procuring his salary." This infuriated the editor. He asserted bluntly that "the apathy exhibited by the councils upon this all-important subject is to us perfectly inexplicable." The words probably came from Hope, who in the same year found himself appointed one of the school commissioners (which did not seem inappropriate to him or to his associates). Shortly he signed a report showing school expenses that year of $11,893.50.

Hope's interest in education was beyond question. But the *Virginian*, with its editor in the lead, was sharply critical of public school provisions in the Underwood constitution of 1868. The newspaper thought the new constitutional demands were likely to produce "a farce." It insisted that "legislation should also prohibit, by unmistakable enactments, the attendance of white and colored children in the same schools. . . ."

In its segregation views the *Virginian* had the full support of Governor Walker. He called himself "an earnest advocate of universal and free education," and he thought that "if the death knell of American liberty is ever pronounced, ignorance will pull the bell cord. . . ." He insisted that for the colored people to exercise intelligently "the elective franchise," the opportunity for education "should, and under our constitution must be, afforded them." But he told the General Assembly that "the true interests of the colored people themselves demand that they should be provided with separate schools." He himself had "in years past, and under the most favorable circumstances, witnessed a fair and impartial trial of the experiment [of placing white and colored children in the same schools] and it proved an utter failure."

The *Virginian*'s "own wish," it said, "is to give the Negro population of the state every advantage of education." It believed "that they are incapable of profiting largely by the system; but at the same time we are willing and anxious to see it attempted. . . . Ignorance is the worst foe which republican institutions have to encounter."

To these views of 1867 the *Journal* added, in an editorial entitled "The Negro in History," an especially sharp and bitter summary of what, three years after slavery, were probably the views of many white people. "If we search to the ends of the earth and explore through the ages of history," the *Journal* declared, "we shall fail to find a single instance of civil government established or maintained by the Negro race. . . . Of all the crimes, of all the treasons, of all the parricides, of all the crimes against nature and reason which the annals of human vice record, there has been none, no not one, so black and monstrous as this abominable crime of surrendering free government to be dishonored and murdered by the negro savage race."

The *Journal* spoke in this vein at a moment when the Freedmen's Bureau had more than 130,000 Negro children enrolled in its schools in Southern states, including schools in Norfolk and in Portsmouth (*Journal*, May 15, 1867). Norfolk itself was preparing two public schools for Negroes which were in operation before 1872. Before then the *Virginian* praised the first Virginia superintendent of public instruction, William H. Ruffner, for carrying out the mandate of the Underwood constitution. It added that "the public free school system, having met a distressing want among the people, was joyfully adopted by the great majority of the counties of the state." The newspaper had changed notably since its strictures on the Underwood constitution hardly a year earlier.

The financial problems were difficult in a state still deep in economic depression. But by 1872 the *Virginian* in a mellow mood could say that the Norfolk public schools "promise, before long, to compare favorably in point of scholastic course, with any private school in the city." Norfolk had four white public schools and two for Negro children then, and there were seventeen private and parochial schools.

Local taxes provided $6,000 for the public schools in the city, and the state gave more. But finding the money was a terrible task even when the pay of teachers was only $15.00 a month (it rose in public schools above $30.00 a month in 1875.) Often teachers did not get it until months later, and many had to turn elsewhere for work, and more would have done so if they could have found work. State officials diverted school funds for purposes they regarded as important until, in 1878, Superintendent Ruffner reported that $1,100,000 had gone this way. A little later he estimated that half the money collected for schools was being diverted. The next year (1879) the number of public school pupils dropped nearly 50 per cent because of lack of teachers.

By that time Virginia was deep in the long struggle of what to do about its public debt, and the public schools, though "the greatest benefaction of which we have any record in history" (in the words of Governor Frederick M. Holliday in 1878), were the innocent victims of that politico-economic struggle.

9 · "THE KING IS DEAD!
LONG LIVE THE KING!"

EVIDENCE BEGAN TO APPEAR IN 1870 THAT ALL WAS NOT WELL WITH THE *Journal*. On May 13 the Norfolk Conservative Party convention nominated the *Journal*'s publisher, Lewellen, for city sergeant. Lewellen was popular and respected, and he won. But it seems unlikely that he would leave the post of publisher to become city sergeant if the newspaper's own position and his relation to it were satisfactory.

On October 26 Lewellen's name as superintendent disappeared from its usual place in the Norfolk Printing-House Company's advertisement in the *Journal*. The next day the designation of the company as the corporation that published the *Journal* disappeared from the newspaper. But not until November 1, 1870, did explanations begin to appear in these words:

> The Norfolk Printing-House Company, having disposed of the Norfolk Journal, its presses, types, material and good will, relinquishes control of the paper with this issue, and begs to commend its successors to the favor of the public.
> The Norfolk Journal has been purchased by five gentlemen of this city who have associated themselves under the corporate name of The Norfolk Journal Company, under whose auspices the paper will hereafter be published. . . .

The new *Journal* still did not announce who the five purchasers were. Nor did it indicate who the editor was or who held other responsible positions.

Some light may have been thrown on this puzzling scene by an editorial appearing on April 14, 1902, in the later established Norfolk *Public Ledger*. The editorial recalled details of early post-Civil War journalism in Norfolk and sought to correct some statements by reminiscent writers of the Richmond *Dispatch* and the Petersburg *Index-Appeal*. Its style and other circumstances suggest that the author was

Joseph G. Fiveash, who was associated with the *Virginian*, the *Journal*, and the *Public Ledger*.

This editorial asserted that "several hundred thousand dollars have been wasted" in newspaper publishing in Norfolk. It stated flatly that the *Journal* "was absolutely given away by Col. Lamb to Henry Ghiselin, who organized a company to run it and that a great deal of money was sunk by that paper before Maj. [C. B.] Duffield representing Gen. Mahone, and John M. Robinson, president of the Seaboard [in 1902], and N. L. McCready, president of the Old Dominion Line, and others purchased it."

Ghiselin was a cotton factor in Norfolk, a director of the Exchange National Bank, and in 1870 a director of the Norfolk Printing-House Company. Duffield, much admired by Hope, was a lawyer. In 1873 he was elected to the state Senate on the Conservative ticket. If he did represent Mahone in newspaper ownership, he would speak for the Atlantic, Mississippi & Ohio and for other Mahone interests, which were numerous and varied. Robinson was president and general superintendent of the Seaboard & Roanoke Railroad in the early 1870's. Later he was president of the Baltimore Steam Packet Company, better known as the Old Bay Line. It operated steamships between Norfolk and Baltimore. A Virginian by birth, he lived eventually in Baltimore. McCready, president of the Old Dominion Line and sometimes called Commodore McCready, was living in New York in 1877 and probably earlier. The Old Dominion Line operated steamships between Norfolk and New York and between Norfolk and nearby localities.

When such men buy newspapers, the normal suspicion, especially in that age, is that they are planning to use their newspapers to serve their other and larger business interests rather than natural newspaper purposes. But much about *Journal* history in the 1870-1873 period is obscure.

William R. Galt, editor of the *Journal* soon after its establishment in 1866, ended his editorship in 1870 or 1871. His had been the chief voice in the policy of accepting the Federal reconstruction program in order to regain membership in the Union and thereafter to seek the removal of disabilities hanging over from the Civil War.

Galt's successor, Major Baker P. Lee, had lived in Elizabeth City County across Hampton Roads. He had not been at the editorial desk long before, in September, 1872, he was nominated by Second District Conservatives to run for Congress against the Republican, James H. Platt, who was much disliked by Conservatives as a leading carpetbagger but was a formidable candidate. The *Virginian* reported on September 25 that Lee "had retired from the editorial management" of the *Journal*. Platt won the election in November by a slim margin. Lee appears to have returned to the *Journal* briefly, for the *Virginian* reported again, on January 24, 1873, that "our friend, Maj. Baker P. Lee, has retired from the Norfolk Journal, of which he was editor-in-chief." The next month he was editor of the Richmond *Enquirer*. Earlier he had been a state legislator, later he was a judge.

The *Journal*'s generally more cautious attitude had led it to criticize Mahone's management of the A. M. & O., whereas the *Virginian* was the consolidated railroad's consistent supporter. When the *Journal* thought in November, 1870, that the railroad was discriminating against Norfolk in freight rates, the *Virginian* promptly published a letter from a writer who had "no sympathy with the Journal and its relentless, unprovoked and unwarrantable warfare against General Mahone." The two newspapers took opposite sides in August, 1871, on a bond issue for aiding the extension of the street railway to Ocean View: the *Virginian* for the bond issue, the *Journal* against it. They disagreed again in April, 1872, when Horace Greeley was trying to rally liberal Republicans to oppose the reelection of Grant. The *Journal* liked the Greeley move and recommended immediately that Governor Walker be asked to join Greeley as the candidate for Vice President—"his name would nationalize the ticket."

The *Virginian* opposed the whole effort, opposed Virginians' going to Greeley's convention in Cincinnati, and even opposed the holding of a Democratic national convention that year. Individual states, it thought, should nominate tickets in opposition to Grant, or support tickets already in the field. But "the moment a certain class in the North realize we are to become participants in the management of affairs, and beneficiaries under the defeat of Grant, that moment the cry of a new 'rebellion' will be raised, and hating us worse than they do Grant, the class referred to will return to his standards." As to the *Journal*'s suggestion, the *Virginian* retorted:

> When the Journal attempts to show that Governor Walker is the 'pride of Virginia' it makes a statement which we challenge. . . . Governor Walker may be a Republican or a Democrat (we regarded him in the latter light after his election), but fish or flesh, fowl or red herring, we do not see how a Conservative constituency can insist on his nomination . . . Virginia has scores and hundreds of men within her borders better entitled to the honor than he is. . . .

When the Democratic national convention in Baltimore adopted
the Liberal Republican ticket of Greeley and Brown as its ticket too,
the *Virginian* hoisted the name of Greeley and Brown to the top of
its editorial columns. Greeley was stronger for universal amnesty
than Grant, and that appealed to the *Virginian* as it did to most
Southerners.

During the campaign the *Virginian* rarely seemed to regard the
outcome as an issue of profound importance. It called Greeley "our
amiable candidate" and seemed in good spirits when it remarked that
he "has been suspected, nay even charged, with being a traitor, a rebel,
a Niagara Falls conspirator, a perfect Guy Fawkes in fact by the New
York Times, but we never expected to hear that he had been a slave
trader. . . . If somebody will only accuse Mr. Greeley of having dined
on a piece of roast missionary, the measure of his iniquity will be
filled."

The *Virginian* printed voluminous reports on the campaign. On
the day before the election, it got down to raw elementals with these
two paragraphs at the top of its editorial columns:

> GREELEY'S LETTER OF ACCEPTANCE—"I accept your nomination
> in the confident trust that the masses of our countrymen, North
> and South, are eager to clasp hands across the bloody chasm
> which has so long divided them."

> GRANT'S WARTIME ORDER TO SHERIDAN—"Do all the damage
> you can to the railroads and crops. Carry off stock of all de-
> scriptions and negroes, so as to prevent further planting. If
> the war is to last another year, let the Shenandoah Valley re-
> main a barren waste."

When the country voted overwhelmingly for Grant, the *Virginian*
could still call Greeley the candidate of "reform, economy and recon-
ciliation" and Grant the candidate of "profligate expenditures, continuing alienation and sectional animosity." It thought the result
"mournful." But it could also return to its original position that the
South ought not to have tried to manage national affairs at all.

Even in the midst of this spirited campaign little incidents could
suggest that the rivalry between the two newspapers ran up and down
their news staffs. Witness the hurt feelings and the warning in a notice in the *Virginian* in June, 1872:

> In the absence of our reporter from the meeting of the Select
> Council on Friday evening last, caused by sickness, the report
> of the proceedings was taken for him by the accommodating
> clerk, Mr. T. B. Broughton, and entrusted to the care of the

reporter on the Journal, who, for some reason, failed to deliver it. As a result, news, legitimately ours, did not appear in our paper on the following morning while it did appear in the Journal. The case will not occur again, as the opportunity for taking such an advantage will not again be afforded.

The *Virginian* was feeling more confident and maybe a little cocky. It asserted in May of 1871 that its circulation, daily and weekly, "is greater than that of any other paper published in Tidewater Virginia. Its city circulation is almost double that of any other Norfolk paper." In June of 1872 it announced that "for nearly two months the presses of the Virginian have been worked by steam. . . . We have at last learned to write serenely over our engine, which puffs and snorts in the most astonishing manner." The *Virginian* could say that it was "the only paper in Norfolk and one of the few in the state worked by steam. . . . Of course, this improvement has been made at considerable cost," but "we are glad to say we have been constrained to it by the large increase in our circulation."

The following year, in February of 1873, the *Virginian* was hammering again on claims of excellence, including "the great accuracy of our market reports and all the fullness of our shipping intelligence and railroad and steamer receipts. We have spared no expense or care to render this department of our paper what it should be—correct and reliable. Our merchants recognize it as a standard to buy and sell by." The spirit of Glennan shines through these words.

This time the *Journal* hit back. It published claims of its own virtues. In doing so it called itself Norfolk's "most enterprising newspaper." That got under the *Virginian*'s skin. It roared back into battle in a harsh, sarcastic spirit that led to one of the most directly personal and severest of all its comments on competitors. "If enterprise consists in originating or apeing [sic] measures and then failing to carry them out, it [the *Journal*] is the most enterprising sheet in the country. Let us examine, neighbor, a few of the undertakings you have attempted and with what result." So to this bitter attack:

> As to your beginnings, did you not commence with an immense corporation, with numerous editors, reporters, clerks, employees, supported by a large number of stockholders, with the promise of being a great paying monopoly from the start, and with what results? Where are your dividends? We have heard old stockholders ask the same question. . . .
> Did you not, in the name of enterprise, commence to give in full, the Sunday sermons delivered in the various churches, with the promise to continue to report them, and how grad-

ually, yet how completely, have you failed to keep up the enterprise?

Did you not establish correspondents at cross roads and by-places, and at all the capital cities on this continent, with Europe, Asia and Africa thrown in, rendering the Abyssinian, Livingstone and Swamp Angel enterprises of the New York Herald small matters compared with yours; did you not receive letters filled with the most interesting news (some made up in the office) ; do you recollect "Our London Correspondence," and have you not dwindled down to the receipt of communications from a few localities?

Have you not attempted to swallow the AM&O Railroad, flay General Mahone, gulp the Seaboard Line and scalp John Robinson, endorse the free railroad policy, and thus injure the interests of our common harbor, and have you not amusingly and ludicrously failed?

The angry mood of the *Virginian*'s attack was far from the polite exchanges, or even the manner in which genuine differences were debated, in earlier years. Even though something has to be discounted for partisanship, the attack includes enough evidence to suggest that the *Journal* had been unable to live up to its hopes.

The *Journal* had tried in various ways to improve its reading appeal. In the later spirit of newspapers it sought to make its front page distinctly a news page and an invitation to read the whole newspaper. As early as 1868 the June 2 issue had only one column of advertisements on that page, the June 3 issue had none at all, and the December 10 issue—this was in a season of much retail advertising—had only two columns. All the rest was news. In September, 1870, the *Journal* took the historic step of publishing on Sundays. At the same time it dropped its Monday issue.

Sunday issues were no larger than the standard four pages, and the price was the same. The *Virginian* had cut its single-copy charge to three cents in 1866 before the *Journal* was born. In January of 1871 the *Journal* went to three cents; a year later it went to two cents. Carrier-delivered papers cost ten cents weekly; annual subscriptions by mail, $5.00. The triweekly *Journal* was $3.00; the weekly edition, $1.50. All these were lower than in the *Journal*'s first year of publication.

The *Virginian*, meantime, was undergoing partnership changes. Solomon Hodges, leader of the printers who took command in 1866, died in 1872. Though he was only forty-one, bad health forced his retirement two years earlier. Edward H. Hodges, who also retired because of bad health, died in 1873. His interest, like his brother's, was sold to the remaining partners. In 1872 the firm changed its name to Glennan, Ruffin & Company. The other partner was J. C. Adkisson.

In December, 1872, Ruffin sold his interest to Glennan—not any part of it to Adkisson—and withdrew from the firm. The name changed on December 14 to Glennan & Adkisson, and Glennan was now the major owner.

The whole town knew Theo Ruffin, and everyone liked him. He was an unusually modest person, but a handy man with either type or local news. The *Virginian* bade him goodbye as a partner with an editorial which said that "we have no words to express the warmth of the friendship which this association has produced. . . . He knows, without any expression of words from us, how deeply we regret the parting. . . ." Ruffin remained in newspaper work in Norfolk for many years.

So the two rivals stood in the early 1870's when the Chicago fire of October, 1871, was big national news and the Franco-Prussian War was big foreign news. The war greatly heightened interest in European affairs, but interest in Europe had existed in Norfolk newspapers (especially any newspaper with which Hope was connected) from their start. The Atlantic Ocean always was Norfolk's front yard.

A byproduct of the Chicago fire was the discussion across the country of the succession of fires that autumn, chiefly in the West. One theory brought the *Virginian* up fighting. "Some of the preachers in New York have seen the 'finger of God' in events which can be accounted for by natural causes," it commented; and "we are told that incendiaries have been at work." The *Virginian* snorted. "This," it said, "is simply preposterous."

Another aspect of the Chicago fire interested the *Virginian* more. Reports of looters led it to assert that thieves "were shot without mercy, or hanged to the nearest lamp-posts when caught—in short, Judge Lynch dealt with them. . . . HOW MANY INNOCENT MEN SUFFERED IN THIS WAY CAN NEVER BE KNOWN." But the moral went further. The *Virginian* declared:

> This is all very well at the North but when a few people of the South under some provocation such as that of midnight arson, murder, or the violation of some poor woman, hang a desperate scoundrel, then all the machinery of the Ku Klux bill is put in operation, and the whole North resounds with eloquent denunciations of our barbarity. It is unlawful to hang and shoot men in Chicago without legal authority. It is wrong

to mete out such justice in the South, but let the world understand that we had the same warrant which the North has for such actions. . . . It was wrong in Chicago. It is wrong here. . . .

The rise of Prussianism had no welcome in Norfolk. The *Virginian's* comments on French defeats in the 1870's reflected regret but generally were realistic. When Prussia's purpose to occupy Luxemburg was reported, the *Virginian* noted that this was being done under the cloak of "military necessity." As to that term, "we are sufficiently familiar with the meaning . . . in this country to understand it as the scant apology which power makes to public opinion, in the perpetration of wrong. . . . as Prussia burns with ambition to become a great naval power, we are prepared at an early date to hear her declaring that Holland and Belgium have been guilty of wrongs which can only be atoned for by submission to the sway of Kaiser William."

A dash of Dean Swift appeared in an earlier (1868) and different kind of editorial based on a report that American Indians were to be herded on reservations. The *Virginian* thought fighting the Indians had proved to be much like chasing the flying Dutchman. It offered "a cheap and comparatively easy method of bringing the business to a successful end." The strategy:

> Let General Sheridan make war on the buffaloes for the same reason which he pleads in apology for the Tilly-like destruction he wrought in the Valley of Virginia. Let him try this on the Indians, and just as soon as they find the skill and art of the white man turned to the destruction of their commissariat, they will begin to be disorganized. This disorganization will break their will, and the destruction of their supply of meat will constrain them to starve, or live by the peaceful arts. If you desire to civilize the Indian you must kill the buffalo.

At home, meantime, the lower Tidewater region was stirring with a new awareness of its natural resources and a new desire to develop them. At Old Point the Hygeia Hotel was rebuilt in 1871. A new hotel with the elegant name of Vue de l'Eau was built in 1872 at Sewells Point, on Hampton Roads opposite Fort Monroe (Cost: $65,000). There was talk of a hotel and more cottages at Ocean View. Northern money was believed to be interested there. But it was local leadership, with A. G. Milhado as president and C. A. Nash as secretary, both Norfolk citizens of repute, that was directing the new Norfolk Turf Association. It built a half-mile track for horse racing south of the Vue de l'Eau and half a mile north of the city line.

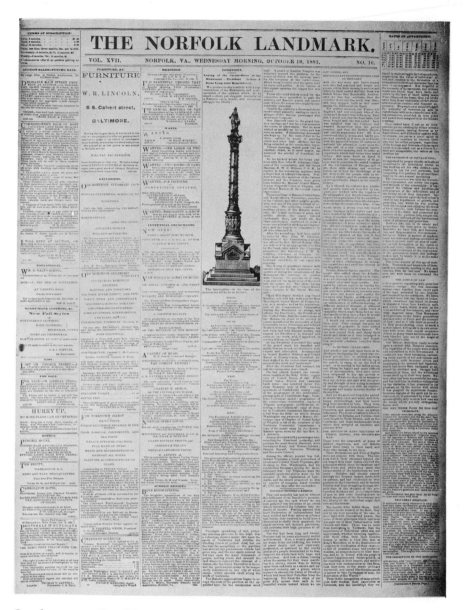

October 19, 1881—How the *Landmark* handled the hundredth anniversary of the British surrender at Yorktown.

Norfolk, 1888—Commercial Place and Main Street.

Portsmouth, 1871—High Street looking west from Crawford Street.

The *Virginian* thought there was "a fair prospect of this business [of hotels and cottages and horse racing and such developments] being overdone." But it recovered well enough to proclaim a little later that "at last Norfolk can offer the Southern people"—other people were still a little alien—"a seaside resort worthy of the name of watering place." It joined vigorously in efforts in 1872 to attract summer visitors. Excursions from Petersburg and Richmond grew popular. A new idea was being born. It would face hard times after the panic of 1873, when the Vue de l'Eau's name could not save the hotel from bankruptcy, but the idea would grow and attain permanence.

In August of 1873 the *Journal* let go one final blast of a circulation claim: "The Journal has a larger circulation in these two cities [Norfolk and Portsmouth] and surrounding country than any and all other papers published here." It set the words in bold type and placed them on top of the editorial columns. But they were much like a death rattle. By the autumn of 1873 the *Journal* had run into such difficulties that its owners were ready to sell. At the same time the coincidence of a death and a will in New Jersey and a resulting inheritance in Norfolk produced an unexpected buyer. News of these striking changes began to reach the public in a series of disjointed announcements.

On September 28 the *Journal* announced that its "establishment, with its presses, types, fixtures and franchises" had passed to other owners. But with that it stopped abruptly. Who the new owners were, and other important and tantalizing questions, it left untouched. Three days later, on October 1, came a second announcement.

On that day the *Journal* reported in a notice at the head of its editorial columns that "the Norfolk Journal Company, under whose auspices this paper has been published since November 1, 1870, is this day dissolved, and the ownership, at the present moment, has passed into other hands." Still, the *Journal* mentioned no name. Instead, after saying that "we sever these relations with reluctance," it launched into two long editorials, one largely of complaint that it had not received more advertising from the city, and the other explaining its political views, in particular its attitude toward the Conservative Party and its candidates.

This was a strange valedictory, querulous and self-exculpatory. But it was overshadowed by the big news of the day. For "A Notice to the Public" by Glennan and Adkisson in their newspaper announced that Hope was leaving the *Virginian*, and Hope's own "A Word of Parting" was his formal farewell. He had been editor since

February of 1867 after being associate editor at the *Virginian*'s birth in November of 1865 and for the five succeeding months.

In spirit both statements were the opposite of the *Journal*'s last words—brief, dignified, and, in the tradition, gentlemanly. "I leave with regret," Hope said. He added an unusual tribute to "my old friend and colleague, T. B. Ruffin, to whose good taste and generous temper the Virginian has been so largely indebted for its hold on the popular affection"—this in spite of the fact that Ruffin had withdrawn from the partnership group ten months earlier. For their part, Glennan and Adkisson wished Hope well.

The glaring lack in all this was Hope's plans and the identity of his successor at the seat of the *Virginian*'s editorial power. The *Journal*'s notice of sale and Hope's notice of departure from the *Virginian* must have indicated to all who could put two and two together what was coming. But a minuet-like formality governed the order and pace of such announcements. Steps must be taken to the music, and the timing of the music was fixed. The town waited for the climax.

It came in the form of a new morning newspaper on the streets: *The Norfolk Landmark,* born October 2, 1873, published by James Barron Hope & Company, erected on such pillars as the *Journal* left standing, but conspicuously different from the *Journal* in spirit and philosophy.

Nothing was designed to proclaim this difference more than the discard of the name of *Journal*, with which Hope clearly did not wish to be associated, and the heralding of a name which the *Landmark* said "was selected after due deliberation, and we believe it will endure to vindicate our selection. We aspire to found an institution, not to attempt an adventure. We are determined to make our own record and blaze our own road."

The new editorial page promised conventionally "to do our best to advance the public interest; to satisfy, so far as we can, the general demand for authentic news, and to give readers . . . well digested opinion on current topics. . . ." But the real message of the *Landmark* —aside from the sheer fact of its birth—was Hope's signed salute under a trumpet-blast of a headline that proclaimed as though from battlements:

THE KING IS DEAD! LONG LIVE THE KING!

This bold and cavalier spirit with its touch of gasconade must have caught the eye of beholders—as assuredly it was designed to do. The words might have stood by themselves, but Hope had something else to say. "In accordance with a time-honored custom in Virginia," he said, "I beg leave to address a few words to the readers of the Norfolk Landmark in my own person and to salute them on taking control of the paper introduced this morning to their notice." The *Landmark*, he said, would "be accurate, candid and exempt from the control of any clique, ring or organization—in short, it will be animated by no considerations, save those born of a diligent study of the public wants and the general necessities of our people."

In an unusual appeal, Hope turned to "my professional brethren" of the press and extended "a respectful salutation." He ventured, he said, "to ask at their hands a continuation of the generous regard with which they have heretofore honored me." Then once more the ringing words of the headline and then the finale:

THE KING IS DEAD! LONG LIVE THE KING!

The Norfolk Journal is extinct and the Norfolk Landmark takes its place to hew out a pathway and make a history for itself as best it may be able. In this endeavor I am not extravagant in the hope that the public will sustain the enterprise which I have this day undertaken to conduct.

James Barron Hope

The highly individualistic nature of this salute disclosed the personal nature and spirit of the *Landmark*. It was Hope's newspaper, not the creation of a group, not the newspaper of stockholders in small numbers or large, but the organ and personality of one man. The incorporators beside Hope were two lawyers, George P. Scarburgh, later a judge, and his partner, Major Duffield, mentioned as the representative of Mahone in Fiveash's account of an earlier purchase of the *Journal*; Commodore Samuel Barron, Hope's uncle; and Colonel Walter H. Taylor, a Norfolk businessman, much esteemed as a staff officer with Lee throughout the four years of the Civil War and an intimate friend of the General. These were obviously friends of Hope but not newspaper operators.

For operating purposes Hope enlisted at the start Joseph L. Young as business manager, Kenton C. Murray as local editor, W. Thompson Barron as reporter, J. Barry King as commercial editor, William H. Stewart as Portsmouth local editor. Some of these rose to much larger responsibilities. But the *Landmark* was Hope, publisher and editor, whose mind, principles, emotions, and taste colored and controlled the whole newspaper.

These steps Hope could take because in the autumn of 1873 he came into an inheritance. His mother's younger sister, Susan Virginia Barron, had married the United States naval officer who rose to be Commodore Jesse Pendergrast. The Pendergrasts had no children. Mrs. Pendergrast was devoted to her sisters, and she maintained close relations with them even during the Civil War. After Hope's mother died, she continued these relations with him. To him she was "Aunt Virginia," and always there was affection between the two. When Mrs. Pendergrast, then a widow, died in Atlantic City, New Jersey, on August 23, 1873, she left funds for her nephew in Norfolk.[1]

Thus armed, Hope acted quickly. No indication appears of a rift with Glennan and Adkisson. The three men were different types, but effective as a team. Lack of funds, almost surely, had been the reason why Hope did not buy in 1866 the interest in the *Virginian* which Lewellen subsequently bought. Now he had funds. The first assumption is that Hope was doing what always he had wished to do: control a newspaper, set its policies, and direct its operations.

His "professional brethren" accepted the *Landmark* definitely as a one-man newspaper. The *Virginian* was courteous in greeting its new competitor, a "welcome visitor to our sanctum . . . edited by our old friend and editorial companion. . . . The Landmark, we are pleased to see, gives evidence in its advertising department of considerable increase of patronage compared with its predecessor, whilst vigor, energy and talent are abundantly shown in its editorial and local departments. . . . We pronounce the paper a decided hit and worthy of the support of the entire community."

Even more suggestive of Hope's position in the eyes of editors were the greetings from newspapers outside Norfolk. The Portsmouth *Enterprise* called Hope "the accomplished and scholarly editor of the *Virginian.*" The Suffolk *Herald* said that "the names of James Barron Hope & Co. are to us a sufficient guarantee that the Landmark will be conducted with distinguished ability." The Petersburg *Appeal*, noting that "our esteemed friend" has transferred "his tripod and his 'Faber' from one sanctum to another in the same city," thought it was not necessary to "reiterate here the high value we set on the virtues of his private character and the ability and brilliancy of his professional qualifications."

In Richmond the *State Journal* expressed "our very best wishes" for the *Landmark* and "its accomplished editor." In Lynchburg the

1. Oral communication, May 30, 1964, to Joseph E. Shank by Anne W. Marr, daughter of Janey Hope Marr and Colonel R. A. Marr, of the Virginia Military Institute faculty, and granddaughter of Hope.

Virginian spoke of "the genial and accomplished Hope"; and the *Republican* thought Hope had "presided at its [the Norfolk *Virginian's*] editorial helm with an ability which has secured for him a reputation extending even beyond the limits of the state. . . . Norfolk will have good cause to be proud of the editorial talent employed on its press."

In North Carolina the Raleigh *News* noted that the Norfolk *Landmark*, "stoutly and nobly manned, full of lusty life, and zeal, and HOPE, lifts it streaming pennon to the breeze . . . it affords us real pleasure to know that we shall not lose from the editorial fraternity the services of the able editor of the Landmark." The Battleboro *Advance* called Hope "one of the finest and most polished writers of the South." It said that he was "well and favorably known in North Carolina, where he has already made his mark."

If some of this was editorial courtesy, more of it was tribute to a much admired editor. Hope had distinctive qualities which on occasion became limitations. Emotions about the Civil War bound him tightly. Republicanism was anathema. Negro suffrage seemed to him intolerable. He looked with deep disfavor on social change of nearly any kind. Women at commercial work never ceased to shock him. Women seeking the ballot box were objects of contempt.

But such was his integrity, so intense were his loyalties, so high was his sense of honor, that men, knowing these innate qualities, respected him even when they disagreed with him. He could be fair when all about him were angry and violent in their language. In personal relations he was the spirit of kindness.

Professionally, his capacities were not equaled by any other Virginia editor of his time. He made scholarship an editorial tool, never an end in itself. Historical and literary analogies, familiarity with men and movements long ago or far away, characterized his writing, but always to illumine and clarify, never to clog the channels of analysis or argument. His humor had a light and gay quality, in contrast to the heavy spirit of the times. His style never obstructed what he wanted to say but carried it forward clearly and directly and with a sense of balance and form. Members of his family thought newspaper work was not entirely congenial to him,[2] and, like other editors in the hard circumstances of those years, he must have wearied. But he seemed to revel in his work, and he performed it with distinction.

Still, he had been an editor, never a publisher, never the com-

2. Janey Hope Marr, in introduction to *A Wreath of Virginia Bay Leaves* (a collection of Hope's poems) (Richmond, 1895).

mander-in-chief of a newspaper, never the administrator of infinite detail. The *Landmark* was opportunity. It was also a hard test.

In appearance the *Landmark* at its start was much like its predecessor, the *Journal*, and much like the *Virginian*, too. It followed the *Journal*, and went ahead of the *Virginian*, by publishing on Sundays, though not on Mondays. All editions carried four pages with seven columns to the page. Its front page disclosed the trend toward making it more of a news page and less of an advertising page. The only advertisements on the *Landmark's* front page were of auction sales. Brief items of local and telegraph news, and items of national and international news, some probably clipped from big-city newspapers, covered this page under small, one-column heads. Typographically, the *Landmark* was more conservative than the *Virginian* at this time and was slow to change later.

Initial prices followed those of the *Journal*: two cents for a single copy, ten cents a week for carrier-delivered newspapers in Norfolk and Portsmouth; $5.00 a year by mail. The *Landmark* printed a tri-weekly edition at $3.00 a year and a weekly edition at $1.50. It used the quarters on Main Street opposite the Academy of Music of that day (where the Selden Arcade was cut later) to which the *Journal* had shifted after its fire in 1868. The *Virginian* and the *Landmark* were close neighbors. Each knew the quality and temper of the other. They girded now for hard competition.

The *Virginian* was under pressure to make up for the loss of Hope with an impressive successor. The choice was Captain John Hampden Chamberlayne, editor of the Petersburg *Index* for the past three years. Earlier he had been associate editor of the *Index* under Cameron, the *Virginian's* earlier editor. When Cameron shifted from the *Index* to the Richmond *Whig* in January, 1871, Chamberlayne succeeded him in Petersburg, and the publishing firm changed to Chamberlayne, Sykes & Co. He was following Cameron's footsteps again as the fifth editor of the *Virginian* in eight years, after Keiley, Cameron, Hanna, and Hope.

Thirty-five years old then, the new editor was widely known as Ham Chamberlayne. He was born in Richmond, won an M. A. degree at the University of Virginia in 1858 when twenty years old, and was an artillery officer in the Army of Northern Virginia. During the war he wrote numerous letters to his family, sometimes sharp in criticism of officers and movements around him, sometimes high in praise, nearly always vivid in expression. Many of them were collected for

a book published nearly seventy years later and were quoted in subsequent Civil War studies.[3]

Three days after Hope left and Chamberlayne took command, the
Virginian reprinted from the Richmond *Dispatch* a mellow, nostalgic
article written anonymously by a veteran Virginia newspaperman.
In the spirit of sentiment that journalists of the time resorted to in
certain moods, this warm-hearted historian recalled pre-Civil War
figures in Norfolk: "Old Commodore Broughton" of the *Herald*; "the
Beacon and the Shieldses;" "that ripe scholar and most courtly gentleman, Hugh Blair Grigsby . . . venerated and venerable;" and William
E. Cunningham, "the handsomest editor in the state." As for the immediate personalities, the veteran wrote affectionately:

> Hope, dear Hope, is a jewel of a fellow, gentle as a maiden,
> confiding and guileless as a child and brave as a lion. He has a
> readiness as a writer and the gift of genius. It shall go hard if
> the Landmark does not succeed with such a helmsman.
>
> The Virginian, a popular journal, in losing Hope, gains our
> young and spirited friend, Ham Chamberlayne, late of the
> Petersburg Index. He has proved his calibre and may be wel-
> comed by the friends of the Virginian. He is an accomplished
> scholar, a forceful writer and an industrious editor. We may
> congratulate Norfolk upon the new arrangement of her active
> daily press. . . .
>
> And now a good voyage to you, young gentleman of the
> Norfolk press.

3. C. G. Chamberlayne, ed., *Ham Chamberlayne—Virginian* (Richmond, 1933).

10 · PANIC, RECOVERY, AND THE *PUBLIC LEDGER*

THE *Landmark* WAS BORN NEAR THE HIGH POINT OF THE VIRGINIA GU-bernatorial campaign of 1873 in which the Conservative, General James L. Kemper, and the Republican, Robert W. Hughes, were the candidates. It plunged immediately into the fight. To neither the *Landmark* nor the *Virginian* did the contest present a difficult choice. Kemper possessed abundant Conservative respectabilities: Confederate background (wounded in Pickett's charge at Gettysburg), old-line Virginia philosophy, ten years' experience in the General Assembly, elevation to Speaker of the House, and full-blown enmity to Radical Republicanism and its Negro allies.

Hughes did not lack character or courage, and he had a Virginia background. But in Conservative eyes he was hopelessly on the wrong side, too intimate with the Radicals, too close to Negro voters, too contemptuous of historic attitudes in Virginia, and too willing to say so. "He is a dangerous leader and an able one," said the *Virginian.* "He takes sides, and that, too, without reserve, with the blacks against the whites, and we shall beat him on his own ground."

The *Landmark* called "the pretensions of the Radical Party a fraud upon the white and colored races." It was confident that Negroes "feel their natural inferiority to the white race." Except for their "good sense" in accepting such segregation, "the railroad trains would soon become a nuisance and cease to subserve the purposes for which they were established." And but for this same good sense, the *Landmark* continued, the public schools would present "the humiliating spectacle of whites and blacks being educated, not in humanities, but in all the horrors of miscegenation." And further: "If a negro can be made President of the United States and his lady mistress of the White House, how, under such circumstances, can social equality be ignored or avoided?"

Blown by such winds the Conservatives sailed to victory. It was gained when one Virginian faced another Virginian in the first election of a governor since Virginia had rejoined the Union. Kemper carried the state by nearly 28,000 in a total vote of more than 215,000. He won Norfolk by 2,341 to Hughes's 1,513, a majority of 828 in a count which showed that the Negro vote was 1,338.

A month after the election John C. Underwood, United States judge for the Eastern District of Virginia and father of the Underwood constitution, died. "To speak of this event with the customary decorum is not easy," the *Virginian* said. "The public life of the dead man was marked by nothing good or upright . . . his whole judicial career proved him an ignorant, a vindictive and a corrupt judge . . . the first judge who had brought infamy to the bench, the first judge to earn the contempt of the state, the first to bring disgrace upon it. . . ." This was probably Ham Chamberlayne at work, with an ax.

"In commenting on this dispensation of Providence," the *Landmark* concluded after reviewing the Underwood career and finding little to approve, "we have only to translate the old law maxim—the act of God injures no man." This was probably Hope, with a rapier.

Within two days (on December 11, 1873), Grant named Hughes to succeed Underwood. The *Landmark* and the *Virginian* were caught short. They had just been damning Hughes when he was a candidate for governor. But now, confronting him as a Federal judge, they had enough respect for his personal and mental qualities, underneath his political partianship, to suspect that he might turn out to be a good judge. He surely seemed to them a welcome native contrast to the alien whom he succeeded.

By the time Judge Hughes first held court in Norfolk, in February, 1874, he had won much confidence from the public. The *Virginian* was reprinting complimentary comment from other parts of the state, and the *Landmark* went further: "We are bound to admit," it said, "that he has borne himself very well in his new position. He is restoring the decency and dignity of his court. . . ."

Five years later Judge Hughes upheld in 1879 the Virginia statute prohibiting interracial marriage in the case of a white woman and a Negro man who were married in Washington, D.C., and were indicted under this law when they returned to Virginia to live. "This decision will add to the deserved reputation that Judge Hughes has earned by his judicial decisions," the *Virginian* pronounced. "We know of no man wearing the Federal ermine in the whole United States who has been so frequently right, so seldom wrong, as Judge

Hughes, and though we have always differed with him in politics, we take pleasure in bearing our testimony to his impartiality and ability as a judge."

The failure of Jay Cooke & Co. and the resultant crash of the stock market on September 17, 1873, brought a one-column report in the *Virginian*. But two days later the story ran to five columns on page one. The *Virginian* admitted that few people were prepared for "the collapse of the great house . . . which has stood for so many years as a sort of financial colossus bestriding the Atlantic." The fault, it explained, was "illegitimate and dangerous railroad speculations."

That brought the crash close. Mahone's A. M. & O. was already feeling the pinch and was not able to complete its Ohio River connection. The Chesapeake & Ohio, aiming eventually for deepwater in Hampton Roads, as well as the Middle West extensions that were engaging it at the moment, seemed in Norfolk to be moving with discouraging slowness. The *Landmark* found it easier to excuse Mahone, the railroad consolidator, whose "energies and genius have given to the state the noblest line of improvements within her borders." But the *Landmark* thought in December, 1873, that the state had alienated the C. & O. for which Virginia had spent "millions." It thought a great wrong was inflicted on Norfolk people who held stock in the C. & O.

"The excuse for this," the *Landmark* continued, "was found in the florid promises that Mr. Huntington [Collis P. Huntington, promoter of the C. & O.] and his friends were going to make the state a paradise. Now we are heartily sorry for Mr. Huntington's stockholders," and "we deplore the great financial embarrassment of the road which he governs." Both railroads were sliding down the hill toward receivership.

Panic or no panic, the Norfolk newspapers had to report and comment on constant changes in a region that was struggling to strengthen its roots and to grow up with the country. In its first week the *Landmark* devoted five columns on its front page to the Virginia and North Carolina Agricultural Society Fair where the grounds were "packed with people." Cotton stirred the *Landmark* and the *Virginian*. They printed records of bales shipped to Norfolk, coming up from the Carolinas and farther south and west, by the Seaboard & Roanoke and the A. M. & O., for shipment by water to Northern and European mills. The report in February, 1874, that Norfolk had risen to the second cotton port in the country, second only to New

Orleans in number of bales received at the port, brought cheers. The Norfolk & Portsmouth Cotton Exchange was established in July of that year. When lumbermen of eastern Virginia and North Carolina held their annual convention in Norfolk that summer, the *Landmark* listed one by one the 147 saw mills they represented.

Another kind of development came with the Masonic Relief Association's lottery (though the association avoided that word) to raise funds for a Masonic temple through a ticket-selling and gift-drawing plan authorized by special legislation. The first goal was $250,000 to be raised by tickets, to a concert, sold at $5.00 each ($2.50 for half a ticket). Hard times cut that figure in half. When the drawing was held in May, 1874, John L. Roper, president of the association, reported to an audience that jammed the Opera House that 34,925 tickets had been sold and $174,625 was on hand. The first prize had to be reduced from $50,000 to $25,000, but that did not prevent the audience's hanging on the results until 1:25 a.m.

The large, red brick building on East Freemason Street stood for nearly ninety years and was the scene, in addition to Masonic activities, of many public and social events, including the Norfolk German Club's heavily formalized germans. Only a few months earlier (September, 1873) the Virginia Club, a men's downtown organization of social repute, opened its "elegantly and tastefully fitted up" club rooms, in the *Virginian*'s words, and began in "the handsome building next to the Custom House" a life that was continuing after other locations nearly a century later.

April of 1874 brought the completion of a telegraph line from Cape Henry to Cape Hatteras. "Now that the telegraph connects the whole coast line, 125 miles, from Henry to Hatteras," the *Virginian* pointed out, "life-saving stations to give and receive information, and furnished with lifeboats and wrecking crews, will soon dot that deadly coast to save property and redeem life." Workmen who completed the telegraph line told the *Landmark* they had counted the wrecks of 125 ships.

The Norfolk Weather Observatory was deemed important enough in June for three columns on page one of the *Virginian*. It was located "in the upper portion of the Burruss, Son & Co. banking house on Main Street." After inspecting instruments and records, the *Virginian* announced—hardly concealing its pleasure—that "Norfolk is not the hottest place in the country." Laredo, Texas, was the reigning champion.

While the country was still quaking from the financial crash of that autumn of 1873, it was shaken by an international incident in Cuba. Spanish authorities seized the *Virginius* near Jamaica while she was flying the American flag, took her into Santiago, charged her with being a pirate ship, and shot her captain and thirty-six crewmen. They did not punish the approximately hundred passengers on what the American press called "an alleged blockade runner."

When news of this "massacre"—the general descriptive—was published in November, 1873, the country flared in anger and warlike threats. The *Landmark* was especially contemptuous of Grant's "muddled" message to Congress. "Any other government," it said, "would have sent its available naval force to Cuba on receipt of the news of the capture of the Virginius to bring her and her surviving prisoners back forthwith—that first and satisfaction afterward. . . . The whole thing is a disgrace to the American nation."

One immediate result was increased activity in the Navy Yard in Portsmouth. The steamer *Dispatch* was hurriedly loaded with "three brass guns, 20-pounders, rifled," and ammunition, for the *Wahopac* at Key West, but the weight "carried her too low in the water and [she] had to be unloaded." The *Mayflower* was being fitted out for a voyage to the West Indies. The sloop of war *Macedonian* came in for overhaul. Day and night work was ordered at the Yard, especially on the *Savannah*, which was expected to be completed in three weeks. Fifteen hundred barrels of beef and pork arrived for dispatch to Cuba.

These excitements led both the *Landmark* and the *Virginian* to run daily a column or more of Navy Yard news. But when Spain accepted Grant's terms in nearly every detail, the excitement subsided. The Navy Yard force was cut in January, 1874, and again in March, this time by 440 men in construction and repair. The *Landmark* reported that "the remaining 345 were suspended for one day to come within the monthly allowance of funds . . . a great misfortune to the yard."

The *Landmark* and the *Virginian* regularly printed much Portsmouth news and regarded the two cities, separated physically only by the three-quarter mile wide Elizabeth River, as one city for such purposes. Back in March, 1869, the experience of a short-lived newspaper in Portsmouth, the *Transcript*, led the Petersburg *Express* (then edited by Holt Wilson, a former *Virginian* and *Journal* man) to comment bluntly on the "want of patronage" which ended the *Transcript*'s career in sixteen days. The *Virginian* reprinted the *Express*'s comment and added that it was "wholesome advice" for Portsmouth.

Whether this public scolding had any economic results is difficult to detect. When the Portsmouth *Times* began publication in August, 1872, the *Virginian* greeted it warmly. It congratulated the proprietors and pronounced the second issue "even better than the first. We are satisfied," it continued, "that with proper management the Times will become one of the established institutions of Portsmouth, and are candid in saying that we can see no reason why it should not receive a handsome support."

The notable Portsmouth newspaper of that era was the *Enterprise*, established in April, 1873, by John W. H. Porter, who had been city editor of the *Virginian*. A little later R. E. Glassett, with newspaper experience in Norfolk and Portsmouth, was associated with him for a brief period. The *Enterprise* merged with the *Daily Times* in 1888 to form the *Enterprise-Times*, which later became the *Progress* and continued into the mid-1890's. Rivalries between newspapers in Norfolk and Portsmouth were inevitable, as they were between newspapers in Norfolk alone; but personal relations were close, and the shifting of reporters, editors, and others from newspaper to newspaper was frequent.

The *Virginian* finally caught up with the *Landmark*'s Sunday edition, publishing its own for the first time on February 15, 1874, four and a half months later. Neither in size nor in content was the Sunday edition significantly different. It was still a four-page newspaper priced at three cents.

That year also marked the organization of the formidably named Publishers and Editors Association of the State of Virginia. Thirty-five publishers and editors met in Richmond on March 25 for this purpose. The *Virginian*'s front pages of the 26th and 27th carried almost full-column reports. Business managers, reporters, proprietors of book and job offices, as well as publishers and editors, "and none others," were eligible for membership at $2.00 a year.

The weather was hot and dry that summer of 1874. Water ran out, not because the new mains failed to bring it into the city from the lakes, but because many landlords did not bring water from the mains into the houses, especially houses rented to poor people. Doing so would increase taxes. Wells had been filled when the mains were laid, and cisterns had dried up. "Is it too much to ask the authorities to relieve the sufferings of so many," the *Virginian* asked, "by providing public fountains?" The city opened a few hydrants from time to time, and "a rush of people" came with tubs, buckets, and pitchers.

Dismal Swamp fires made the autumn worse. In November the *Virginian* reported wearily that "we have had the longest and warmest Indian summer within the memory of the oldest inhabitant. The air, naturally smoky at this season, was for weeks smokier by the woods being on fire, especially was the great Dismal Swamp the scene of miles and miles of blazing timber, and so dry was the peat soil that many large and deep holes have been burnt out several feet deep in places usually covered by water. . . . We can't tell when our people were more relieved when . . . came the refreshing rains that put out the fires in the forest and at least partially filled the cisterns in the city."

Through this murky heat came in October the electrifying news that two former Confederate generals of combat distinction and postwar prominence, William Mahone and Bradley T. Johnson, were on the point of fighting a duel. Johnson, earlier a Marylander, was state senator from the Richmond district. To stir Tidewater Virginia the more, the report said they might turn for a field of honor to North Carolina soil less than forty miles south of Norfolk.

In the midst of this excitement the *Virginian's* Michael Glennan received a telegram from the Richmond correspondent of the New York *Herald* inquiring whether Mahone and Johnson were already in Norfolk. Armed with this inquiry, Glennan went to Mayor John B. Whitehead. Whitehead investigated and learned that Mahone was in the National Hotel. He issued a warrant for his arrest and accompanied the constable ordered to serve it.

These two, the mayor and the constable (though if Glennan was in the offing it would not have been surprising), went to Mahone's room. They found him in bed asleep. Whitehead served the warrant himself and set a bond of $10,000 to assure Mahone's keeping the peace. Three of Mahone's friends in Norfolk, Walter H. Taylor, Richard C. Taylor, and Benjamin P. Loyall, all estimable citizens, provided the money for the bond.

The warrant and the bond halted movements on the surface. But under the surface the activity grew intense. The *Virginian*, following events like a hound on the scent, reported that Hope, its editorial competitor, had been drawn into negotiations on behalf of Mahone. He caught a Seaboard & Roanoke train and rode to Weldon in North Carolina. There he conferred with two renowned Confederate generals, Jubal A. Early and Matt W. Ransom, the latter a United States senator and later minister to Mexico.

Early was reported to be representing Johnson, Ransom to be

drawn in because he was a friend of both men. Obviously matters of
high importance under the code were at stake. "It was said to be the
purpose of Captain Hope's visit to Weldon," the *Virginian* continued,
"to present the position of General Mahone to the opposite party, and
to say that if a meeting was demanded General Mahone would forfeit
his bond and grant it."

The reports raise questions not clearly answered, and not all the
formal maneuvers are part of the public record. But the duel did
not take place. In the words in the *Virginian* on October 3, quoting
from the Petersburg *Index and Appeal*, "we hear now, gladly, that
neither of the distinguished gentlemen is free to act in a manner that
would result in the death or disqualification of the other."

In later years the affair was cited among other threats of duels that
did not eventuate as evidence of more bluster than blood in these
affairs. Newspapers in New York especially increased their derision
of the code. They probably made it easier for Virginia newspapers,
and public opinion in general in Virginia, to harden attitudes against
dueling. Glennan thought that Mahone did not seek to evade requirements of the code. No evidence is known to suggest that Johnson did. It was the law as an instrumentality of public opinion that
exerted the controlling influence.

But scandal was not on the way out. When Theodore Tilton
made his charges in July, 1874, that the Rev. Dr. Henry Ward Beecher
of the Plymouth (Congregational) Church in Brooklyn, one of the
best known American ministers, had engaged in adultery with Mrs.
Tilton, the *Landmark* needed three columns on its front page to tell
the tale. When Beecher denied the charges, the *Landmark* needed
three more front-page columns. When Beecher submitted a formal,
detailed defense in August, the *Landmark* gave over its entire front
page, plus a column inside, to that news. That was more than half
of the news in the newspaper—an unprecedented allocation of space
for any story.

The *Landmark* was a conservatively edited newspaper that claimed
a circulation "superior in character" to that of any other newspaper
"in the same field." Beecher had, before these events, an aura of
high respectability and was much admired in many respectable homes.
But this was unavoidable news. Hope himself had powerful views
on personal behavior. To him Tilton's making such charges public
was an inconceivable violation of the code of a gentleman. He wrote:
"Whether the accused are guilty or innocent, Tilton ought to be tied
to the tail of a cart and lashed from the Battery to Central Park in

open day and then branded as the basest of his kind with a red hot iron."

As for Beecher, after he had asked for an investigation by a committee of church members, "he knew he could not confine it. . . . Having made carrion of themselves they cannot complain that the buzzards are on them." The *Virginian* could not keep up with such scorching words, but its front page often was dominated that summer by Beecher news.

The Christmas season brought the gift of new advertising highs for the *Virginian*. On October 4 it included with its regular four pages "an extra sheet as a supplement" necessitated by the pressure for advertising space. An announcement said "these advertisements reach a large portion of North Carolina and all of the eastern coast of Virginia." The *Virginian's* circulation at this time was not more than three thousand copies. But when the *Virginian* added a two-page supplement from December 20 to New Year's Eve, distributing in effect a six-page newspaper, it probably was doing more than any predecessor, and certainly any current competitor, had done.

The *Virginian,* which rarely overlooked an anniversary of its own, reflected on November 22, 1874, as it entered its tenth year, that "nine years ago the prospect was dark indeed, a country devastated, industries lying in ruin, hopes blasted, a past painful, a future black, a present oppressed by evil laws and more evil law-givers. Such was the period when this journal was established and essayed to represent the people." Norfolk had come a long way from that period, and so had the *Virginian.*

In the next year it found strong satisfaction in celebrating the hundredth anniversary of the American Revolution. It published articles on events in 1775: the movements of British and Virginia forces, the battle of Great Bridge, the burning of Norfolk, the subsequent British fleet activities, much other local history, and in June much about Bunker Hill. To participate in the Bunker Hill celebration the Norfolk Light Artillery Blues traveled to Massachusetts. Glennan of the *Virginian*, C. E. Perkins, city editor of the *Landmark*, and W. E. Foster of the recently established *Evening Times and Advertiser*, accompanied Norfolk's elite military unit—the first example of so many Norfolk newspapermen dispatched to cover events at such a distance.

The city still lived close to the Civil War. A review of a history of the *Merrimac* (*Virginia*) written by Lieutenant Catesby ap R. Jones, her executive and ordnance officer and her commander during the duel with the *Monitor*, required two and half columns in the *Virginian*. When Foley's statue of Stonewall Jackson, the gift of "English gentlemen" as the inscription records it, was unveiled in the Capitol grounds in Richmond in 1875 (the Blues were present there too), the *Virginian* used half of its front page on October 27 to report the proceedings. But the weight of the historical articles of 1875 was on the centennial of the Revolution. They reflected patriotic pride and a glorying in national achievement, the greater because those who felt thus were living in the shadow of more recent defeat. Virginians in 1875 found special compensation in turning back to their ancestors' role in the birth of the republic.

But 1875 was also a year when the depressing effects of the panic of 1873, increasing in severity as they continued year after year, tightened their grip on new and undeveloped railroads. By November the Chesapeake & Ohio management confessed the railroad was bankrupt. Although the C. & O. had not yet started its tracks eastward from Richmond toward Hampton Roads, Norfolk hoped greatly that when it did it would place its terminal in Norfolk. Nearly three years earlier the city government set up a committee "to take into consideration the propriety of purchasing a wharf front and donating it" to the C. & O. if the railroad would do so.

When the vice president of the railroad, W. C. Wickham, was appointed receiver, the selection shocked the *Virginian*. It exploded in these words:

> The whole management of the Chesapeake & Ohio since 1867 has been a fraud upon the State, has cost the State millions, has swept away the private means of many of its citizens, has destroyed almost all of the fund left by the late Mr. Miller to the University of Virginia,[1] has crippled the Hampton school, has allowed endless speculations on the part of people connected with its inner workings, has wasted or diverted to individual uses the vast property conveyed to Huntington and his associates by the State of Virginia, has gotten Richmond into a great, and so far, useless expenditure, and finally has utterly failed to answer the purposes it promised to subserve. . . .
>
> During all these years William C. Wickham has been vice president of the company, and consequently, either a dupe or cat's paw or something worse. Yet he is now made receiver, to inquire into the wrongs he consented to or was blind to, and to right the evil done under his nose.

1. The reference is probably to the gift of $100,000 by Samuel Miller, of Charlottesville, for a school of agriculture.

Two weeks after news that the C. & O. was in financial trouble came news that the A. M. & O. was in the same plight. A receivership seemed a strong possibility. Mahone had made an arrangement in 1871 with British financiers to dispose over three years of bonds with a face value of $9,500,000. The British ultimately took better than half of that amount. Now Mahone wrote to British bondholders that he had hoped to pay one half of the interest due on October 1, 1875, but, because of the depression that began in 1873, this had proved impossible. He hoped the bondholders would show "forbearance."

The city of Norfolk had invested $500,000 in the railroad. About this the *Virginian*, which feared the A. M. & O. would be taken over by larger railroads, had something to say in March, 1876:

> The object of the State in chartering the various original roads which now constitute of A. M. & O., and giving them State aid to the amount of so many millions, was to open up new avenues of commerce throughout South-side Virginia . . . and especially to build up here in Norfolk a great commercial port. . . . It was the evidence of the advantages of such a connection that induced the city of Norfolk to overwhelm herself with debt beneath which she has staggered ever since its creation, and now just as the city is beginning to feel the good effects of the all-rail connection with the South and far South, and Norfolk is looming up as a cotton port as never before, this movement is made, which, if not properly directed may eventuate into converting the Atlantic, Mississippi & Ohio Railroad into a mere feeder for the hostile roads of Tom Scott [of the Pennsylvania Railroad] and Garrett [John W. Garrett, of the Baltimore & Ohio Railroad], and in depriving Virginia and Virginia cities of the trade and commerce it was created to foster.

These words represented a fundamental of newspaper thinking in Norfolk as manifested many times in both the *Virginian* and the *Landmark*. To hold the A. M. & O. to the development of Virginia and Norfolk, and not to permit it to be a mere adjunct of railroad systems in Pennsylvania, Maryland, or anywhere else, was, in their opinion, the prime necessity. They were always ready to go to war on this issue. When the railroad emerged from receivership as the Norfolk & Western in 1882, Norfolk felt better. And when a year later, in 1883, the Norfolk & Western sent its first carload of coal to Norfolk, where it had a thundering reception, an entire new era began.

The good feeling for Federal Judge Hughes's influence in these developments during the receivership was very high. They were even more significant because by the early 1880's Virginia was riven by political struggles over the state debt, and the *Virginian* and the *Landmark* found themselves far from Judge Hughes's views on those struggles, and even further from Mahone's. But the A. M. & O.–N. & W. record led the *Landmark* to say that "Judge Hughes, long before he could have dreamed of making his home in this city, was the wise and fearless friend of Norfolk, and that, too, in days when men did not find their fortunes promoted by such opinions as he has been in the habit of declaring, and which were all the more helpful to our town because set forth in a style which combined the grace of Addison with the energy of Swift."

Of Mahone's development of the A. M. & O., the *Landmark* said on March 2, 1881—at a time when it was highly critical of his political maneuvers—that:

> *Norfolk then saw,* for the *first time in her history,* a reasonable hope of a great future.
> Mahone realized for her the dreams of Virginia's greatest statesmen, and gave us, and gave the state, western connections with coast deliveries. . . . Any candid person who knows the history of that remarkable achievement must admit that no man in Virginia, at any time in her civil history, ever performed a more honorable act . . . we repeat an oft-made but by no means popular declaration of ours that the time will come when Virginia will do him honor as the hero of the Crater and the hero of consolidation. On one occasion he saved Lee's army. On the other he laid the foundation of fortune for this city and state.

Like the *Landmark,* the *Virginian* disagreed—and even more emphatically than the *Landmark*—with Mahone's fight to readjust the state debt. But "in his last efforts to prevent Virginia's great railroad from falling into inimical hands," the *Virginian* declared, "he is deserving of full credit, which should be cheerfully and not grudgingly awarded him." Though Mahone had been denied the office of receiver, he exercised strong influence on decisions made during the receivership.

In January, 1880, the *Virginian* was still fighting to induce the C. & O. to extend its tracks into Norfolk. The line should run between the two major cities, Richmond and Norfolk, it argued. Norfolk business men set up a committee to carry the argument directly to the C. & O.'s high command. They knew that Hampton and Newport News on the lower Peninsula of Virginia were striving for the terminal too, arguing that the Peninsula route would be shorter and cost less and would face no competing parallel line. These were the views that prevailed. The plum went to Newport News, then a young city and still carrying its historic name of Newport's News.

But railroad receiverships and the loss of the C. & O. terminal to a neighbor across Hampton Roads could not hold back the combination of Norfolk's rising economic growth and Norfolk's rising maturity about—among other things—municipal credit. On January 1, 1875, the *Virginian* printed a letter signed "Countryman" demanding to know, "What is the matter with Norfolk?" Every other city or town of any size or respectability that he knew of, "Countryman" declared, "is paying or trying to pay a part of the interest on its bonds. But Norfolk, since early in 1872 . . . has paid nothing and says nothing about paying. . . . Perhaps they are going to pay soon, for I see the Richmond papers quote Norfolk city 6's at 38 with a rising tendency."

"Countryman" was no fool. Another year was needed, but early in January, 1876, the *Virginian* could let out a cheer: "We gladly call attention to the notice given by the city treasurer in our advertising columns that he will be prepared to pay, on January 10, the interest due on the registered bonds of the city." The end of another era had come.

It was a new era too for the newspapers in Norfolk.

An evening newspaper had been born the previous year (May 3, 1875): the *Evening Times,* published by Mack Nicholson and I. L. Nelson, with W. E. Foster as editorial director. Foster had been associated with the *Day Book* before the Civil War and later was elected to the House of Delegates and the Senate of the General Assembly. In 1876 a newcomer to Norfolk, Oscar Baring, obtained an interest. Then the house fell in. The *Virginian* printed on March 3, 1876, this item: "ABSCONDING NEWSPAPERMAN—Yesterday afternoon the report was current that Oscar Baring, senior proprietor of the Evening Times, had absconded, much to the regret of several merchants, hotel keepers and others. Today it was learned that he had taken the Baltimore boat night before last."

H. W. Burton, better known as "Harry Scratch," a reporter for several Norfolk and Portsmouth newspapers, added frank details in his history of Norfolk: "This accomplished young thief came here a month or two previous to his sudden flight, and bargained for an interest in the *Evening Times,* a penny paper which was then being published by some enterprising and honest young men. . . . Besides buying goods which were to be paid for in advertising, and borrowing

. . . he stole several gold watches, ran up a large hotel bill, made love to some 'ladies fair,' and vanished like a sora."[2]

Two weeks after the disappearance of Baring, T. B. Ruffin joined the *Evening Times'* staff, and the *Virginian* greeted him warmly: "This sprightly paper made its appearance last evening in improved form. . . . No more faithful and industrious worker than Mr. Ruffin could be secured . . . we welcome him back into the newspaper field." But the chief significance of these events was not the likeable Theo Ruffin's aid to the staggering *Evening Times* or the ultimate fate of that newspaper, which lasted only a few months longer. It was the evidence of increasing attention to the evening field in which, in Norfolk, the ineffective *Day Book* had been operating alone.

In the same March of 1876 changes of large importance began successively to appear in the *Virginian's* organization. Ham Chamberlayne resigned as editor after two and a half years. Michael Glennan bought out his only partner, J. C. Adkisson, and at thirty-two years of age stood up as sole owner of the *Virginian*. John S. Tucker, who at the moment was running for mayor of Norfolk, succeeded Chamberlayne as editor of the *Virginian*.

For reasons nobody undertook to explain, Glennan, the new owner, did not announce the choice of a new editor until other newspapers had reported it and commented on it and the whole town must have been talking about it as part of these striking alterations in the ownership and editorial operation of Norfolk's largest newspaper.

Chamberlayne's departure had the look of a normal development. In Norfolk he had the difficult role of editing a newspaper in competition with Hope. But he made his mark. When he did withdraw, it was because of an opportunity that would have moved many another editor: the opportunity of owning and editing his own newspaper, and in the state capital too. Chamberlayne named his newspaper the *State*. He published it—a little later in association with Richard F. Beirne—until his early death at the age of forty-three in 1882.

Glennan's rise to the top was announced on March 25 in these words: "The partnership heretofore existing between M. Glennan and J. C. Adkisson has been this day dissolved by the withdrawal of James C. Adkisson, who has disposed of his full title and interest in the Norfolk Virginian newspaper and job printing office to M. Glennan, who assumed the full proprietorship. March 24, 1876."

2. H. W. Burton ("Harry Scratch"), *The History of Norfolk, Virginia* (Norfolk, 1877), pp. 165-66.

It had taken Glennan nine years, since he came in from teaching a three-pupil school in Portsmouth, to rise to sole ownership and command of the *Virginian*. He had seen all of the printers who hired him early in 1867 withdraw or die, and had bought out their interests until now he ruled supreme. His talent for promotion, his shrewdness in seizing opportunities, his awareness of the value of breadth of appeal, all these helped a young and struggling newspaper. He had close associations with the business community, whose interests he fully recognized and aided, but he did not take on the normal conservatism of many business men. In planning and pushing ahead he was bold and imaginative, and when he began to exploit an idea or argue for a program, he was formidable. He lacked large financial resources, but at that stage of the *Virginian*'s history he did not need a great deal. No one else commanded a fortune either. He did have energy, confidence, and determination, and these he had put to work.

Chamberlayne's resignation was announced March 18, Glennan's proprietorship on March 25. But it was the *Landmark*, not the *Virginian*, that first reported the news of the new editor. On March 24 the *Landmark* published this item: "CAPTAIN JOHN S. TUCKER—For some days we have known that this gallant gentleman, with the empty sleeve and the full head, had succeeded Captain Chamberlayne as editor of the Virginian. . . . We bid our gallant friend welcome to the profession of journalism."

Captain Tucker's sleeve was empty because he had lost an arm at Corinth, Mississippi, in May, 1862, while fighting under Beauregard. Newspaper work was as new to him in 1876 as soldiering had been in 1861. In Norfolk he was a lawyer and a popular orator who was called on many times, especially for memorial occasions; and he had been a member of the three-man Board of Water Commissioners before running for mayor. In the election in May he won, and on July 1 he took office without giving up his editorship.

Apparently Glennan saw no reason why his editor should not continue in both positions, though when Glennan took public office later he himself gave up the editorship he then held. Nor did Hope see any reason later why he should not be Norfolk's public school superintendent while he was editor of the *Landmark*. On such matters opinion shifted much later.

All of Tucker's predecessors—Keiley, Cameron, Hanna, Hope, and Chamberlayne—had been newspaper men before they were editors. But the Suffolk *Herald*'s greeting to Tucker as "no partisan bigot but a free and fearless man" reflected a widely held sentiment.

In the first month of his administration Mayor Tucker stood on the stage of the Opera House to welcome to their reunion the men of Mahone's Brigade. Beside him stood his fellow editor, Hope, to read an original poem dedicated to the brigade. And beside these two stood their friend, formerly of the *Virginian* and formerly of the *Journal*, J. Richard Lewellen, ready to deliver the major address of the reunion. This was July 31, 1876. At that moment Lewellen must have been thinking not only about the oration he would deliver but also about the plans he and two associates were making for a new afternoon newspaper in Norfolk. Within three days that newspaper was born.

The Public Ledger, an afternoon newspaper published by J. Richard Lewellen & Co.—familiar name in a new setting—appeared August 3, 1876, bowing cheerfully and in friendly spirit. Lewellen's partners were Joseph G. Fiveash and Walter A. Edwards. All three were experienced in newspaper publication and familiar with Virginia and the local scene. All three could set type and write news, and on occasion they did both.

Sixty-one years later the *Ledger-Dispatch* published (October 27, 1937) a copy of the original agreement among these three newspaper proprietors. Each provided $500 in capital, to be used in buying type and other equipment. Gains or losses were to be shared equally. For personal use they would draw out equal amounts, the sizes of which were to be agreed upon "from time to time as the conditions of the business will justify."

In an interview published by the *Ledger-Dispatch*, January 1, 1914, Edwards said:

> . . . at the outset eleven men were employed to get out the Public Ledger. This included the reportorial staff, the printers and pressmen as well as the staff in the business office. We thought that was a pretty good force. . . . The paper was run off on a Campbell flatbed press, which had a capacity of 1,000 copies an hour, so you see that going at full speed, it would take us three hours to get off the 3,000 papers. . . . Although the capital stock of the Public Ledger Company was only $1,500 at the time of the organization in 1876, Mr. Fiveash and I paid $3,500 for Mr. Lewellen's share when he went to Danville to take charge of the Register. . . .

That was in 1885. In less than nine years Lewellen's stock had risen 700 per cent in value. Edwards' recollections suggest how easy it was, financially, to start a daily newspaper in the mid-1870's. But all three of these men could put much experience and competence into the organization.

After one term as city sergeant, 1870-72, Lewellen had turned to farming in Norfolk County, operated a crockery business in Norfolk, run for the General Assembly in 1875 from Norfolk County but was beaten by Miles Connor, a Negro, and lectured for the State Grange. A dispatch in the *Virginian* from Staunton, where he had lectured, described him as "a man over six feet in height, of fine personal appearance, made venerable by white hair and beard, and has an eye full of fire." Lewellen could do many things, but he was preeminently a newspaper man. Now fifty-five years old, he wrote the *Public Ledger*'s editorials, and as he was senior among the partners he was more the general manager than the other two. In its early period the *Public Ledger* carried a slogan at the top of its editorial columns, declaring, "For the right that needs assistance, against the wrong that needs resistance, for all the good that we can do."

Fiveash, who spent most of his youth in Portsmouth, had blockade-running experience in the Civil War. He joined Lewellen and his associates as circulation "agent" when they established the *Virginian*, followed Lewellen to the *Journal*, and followed him again as deputy when Lewellen was city sergeant. He had some bookkeeping experience with a cotton broker too, but newspaper work was his first love. He was in charge of the *Public Ledger*'s news.

Edwards was a printer par excellence—and he could prove it. While foreman of the *Journal*'s composing room in 1871 he won second place in a national contest for speed in setting type "at the case"—that is, picking up each piece of type with the right hand and putting it into a holder in the left hand to form lines. He had been a first sergeant in the Civil War—Sixth Virginia Infantry, Mahone's Brigade. Now he took charge of the mechanical work of the *Public Ledger* at its modest quarters on the second floor at 126 Main Street where the Virginia National Bank building was standing in the middle 1960's.

Typographically the *Public Ledger*'s four pages with six columns each were not essentially different from those of its contemporaries. The small, single-column heads and the play of the news were more conservative. But the new newspaper was different in one significant respect. It sold on the streets for a penny. Its charge for carrier-delivered copies was six cents a week and for a year's subscription by mail was $3.50. These were lower figures than the *Virginian* and the *Landmark* charged. The latter had a two-cent price since its establishment in 1873. The *Virginian* went to two cents in May, 1876. Both charged ten cents a week for carrier-delivered copies and $5.00 a year for mail subscriptions. The morning newspapers had no Monday edition, the *Public Ledger* no Sunday edition.

Two afternoon newspapers already were being published in Norfolk, the old *Day Book* and the new *Evening Times*. But neither was as strong—and probably the two combined were not as strong—as either the morning *Virginian* or the morning *Landmark*. Afternoon newspapers began to increase notably in the 1870's. The Civil War had stimulated their growth (almost had created them) because of the new emphasis on news and telegraphic dispatch of news, and the improvement in the speed of printing and distribution. The growth continued during the 1880's and 1890's, especially in smaller cities. By 1890 afternoon newspapers throughout the country exceeded the number of morning newspapers.

But in 1876 afternoon newspapers were still rare in Southern states. Fifteen years later the *Public Ledger*, celebrating its anniversary, recalled afternoon newspapers only in New Orleans, Memphis, Nashville, Richmond, Alexandria, and Norfolk when it was born. Even in 1891, "the total is still small," and

> Indeed in cities much larger than Norfolk attempts to establish afternoon papers have resulted disastrously to those engaged. Charleston, which has a population exceeding 50,000, has never supported an afternoon paper. In Savannah repeated failures have been made in attempts to establish one such paper. The same has been true of Atlanta, the present venture being the first successful effort to give that city the latest local and general news. Richmond, with its 80,000 inhabitants, has never done more than support one afternoon paper. Washington, Baltimore and Brooklyn, with much larger populations, have only one afternoon paper each. [Norfolk's population in 1876 was about 20,000; in 1891, about 35,000.]
>
> In mentioning these facts we deem it not amiss to state that the Public Ledger has, from the day of its first issue until the present time [August 3, 1891], published all the dispatches furnished by that greatest of all news gathering organizations, the Associated Press, and were it possible to obtain fuller reports from the same association, we would do so.

The *Public Ledger* was not only a *news*paper: it was also well managed and vigorous in its advertising and circulation departments. Hard going faced it in its first year or so, especially in 1877 when it had to dismiss its only reporter and rely on its owners (all of whom were well qualified for such additional duties) in covering local news.

But in two or three years its position was solid and, within reasonable limits, assured.

In time new competition did develop. The morning newspapers faced eventually a lusty new rival which itself affected newspaper history in Norfolk. The *Public Ledger* faced in its afternoon field fresh and spirited rivalry. Changes did come. But once the *Public Ledger* was firmly established, as it was before 1880, its position as the major afternoon newspaper, and the positions of the *Virginian* and the *Landmark* as the major morning newspapers, were fixed for the next fifteen years; and all three in merged form survived to the present.

The period did not come about by chance. Norfolk and Virginia were experiencing new growth and establishing new relationships. The years since the South and the North had laid down their arms had brought major changes. The reorganization of life had advanced far. New understandings, new acceptances, new energy, new efforts in many directions made 1880 vastly different from 1865. Norfolk gained 14 per cent in population between 1870 and 1880. It gained 60 per cent between 1880 and 1890. Its economic resources rose sharply. Its confidence kept pace—sometimes leaped far ahead. At times it would be set back on its heels. But the bleakness of the postwar years had gone forever.

SUPPORT FOR THE DEMOCRATIC TILDEN-HENDRICKS TICKET AND OPPOSITION
to the Republican Hayes-Wheeler ticket in 1876 flowed almost automatically from the *Virginian*, the *Landmark*, and the new *Public
Ledger*. They were less enthusiastic about Tilden than critical of the
dying Grant administration and hostile to nearly anything carrying
the Republican name.

The *Virginian* especially had a low regard for Grant, whom much
earlier it had admired. "Darius is marching upon Babylon; let Bel-
shazzar tremble," it thundered. Then, getting close to earth and ob-
serving that "the Radical papers say in praise of Governor Hayes that
if he is elected he will carry no pledges into the White House," it
added this caustic comment: "Let us hope he will carry a temperance
pledge there, for he will find none on the premises." And when
Hayes said in his acceptance speech, "I understand very well that it
was not because of my ability that I was chosen," the *Virginian* commented sardonically, "That may be called a campaign truth." But it
was the close balance in the presidential voting, the issues of honesty
in vote counting, and the question of who would be President that
galvanized the press into new activity and fiery criticism.

For days the result hung in doubt. Then the *Virginian* announced
the election of Tilden. That afternoon the *Public Ledger*—much more
flexible in its press work than earlier Norfolk newspapers—made over
its column of telegraphic news, inserted a "SECOND EDITION"
slug over a bulletin announcing that President Grant had ordered
troops to Florida and Louisiana, and made over its editorial page to include this: "THEIR GREAT AIM—From all the facts before the people now, it is the almost universal sentiment of the masses that the
great aim and objective of the Republican party is to make false election returns in the states of Louisiana, Florida and South Carolina. To

aid this great object Grant has sent troops to New Orleans and Talla-
hassee to 'protect the returning boards in the faithful discharge of
their duty.' "

Two days later the *Virginian* declared: "The reputation of the returning board in Louisiana is so well known to the whole country
that we cannot but expect a fraudulent count from it if left to itself.
In 1872 and 1874 their frauds were so glaring they were repudiated
by a Republican congress."

When the electoral commission handed down its eight-to-seven decision, perilously close to inauguration day in March, newspapers in
Norfolk—perhaps exhausted by anxiety, like much of the country—
accepted the result quietly though not happily. The *Public Ledger*
was "disappointed and mortified." The *Virginian* saw one consola-
tion, "and that is the exit of Mr. Grant." The *Public Ledger* agreed
that "as far as the South is concerned, any change must be for the
better."

But it was not national or congressional elections that engrossed
government, public life, and politics in Virginia for twenty years after the Civil War. The struggles that shook the state most—with the
exception of new racial relationships—grew out of the unmanageabil-
ity of the state debt. Some legal issues rising out of the debt hung on
for fifty years. Not until 1918 did the Supreme Court define all details of West Virginia's responsibility for obligations assumed when
the two states were one.

In 1860 the bonded debt of Virginia was $33,000,000, nearly all
spent to build canals, railroads, and highways. It was not a serious
burden so long as economic conditions were favorable. Bonds sold
above ninety. But the war drastically reversed the situation. Public
works for which the money had been spent were heavily damaged if
not destroyed. West Virginia, a third of prewar Virginia, had gone its
way. Emancipation of the slaves, invalidation of the Confederate
bonds, and property losses in war eliminated much of the capital. Virginians generally were reduced to poverty. Private borrowing was difficult when loanable funds drew from 20 to 30 per cent interest. Tax
increases were politically impossible.

The General Assembly that met in December, 1865—the last to reflect the prewar life of Virginia, and, in postwar Virginia, an anomaly
—assumed full responsibility for the principal of the debt and ordered
the funding of the wartime interest that had not been paid. The two
together lifted the debt total to $38,000,000. But the legislators ig-
nored the need for new revenue.

The continued lack of revenue to pay interest on the debt, to operate the government, and to maintain public schools, which the new
Underwood constitution required and the people were demanding,
drove the state into yearly deficits and raised the debt total by 1870
to $45,000,000. The General Assembly followed Governor Walker's
recommendations for funding the entire $45,000,000 of principal and
unpaid interest, with interest-bearing coupons instead of bonds for
one-third of the debt, which was held in Virginia to be West Virginia's share. It simultaneously authorized the sale of the state's assets in railroads and other properties, which were yielding no returns.

A year later, in 1871, the legislators had second thoughts. They
repealed the funding act only to have Governor Walker veto the
repeal. When the legislators prohibited the acceptance of coupons
for taxes, the state's high court ruled that the authorization of coupons for tax payments constituted a contract between the state and
those bondholders who bought their bonds—called "consols"—before
the attempted legislative prohibition. But no one produced the essential revenue for a state government that was running a deficit year
after year.

When Governor Kemper came into office in January, 1874, that
hard fact stared him in the face. He proposed paying interest at the
rate of 4 per cent instead of 6 per cent and asking creditors to wait
for the other 2 per cent. The *Virginian* swelled with anger. It had
devoted five columns to the governor's message, but "if we are to return to solvency only through bankruptcy," it said editorially, "let
us face the bankrupt court, declare that self preservation made it
necessary, and at least quit the shifts and evasions, the excuses and
idle promises to pay, which have been the rule with us for years past.
. . . Do not, at least, let it be said of us that we had not the sense
and spirit to direct our affairs, but suffered ourselves to fall, to drift,
to sink passively into repudiation. . . ."

Kemper's attempts at persuasion brought firm dissent from "con-
sol" holders. It was a sign of the times. For the lines were hardening
on both sides. The panic of 1873 had made economic life painful
throughout the state. Farmers especially began to organize in granges.
Men who thought readjustment of the debt the only hope talked
more firmly and louder.

High among them—some people called him the father of readjustment—was John E. Massey, better known as "Parson" Massey. Son
of a small farmer and mechanic, and well educated himself, he was
by turns teacher, lawyer, preacher (sometimes regular, sometimes itin-

erant), who turned farmer in Albemarle County and soon was in the General Assembly. Amiable and a little rustic in appearance, but energetic and fervent, he was a stump-speaker unequaled in the Virginia of his times. Now he was convinced that the General Assembly was not paying enough attention to the interests of the people. He began to say so, and people began to listen to his homely and evangelical economic dissertations. Those who had their wits about them knew that something was brewing.

As the sentiment for readjusting the debt grew swiftly, certain pieces began to fall into place. The A. M. & O. receivership in 1876 left Mahone free to pursue other goals. His years of railroad experience had made him familiar with state government. Now he turned definitely toward politics. He lacked the talents of Parson Massey on the stump, but he could write; and he had organizational talent, managerial capacity, ability to put young men to work, and few scruples about his weapons.

Mahone faced the political scene in time for the elections of 1877, gubernatorial and legislative, when Republicans, discouraged by losing ground ever since the state began to rebound politically after the Reconstruction period, did not put up candidates for state offices. Suddenly Mahone was a candidate for the Conservative nomination for governor.

Lined up against him were three eminents: F. W. M. Holliday, John W. Daniel, and General W. B. Taliaferro. But it was Mahone who drove the press to fury. "No radical candidate was ever pursued with more remorseless severity," the *Landmark* declared. This was easy for the *Public Ledger*, which did not like Mahone's railroad record and viewed the possibility of his becoming governor with cold anger. "The Richmond Whig throws out its banner for Mahone for Governor," it said in March, 1877, "and other papers, hitherto too timid to openly espouse the cause of the dethroned king, will probably follow suit. . . . His record on the railroad question makes his defeat certain and overwhelming."

The *Virginian* disapproved these *Whig-Public Ledger* exchanges. "In the interest of Virginia we protested and again protest," it said, "against the unseemly quarrel between the friends and enemies of General Mahone. . . . The Conservative party cannot afford to break up into Mahone and anti-Mahone factions." It intended to support whichever candidate the Conservatives chose. But against debt-scaling it was adamant.

The *Landmark* thought it unfair to damn Mahone because the

A. M. & O. had gone into receivership. It quoted the Petersburg *Post*'s comment that almost all railroads in Virginia were in the hands of receivers. Mahone, said the *Post*, "shared the same fate at the ruthless grasp of foreign bondholders." The *Landmark* had not heard C. P. Huntington of the C. & O. and John S. Barbour of the Virginia Midland "abused for having been caught in the panic of 1873."

But the *Public Ledger* would have none of that. "When the presidents of other bankrupt railroads ask the voters of Virginia to endorse their lack of administrative talent by making them governor of the state," it declared, "the Public Ledger will dare then, as it dares now, to show the people that the failure to manage one interest properly is by no means the best recommendation that the delinquent is really the fittest of all men to have charge of all the interests of the state."

To Hope repudiation would be a violation of honor. But the *Landmark* under him stressed the difference between repudiation and readjustment. It did not object in principle to readjustment; it insisted only that the readjustment should be done with the consent of the bondholders. In comparison with the views of the *Virginian* and *Public Ledger* this was moderation indeed. The *Virginian* demanded not readjustment but payment in full. It declared in August, 1877: "We have no sympathy with those who would sacrifice both [the state's faith and honor pledged to the holders of the bonds] rather than pay sixteen and two-thirds cents on the dollar [*sic*] in addition to the taxes now levied. If there is a person who would rather see his State disgraced, her faith forfeited, her honor dishonored, than pay out of his own pocket sixteen and two-thirds cents out of every hundred dollars he possesses, we have no sympathy with that man. To us he is as devoid of honor as he is of common sense."

In the Conservative convention Mahone led the balloting, closely followed by Daniel, with Holliday further back and Taliaferro trailing. After five ballots Mahone, sensing he could not win in a contest that pitted Mahone against the field, withdrew and threw his strength to Holliday. (In a dramatic moment Cameron, the editor, announced Mahone's decision to the convention.) In November, 1877, Holliday was elected governor. But at the same time voters elected majorities of readjuster candidates in both houses, and most state officers sided with them.

The revolution had not gone full turn, but it was on its way. Holliday still possessed the veto, and the Conservatives—called Funders on this issue—still retained powerful strength in the General Assembly and in the state. They included old-line Virginians, most of the business and banking leadership, and monied people generally. Nearly all the larger newspapers were on their side. Their contention that the state's credit and its good name required payment in full was a strong argument in a state with a record of financial stability, an excellent credit position in earlier years, and a personal code of historic lineage.

Now the Funders faced challenges on complicated and tough issues from a loose federation of small farmers, little-business men, Republicans, Negroes, independents, and many people of all types, including some of the old families who were suffering severely from bad times. These groups held that justice to all, the interests of the public schools in particular, and inability to meet all demands in the prevailing economic conditions required the debt to be scaled, or readjusted. In Mahone they found a leader with the capacity to weld them into an effective force.

Early in 1878 the General Assembly, under readjusting pressures, approved the Barbour bill which put "the constitutional obligation to support the system of public schools" ahead of "the payment of the present rate of interest on the amount claimed as the principal of the public debt." Governor Holliday vetoed it. Free schools, he declared, "are not a necessity. The world for hundreds of years grew in wealth, culture and refinement without them." The *Virginian* thought that "Governor Holliday has saved Virginia from the disgrace of repudiation."

But the Readjusters came within five votes of overturning the veto. They were disappointed but not broken, and they turned again to more systematic organization of the state. So did Conservatives. Before 1878 ran out they established a new society "to preserve the credit of the state," with thirty-nine well-known Virginians as its sponsors, including several ministers and two Republican judges. Out-of-state and foreign bondholders, who held two-thirds of the bonds, produced a plan named after its chief designer, former Secretary of the Treasury Hugh McCulloch, then chief agent for New York banks interested in the debt.

Mahone countered by calling for a convention of Readjusters. Representatives from sixty of the ninety-nine counties (none from Norfolk) met in Mozart Hall in Richmond, listened to statements, adopted resolutions, and emerged as a formal political party.

Most of the press tore into this gathering. "The odds and ends of the Conservative and Republican parties," was the *Public Ledger*'s de-

The *Virginian-Pilot* scooped the world with this famous story of man's first flight. The picture of the plane is superimposed.

Virginian-Pilot.

VOL. XXIII. NO. 24.   NORFOLK, VA., SATURDAY, APRIL 27, 1907. SIXTEEN PAGES.   THREE CENTS PER COPY.

JAMESTOWN EXPOSITION, UNDER BRIGHT SKIES,
OPENS WITH ATTENDANCE OF 60,000 VISITORS

*President's Speech, Naval and Military Reviews, Booming of Cannon, Presence of World's Great and
Tremendous Throngs of Sightseers, Mark Auspicious Inauguration of Ter-centennial
Celebration on Shore of Historic Hampton Roads.*

Characteristic Forensic Poses Of Theodore Roosevelt In Delivering His Speech From Grand Stand

THE NORFOLK LANDMARK.

VOL. LXIV—NO. 47.   NORFOLK, VA., ... MORNING, APRIL 27, 1907.   16 PAGES   PRICE—THREE CE...

AMID SCENE OF BEAUTY
THE EXPOSITION OPENS.

President Opens Celebration of Ter-Centennial of Landing at Jamestown.

HEAD OF NATION REVIEWS FLEET.

Virginia's Sons Pay Lasting Tribute to Founders of a Great Republic—Weather Was Auspicious—Diplomats Representing
Many Nations Participated in Exercises.

Commemorating the three hundredth anniversary of the first
landing of English speaking people at Jamestown Island, the ...

PRESIDENT WAR
THE WRONG D...

**Welcomes All Nations
Ter-Centenary.**

WOULD CURB CORPORA...

Judge Each Man by His De...
Says—He Also Discuss
...mieration and Dangers
preparedness for War.

In a speech replete with stri...
tenanted, a warning to the wo...
whom he declares shall ...
marcy at his hands. Presiden...
dore Roosevelt yesterday a...
formally opened the Ter-Cen...
The President held the close...
tion of the many thousands...

THE LEDGER-DISPATCH.

EXPOSITION
EDITION

CIRCULATION
Daily Average for March, 1907.
2 1 , 6 1 7

VOL. LXII.—NO. 71.   NORFOLK, VA., FRIDAY AFTERNOON, APRIL 26, 1907.   PRICE ONE CENT

VIRGINIA WELCOMES WORLD TO JAMESTOWN

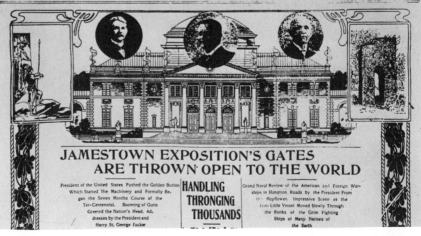

JAMESTOWN EXPOSITION'S GATES
ARE THROWN OPEN TO THE WORLD

President of the United States Pushed the Golden Button
Which Started the Machinery and Formally Be-
gan the Seven Months Course of the
Ter-Centennial. Booming of Guns
Greeted the Nation's Head. Ad-
dresses by the President and
Harry St. George Tucker

**HANDLING
THRONGING
THOUSANDS**

Grand Naval Review of the American and Foreign Warships in Hampton Roads by the President From
the Mayflower. Impressive Scene as the
Trim Little Vessel Moved Slowly Through
the Ranks of the Grim Fighting
Ships of Many Nations of
the Earth

How three Norfolk dailies reported the opening of the Jamestown
Exposition.

scription of the delegates. They had assembled, it said, "to clothe these arch conspiritors with legislative power to further forage upon the treasury." The *Virginian* called them "the flower and chivalry of forcible readjustment . . . uneasy, self-seeking politicians . . . this piebald convention," with which "the wise and sagacious men of the state have no sympathy."

The *Landmark*, as usual, was more moderate. It wanted to see the Conservative Party "stand together and . . . adjust the debt question within its own ranks, and this, we believe, can yet be done by moderate language and prompt action. . . . We think the Readjusters are making a stupendous blunder by going outside the party."

The McCulloch bill won legislative approval. It divided outstanding bonds into two classes, provided for their funding into new ten to forty-year bonds on which interest was cut to 3, 4, and 5 per cent for ten, twenty, and thirty years, respectively, with funding arrangements assigned to New York and British groups under specified terms. West Virginia's supposed one-third of the debt was set aside. From 1885 a new tax would channel money into a sinking fund.

The *Virginian,* the *Landmark,* and the *Public Ledger* all approved the act. It had substantial advantages for the state. But it depended on the funding arrangements, which left uncertainties, and on the state's ability to pay even the reduced interest, which the Readjusters were confident the state could not do. A judgment on all these issues, it was clear, would be passed on to the voters in the 1879 election of legislators.

The *Public Ledger* admitted that "Virginia Conservatives did compromise the debt," though "with the consent of her creditors. The present quarrel," it continued, "is not really so much against that [McCulloch] settlement as it is for the purpose of raising a flood of political agitation upon whose waves it is expected to float into the United States Senate the leader of the Mozart hall agitators."

The campaign stirred the state. When Major W. T. Taliaferro and Colonel L. D. Starke undertook to explain the McCulloch plan to a Norfolk mass meeting, the *Landmark* used two and a half columns to report the explanations. When three Conservative speakers (one of whom was the *Virginian*'s recent editor, Ham Chamberlayne) and three Readjusters (two of whom were Mahone and Parson Massey) debated in Suffolk, the largest crowd ever assembled there listened to hours of argument. Some of the debaters came the next day to Norfolk where Massey alone needed two hours to state his case, and, said the *Landmark*, was listened to with great interest and was frequently applauded. A Portsmouth debate in September was still going strong at 12:45 a.m.

Election day in November of 1879 found the *Virginian*, the *Landmark*, and the *Public Ledger* standing side by side. "Vote for the maintenance of Conservative principles," the *Public Ledger* urged. But the other two sought more moving appeals. "Vote as you shot— for the honor of Virginia," pleaded the *Virginian*. "Virginians will pay a just debt," the *Landmark* insisted, "though they walk barefoot to the polls to vote the way Marse Robert would vote were he today among his people."

But newspapers could not stop the turn of the revolutionary wheel. Norfolk elected Readjuster legislators, though by thin margins; the state chose small Readjuster majorities for House and Senate. Norfolk newspapers were shocked and, save for the philosophic *Landmark*, bitter. They placed the blame in Norfolk on the failure of some five hundred registered white men to vote. Those who did not vote, declared the *Virginian*, "have helped by their indifference to crucify the honor of the Commonwealth."

Bitterness increased when the new General Assembly, in December, 1879, began displacing Conservative officeholders with Readjusters, sometimes with Negroes. "It now turns out," the *Virginian* charged, "that the leaders of Mozart hall had made a covenant with the Negroes of the state by which they guaranteed all the demands they had ever made. . . . The debt question was a mere pretext. The great object was the destruction of the Conservative party and the construction of a party that should be owned by Mahone, Cameron and Company."

The *Public Ledger* was even more fearful: "General Mahone will be elected United States senator. God save the Commonwealth!" The *Virginian* produced a new analogy: "Judas Iscariot went out and hanged himself. General Mahone will never pay the same tribute to his conscience if any he has. Score one for Judas Iscariot." But the *Landmark* would not follow this lead. It admitted that "the outlook is distressing, but we rely with confidence upon the sober second thought of the people. It may be delayed, but the swing of the pendulum is not more certain than the popular reaction which we foresee."

This calm voice did not keep tempers from exploding. The *Virginian*'s opposition to debt readjustment during the campaign had created indignation among Readjusters. When their convention in

Norfolk nominated legislative candidates, it adjourned "with three groans for the *Virginian*." When the *Virginian* attacked "the distribution of the spoils" in Richmond after the election, a meeting was called for Norfolk, but never held, to deliver formal criticism of the newspaper's course. Some of the Readjusters "gratified their ambition by 'stopping the Virginian,'" the editor wrote, but "to this we patiently submitted in the belief that if they could stand it we could. . . . These and other manifestations we accepted as tributes which we prize as proof of efficient work in a good cause."

The fires grew hotter. In December, 1879, night prowlers and small mobs went into direct action against the *Virginian*. They threw rocks and bricks against its building and fled in the darkness. Growing bolder, they hurled stones at the windows, broke panes, shattered the skylight of the press room, and narrowly missed compositors at work. With that the *Virginian* let loose:

> We have heretofore avoided making any mention of this matter in the hope of being able to find out the cowardly perpetrators of these outrages, but we have been baffled in our efforts to detect them. . . . This is a mode of warfare to which we are not accustomed.
>
> If the cowardly scoundrels who have thus attempted to injure our employees, who are in no way responsible for the sentiments expressed in this paper, will muster enough courage to come to the front of our office and attempt in daylight the outrages they have perpetrated under cover of darkness, we will give them an appropriate welcome. Meanwhile, we notify them now that if they continue these annoyances any longer they must be prepared for the summary retribution such ruffianism deserves.

The local furies in Norfolk abated, but the Readjusters went about their business in Richmond. The new General Assembly elected Mahone United States senator (in December, 1879). Following the timetables then he did not take his seat until a special session in March, 1881, after the election of Garfield and Arthur. The organization of the new Senate hung in precise balance between Republicans and Democrats, and the nation watched in fascination to see which camp Mahone would vote with. He called himself then a Democrat or Conservative and in the 1880 campaign in Virginia he had worked through Readjusters against the Republican ticket. But he insisted that he had been elected a senator by Readjusters and not by Democrats or Republicans, and was beholden to neither national party.

On the showdown in the Senate Mahone voted with the Republicans. As he did so, honors showered down on him: flowers from the President, the chairmanship of the Committee on Agriculture, and high-ranking membership in three other important committees— unprecedented honors for a newcomer. At home old-line Democrats damned him for a traitor. Joining the Republicans! Mahone denied that he had, but denial made no difference. Forever afterward, in the minds of old leaders of Virginia, he was a ruined soul.

In the *Virginian's* judgment Mahone belonged now to "the state's enemies and traducers." The *Public Ledger*, in March, 1881, declared: "Now that he has definitely made his choice, we may congratulate ourselves at his departure, and rejoice to know that he will do more to destroy the Republican party than any other person of whom we have any knowledge."

In Richmond, meantime, the Readjuster-controlled General Assembly passed a new debt bill presented by Senator H. H. Riddleberger, a newspaper publisher from the Valley of Virginia. Governor Holliday vetoed it, and the *Public Ledger* thought "the repudiationists have received a setback from which they will not soon recover." The *Virginian*, for its part, was more succinct. "Thou has kept the faith," it informed the governor. If the Readjusters were to write their views into law, they would have to elect more legislators or a governor. They set about getting both, chiefly a governor.

In the Readjuster state convention of June, 1881, Parson Massey of Charlottesville and Cameron, the Norfolk, Petersburg, and Richmond editor then in his third term as mayor of Petersburg, were the principal candidates for governor. Cameron won. The *Public Ledger* greeted him and his associates with a blast: "All the Readjuster nominees are tarred with the same stick . . . a trinity of demagogues emphatically of the genus political best described as chameleon." The *Virginian* knew Cameron better than that. It pronounced him "a chivalrous, gallant gentleman." But "as the nominee of the Mahone party [he] has not the strength that some of the others mentioned might have commanded [a reference to John S. Wise, of Richmond, and General V. D. Groner, of Norfolk, who were also candidates for the nomination]. His former bitter and relentless war against the Republican party . . . will prevent him from securing anything like full support from adherents of that party . . . a weaker ticket could not have been selected."

The *Landmark*, though it had no love for Readjusters, could present a different picture of the ticket, especially of Cameron:

The Readjusters, we think, have put up one of their strongest and most adroit leaders. He is personally attractive, his manners are genial, his pen ready, his speech fluent and graceful, and altogether, we think, the enemy did, for their interest, a wise thing when they put forward Colonel Cameron. It will be easy to bombard him with quotations from his own writings when he was "after" the Republicans like a political Saul of Tarsus; but it will not do to rely too much on these—the masses have short memories and forgiving tempers. We must organize our party.

But when Cameron declared a few days later that "I do not intend to carry the war into Africa, but Africa into the war," the *Landmark* was shocked. "We doubt if any man in his party could have stated the real issue in fewer words," it said. "Under this neat phrase there lies a meaning, the repulsiveness of which no glitter of words can abate or modify, for it means just this: Colonel Cameron and his party intend to lead the negroes, ignorant and unfit for self-government, in a 'war' against the white debt-paying Democrats especially, and against all debt-payers in general."

The Funders, who earlier had been Conservatives for the most part, were going back now to the traditional designation of Democrats. They nominated John W. Daniel, of Lynchburg, for governor. Norfolk newspapers immediately announced their support, though the *Landmark* had preferred John Goode, of Norfolk. The *Virginian* now was opposing its earlier editor, Cameron; the first *Virginian* editor, Keiley, now chairman of the Democratic State Executive Committee, was leading the party fight against his old editorial protégé.

The campaign threw Daniel, an orator of wide fame, against Cameron, a shrewd debater. They met in headlong debate many times. Early in these excitements the *Public Ledger* complained of partisan and inaccurate reporting. "Since the canvass was opened in the Southwest," it noted, "reports have been furnished the central organ [the Richmond *Whig*] glorifying the Mahone candidate for governor, and where discussions have been held the Democratic reporters have assured the public that Cameron was either skinned or wiped out." It continued:

> We don't fancy this style of reporting. It does no good to either party, but, on the other hand, creates a faulty impression. The fairest way to report discussions, and the plan this paper has always adhered to, is to give as full a synopsis as possible of what each candidate actually said, and then to leave the public to decide who was the victor and who the van-

quished. The newspapers should deal fairly with all speakers. The wishes and prejudices of the reporters should have nothing to do with what they write.

The *Public Ledger* struck this high note far ahead of its times. It was championing essential principles and policies which in time most newspapers espoused and sought to perfect. In 1881 this was a historic utterance.

Election day brought a Cameron victory and renewed Readjuster majorities in the General Assembly, though slim ones. Cameron's margin was 13,000 votes out of about 212,000. Once again the Norfolk press blamed nonvoting whites. Once again it prophesied gloomily. Even the *Landmark* was depressed:

> We can see nothing [the *Landmark* said] to cheer up the people . . . we have now and for the first time fairly entered on the revolution foreshadowed at Appomattox. One after another the conservative checks and balances of the state have been broken, until now the executive and legislative branches of our government have passed into the hands of a majority of our population, made up of blacks and whites, with the former in marked preponderance. . . .
>
> But the worst has not been told. The judiciary is to be made a partisan machine. We are confronted by a horde of negroes who hold the balance of power and are to be rewarded. Colonel Cameron led them into "the war," and they are to be paid bounties and rations, and will have them. The town charters are to be tampered with, the poll tax to be taken off, the juries are to be mixed, the courts are to be packed. . . .
>
> What then can we do? We can resist by all lawful means each and every encroachment. We can band together and exercise a moral power, and, if we can do nothing else, we can show that we are men enough to try and protect society from the calamities which threaten.

Governor Cameron's message to the General Assembly in January, 1882, called for a revised Riddleberger bill, citing as he did so the diversion of funds from the schools and the need "to preserve the school fund from future invasion, and to restore to it, as speedily as possible, the amount which has been diverted." He urged repeal of the poll tax as a prerequisite to voting, revision of registration laws to encourage voting, and judges of elections chosen from opposing parties. Neither the *Virginian* nor the *Public Ledger* found fault with these latter proposals. They emphatically opposed the new Riddleberger debt bill.

But much of the opposition in Virginia lacked the old fire. With

Readjusters in control of both houses of the General Assembly and the governor's chair, a new debt bill was inevitable. Among many Funders who themselves had accepted the idea of some degree of readjustment, although proclaiming always their enmity to repudiation, the recognition was growing that continued and long-range opposition did not carry promise of success.

So the Riddleberger bill moved surely through the legislature and received promptly Governor Cameron's approval. It rested on the premise that in July, 1882, after all previous payments had been taken into account and a third of the debt had been allotted to West Virginia, the Virginia debt would be $21,000,000. It authorized new 3 per cent, eighteen to fifty-year bonds (popularly called Riddlebergers) and offered them in exchange at varying ratios for outstanding bonds. Accompanying coupon-killer acts sought to restrict the use of coupons for paying taxes and to establish their genuineness when presented—an old problem. The effect was to scale down the principal, lower the interest, and tighten the handling devices, as compared with the McCulloch bill. The bill could not assure that die-hard bondholders holding out for face values, many of them living abroad, some of them bond speculators, would exchange their bonds for the new Riddlebergers. But the new bill quickly gained acceptance from the Democratic leadership.

The Democratic state convention declared in July, 1883, that "the Democratic party accepts as final the recent settlement of the public debt . . . and will oppose any further agitation of the question, or any disturbance of that settlement, by repeal or otherwise."

Later in 1883, after the Democrats had won the General Assembly in the elections of that autumn, they carried a resolution through the legislature reviewing thirteen years of "political contests which have convulsed the popular mind, given repeated and ruinous shocks to the business interests," and "retarded prosperity." The resolution recalled "persistent, repeated, and earnest but unavailing efforts" to recognize a larger debt principal. But it also noted that the Riddleberger bill had received numerous endorsements from the people and the courts. It rose to the point in these words: "Any expectation that any settlement of the debt, upon any other basis, will ever be made or tolerated by the people of Virginia, is absolutely illusory and hopeless," and it concluded that the bill's acceptance was required in the interest of bondholders and the state.

The *Landmark* acted more quickly. It declared in March, 1882, shortly after passage of the bill, that the debt question had been settled by the Riddleberger plan and "can only reappear in the courts."

But the *Public Ledger* was more reluctant. After the Democratic state convention in July, 1883, had pronounced the settlement to be "final," and the Baltimore *American* had declared that "the old Virginia Democracy" had disappeared—"they are all Readjusters now," it said—the *Public Ledger* replied in these words:

> We accept the debt settlement as we have been time and again forced to accept impositions and insults in which we had neither part nor lot. Step by step, readjustment of the debt was fought by the Virginia Democrats in convention, before the people and at the polls. But whenever or wherever the contest was waged we had not only to oppose the whites who honestly differed from us on the question, but men calling themselves Republicans were leading the colored voters in a solid phalanx against us, backed by northern money given to the "Boss" to buy votes and corrupt the ballot box. . . . Defeated at every turn by Mahone and his northern radical allies, we were forced to accept the decision of the highest court of the Union . . . and [we have] left the debt question with the courts and the responsibility of its settlement with Mahone and his stalwart friends of the north. . . .

The debt had been settled as a generator of storms. Some holders of older issues of bonds still refused to turn them in for the Riddlebergers, and their efforts, especially those of British bondholders, continued. In 1891 this unhappiness produced meetings of a state commission and a bondholders' committee, with an advisory board for the creditors on which sat, among others, Grover Cleveland and former Secretary of State Thomas F. Bayard.

Out of these amicable efforts came the settlement named for Frederick P. Olcott, chairman of the bondholders' committee. Built on the Riddleberger plan, it lifted the principal somewhat and thus made more likely exchanges of old bonds for new one-hundred-year bonds called "centuries." Because the proposals were more agreeable to the bondholders they removed, at least in the minds of many Virginians, any taint of repudiation. The interest rates were lowered. But the real point was that both sides desired a settlement. The earlier battles had created that spirit.

In Norfolk the *Virginian* declared on November 20, 1891, that "yesterday was indeed a glorious day for Virginia. Bonfires and salutes of cannon should testify to the peoples' gladness." The *Landmark* exclaimed "Debt settled! Happy declaration!" and prophesied that "this state administration and the year 1891 will be memorable in the history of Virginia." The *Public Ledger* thought "this is the most favorable offer the state has ever received." A mass meeting in Mechanics Hall asked the General Assembly to accept the settlement without delay. The legislators ratified the settlement February 20, 1892.

This, too, was fruit of the readjuster movement. But the height of the Readjuster Party's power came in 1882 and by 1891 was long past. It had elected Riddleberger to the United States Senate in 1881 to join Mahone there. It sent members to the House of Representatives. It won acceptance of its major premise from many old enemies. It instituted reforms of value, chiefly liberal in philosophy and designed to aid new elements in postwar Virginia, including Negroes. These actions carried the party into general political life where it lacked the unity and dedication of the readjusting cause. It suffered from dissension.

Mahone's leadership, often effective, sometimes brilliant, was always rough and tough; and his discipline was iron. Thereby he lost valuable lieutenants: Massey, Cameron, Riddleberger, among others. His displacement of well-regarded officials—William H. Ruffner, state superintendent of public schools, for one—created enmities. The frank Republicanism which Mahone adopted increased defections. Virginians who followed him in readjusting a burdensome debt would not necessarily follow him into a traditionally disliked political party. From 1883 the whole movement declined.

The Massey revolt had ironical aspects. In 1882 one congressman had to be chosen at large. Massey sought to be the Democratic choice for that candidacy. The very suggestion brought the anti-Massey *Public Ledger* up fighting: "We regret to know that any true Democrat in Virginia has ever thought, even as a matter of expediency, of nominating Parson Massey for Congressman-at-large. . . . We turn from the bait with loathing and disgust. . . . With Massey as our standard-bearer, success is utter disaster to the Democratic party, even if it were possible to elect him."

But the state Democratic committee refused to name any candidate, and Massey was by default the Democratic candidate. The Readjusters named John S. Wise, son of a Democratic governor and a formidable campaigner and personality who had to take time out at the beginning of the campaign to fight a duel. His opponent was the commonwealth's attorney in Wythe County, John S. Crockett. They exchanged two rounds, both missing on the first round and Wise's pistol failing to fire and Crockett missing on the second round.

Neither admitted satisfaction, but the duel was over. A dispatch to the *Virginian* reported that "the fight had every indication of being a genuine combat, though bloodless."

Neither Wise nor the Parson missed often in the rounds of debate in which both of them—and the state too—reveled. On platforms they argued for hours to the delight of thousands of listeners. Massey, it turned out, could fire as heavy guns against Mahone and Riddleberger as he had fired at Funders. The results were a little unusual.

For whereas the *Public Ledger* had declared in July, when the state committee had refused to name a candidate, that "we regard this action as suicidal to the best interests of the Democratic party in Virginia," now it began to take second thought. And whereas the *Landmark* had said then, "We warn our friends on the central committee of our party that the people are not prepared to take Mr. Massey as an exponent of their principles," now in October the picture seemed different. As for the *Virginian*, Michael Glennan as a member of the state committee had opposed its decision to name no candidate.

By October readers of the *Public Ledger* were learning that "Mr. Massey is a wonderful old man and without doubt the best stumper in the state . . . [his] speech was listened to by at least 3,000 Democrats. It was well delivered, and the 'old man's' points were mighty clear." In the end the *Public Ledger* based its championship of the Parson on the conviction that "the supreme object of the Democratic party in Virginia is the defeat of Mahoneism—which is Republicanism in its most corrupt form," and that "no man can do more toward the accomplishment of this desirable end than John E. Massey."

Not even this somersault was enough. Wise won the state, though he did not carry Norfolk. The embarrassment in Norfolk editorial offices must have been mixed. The candidate they had endorsed had lost, and in Wise they had one more Readjuster congressman to contend with. But they could never have been really happy in thinking of the Parson as their Democratic representative—any more than they could have been happy with the news just in from Massachusetts. Democrats there had just elected Ben Butler as governor.

IN MAY, 1878, THE *Virginian*, STILL BEMUSED BY THE DREAM OF A CON-
tinental railroad, Norfolk to California, grew excited over the Texas
Pacific railroad bill in Congress. "There is no other question now
before the country," it said, "in which the people of Norfolk are so
much interested. All other issues are subordinate to the construction
of a Southern Pacific railroad that shall strike the Mississippi River
at or near Memphis and then, connecting with the system of railways
that terminate at our wharves, make Norfolk the great American
trade center where the commerce of Europe and Asia shall meet. This
is the great consummation in comparison to which all other matters
sink into insignificance."

The thinking smacked of the late 1860's. But closer at hand many
dreams were coming true.

The arrival in 1883 of the Norfolk & Western's first car of coal
was followed shortly by Chesapeake & Ohio coal that rolled across the
state to Newport News. In 1909 a third coal-carrying railroad, the
Virginian, was pouring its tonnage into Norfolk coal piers. By that
time Hampton Roads was the world leader in coal shipments. (In
the early 1960's the Norfolk & Western acquired the Virginian and
merged the two into one operating railroad.)

Rail service for the few miles to Ocean View on Chesapeake Bay
was established in 1879. The Elizabeth City & Norfolk was opened
in May, 1881, with excursions carrying hundreds of celebrating passengers from Norfolk to Elizabeth City one day and from Elizabeth
City to Norfolk the next day. The line extended to Edenton the
next year, changed its name to Norfolk & Southern (later Norfolk-
Southern), and was peering deeper into North Carolina. First spike
in the Norfolk-Virginia Beach line, a narrow gauge then, was driven

in February, 1883, and in July, Norfolk was enjoying the ocean by rail.

The Norfolk & Western built a new station in Norfolk in 1882 with an eighty-foot tower carrying an illuminated four-face clock six feet across. The railroad was planning to circle Norfolk from its Main Street station to its coal terminal on the Elizabeth River at Lambert's Point. By 1884 the New York, Philadelphia & Norfolk—which Norfolk, sounding the first letters, like to call the Nyp 'n N—sent its rails southward down Virginia's Eastern Shore to Cape Charles and used ferries and barges to reach the Norfolk side of Chesapeake Bay. This Pennsylvania-controlled line cut the Norfolk-New York passenger trip by five hours.

In 1883 ground was broken for the Atlantic & Danville, the first link of the Great Western dream of the 1860's. Portsmouth voted $150,000 participation by 1,399 to 316. But progress was slow, and the line did not open until 1890. The next year, the N. & W. was building a larger station and warehouses at the foot of Main Street, filling in Mahone's Lake to do so. The Norfolk & Carolina built its line to Tarboro in North Carolina in 1890, and Norfolk's connection with the Atlantic Coast Line was assured.

Late in 1895 the Southern Railway came into Norfolk over that line (later over the Atlantic & Danville), looking for deepwater and adding for a time a Pacific passenger train. The Seaboard Air Line had established its Florida connection by 1891, and when it and the Southern arranged coast-to-coast connections, the *Virginian* cheered (February 21, 1896):

> The recent departure of a through passenger train over the Seaboard Air Line to San Francisco on the Pacific coast without a break, carrying a portion of the crew of the battleship Texas, was an event that was very properly heralded throughout the country.
>
> The recent arrival over the Southern Railway of the first solid passenger train from San Francisco to Norfolk, carrying the 119 sailors and five officers of the United States ship Baltimore, late in Chinese waters, making the run in five days and nine hours, was another exhibit of the wonderful railway advantages now possessed by Norfolk. . . .

In 1893 the C. & O., which had been using barges and ferries between Newport News and Norfolk (and continued to do so), bought heavily in Norfolk's Brooke Avenue area and built a half-million dollar terminal there. Eventually, in the later 1890's a belt-line railroad circled the Norfolk-Portsmouth area to make interchange efficient.

The high tide of railroad development left mistakes that dragged some of the lines into receivership, especially when the panic of 1893 shook business to its foundations. But in the historical sense these were temporary setbacks that did not keep the trains from running. The 1880's, with a start earlier and some filling in and rounding off later, wrought a Norfolk revolution. No longer had the city been forced to fight its way, or to beg with hat in hand for railroads: they had come of their own will and sometimes fought among themselves to reach Norfolk.

The *Virginian* and the *Landmark* pumped hard for every step in these developments, though the *Public Ledger* had its doubts about the virtues of urban growth. "We do not think there is a city in the United States so much commented on during the last few years by the press of the country as Norfolk," the *Virginian* declared on November 30, 1880. "Nearly every paper has something to say about her wonderful growth, the astonishing amount of business she transacts, and the splendid field she presents for the investment of capital." To the *Virginian*, no influence in these changes in Norfolk was as great as "the unceasing efforts of her newspapers."

For its part, the *Virginian* undoubtedly had tried. It systematically published trade editions and other special editions, nearly always at the start of a new year and on anniversaries, but whenever it could find a reason. In late December, 1880, it boasted:

> Previous to these trade issues the growth of Norfolk as a cotton port was only considered, but when we summarized its business in cotton, lumber, peanuts, groceries, dry goods, fruits and vegetables, general merchandise, liquor, grain and notions —when we pointed out its increase in population and building—the business of its railroad and canal lines—when by attractive maps we exhibited the proposed extension of its limits and its magnificent trade area—and then spread broadcast this information in issues of 10,000 copies, mailing to the press of the country marked copies, with the request that if they saw fit to notice its contents we would be thankful; the fruit of our work was recognized, and from one section of the country to the other, generous and at times elaborate allusions by the press were made to the prosperity of Norfolk.

An eight-page trade edition in October of 1880 included a five-column map of the Norfolk trade area on the front page with railroad, canal, and highway connections. (Glennan liked maps and was skilled at using them.) Ten thousand copies were distributed free in eastern North Carolina. The *Landmark* had published a special edition (rare for it) in April of 1880, full of tabulated statistics to show Norfolk growth, advantages, and opportunities, and, by intimation, to invite readers to come and see.

The *Virginian* had made the invitation more direct in 1879 when some fourteen hundred North Carolina business men, invited by Norfolk merchants and other business men, came on excursion trains to Norfolk for inspection and entertainment. The *Virginian* published a twelve-page edition then, an unusual accomplishment for the times. The *Public Ledger* pronounced it a "magnificent special edition, which has been in preparation for some weeks, and a really splendid paper it is," distinguished by "photographic views" and much local history. It included, as the *Virginian* always was sure to provide, a good deal of history about the newspaper itself. The *Public Ledger* noted "the abundant evidence that it is a pecuniary success." Generally, half the space in such editions was used by advertisers.

A *Virginian* special edition of January 1, 1884, included, in addition to the standard kinds of material, some of the "links which connect the Virginian with the press of this and other states, furnishing, as it has, so many of those who have been associated with it, to edit and conduct and manage the departments of successful and enterprising journals." It called a long roll:

James Barron Hope to edit, S. S. Nottingham, Jr., to manage, and J. S. Barcroft to superintend the job department of the *Landmark*; Lewellen, Fiveash, and Ruffin of the *Public Ledger*; W. S. Copes of the Norfolk *Weekly Herald*; John W. H. Porter and M. W. Concannon of the Portsmouth *Enterprise*; R. E. Glassett of the *Landmark*'s Portsmouth office; J. C. Wilcox of the Portsmouth *Weekly Observer*.

To these the *Virginian* added Governor Cameron, who had been editor of the Petersburg *Index*; W. S. Copeland of the Petersburg *Mail*; Chamberlayne (who had died in 1882) of the Richmond *State*, along with "that brilliant journalist, the lately departed 'Brevity' Bennett"—Col. A. P. Bennett; Maj. James F. Milligan of several Norfolk newspapers; Henry S. Brooke and Alex Bell of newspapers in New Mexico and New York, respectively, and "there are others whose names we cannot recall."

Yet the *Public Ledger* under Lewellen was disturbed by some signs. "We can hardly take up a Virginia paper," it said in January of 1881, "in which we do not meet with paragraphs boasting about the growth of our towns. We can remember when such towns as Danville and Staunton were mere villages." Then to the doubt:

> This prosperity sounds very well. In some respects we rejoice at it. Nevertheless, Jefferson never uttered a truer saying than that the "cities are sores upon the body politic."[1] Whenever we find them we find social and political corruption to a greater or less extent, and though our cities are not yet large enough or numerous enough seriously to affect the moral status of Virginia, we shall see another picture developed even by the end of this century, when the city population of Virginia shall have so greatly increased that it will have a great influence in demoralizing our people. . . . We shall become a richer but a less reliable people and the future historian will be compelled to acknowledge that the high moral and political character of Virginia departed when we ceased to be a purely agricultural community.

On this issue the *Public Ledger* seemed in Norfolk almost a lonely voice then. But the echo could be heard in rural parts of Virginia more than eighty years later.

The end of the *Day Book*—last of the prewar newspapers, suspended during the war, and never its old self subsequently—came on January 5, 1881. The *Virginian* said it died after "a long and manful struggle," but the *Day Book* itself was blunter. The reason, it declared, was "lack of means."

None of the other daily newspapers established in the 1880's could make real headway against the *Virginian* and the *Landmark* in the morning and the *Public Ledger* in the afternoon. The *Liberal*, which began publication in 1880, and the *Daily Review* in 1882, both Readjuster journals; the *Evening News*, starting in 1882, first of two newspapers to carry this name; the *Evening Telegram* of 1888 and the *News and Courier* of 1890, which changed its name to the *Evening News* in 1896—all these had short careers, in one instance only three months, in no instance more than seven years.

Weeklies did better. The *Herald*, with intelligent direction from W. S. Copes and, for a time, with a much respected editor, N. B. Webster (often called Professor Webster, because he had taught school), the *Sunday Gazette* (later the *Gazette*), and the *Journal of Commerce*

1. The Reference Department, General Reference and Bibliography Division, the Library of Congress, has not found the above quotation that is attributed to Jefferson but has noted on page 276 of Burton Stevenson's *The Home Book of Quotations; Classical and Modern* (9th ed.; New York: Dodd, Mead, 1958), the following statement by Thomas Jefferson: "The mobs of great cities add just so much to the support of pure government as sores do to the strength of the human body."

were solid publications for many years even though they had strong competition from weekly editions of the *Virginian* and the *Landmark*.

Portsmouth lost the daily *Record* in 1888 after four years of publication, but the *Daily Enterprise*, which began in 1873, and the *Times*, from 1877, merged into the *Enterprise-Times* in 1888 and continued, eventually under the name of the *Progress*, until 1895. In 1894 the Portsmouth *Star*, guided by Paul C. Trugien, aided two years later by W. B. Wilder, began a long career.

The *Landmark* argued repeatedly that Norfolk had too many newspapers. When the Portsmouth *Record* ceased to publish in 1888, the *Landmark* asserted that "just as long as men will foolishly invest their money where competition is already too great, and in a business which they do not understand, just so long will they see their substance ascend in the smoke and ashes of financial failure."

Four years earlier, the *Landmark*, irritated by criticism of Norfolk newspapers as compared with big-city newspapers, recalled that "Sir Walter Scott said that 'every man thinks he can drive a gig'," and added that "we paraphrase this by saying that large numbers of critically inclined persons think they can edit a newspaper." Rolling up its sleeves, the *Landmark* went to work (September 21, 1884):

> In Norfolk there are four newspapers which are published daily and four which appear once a week. They are all competitors within a narrow limit, and the effect of this is shown by the very low rates for advertising . . . . Norfolk has a population of 25,000 (half Negroes), but say it includes all the settlements on the Elizabeth River, and this will give an aggregate of about 40,000 inhabitants, white and colored.
>
> This being done, we must add five more papers to the list, two daily and three weekly, for Portsmouth, which makes a total of 13 candidates for public favor among some 20,000 white residents (not including the weekly editions of the Landmark and the Virginian). We make the distinction of color because it is justified by the facts, and patronage of the newspapers is practically limited as indicated.
>
> Take Baltimore by way of contrast to Norfolk. That city has 323,313 population and three morning papers. Turn to Cincinnati with 255,139 and we see there only six papers for that number. As a consequence the Cincinnati Enquirer can afford to pay from $2,000 to $2,500 a week for telegraphic service alone, but it would be unjust to contrast a morning newspaper here with one printed in the Queen City of the west, or in New York City. And yet people do compare a Norfolk paper with those printed in the greatest town on the continent . . . . It is plain that such comparisons are unjust, and that the critics are unfair or ignorant.

Take the Landmark, for example, any day in the week, and you will find that it anticipates in its telegraphic columns much of the news read the night of its publication here in the [New York] Herald . . . . Compare it with any paper in the state, and you will find that the Richmond Dispatch is the only journal in the Commonwealth, save the Landmark, which receives the after-midnight dispatches. This is costly service, and the sum paid by us for regular telegraphic news . . . is a great deal more than is expended for telegraphic press service by any morning paper in the state, the Dispatch always excepted. Moreover, Norfolk is the most expensive place in the state, all things considered, for the publication of a daily morning newspaper . . . .

The *Virginian* took off its hat to this presentation of the case: "a most excellent article on the press of the two cities." It too thought the number of newspapers in Norfolk and Portsmouth was "too many, by far," to be supported by a white population not exceeding, by the *Virginian*'s count, thirty thousand.

By September, 1887, the *Virginian* began calling rolls too. It counted four daily newspapers in Norfolk and two in Portsmouth, plus the weekly editions of the *Virginian* and *Landmark*. Then it listed nine weekly newspapers, although it had to include some special publications, like *Our Railroad Men*, *The Christian Voice*, and the *Norfolk Pioneer*, a German weekly, to reach nine. To these it added a group of monthly publications and arrived finally at a grand total of twenty-seven.

Norfolk had a population of 21,966 in 1880 and of 34,871 in 1890 (after the annexation of Brambleton) ; and Portsmouth had 11,390 in 1889 and 13,268 in 1890. The *Landmark* thought 20,000 people were "necessary to sustain one fairly good newspaper."

What the number of newspapers and the thinning out of readers were doing to bold circulation claims was a question the town could not answer before 1882 and could not answer accurately for a long time thereafter. In November of that year an advertising contract with the city was at stake, and the city demanded figures. The *Public Ledger* reported subscriptions and daily sales of 2,340; the *Virginian*, 2,033; and the *Daily Review*, the short-lived Readjuster newspaper, 1,000. The *Landmark* at first refused to make any figure public. "If an abatement in rates is expected, the Landmark is not a competitor," it declared. Two days later it shifted ground. Its circulation on October 25 was 2,075, it reported, but by November 10 it raised the figure to 2,400.

Claims and counter claims continued. In December, 1885, the *Virginian* reported 2,900, and in 1887 it reprinted a report in the Raleigh *News and Observer* that in ten eastern North Carolina counties nearly every farmer, wayside merchant, and crossroads store received the *Virginian*. In the same year the *Public Ledger* claimed the largest circulation in Tidewater, and the *Virginian* came back with a claim to the largest in eastern Virginia.

The *Landmark*, meantime, remained aloof from those contentions. In February, 1888, a rash of *Virginian* and *Public Ledger* assertions stirred it to make fun of both newspapers. "The Virginian," it said, "has intermittent circulation fever. . . . This disease prevails extensively in some of the larger northern cities. The Virginian is the only well-developed and thoroughly marked case in the South that we recall." It placed its own circulation at 3,792 and said that was more than the *Virginian*'s. Not until January, 1892, did any Norfolk newspaper (the *Virginian* first) claim a circulation of more than 5,000,

Not only were the circulation and advertisements of Norfolk and Portsmouth newspapers spread thinly: the cost of doing business was rising. The need for more space drove the *Virginian* in 1878 to find a new home, its third, which it flung open with a celebration on January 1, 1879.

This was a four-story brick structure at the southeast corner of Main and Commerce Streets, the most conspicuous site and building the *Virginian* had ever enjoyed. It kept the corner office for what it called its "counting room," rented out most of the street floor and all of the second, and used the third and fourth floors for editorial work and mechanical operations. In the rear of the main building it built a press and engine room. Its first press (in 1865) was a Potter, its second a Cottrell and Babcock drum cylinder press. Now it had a Campbell two-revolution press. The cost of the buildings, their improvement, and the new press was, as the *Virginian* recalled reminiscently eighteen years later, "nearly $20,000."

Thus equipped, the *Virginian* expanded in December, 1882, to eight pages regularly. It proclaimed as it did so that "excepting New Orleans, Atlanta, and Louisville, there is no paper south of Baltimore as big as the *Virginian*." But it had moved too fast, and by the following April (1883) it dropped back to four pages except for special editions or unusual situations. Thus the eight pages of January 1, 1884, celebrated "Norfolk's $55,000,000 business total during 1883" and the *Virginian*'s own recently acquired "Brown's folding machines, by which the Virginian is instantly and beautifully folded as it comes from the press." No other newspaper in the South had such facilities, it reported, save "perhaps" the Atlanta *Constitution* and the New Orleans *Times and Democrat*.

These improvements and its own needs spurred the *Landmark* to action. In December, 1883, it installed a new press which, it declared, "would print papers faster than any other piece of machinery in this region." Six years later, in January, 1890, *Landmark* directors approved plans for buying a Hoe double cylinder press and Dunbar folders.

The *Virginian* jumped faster. It appeared on August 12, 1890, in eight pages, which it was running regularly then, printed by a new Stonemetz web perfecting press "at the rate of 10,000 an hour, the motive power being a 20-horsepower engine, and the paper a continuous sheet or roll from three to five miles in length, printed on both sides and issued from the press already folded." This press was formally named "The Willie Glennan" for Michael Glennan's brother, who until his death had charge of the press room. The number of columns had been reduced from nine to seven, and six inches were cut from the length.

The *Landmark*'s new press was ready in November of 1890. At the stockholders' meeting in March of 1891, the *Landmark*'s general manager then, S. S. Nottingham, Jr., reported that "these and other expenses were made necessary by the enlargement and improvements made by our morning contemporary and competitor, The Virginian, in August last."

Oddly enough, the *Landmark* expanded to nine columns just when the *Virginian* was contracting from nine to seven. The *Landmark* was first with a leased wire (February 18, 1891) for its enlarged Associated Press report of news. The *Virginian* followed suit with a leased wire carrying the United Press's report. (This was not the modern United Press, which later became United Press International, but a recently established news-supplying organization competing with the Associated Press of that period, itself a predecessor of the modern AP.) The *Landmark* jumped ahead of the *Virginian* with type-setting machines, in August, 1894, but three years later gave up these unsatisfactory Thorne machines for newly developed Mergenthalers.

The *Public Ledger*, with less vigorous competition from other afternoon newspapers, moved slower. It shifted quarters at the start of 1885, from 126 Main Street to 24 Bank Street—"for the better convenience of its patrons, and to add to its own facilities." The new home was close to the Main Street axis. The *Landmark* felt sure that the *Public Ledger*'s "gallant editor has troops and hosts of friends who are willing to follow him anywhere." When the *Public Ledger* began its nineteenth year, August 3, 1894, it was the oldest afternoon newspaper south of Washington except the Richmond *State*, which itself ceased to publish three years later.

To the rising costs of such mechanical improvements were added demands for higher pay by printers. In September of 1878, the *Public Ledger* reported disagreements between union printers and printers working "at unfair rates." At a meeting of the local typographical union, a resolution, which referred to the "depressed state of trade," suspended the scale of wages and freed members to work "for whatever they may choose." This brought protests from some union members and an appeal to the international president. The subject was lively too in Richmond where the *Dispatch* was reported paying printers $3.00 a day and the *Whig* $1.87½.

Four years later, in 1882, the *Landmark*, under a headline reading "LANDMARK REJECTS PRINTERS' DEMANDS," apologized for "very little in the paper" and explained that "this results from a most unjustifiable exaction made by some of the printers in this office, who gave us an hour and half to consider their ultimatum for increased pay. It was considered and acted on at once by the prompt rejection of their demand."

In 1887 the *Virginian* had a long controversy with its printers. Michael Glennan said on September 3 that "a severance of business relationships . . . on the part of the compositors of the Virginian with the paper" had taken place. The printers had asked for a higher scale of pay: for morning newspapers, from thirty to thirty-five cents per thousand ems (a form of measurement of the amount of type set); for afternoon newspapers, from thirty to thirty-four cents per thousand; for book and job offices, $2.50 per day. The proprietor replied that the *Virginian* was not able to meet the increases. Glennan added that he "would hereafter manage his business free from the actions or decisions of outside parties having neither pecuniary interest or business relations with the office."

When informed that a strike would take place if the demands were not met, Glennan telegraphed the National Printers Protective Fraternity, and shortly other printers arrived and went to work in place of those whom he had dropped. Glennan produced a two-and-a-half column front-page explanation on September 6, including more figures. The foreman and six journeymen compositors had received over twelve months a total of $5,445.77; the foreman, $1,060; the lowest paid printer, $523.50; the average for the seven men, $777.97, which was said to be "greater by more than $200 than the average earned by union printers throughout the country."

In Southern cities, Glennan continued, the pay for composition ran from thirty to forty cents per thousand ems, but generally the type elsewhere was larger and easier to handle, and subscription and advertising prices higher.

In addition, Glennan said there were disagreements on pay for what he called unnecessary work—in more recent times, feather-bedding. He explained: "If an advertiser furnished a plate advertisement to occupy a full page, the printer would demand full pay for setting the page, although he never touched a type."

The controversy dragged. Glennan offered to submit "every detail of my business so they may judge of the justness of my course" to a committee, but he thought it necessary to explain again (September 13) why he had sent for aid from the protective fraternity, "whose union has as much right to exist as ITU"—International Typographical Union.

With that, the *Virginian* reported no more about the disagreements. The printers issued a circular earlier, but the *Virginian* did not disclose its contents, and they are lost. The *Landmark* and the *Public Ledger* ignored entirely this most widely publicized newspaper labor controversy Norfolk had experienced.

The newspapers themselves were changing in content and presentation. In November, 1882, the *Landmark*, fighting against slow handling of the mail, used cartoons, one showing letters looking for a place to go and another with coals of fire being heaped on a terrapin's back. In 1885 the *Virginian* began to publish serialized fiction —*Dark Days* and *In Luck at Last*, for the first two novels. It increased its use of pictures with a series of biographical sketches in 1888, furnished by a feature syndicate, and again in 1889 when it ran a three-column layout of five possible candidates for governor.

News about sports was getting more attention, including baseball, chicken fights, and bicycle racing. By 1880 the *Virginian* was publishing a column (on page one then) under the head, "IN THE SOCIAL WORLD," which a year later was renamed "OUR SOCIETY DEPARTMENT." The *Landmark* published later in the same year a column under "SOCIETY NOTES OF THE WEEK—How the Week Has Been Utilized—Delightful Entertainments—Coming Events." In September, 1891, the

Virginian was printing syndicated articles aimed at women readers—the fall styles, for an early example.

But ten years passed before the later *Virginian-Pilot* engaged its first "social correspondent," Annie K. Henry, and then only after full discussion by the board of directors and with formal action by it on November 19, 1901. She is not only the first identified society editor but the first recorded woman in news work in Norfolk.

The most notable single instance of Norfolk newspaper influence in all this period was Michael Glennan's urging in the *Virginian* that the nation pay due tribute to the hundredth anniversary on October 19, 1881, of the surrender at Yorktown.

The events at Yorktown were receiving then routine attention. The site itself was difficult to reach, the only practical approach being over water. For visitors the attractions on the spot were meager. The area of the siege and the surrender were poorly marked. It lacked statuary or monuments. In the popular mind the Fourth of July reflected best the meaning of the American Revolution, and it was a Fourth of July celebration that set Glennan's promotional mind to working.

In the *Virginian* of July 9, 1879, Glennan pointed out (not without a keen eye to the economic aspects) that the Fourth of July five days earlier "brought to our city immense crowds of excursionists from the interior of our state and from North Carolina . . . probably 10,000 people. . . . Thirty-eight carloads of excursionists were brought down over the Seaboard and Roanoke Railroad and nearly as many more on the Atlantic, Mississippi & Ohio Railroad. From Baltimore, Washington, Richmond and the villages and counties connected with us by water, boat after boat brought its load of pleasure seekers and from our own immediate back country, carriages, buggies, and wagons by the hundreds poured their living contents into our midst. . . ."

Here was the evidence, the *Virginian* continued, of "the accessibility of our city and the ease with which immense crowds can be concentrated here for any purpose of pleasure or patriotism. . . . With this proof before our readers we desire to suggest the celebration of a day not far off that should be as dear to Americans, and especially to Virginians, as the Fourth of July itself." For

> The Fourth of July, 1776, would not be known to history had it not been for the 19th of October, 1781. What the pen of Jefferson enunciated on Independence Day, the sword of Washington worked out to glorious fruition on Consummation Day . . . . When the old bell at Independence Hall rang out

the Declaration of Independence, it was a glorious sound falling upon willing ears, but more glorious still was the cry of the sentinel that rang out on the night of October 19, 1781— "Past 1 o'clock and Cornwallis is taken . . . ."

The 19th of October, 1881, will be the centennial anniversary of the capture of Cornwallis, and the American nation owes to itself and the memory of the men who achieved its liberties, that it should be celebrated with a pomp and circumstance worthy of the event it commemorates . . . .

Virginia newspapers and public officials gave the *Virginian*'s editorial strong support. Others had been thinking of the Yorktown centennial, but by July 20 the *Virginian* could say that its plea "is generally received with favor all over the country." Glennan had talent for stimulating responses, and he gave heavy play to comment elsewhere: the Philadelphia *Record*'s strong endorsement, for example. Virginia's Governor Holliday began to build up preliminary Yorktown anniversaries with proclamations and increasingly elaborate ceremonies.

The governors of all thirteen original states met in Independence Hall in Philadelphia to plan for the centennial celebration, then proceeded to Yorktown for the observance of 1879. Afterward Glennan presented a resolution, which was adopted, asking Congress to "give practical effect" to a resolution originally offered on October 29, 1781, by Edmund Randolph, of Virginia, for "a marble column adorned with the emblems of the alliance between the United States and His Most High Christian Majesty and inscribed with a succinct narrative" of the surrender events.

At home the *Virginian* reported the ninety-eighth observance in five columns, starting on page one. In June, 1880, Congress approved the "marble column" in principle. In the following December the *Landmark*—for the march of events had then embraced all Norfolk newspapers—described in detail "the ornamented Corinthian column, surmounted by a Corinthian capital, upon the top of which is a statue of Liberty."

A long struggle followed to provide enough money from Norfolk, Virginia, and the national government itself. But when the centennial arrived in 1881, the celebration was a huge success. It spread across four days ending with military and naval reviews; it brought President Arthur, the French minister, Maxime Outrey, and the Massachusetts historian and former Senator Robert C. Winthrop for addresses, presented Paul Y. Hayne of South Carolina for the ode and

James Barron Hope for the poem, and laid the cornerstone for the monument to Liberty, all before many thousands of visitors. Hope's poem, entitled "Arms and the Man," ran to more than a thousand lines, extending over twenty pages in the official report of proceedings. It reached its climax in the last six lines:

> Give us back the tides of Yorktown!
> Perish all the modern hates!
> Let us stand together, brothers,
> In defiance of the fates;
> For the safety of the Union
> Is the safety of the States!

No one enjoyed the celebration more than Glennan. Governor Holliday had appointed him commissioner to represent Virginia at the centennial. The acclaim he received for his role in directing attention to the centennial and lifting it to a high status was a source of great pride to him forever afterward and was, in fact, an impressive tribute to newspaper influence.

Glennan had taken on the duties of editor of the *Virginian*, in addition to the duties of proprietor and general manager, on March 21, 1880. Tucker, after four years as mayor which coincided closely with his four years as editor, faced heavy opposition in the primary from Colonel William Lamb and resigned to prepare for it or because he or Glennan thought his dual role as editor and mayor was a handicap to him or to the newspaper. Lamb won the nomination, and Tucker was appointed secretary of the Yorktown Centennial Commission, which took him to Washington. He practiced law there later and was an official in the General Land Office.

Glennan clashed violently with Lamb in September, 1882 (in a Readjuster campaign), over the *Virginian's* report of a speech Lamb made at Surry Court House. According to the *Virginian's* account, Lamb was "completely demolished, whipped out, routed . . . by those two negroes" who replied to his speech. The pugnacious Lamb would not stand for that. He published a circular in which he declared that "I deem it my duty to denounce the author of that communication [the report of his speech] as a wilful and infamous liar, it being from beginning to end a series of falsehoods, and I pronounce M. Glennan, the owner of the Virginian, a base ingrate and contemptible scoundrel for giving circulation to such slanders against one who has treated him from his youth up with nothing but disinterested friendship."

In fine, Glennan "shall be treated by me, if he goes too far, precisely as I would treat a mad dog that attacks me."

Lamb's reference to Glennan's "youth" and his own "disinterested friendship" for Glennan grew out of Glennan's boyhood employment by Lamb before the Civil War when Lamb was an editor of the *Daily Southern Argus*. This, more than anything else, aroused Glennan to an extraordinary response.

His reply spread across six columns of the *Virginian*'s front page of Sunday morning, September 10, by far the greater part of the page and in massiveness alone a display that must have set the town to talking. There under a single-column head, "A PAPER, Which Includes a Sketch of Two Lives and a Reply to a Card," Glennan picked up the old relationship in order to describe his own life with almost boastful humility and to depict Lamb's as that of a "character blasted" and a "reputation smirched." He began with Victorian solemnity: "There are two men in this community whose daily life and walk are well known. One was reared in the lap of affluence, with all the advantages of wealth, social position and high station. The other was the child of poor but honest parents, whose way through life has been one of hard and unremitting toil—a struggle throughout."

From this beginning Glennan traced his boyhood admiration of Lamb, his wartime service under him, his gradual disillusion, and—with his anger mounting—his depiction of Lamb's errors as he saw them, from ingratitude and selfishness to deception as a banker, tyranny as a public official, and cowardice as a man, and finally this: ". . . he has made his threat with an evident purpose of bulldozing not only the freedom of opinion but the freedom of the press. I tell him now, tyrant and demagogue that he is, that no threat from him can intimidate or silence me . . . and that in the face of his cowardly threat I shall consider myself justified in being prepared to meet him, defending myself by the rights that God and the law give me."

Lamb promptly took note of the six columns in the *Virginian* by issuing a pamphlet, as the *Public Ledger* reported on October 7, which Glennan in turn said he would answer. But the quarrel faded. The *Landmark* ignored the whole affair.

The editor of the *Landmark* had come close to a duel with Lamb in the first week of Lamb's term as mayor (in August, 1880). The new mayor had dismissed a policeman. Lamb contended that in ordering the dismissal he had said the policeman had a right to appeal to the police commissioners. The *Landmark*'s account did not include this, and C. E. Perkins, its city editor, said it was not in the order that he had read. Lamb turned to the *Day Book*, which was friendly to him, and in its columns charged the *Landmark* with "deliberately falsifying the public records of a court of justice for political purposes."

To Hope these were unforgivable words. He was away from Norfolk at the time. But when he returned, correspondence looking to a "hostile meeting" began, and arrangements were made to go to North Carolina by boat for the duel. The word got out. A justice issued warrants for their arrest and policemen guarded their homes to prevent their departure. A Negro oarsman carried Hope from the rear of his home at night to a boat in the marsh, and he headed southward as far as Great Bridge. Lamb was discovered at 4:00 a.m. trying to reach a boat at the foot of York Street. Ultimately both men were placed under bonds of $20,000 to keep the peace. There was no duel.

The *Virginian* printed four columns about this affair before the arrest of the principals and full texts of all statements later.

Glennan was involved during February, 1884, in a controversy that seemed likely to eventuate in a personal clash. John W. H. Porter, editor of the Portsmouth *Daily Enterprise* and a member of the Virginia House of Delegates, wound up a newspaper argument about some harbor business by declaring in print that Glennan was "a conceited ass and liar."

This time Glennan collected a friend and headed straight for Portsmouth. When he discovered that Porter had gone to Richmond, Glennan and his friend followed as fast as a train would take them. In Richmond Glennan learned that Porter was registered in Ford's Hotel. He stationed himself in front of the hotel to wait for Porter's appearance and kept post there for two hours.

By that time word had reached the Richmond police by telegram from Norfolk. They arrested both Glennan and Porter, and a justice put the two editors under bond. "Mr. Glennan is opposed to the 'code,' as is well known," said the *Landmark*'s account of February 22, "but his personal courage has never been questioned." What would have happened if Porter had shown up in front of the hotel does not exactly appear.

Glennan had been heavily involved in politics in 1883 as chairman of the Second District Democratic Committee, and, as he wrote after the election, "the editorial columns were, to a large extent, in charge of Captain Henry E. Orr." Before the Civil War Orr had been an apprentice in Lynchburg with the *Virginian* and the *Republican*. He came to the Portsmouth *Transcript* in 1858, and was four years in uniform during the war. After the war he was with the Raleigh

Progress as an editor and with the Wilmington (North Carolina) *Star* as foreman, showing a not unusual capacity then to double in brass. In Norfolk in 1879 he worked briefly with the *Evening News* but later with the *Virginian* as associate editor and substitute editor until his death in 1892.

When Cleveland was elected President in 1884, to the jubilation of the Norfolk press, an immediate question was who among the newspaper stalwarts would win Federal appointments. The *Public Ledger* announced quickly (November 11, 1884) that Lewellen did not seek and would not accept a Federal appointment, nor would his associates. He had been mentioned for superintendent of public printing. Hope was spoken of as a possible collector of customs in Norfolk, but "my first duty," he said, "is to protect the interests of the Landmark and my fellow shareholders." The *Public Ledger* thought Glennan deserved a reward. He has "labored in season and out of season, to the neglect of his private business, for the success of the Democratic party," it pointed out.

In time the White House heeded such views. In June, 1885, Glennan was appointed Norfolk postmaster. The *Virginian* said he had not sought the post but had received many endorsements. He took it, but taking it required him to find an editor. Cleveland had laid down the principle that postmasters serving as editors of Republican newspapers could be removed for partisanship, and the principle worked both ways.

After the *Virginian* announced July 2 that Glennan had retired as editor, it said nothing about a successor until five months later. But Norfolk was too small for this kind of reticence, and the *Public Ledger* could promptly say that "we learn" of the choice of Captain Orr, and added that he was "well qualified for the position." The *Landmark* waited until July 21 to greet the new editor in these words: "Captain Henry E. Orr has become the editor of the *Virginian*, and we would have announced the fact at an earlier day but for the impression, derived from the proprietor's notice, that impersonal journalism was to be the rule with our contemporary. But as others have referred to Captain Orr's succession to the editorial management of the Virginian we feel it a pleasure to bear testimony to his fine abilities and entire fitness for the place he now adorns."

Glennan was not immediately confirmed by the Senate. Mahone opposed him there, and the confirmation was held up for nearly two years. But on the day Mahone's term ran out, March 4, 1887, Glennan won his confirmation. He himself went out in July of 1889 for political reasons instead of holding an appointment that normally would have lasted to 1891.

More important changes were taking place in the *Landmark*'s organization. For reasons not publicly explained, the James Barron Hope Company, which published the *Landmark*, reorganized in March of 1882 and became the Norfolk Landmark Publishing Company. Hope's original incorporators in 1873 had been chiefly relatives and intimate friends. The incorporators of the new company, in addition to Hope and Barron, were James Elliott Heath, Barton Myers, and Charles G. Elliott, able and much respected citizens of the community. Barron had been with the newspaper from its start. In January of 1878 he bought an interest and moved into management.

A month after the reorganization the new directors were announced as L. D. Starke, John H. Core, C. A. Nash, D. S. Burwell, and W. A. S. Taylor—an impressive group with business and legal talents. Hope was president, and Barron was secretary and treasurer. The company announced that its indebtedness was "very small" and "will be paid off as presented."

Another significant change came in January of 1883. S. S. Nottingham, Jr., after seven years with the *Virginian*, moved over to the *Landmark* and was identified as a "large stockholder." Eight months later he was associate editor and business manager. He would be an important figure in *Landmark* history.

Three years later Hope, while continuing as editor and president, accepted the superintendency of Norfolk's public schools. Fellow editors around the state gave him such a fine salute that, on a day when Hope was out of town (as Nottingham explained in print), the *Landmark* reprinted a great batch of these friendly greetings. No one seemed to remark that the simultaneous responsibilities of editor and school superintendent raised questions of conflict of interest which later eras would regard in a different spirit.

Hope may have paid a price for the extra work. Though only fifty-seven years old, he was not in good health. Twenty months later he completed his long poem designed to be read in a few weeks at the laying of the cornerstone of the Lee monument in Richmond. After a normal day in the *Landmark* office, where he attended to editorial duties and spent an hour in the counting room, he went home in early afternoon and took a nap. When he woke and sought to rise from the bed, he fell back and quickly died (September 15, 1887).

For the first time since the death of General Lee, both the *Virginian* and the *Landmark* turned their column rules—the old newspaper tribute to the dead expressed in heavy black lines between the columns of type. City hall flags went to half-staff. The public schools closed until after the funeral, at which the Rev. Beverley D. Tucker read a tribute in verse which he had written. Six years later friends of Hope dedicated a tall marble shaft which they had erected in Elmwood Cemetery in his memory: "To the Poet, Patriot, Scholar, Journalist and Knightly Virginia Gentleman."

Nine months earlier, J. Richard Lewellen, a leading figure in the establishment of the *Virginian*, the *Journal*, and the *Public Ledger* in Norfolk and of the earlier *Index* in Petersburg, died (December 4, 1886) in Danville where for eighteen months he had been editor of the *Register*. "As a journalist," the *Landmark* said in words that probably came from Hope, "he was admirably equipped for his profession, combining, as he did, independence, courage and patriotism with a fine practical sense and a trenchant popular style. A Democrat of the old school, he lived by the ancient landmarks and his weighty blows will be missed now when they are most needed."

Hope and Lewellen were strikingly different: Hope, the man of mind and spirit, sensitive and intellectual, who lived by honor; and Lewellen, the printer-editor-owner type of all-'round capacity, "able and ready," as an associate said, "to start a newspaper, write for it, or set type." But they were alike in being survivors of the Civil War who in newspaper careers in Norfolk for twenty years of struggle in difficult times contributed substantially and with great labor to the slow recovery and rehabilitation of all life.

13 · AS EVIL AS OMAHA?

LEWELLEN'S DEPARTURE IN MARCH OF 1885 FOR DANVILLE A YEAR AND A half before his death had created little change in *Public Ledger* policy. The loss of his pen was felt. So was the personal touch he gave to a newspaper that otherwise was rarely personal. But Fiveash took on the editorial duties, and he and Edwards continued to conduct a modest, efficient operation. In the afternoon the *Public Ledger* did not face serious competition. Its owners were willing to pace their own field.

The death of Hope was a more serious blow to the *Landmark*. He was the heart and soul of that newspaper. Colonel Lucien D. Starke, who had been elected a director in the reorganization of 1882, now was elected president of the corporation. (He was the older of two men of the same name long associated with Norfolk newspapers; his son later was associated with the *Virginian-Pilot*, ultimately as president of its publishing company.) Starke had early newspaper experience, starting as a Hanover County boy with the Richmond *Enquirer*, then in Norfolk as foreman of the prewar *Argus*, and in Elizabeth City, North Carolina, where he established the *Democratic Pioneer*. But when he came back to Norfolk after the war he was primarily a lawyer. As *Landmark* president he was neither a large stockholder nor the chief executive. The chief figure in the *Landmark*'s organization was Smith Severn Nottingham, Jr.

Thirty-five years old then, Nottingham had come to Norfolk from Northampton County on the Eastern Shore when quite young and worked seven years with the *Virginian*, chiefly in the business office. When he shifted to the *Landmark* in 1883 he showed capacity in both news-editorial and management areas. On Hope's death he was elected secretary and treasurer, which under *Landmark* by-laws made him general manager. He was the principal personality in the *Landmark*'s command, a man of strength, conviction, and firmness, for the next twenty-five years.

On the choice of an editor the directors hesitated briefly. After Hope's death Kenton C. Murray took over the chief editorial duties, and these he continued to hold without the title. He bought some stock and was elected to the board. Four months later (January 3, 1888) the directors named him editor, though without increasing his salary of $20.00 a week. In another six months they elected him president (July 17, 1888), and this time his salary went up from $1,040 to $1,200 a year. Starke had asked to be relieved of some responsibilities, but he remained on the board and later was elected president for a second time.

Murray was the second largest stockholder, Nottingham the largest. The other directors—Starke, James Elliott Heath, W. A. S. Taylor, John Vermillion, and D. S. Burwell, all well known and respected citizens—had very small holdings. Nottingham and Murray exercised control.

Yet Murray had little newspaper experience. As a boy in Botetourt County west of the Blue Ridge he had studied telegraphy and worked as a railroad telegraphist and for Western Union in half a dozen localities, including Norfolk. Later he lived in Chattanooga, acquired an interest in the *Times* there and also practiced law, and still later lived in New York. When he came to Norfolk in 1883 he was stenographer and claim agent for the Merchants and Miners Transportation Company, a shipping line. For a time he taught typewriting and was a public copyist, and he began journalistic work.

During an early period with Western Union in Farmville Murray was a close friend of Philip W. McKinney. When McKinney ran against Mahone for governor in 1889, Murray managed his campaign; when McKinney went into office Murray went with him as private secretary. But he stayed with Governor McKinney only a few months. In 1890 the State Board of Education named him superintendent of the Norfolk public schools, as it had named his editorial predecessor, Hope. The superintendency paid $1,200, so that Murray, with $2,400 a year, had a larger income as editor and school superintendent than Nottingham, the general manager, whose salary then was $40.00 a week, or $2,080. Murray was two years older than Nottingham.

Both men reflected the Hope philosophy. They were careful in making up their minds, fond of accustomed ways, and especially dubious about social change. Lack of capital was a handicap. They were forced to publish a smaller newspaper than the competing *Vir-*

ginian, but they sought with considerable success to make a virtue of their limitations. Their own standards were high, and they emphasized quality and appealed to intelligent readers. Both had independent minds, and they did not lack courage.

The operation was still small. The *Landmark* corporation's capital stock at this time consisted of sixty-eight shares with a par value of $100 each. From bookkeeping as modest as the totals of the figures, stockholders and directors learned that "excess of earnings over expenses" in 1888 was $3,063.26. Resources were put at $21,501.02. They jumped in 1890 to $27,583, and at the end of 1891 were up to $31,108.38. Earnings had risen to $5,231.50. Dividends had been running at 6 per cent, but for 1890 they were up to 9 per cent, and at the end of 1892 the directors voted an extra dividend of $20.00 a share. There was no increase in the number of shares until April of 1896 when each of six directors took one additional share, lifting the total to seventy-four. By 1899 resources climbed above $45,000, and the next year earnings passed $10,000 for the first time.

The *Virginian's* operation was larger and more costly, probably by a considerable amount; the *Public Ledger's* was, on the surface, near that of the *Landmark's*. All three were growing with a city and a surrounding region that were increasing in population and business activity and had improved in economic health.

Norfolk was growing too in lustier ways. It was the city of the region, and people turned to it for relaxation and pleasure, and for exploitation too. As a commercial and naval port, it always had within it large numbers of young men far from home who, after long periods at sea, embraced life ashore with historic gusto. Its liquor business was expanding not only commercially but as a political force, often with disregard of public opinion. Prostitution was taking on the aspects of important industry. It spread throughout much of the older town and acquired a reputation that attracted business from far beyond Norfolk. Gambling built up large patronage. It grew more elegant, and it grew bolder.

Alliances among these businesses, organized to protect their investments, turned toward government as a kind of insurance. They influenced for the worse the looseness and fraud in registration, voting, vote counting, and all the political manipulation that prevailed after the war, involving, but by no means limited to, new Negro voters. The war had left a residue of violence, and in a pistol-carrying era the inevitable results could be—and frequently were—murderous.

The collision of all these forces and influences with people more

Samuel L. Slover, publisher, photographed while he was mayor of Norfolk from March, 1933, until March, 1934.

NORFOLK LEDGER-DISPATCH

THE WEATHER

VOL. LXXXII—NO. 57.   NORFOLK, VA., FRIDAY AFTERNOON, APRIL 6, 1917.   26 PAGES   PRICE: TWO CENTS

PRESIDENT SIGNS WAR DECLARATION

Interned German Steamers Seized

NAVAL RESERVE IS CALLED TO THE COLORS

Also Issues Proclamation Calling Upon American Citizens to Give Support to All Measures Adopted by the Government—Navy Department Flashes Order to Warships to Begin Hostilities.

Washington, April 6—President Wilson today signed the resolution of Congress declaring a state of war between the United States and Germany.

All the naval militia and naval reserves were called to the colors with the President's signing of the war resolution.

German Crew Of The Arcadia Reach Norfolk

United States Customs Officials Take Possession of Scores of Freighters and Liners Which Snugly Refuge in American Ports When the European War Began.

Washington, April 6—Seizures of German merchant ships in American ports, according to official statement today, are measures of safety for the ships themselves and adjoining property. The crews aboard are regarded as German reservists on German territory.

War Proclamation

Washington, April 6—After signing the declaration of war adopted by the House and Senate, the President today issued the following proclamation calling upon all Americans to support the measures adopted by the government:

Virginian-Pilot
AND
THE NORFOLK LANDMARK

BIG LEAGUE BOX SCORES ON PAGE 9

VOL. LXIII—NO. 75   NORFOLK, VA., WEDNESDAY, JUNE 13, 1917, TWELVE PAGES   THREE CENTS PER COPY.

GREAT NAVAL BASE ON OLD EXPOSITION SITE NOW ASSURED;
KING CONSTANTINE ABDICATES IN FAVOR OF PRINCE ALEXANDER

GREEK KING'S ACTION DUE TO DEMANDS OF ENTENTE

Prince Alexander, Second Son, Named By Retiring Monarch As Successor—Crown Prince George Eliminated Because Strongly Pro-German In Sentiment

CLIMAX PRECIPITATED BY FRENCH SENATOR

ABOUT NEW KING

No New Arrest In Keet Abduction and Murder Case

PROGRESS OF LIBERTY LOAN SINCE FRIDAY GRATIFYING

Treasury Officials, However, Unable To Estimate Total Subscription Owing To Failure of Banks To Report—Urgent Call Goes Out

BIG EFFORT NECESSARY; AN APPEAL ISSUED

TWO MILES OF TRENCHES TAKEN BY HAIG'S MEN

Sketch of King Constantine, of Greece

KING CONSTANTINE I, of Hellenes, who yesterday abdicated the throne of Greece in favor of his son, Prince Alexander.

HOUSE ADOPTS AMENDMENT TO WAR BUDGET BILL EMPOWERING WILSON TO PURCHASE TRACTS

Maximum Price Fixed at $1,200,000—If Owners Refuse Price, Government to Occupy Property While Courts Decide Issue

$1,600,000 ALSO PROVIDED FOR IMMEDIATE DEVELOPMENT OF BASE

Lower Body's Action Quickly Follows Receipt of President Wilson's Letter Endorsing Proposal and Urging Immediate Action

Washington, D. C., June 12—with a most convincing demonstrability with its adverse temper as shown last Thursday, the

---

NORFOLK LEDGER-DISPATCH

THE WEATHER

VOL. LXXXV—NO. 88.   NORFOLK, VA., SATURDAY AFTERNOON, NOVEMBER 9, 1918   22 PAGES   PRICE: THREE CENTS

ABDICATION OF KAISER IS OFFICIALLY ANNOUNCED

Paris, Nov. 9, 6:45 P. M.—The abdication of Emperor William is officially announced from Berlin, according to a Havre dispatch from Basel.

CONFIDENT HUNS WILL SURRENDER

(BY ASSOCIATED PRESS)

Germany's answer to the allied terms for an armistice is not expected to reach Marshal Foch's headquarters since the middle of this (Saturday) afternoon at the very earliest. The courier left for Spa, the German headquarters, immediately after the terms were delivered and the enemy had been given seventy-two hours in which to send his answer.

Few details of the terms have been divulged, nor have any of the triumphs elements of the scene at the allied commander-in-chief's headquarters been reported. Nothing but the briefest dispatches have told of an event, the consequences of which will affect the whole subsequent history of civilization.

Surrender Seems Certain

Germany Crushed

(BY ASSOCIATED PRESS)

While the German government is considering the allied armistice terms the British, French and American armies are carrying on successfully the last of freeing French soil from the invader.

On the north the British have captured the fortress of Maubeuge and above them the Germans back the Belgians in the region between Maubeuge and Mons. Along the Schendt in Belgium where the British hold part of Tournai, the Anglo-American forces have crossed the river on a nine-mile front north of Tournai.

German Empire Crumbling Fast

BY WALTER DURANTY

Joint Special Cable to the Ledger-Dispatch and New York Times.

With the French Armies, Nov. 8—Germany is beaten on the front and at home.

British Capture The Fortress of Maubege

Haig's Forces Are Pushing Forward Rapidly After Taking Great Stronghold

Gives Up Throne

London, Nov. 9—The British forces have captured the fortress of Maubeuge, Field Marshal Haig announced today.

South of Maubeuge the British are pushing eastward and are well beyond the Avesnes-Maubeuge road.

NO MORE SUNDAY WORK

Washington, Nov. 9—The Navy Department today issued an order abolishing Sunday work, except at navy yards and other stations of the navy. The

---

World War I brought tremendous growth to Norfolk when the old Jamestown Exposition site became the great Norfolk Naval Base.

strict in attitude and behavior and restrained by religious convictions and associations mounted during the 1880's and 1890's into hard-fought struggles for control that affected the life of Norfolk in numerous ways.

Before William Lamb was elected mayor in 1880, the *Virginian* and the *Public Ledger* disagreed about whether Norfolk needed more policemen in proportion to its population than other Virginia cities. The *Virginian* was confident of the need for more. "No other Virginia city," it argued, "has men-of-war lying in her harbor at all seasons of the year. In the last few days [in August, 1877] this city has been full of sailors on liberty, and when Jack goes on liberty he is very likely to wind up in the station house. We all remember the visitation of the Russian fleet here last winter."

(Early in 1877 two Russian frigates, *Swetlana* and *Bogatyr,* spent two months in Norfolk waters. It was a period of heroic entertainment, not all of it confined to the princes, grand dukes, and admirals of the Imperial Russian Navy who were in Norfolk.)

Lamb had hardly settled in office when he suspended the assistant chief of police and a sergeant for violating regulations. The policemen thought they were being punished for supporting the reelection of Mayor Tucker, whom Lamb had defeated. The newspapers reported in detail these and other police changes and charges that indicated a large degree of political activity by policemen. The clash between Lamb and Hope (already noted) sharpened press attitudes. So did the mayor's withholding of police reports and other abrupt actions. Efforts to control the town's prostitution business led to frequent turmoil. The *Virginian* and the mayor were at odds over this problem in December, 1881, when the *Virginian* protested: "Mayor Lamb is mistaken when he says that when he cleared Cove Street of improper characters we failed to render him support. . . . His action was warmly upheld, and at the same time we asked him to continue his good work in cleaning Washington, Nebraska and Church streets of these people. Yet these locations are still the haunts of harlots."

Lamb retorted immediately:

> I am censored because I do not suppress houses of ill fame. I only know of their existence officially from testimony under oath in my court. Whenever they are thus reported I have always fined the offending party, and I know of no house of ill repute in Norfolk that has not, by one or more fines, impartially imposed, been practically informed that they were violating the law. I have cleared Cove and practically Cumberland

streets, the necessary approaches to our places of worship and the resting place of our dead, from all improper characters known to me, and in doing so have incurred enmity and hatred, and have looked in vain to the editorial column of your paper for support. Wolfe and lower Church street have no unseemly sights in them now to offend passing strangers.

Liquor, saloons, and a rising temperance spirit were creating more problems and more news. The General Assembly tightened regulations for the control of saloon operations. The Roman Catholic bishop of Virginia induced Catholic liquor sellers to pledge not to sell on Sundays and not to sell to intoxicated persons at any time. The Virginia Temperance Society was organized in Norfolk in February, 1881. The *Public Ledger* reported in the same month that "the prohibition movement has been started and is gaining in popular favor." A local option bill was approved by the General Assembly in February, 1886. Before May elections had been held in eight Virginia localities, two of which voted dry. Norfolk liquor dealers discussed Sunday sales problems, though with no solutions. It was a touchy subject because many people who did not object to open saloons on other days did object to selling on the Sabbath. But for saloons this was the banner day of the week when sales often were larger than on all other days combined.

The reform spirit extended in other directions, with attempts to close down the Sunday operation of freight trains, excursion trains and vessels, and Sunday newspapers, though the newspaper target was quickly taken off the list.

Powerful evangelists and revivalists reflected and stimulated the popular mood during these years. A campaign by Sam Jones in Georgia attracted wide attention in other states. When he moved on to St. Louis and Chicago, newspapers in many Western cities printed his sermons. An assistant to Sam Jones was Sam Small, whom the *Landmark* called "the brilliant Georgia journalist." Norfolk would know him well.

In this same April of 1886 Dwight L. Moody and his song leader, Ira D. Sankey, swept Norfolk in five days of meetings. The largest crowd the city had known jammed into a railroad warehouse, and overflow meetings tried to take care of those who could not get in. "It is not to be doubted that the seed they have sown will bear rich and desirable fruit," the *Virginian* pronounced.

But whereas Moody preached in 1886 to his four thousands in Norfolk, Sam Jones preached in 1890 to his eight thousands and once to an estimated twelve thousand. A tabernacle was built for him on the northeast corner of Queen (later Brambleton Avenue) and Chapel Streets. He was particularly severe, the *Public Ledger* reported, on "gamblers and saloon keepers. He said Norfolk was under the domination of the liquor ring, which is one of the worst and most corrupting elements on the face of the earth." The *Landmark* quoted him thus: "The day will come when every drop of liquor will be cleared out of this country and prohibition will reign from Maine to Florida. I wonder if there is a member of the church here who rents his house to a liquor dealer. The fellow who makes it, the fellow who sells it, the man who rents his house, the man who votes for it and the man who drinks it, if they don't all go to hell I haven't read my Bible right. What do you old demijohncrats say to that?"

The *Virginian* and the *Landmark* split far apart on these meetings: the *Virginian* sharply critical, the *Landmark* laudatory. But the enthusiasm with which a large part of Norfolk embraced the preaching of the evangelists was in striking contrast to the thriving condition of the liquor, gambling, and prostitution businesses, to the cynical manipulation of voters and votes, and to spectacular crimes.

Some of these characteristics came to light in the city election of 1888 in which the Democrats split into factions supporting John R. Ludlow, a former mayor, and R. Y. Zachary, an ardent reformer. When Zachary lost a hot primary fight to Ludlow, his backers produced 299 citizens who declared they had voted for Zachary in a ward where his total vote was reported at 195. Eventually Zachary was nominated but only after such infighting that in the election Major R. G. Banks, a Republican, won the mayoralty though all other winners were Democrats.

The *Virginian* reprinted with obvious approval a comment of the Fredericksburg *Free Lance* that "in many portions of the South, Norfolk among them, the Democrats are so prone to commit fraud at the polls, that if they have no one else to cheat they cheat each other."

Two months later a Main Street killing at 3:00 a.m. shocked the town and stirred the newspapers into biting comment. Two young men had begun by scuffling and ended by firing five or six shots at each other. "Duelling in the Dark" the *Virginian* called it, and then plunged into the background: "Such occurrences may well be expected when open and flagrant violations of the law are permitted here in the shape of policy shops, gambling dens, dance halls, gilded houses and horrible resorts of prostitution and a shameful disregard of the Sunday liquor law in permitting bar rooms to keep almost open doors on a day consecrated to the worship of God. These wrongs against law should cease."

The *Landmark*, which reported the two fighters to be "young sporting men, well known around town, and it is said there had been rivalry between factions headed by them," added to the indictment:

> The fact that the laws forbidding gambling and forbidding the sale of liquor to minors and its sale on Sunday are believed to be openly and defiantly violated is enough to arouse great indignation in the community. . . .
>
> If the present police facilities are not adequate, let them be increased. If they are sufficient in numbers but not in activity, let them be replaced by others. If necessary, let the councils appoint inspectors with special powers to investigate, inform against and prosecute the violators of the law. There should not be any difficulty in the way of a grand jury reaching the evils.

But former Mayor Lamb, when interviewed by the *Virginian*, doubted the prescription:

> Gambling and Sunday tippling are moral plague spots in our community and you cannot expect to wipe them out as long as a majority are not opposed to them. When you see the heads of party organizations and favorite candidates who are overwhelmingly endorsed at the polls frequent bar rooms on Sundays how can you expect the youth of the city to resist their example or the officers of the law to enforce statutes unsustained by public sentiment?
>
> . . . With a few exceptions, on this question of social evils, the present police force is rotten to the core, and to call on Mayor Banks to suppress gambling and liquor tippling and keep vice within bounds with the present force is a roaring farce. The judge may charge the grand jury, but how can the grand jury effect anything when some of its members are patrons of Keno and drink on Sundays at the nearest bar?

The *Landmark* reported a week later, however, that "SUNDAY WAS THE DRYEST DAY EVER EXPERIENCED IN NORFOLK." It was confident that "the police department entered fully into the spirit of reform which lately has possessed our people." In the same issue the *Landmark* reported that the pastor of Freemason Street Baptist Church, Dr. J. L. Burrows, had expressed the hope in a sermon "that we may have in Norfolk at least one paper independent enough to sever all connections with Rum and Ring Rule."

The newspapers leaped up in anger at these words. The *Public Ledger* informed the minister tartly of its record of demanding liquor law enforcement, "unaided and alone," before he came to town. The *Landmark* cited statements of its own. Nevertheless, Dr. Burrows' words had more significance than either he or the newspapers which replied to him realized.

When the prohibitionists held a state convention in Roanoke in October of 1890, the *Virginian's* headlines read: "THE COLD WATER PARTY. Prohibition Convention at Roanoke. They Straddle All the Barbed Wire Fences at Once and Adopt a Platform Partly Republican, Farm Alliance and Dry." When the Women's Christian Temperance Union of Virginia met in Norfolk, Kenton Murray, the *Landmark* editor, addressing the convention, informed it that "temperance begins at the cradle, not at the polls . . . a matter of growth, not a matter of violent compulsion." But when the temperance campaigner, Francis Murphy of Iowa, conducted a series of meetings in the Sam Jones tabernacle, three thousand men and women signed total abstinence pledges and five thousand listened to him on a Sunday afternoon.

Main Street could always supply more fuel. On Christmas night in 1890 a wife gathered her children and carried dinner to her husband, Charles J. Calcutt, a watchman in a business house near Main Street. He had formerly been a policeman. Into this quiet family scene, on this day of all days, a man named James E. Brady stormed up to the watchman. He demanded the arrest of someone with whom he had quarreled in a saloon. When the watchman said he had no such authority, a new quarrel blazed. In the end the watchman fell under gunfire and died while his family looked on.

"It is to be hoped," declared the *Public Ledger*, "that the feeling of indignation aroused by the atrocious murder . . . will insure not only the swift punishment of those who commit the graver offenses against the law, but also suppression of nests of crime as well . . . places which are forbidden by law, where the unthinking youth of the city receive their first lessons of lawlessness. . . ."

Judge D. Tucker Brooke instructed the next grand jury (February, 1891) to find out if there was "anything rotten in Denmark," but the grand jury's report was stronger in words than in actions. Its findings about the "admitted inability of the police commissioners to correct conditions" was referred to the Select and Common Councils. The grand jury was especially vivid in describing "the unbridled license allowed prostitutes to infest every part of our city." It proclaimed: "When these women parade the public thoroughfares, infest public places and openly display themselves clad in extravagant finery riding in open carriages with coachmen in livery, they . . . openly advertise themselves and their avocation. We believe that these women are no less depraved, but only less unfortunate than she who prowls the streets by night in her rags and is known to the police as a street walker, and whom the police arrest without ceremony."

By May after the Christmas killing the time arrived for renewing saloon licenses, and this time Judge Brooke directed a grand jury to investigate whether present sellers had violated law. And this time the Women's Christian Temperance Union came forward with a list of 52 persons believed to know about violations. The city sergeant reported trouble in locating some of these potential witnesses although other people saw them on the streets. But in the end the grand jury reported that 22 liquor dealers had sold liquor on Sundays. Judge Brooke denied license renewals to 20 of these as well as 7 others, but 85 bars, 22 retail dealers, and 10 ordinaries were virtuous enough to win renewals. Prohibitionists charged in 1893 that Norfolk had 250 saloons, bar rooms, clubs, and brothels where liquor was sold.

The long struggle—stirred by much talk of prohibition in the presidential election of 1892—mounted to a climax early in 1893. The *Landmark* led off on February 22 with a thoughtful look at city government in general:

> No question of the present day is receiving more attention from thinking people than that of municipal government. Very many of the cities of this country are badly governed. They are ruled merely for spoils. The dominant party, whichever it may be, looks upon the municipality as its legitimate prey. The people, to use the common slang of the day, are "not in it." They must praise God for what they get and stand aside. They must pay their taxes and keep silent.
>
> In many cities inquiry has arisen whether it is not worth-while to inaugurate a business system of managing municipal affairs. Citizens associations are being formed. . . . This is a subject of keen interest, and it is not surprising that it is being agitated in many places.

The *Public Ledger* and the *Virginian* quickly picked up this lead. "Bad government is the result of the indifference of good men," the *Public Ledger* quoted Thomas Dixon as saying. "If the law-abiding citizens of Norfolk would make the proper effort they could rid the community of many of the evils which tend to bring the city into disrepute."

But it was the *Virginian* that exploded. In news columns and in editorials it went to work with such headlines as "Clean out the Dives," "Pertinent Facts for the Police Department," and "The Plague and the Remedy." It quoted a woman as telling a policeman that "I took the law into my own hands because, in Norfolk, women can't get justice and virtue is not protected." It recalled the old saying that law violators in a seaport were "characters who are here today and gone tomorrow," but police records in Norfolk "reveal that the stranger is nearly always the party assaulted or robbed. The offenders are thieves and murderers who live and flourish on vice in Norfolk. In Norfolk gambling houses are almost as public as drug stores and houses of ill fame as open as hotels. If any man doubts this, let him investigate."

"IS THE LAW ENFORCED?" the *Virginian* continued to demand (February 26, 1893.) The newspaper did not think so—not in a city in which "low variety theaters, where women hustle for drinks, are bringing down to the gutters some of the most promising young men of the city. . . . Twelve months ago great reform was promised, and yet, yesterday, a prominent liquor dealer said, 'I am ashamed to proclaim the character of my business for fear that I may be thought to have an interest in one of the numerous places of vice known as concert halls.' "

The *Landmark* joined the attack with the declaration two days later that "there never was, is not now and never can be any excuse for leaving the laws of the city and state unenforced." The *Public Ledger* followed the next day with "the time to act is now." The time to act was a little earlier, before a Petersburg visitor, who came on a "pleasure trip," was robbed of $970 in the Novelty Theater.

That brought Mayor Augustus B. Cooke before Judge Brooke with a request that he revoke the Novelty's liquor license and also the license of a saloon called The Slide. The *Virginian* printed some of The Slide's history. When its owner thought he might lose his license, the newspaper reported, he transferred ownership to a clerk. When he heard that the skies had cleared, he resumed ownership. Numerous charges in this period indicate dealing in licenses and saloon ownerships, from one man to another, sometimes to dummy figures, until the law, when it did act, could not always find out where to crack down.

And not always did the law's agents try very hard. John Whitehead, city editor of the *Virginian*, was also Norfolk correspondent of the Richmond *Times*. He reported to the *Times* during this February that Norfolk police were afraid, "they boldly state, to execute the law, because removals will, in certain cases, follow." This, the *Virginian* reported, caused "rather a stir."

The police commissioners called in Whitehead for questions. The hearing attracted a large share of the press plus a number of policemen and the Methodist ministers in a body. Whitehead refused to give any names, though he said he would tell a grand jury, and he did cite certain types of transfer. He did not believe the mayor could stop this sort of thing, and, he added, the mayor had said as much.

With that the fire blazed hotter. When did he say it? the mayor demanded. In the *Virginian's* office, Whitehead replied immediately. He called another *Virginian* man, R. E. Turner, who was present, to confirm it. Turner did so. H. S. Bailey, city editor of the *Landmark*, added testimony of a similar nature. The Methodist Ministers' Association shortly pledged support of "impartial law enforcement." The Baptist ministers followed with a pledge of aid and moral influence, "especially to members of the press" in their efforts. In a few weeks the Presbyterian ministers added their support. And on March 8 the *Virginian* fired again:

> In writing up dives, only places of great notoriety have been mentioned . . . they are the greatest offenders and the character of these houses is known to the people and to the executive officers. For more than 10 days a continuous fire has been kept up. The law published in the Virginian February 25 and 26 should be enforced. . . . Now if the mayor, commissioners and chief of police will assert that so far as they are concerned they intend to let these dens of vice remain, the Virginian will clean out every dive from Main and Union to Church Street, and, if necessary, will continue the work in other parts of the city. . . . Gentlemen, what do you intend to do?

What a grand jury did was plain. It recommended that the licenses of The Slide at 209 Main Street and of the Novelty at 80 Church Street be revoked along with the licenses of thirty other saloons. It heard 350 witnesses and returned 150 indictments. It summarized the Norfolk situation in such words as these:

> Saloons have been kept open on Sunday and liquor sold to minors so openly that we have found no witness who would say that he could not procure liquor if he desired to do so.
> Houses of ill fame have thriven in many portions of our city, and especially upon Wolfe and Avon Streets, in sight of police headquarters.
> Gambling has been conducted almost as openly upon some of our principal streets.
> In the lower portion of our city, particularly upon Church Street, between Main and Union, the condition of affairs is a disgrace. There liquor is sold on Sunday, houses of ill fame

exist and concert halls and dives are run so openly as to attract the attention of even the casual passerby.

We also report that we have had testimony before us to the effect that Charles E. Pettis, Chief of Police, has been seen under the influence of liquor drinking with women in "The Slide" saloon and in the police station. . . .

The *Public Ledger*, which had published an extra edition when Whitehead testified, published another extra to carry the grand jury's report. Editorially, it praised the grand jury, blamed the police commissioners most, and declared that "the law-abiding people will have to supplement their [the grand jury's] work at the polls." The *Landmark* reminded the town that the people "have the power to make a clean sweep at the next election." The *Virginian*, much pleased, printed a resume of its articles and concluded that its shot had good effect.

But the enemy gave ground slowly. Although Judge Brooke revoked the licenses of the Novelty and The Slide, the *Virginian* was "astounded" to find both open and in business two days later. "DIVES IN FULL BLAST," its headline cried. Mayor Cooke explained that the license revocations affected bars only. He had given permission for a theatrical performance in the Novelty, and what was wrong with selling soft drinks? Some people assumed that soft drinks included beer.

Hardly by chance, a police justice chose this moment to order the arrest of people in general found working on Sunday. The police rounded up some fifty railroad, steamship, and telephone employees. The *Virginian* heard "that next Sunday the police would raid the Virginian and the Landmark and arrest all printers, reporters, and clerks found at work on Sunday editions." This the justice denied.

Another raid did take place. At the instance of an anti-gambling society in New York, Norfolk police, led by a Washington detective, who had been investigating for the society, walked into the offices of the Dismal Swamp Lottery Company, which—was this coincidence too?—were on the floor above the Novelty. Its charter from the General Assembly of Virginia had been revoked, but the lottery company kept on doing business. The Washington detective called it "the worst fraud east of the Mississippi." "The general verdict," said the *Public Ledger* "is that last night Norfolk's moral wave reached a shore that needed washing badly." The *Virginian* reported events in a two-column story. The *Landmark* asked bluntly, "Why was this not done before?"

The Board of Police Commissioners investigated, meantime, the charge of drinking against Police Chief Pettis. He told the board that all he drank in the Novelty was ginger ale. The reason he was there in the first place, he continued, was that the husband of a woman employed there had asked him to "keep an eye on her." This the chief said he did in line of duty. The board thought this reasonable. It pronounced the charges against the chief to be "wholly unsustained." But on hearing the verdict the *Virginian* recalled that a few weeks earlier it had asked "who was responsible for the state of affairs, the chief of police, the board of police commissioners, or the mayor? The board has investigated the chief and declared he is OK. Has anybody investigated the board?"

Another discovery of the times was the meaning of "one day" when used in fixing jail sentences. Fourteen women had been found guilty in Corporation Court of operating houses of ill fame. They were fined $20.00 each and the costs, which lifted the total to $34.00 for each, and were sentenced to jail for a day. In the words of the *Virginian*: "Last night at 11 o'clock these persons were taken to jail, where they were confined until after midnight, having served from March 30 to March 31."

But there were signs for those who could read them. Norfolk Prohibition Club No. 1 was reported in April, 1893, to have decided to establish its own newspaper. The club announced that some of its members had cast votes for the prohibition candidate for President in 1892, but it had looked in vain for any such votes in the returns of election judges in Norfolk. Norfolk ministers began holding closed-door meetings on what to do about crime. At one meeting, "about 150 businessmen, the bone and sinew of the city, were present. . . . The newspapers were again informed there was nothing for publication," the *Virginian* reported. A prohibitionist ran for governor of Virginia in 1893, though he trailed far behind, and the *Landmark* declared:

> There is no doubt whatever that a large proportion of the people is convinced that something should be done to restrict and limit very much the great privilege now enjoyed by liquor dealers and liquor drinkers. . . . It has grown to be a public conviction that the promiscuous sale of intoxicating beverages is nothing more or less than a public calamity. It is not that so many persons favor prohibition as the best method to deal with the subject but that it has so far seemed the favorite system.

Outright prohibitionists were still a small segment of the Norfolk population, but the rising resentment against political methods was creating a formidable opposition. "We want elections which and election officials who will insure a fair vote and an honest count," the *Landmark* declared in December of 1893. "This the majority of Democratic voters believe cannot be gotten under the present local dispensation of party politics. . . . They believe that the party machinery has been wrested from the people to be used for factional interests." Suspicion grew when the Negro Democratic vote in Norfolk's Fourth Ward, which had not exceeded 171, shot up in 1893 to 822. "Some machine work there," the *Virginian* thought.

After Norfolk prohibitionists in January, 1894, nominated C. W. Pettit for mayor in the May election (a former Methodist minister, then in an iron works business), they criticized the controlling Anderson-McCormick statute as one that was "framed and retained in order to enable a few extreme partisans, in the interest of the worst elements of society, to disfranchise our best citizens. . . . appointing as judges of election the most corrupt men to be found in the city." This was straight newspaper doctrine. But David Humphreys, a prohibitionist leader, charged the press with "upholding" the saloons.

Prohibitionists and the press were unmistakably allied in criticism of election management. When two of three members of the city's electoral board retired, a Democratic citizens' group, not representative of party management, went to Richmond to urge the General Assembly to select new board members of their choice. The petitioners included Colonel Starke, of the *Landmark's* board, and three editors, Glennan of the *Virginian*, Fiveash of the *Public Ledger*, and Murray of the *Landmark*, as well as important citizen leaders, among them Barton Myers, the former mayor. But Norfolk legislators were allied with the professionals, and the General Assembly followed their wishes, not the newcomers'.

The electoral board member reelected was Napoleon Bonaparte Joynes, at the moment under indictment on charges growing out of a prizefight in Norfolk County. Among those who defended Joynes was a young politician named James V. Trehy, who had been called a saloon owner in one of the Corporation Court investigations. Both names were destined to become familiar in the political history, lore, and legend of Norfolk.

All three newspapers rang during early 1894 months with denunciations of "boss rule," "the machine," and "the ring." Anger rose when General Assembly Democrats held on to the Anderson-McCormick election statute and attached the Walton bill providing for a "reader" at each precinct to mark ballots for illiterates—an opportunity believed to have extensive and tempting potentials, especially if election judges were short on virtue. Some steps toward the Australian ballot and stronger primary statutes seemed better. But these were not enough for the aroused Norfolk electorate.

So aroused were antimachine Democrats that, turning their backs on machine Democrats on the one side and prohibitionists on the other, they formed their own Democratic Association under the leadership of Barton Myers and set about putting their own candidates in the field. The new group had support from many businessmen and moderates, and from the *Virginian,* the *Public Ledger,* and the *Landmark.*

Another series of Moody-Sankey meetings in March of 1894 improved the climate for both the prohibitionists and the Democratic Association even though Moody refused to preach politics. But Sam Small came in April, and he preached hardly anything but politics, wielding, in the words of the *Virginian,* "a double-edged sword with which he smote Democrats and Republicans alike." He announced from the start that he would show that "the police of Norfolk protect saloons in violation of the law, because they are controlled by a police board which is under the domination of the liquor interests." About this the *Virginian* commented: "If Mr. Small will announce the day and hour when he proposes to make the expose his audience will fill a ten-acre lot."

This was Small's first appearance in Norfolk, but far from his last. Born in Knoxville in 1851, he graduated at Emory and Henry College and acquired degrees elsewhere. He also acquired skill as a stenographer that led him to become President Andrew Johnson's secretary for a time, a proceedings-reporter in the United States Senate, and secretary to the American Commission to the Paris Exposition of 1878. Journalism excited him in Atlanta, and he worked for the *Constitution* as city editor. But he was born for movement, controversy, and the evangelical pulpit.

Detached scenes of his life include those in Guthrie, Oklahoma, where he had "a lively time" in newspaper publishing and in seeking a United States senatorship; in Oklahoma City, where he founded a newspaper; and in Cuba, where he was charged with swindling and asked to leave. He was thirty-four years old when he joined the popular Sam Jones. Thin, pale, terribly in earnest, a chain smoker of cigarettes before he renounced tobacco, a fiery public speaker, supremely confident in himself and unruffled by opposition, Old Si (as admirers called him) plunged in where most other angels feared to tread. He possessed, said a sketch of him in the *Virginian's* weekly edition, March 18, 1886, "the grace, elegance and refinement which Mr. [Sam] Jones lacks." He possessed also a willingness to get right down to cases: the names of sinners, the nature of their offenses, the degree of their villainy. He was often in trouble, sometimes in fist-fights, sometimes in court, but most of the time Old Si could talk his way out. In action he was a fascinating performer. The Norfolk of 1894 took him to its bosom, and each felt at home.

The campaign mounted in a strange fury of religious fervor, prohibitionist crusading, election purifying, and old-fashioned, down-to-earth organizing, maneuvering, name-calling, and vote-coralling. The prohibitionists imported speakers from far across the country and held as many as five meetings a day.

At one of these the chairman of the National Prohibition Party, the Reverend Mr. Samuel Dickie, addressing a full house in the Armory with Sam Small by his side, declared that the American city with which hitherto he had associated the grossest crimes was Omaha, Nebraska. Omaha, he thought, was one of the worst cities in the country. There the police did not see many of the shameless crimes which citizens did see because the rottenness of the government in Omaha blinded policemen. But now, the Rev. Mr. Dickie told his Norfolk audience, he was not so sure about relative standings. "The same cancerous disease has reached this seaport city." Norfolk, he feared, was as evil as Omaha.

Small spoke at one series of meetings in April, a second series in May. The *Landmark* called him "an orator of uncommon ability" and was sure "he has made a strong impression upon his audiences." For the most part he was more of a prosecuting attorney than an orator.

Thus Small cited by name a Norfolk councilman who, he said, voted in an earlier election in the Fourth Ward and later in the day in Norfolk County. He read a list of names of Norfolk people recorded as voting who said they had not voted. He read another list, 116 names this time, of people recorded as voting who could not be found. He quoted an election judge, one Lewis, as saying that it did not matter who voted—he would "count them out." To vary the attack, Small charged the city councils with "robbing the schools of $50,000" (the *Public Ledger* thought this too much but agreed the schools had been bled) and characterized Norfolk as "the only city in the United States that has no public high school." Its school buildings, he said, were "inferior to those of any city of its size in the United States."

In the midst of these attacks, when charged with being a nonresident who was interfering in a local election, Old Si replied grimly, "If they fool with me I'll stay here." He soon had new and more formidable opposition than local talent could provide.

For just before the Democratic primary for the nomination of candidates for the Common and Select Councils who would be elected on May 24, the City Democratic Executive Committee announced, on advice of counsel, that no such primary could be held. Earlier in 1894 the General Assembly had authorized primaries, but the time was said to be too short to set up this Norfolk primary. Nominations for councilmen, accordingly, would revert to the old ward meetings. The *Landmark* recalled these as being "held sometimes in a room too small to hold half the Democrats in the ward, sometimes in the vestibule or hallway of the Armory, and often attended by men of other wards who help vote down every proposition for fair methods of casting and counting the ballots."

The belated discovery did not affect salaried city officials. In the opinion of the Democratic Association leaders it did create too heavy handicaps to the nomination of their own Democratic candidates for the councils, and they withdrew all their candidates.

The effects were far-ranging. For whereas a three-way contest was in prospect, with the antimachine vote divided between the prohibitionists and the Democratic Association, now antimachine sentiment coalesced behind prohibition candidates. In alarm old-line Democratic leaders turned to the state Democratic organization. That body sent to Norfolk as chief opponent to Small the stump king of readjuster years, now state superintendent of public instruction, Parson Massey.

These two professional platform warriors, Massey and Small, met head-on for the final week of the campaign, not in joint debate, but with nightly blasts that amounted to almost the same thing, Small using the big Armory as his base, Massey the smaller Academy of Music. Massey sought to make up for smaller audiences by scoring the personal point. "The gentleman here advocating prohibition" had been "thrown in the mire by whiskey," he charged, and "he is a fine man to be advocating good morals, isn't he?" But when Small, standing before six thousand men and women in the Armory, was handed a list of charges made against him by Massey, the *Landmark*'s reporter described the scene in these words:

For about 15 minutes he gave Massey one of the most terrible excoriations ever heard from the lips of man. As he dis-
proved each charge and made the most severe counter-charges,
the vast audience was gradually enthused to such an extent
that when he hurled his last thunderbolt pandemonium held
full sway.

Men cheered and threw up their hats, ladies threw up their
fans and screamed. People all over the building rose to their
feet and shouted themselves hoarse, and it was fully 10 minutes
before the effect of the denunciations had worn off.

When Massey charged that Small ran for Congress in Atlanta but
landed in jail, and that Small had been described as "once a Methodist
minister, and then an Episcopal minister," and then was appointed
president of a female college, and "when his books were examined
some $8,000 failed to appear," and "this I have never seen corrected
either," Small replied with these words, "Now I brand him as the
most infamous liar who ever lived." The *Virginian*'s headline followed the story: "MASSEY SCORED—Sam Small Calls Him an Infamous Liar."

Throughout the campaign Small repeatedly praised the records of
the *Virginian*, the *Public Ledger*, and the *Landmark*, and conspicuously on three occasions. At the last of these, just before the election,
he called these newspapers "pioneers in this reform movement" and
declared that "their fight for it within their party has been heroic . . .
they are for reform."

So were the voters. On May 24, 1894, they elected all prohibition-
reform candidates for contested offices and added emphatic majorities
in the two councils. The voting ranged up to nearly 6,300 votes, and
the ratios of prohibition-reform victories in most instances were of the
order of three to two. Since the new registration before the election
had enrolled the names of 5,636 white men and 2,658 Negroes for a
total of 8,194, approximately 77 per cent of the registered voters went
to the polls, a high percentage by American standards.

Opinion divided as to how much the prohibitionist sentiment
counted and how much the general reform spirit. The newspapers
had no doubt. The *Virginian* noted that prohibitionists had polled
only 700 votes for their legislative ticket in 1893. In 1894 they went
to work earlier, provided far more spirited leadership, and broadened
their appeal with candidates pulled out of old parties. But the *Virginian* thought that: "Possibly in no other city in Virginia could the
Prohibitionists have been so successful. In no other city could they
have found the rank and file of Democrats clamoring . . . for relief

from the injustice of ring rule. In no other city were the police more officious in politics . . . the officials more indifferent to . . . the people."

The *Public Ledger* stated flatly that "the result was a distinct uprising of the people in favor of good government and against misrule." The *Landmark* quoted the mayor-elect, Charles W. Pettit, as saying that he ran for office not as a prohibitionist or a Democrat but as a man doing his utmost for the city.

Still, the victors had to learn that winning an election is one thing and establishing an effective government is another. When the Pettit regime took office July 1, it could not find the right chief of police, an appointment of critical importance after the kind of campaign that Norfolk had just endured. Then other troubles erupted.

The new Board of Police Commissioners consisted of the mayor (by virtue of his office) and two councilmen elected by the councils, one of whom was C. A. Verdier. Within his first week in office the town was "shocked to learn," according to the *Virginian*, that Verdier had not attended a recent board meeting because "he was at the horse race track at Suffolk, and that his fine nag was the winner of a $100 purse."

In vain did Commissioner Verdier, of the prohibition-reform ticket, protest that his horse was taken to Suffolk by his driver, who entered the horse and received the winnings. He himself had gone to Suffolk simply to see how the horse would run.

"Commissioner Verdier is a handsome young man, who has admiration for fast horses and game chickens and is a good judge of both," the *Virginian* reported in a free-wheeling account. "Some naughty things are being said about this dashing young commissioner. There are fellows in Norfolk who prefer cards to horses, faro to horses, and some crap to horses. They can't see much difference when there is a question of winning or losing money. All are termed sport." The next day the *Virginian* came down hard on its point:

> For a police commissioner, Mr. Verdier's usefulness as a correction of policy shops, crap institutions and gambling establishments is gone. The man who presents himself as the bettor of horses is not the man who, by the requirements presented by the Rev. Mr. Small, is qualified to correct the evils he so vividly pictured as affecting the good government of Norfolk. What a picture Mr. Small could present of Mr. Police Commissioner Verdier! His resignation should be called for.

Mr. Verdier's race horse was only one of many problems for the reform administration. People were clamoring for jobs. The new leaders felt obliged to rid the government of undesirables, but when they supplanted some white street workers with Negroes, the discharged men paraded with banners and soon were an army. The new chief of police, C. J. Iredell, a former Confederate cavalry captain, found himself at odds with two of the police commissioners about whom to discharge, whom to keep.

Soon Iredell was charging that Verdier had given permission for the playing of a piano in a bawdy house in spite of a general order against such music in such concert halls. Verdier explained that a request had indeed come to him—from a prominent Democrat, he said—for the use of a piano from 9:00 to 11:00 p.m. at a certain address because of a birthday celebration there. But he said he had referred the request to the police chief.

The *Virginian* concluded that if Verdier had not granted the piano request he had certainly suggested it and had called it "harmless recreation, not conducive to immorality." The *Virginian* pointed out that "this is a new phrase for life in houses such as this on Smith Street."

The circus affair confused the situation too. Mayor Pettit had given a circus permission to pass through Norfolk streets on a Sunday morning to its tent area provided it did so by 8 o'clock. But the circus was two hours late in arriving. When it did arrive, some of the new social clubs (which, because of the reform administration, were taking over the Sunday saloon business) showered circus people with tickets to their clubs, where members and properly introduced visitors could buy drinks at will. Iredell faced a problem. In the end he solved it by waving the circus on, and it clattered through the town during church hours on Sunday morning far past the mayor's deadline. When called up for an explanation, the chief said that he thought it better to keep the circus moving than "to have them all on the street drunk."

The chief was out by October, and his command went to the not yet qualified assistant chief, Murray by name, but within ten days he was suspended and then discharged.

The newspapers found it difficult to treat these items of public business with complete journalistic sobriety or, indeed, with sympathy. The new municipal leaders, who held that voters had put them in command and they were entitled to reorganize the city government, resented newspaper criticism. As early as August, the month after the new administration came into office, a prohibitionist mass meeting adopted resolutions condemning as

> unwise and unfair the attempt of the daily papers to disparage and prevent the organization of the various departments of

the city government and denouncing the course of the Virginian for its abuse and misrepresentation of the personnel as well as the measures adopted by the Prohibition-Reform party, and calling upon all good citizens and fair-minded men to disregard as unreliable the efforts of partisan newspapers to exalt to the skies every man who is displaced, while nearly every man who is put in office is defamed or pronounced unfit for the position.

To this the *Virginian* replied immediately in an editorial summarizing actions of the new government to which it had objected. It declared that "a large proportion of the officials and councilmen elected with the reform group were Democrats who won on the broad issue of good government, and this the people expect at their hands." When a prohibitionist leader, David Humphreys, charged that the editors of the *Virginian*, the *Public Ledger*, and the *Landmark*, had conferred and agreed on a course to be followed by all three in dealing with prohibitionists, denials came quickly from the editors.

The enmity was growing. The greater must have been the anticipation in the prohibitionist leaders' knowledge that already they were forging a weapon of their own—a newspaper dedicated to the cause of prohibition—that would be useful against the not too respectful Norfolk newspapers. The forging began before the open break of prohibitionists and the press, and the original motives and purposes were much broader. For the Prohibition Party of Virginia now had high hope of marching out from its Norfolk base, secured by the recent victory, to other targets across the state and ultimately to the capture of the state itself. In these hopes and plans the reform elements which had joined the prohibitionists in Norfolk during the campaign, but had not absorbed the philosophy of prohibition, had no part. A new newspaper would not necessarily speak for them.

Planning of this nature could not be kept secret. The *Virginian* reported on July 6, six days after the new regime took command in Norfolk, the purpose of the prohibitionists to establish a newspaper of their own. The editor? None other than Sam Small! The *Virginian's* report:

> Last night it was stated that all arrangements had been completed to start a joint stock company with a capital of $50,000 to publish a daily upon the pattern of the Washington Post, with the Rev. Mr. Small as editor-in-chief and a corps of able and experienced assistants. The stockholders are mostly of Norfolk but there will be some outside money in the enterprise. The paper will be the organ of the [Prohibition] party in

Virginia, and it is likely that the headquarters of the state committee [of the Prohibition Party] will be transferred from Staunton to Norfolk.

So Sam Small had indeed decided to make Norfolk his home, he
who during the campaign had said, "If they fool with me, I'll stay
here." In important respects the victory—however much it was aided
by a broader reform movement—had been a widely heralded triumph
for prohibitionists in even a national sense. It gave great zest to prohibitionist efforts and stimulated many ambitions. To those looking
for opportunity it seemed to open large possibilities. Old Si was one
of these. He had been a wanderer on the face of America. Now in
Norfolk, where people admired him fervently, and his influence was
powerful, and his campaigning may even have been the decisive factor in a striking victory, he had found a home.

The new newspaper was *The Daily Pilot*. It appeared first on October 6, 1894—a morning newspaper, but (this was an innovation) an
afternoon newspaper too, and a Sunday newspaper to boot. Its chief
editor was Small. Its business manager was W. W. Gibbs, who, as
state chairman of the Prohibition Party, had come from Staunton for
the Norfolk campaign, in which he worked with vigor. "A huge, fine-
looking man," he survived the animosities of the campaign and won
respect in Norfolk. The financial basis was the Pilot Publishing Company, with many stockholders and a directors' board of fifteen members (some of whom said six months later that they had never attended a meeting). The location was 8 Hill Street, a few steps off
Main Street and near the heart of the business life of old Norfolk.

Among the courteous, though somewhat cool, greetings of contemporaries was the *Landmark*'s report of October 7 that the *Daily
Pilot* "is a clearly printed, well gotten up, seven-column, four-page paper . . . prohibitionist in politics, and we infer from the editorial ex-
pressions of its first number that it means to make things lively for
both the old political parties." The *Virginian* and the *Public Ledger*
made their bows, but they said little. The *Public Ledger* thought the
Daily Pilot was "neatly made up and presented a handsome appearance, especially its first page, which is devoid of display advertisements." The *Public Ledger* had never printed display advertisements
on the front page, but the *Virginian* and the *Landmark* continued to
accept a column, sometimes a little more.

A pointed comment of the day was the *Landmark*'s note that
"Norfolk now has three morning and three afternoon papers, and

would be a point of curiosity for the students of many phases of the newspaper problem": the *Virginian*, the *Landmark*, and now the *Daily Pilot* in the mornings; the *Public Ledger*, the *News and Courier*, and now the *Daily Pilot* in the afternoons. The *Landmark* could have added that now there would be three Sunday newspapers too. This was going too far for economic law, and the *Daily Pilot* learned as much. In a month, it dropped afternoon publication and held to its morning and Sunday editions.

The directors included prohibitionists like Luther Sheldon, R. Y. Zachary, David Humphreys (Major D. Humphreys in most identifications), Ira B. White, and T. C. White; substantial business men of much energy in tackling public welfare problems like John L. Roper and S. Q. Collins; one at least with newspaper experience, W. B. Wilder, well known in Portsmouth journalism and an associate of Paul C. Trugien in the establishment of the Portsmouth *Star* only a month earlier; the much discussed police commissioner who liked a horse race, C. A. Verdier. All told, it was a formidable body for many purposes, but whether for operating a newspaper only time would tell.

For it was clear from the start that in what it published the *Daily Pilot* was largely Samuel W. Small and not often anyone else, and that it would rise or fall on his leadership and judgment in directing a daily newspaper dedicated to prohibition in a highly competitive field in which other newspaper publishers and editors did not lack capacity.

THE *Daily Pilot* CAME IMMEDIATELY TO THE SUPPORT OF THE NEW CITY administration. But this was defense, and Sam Small's forte was attack. If there was a lessening of ardor about these somewhat routine duties it would not be surprising in an editor of his temperament.

Gibbs, the business manager and a deep-dyed prohibitionist, was eager for his party to merge with the Farmers' Alliance. The Alliance had been preaching the Populist philosophy in Virginia with less success than in some other Southern states hard hit by the depression of 1892-93. An attempt was made in that summer of 1894 in conventions in Lynchburg to consider such a merger. But it got nowhere. (One explanation ran that it was "not in the Populist nature to do anything quite as ascetic as" prohibiting the liquor traffic.[1]) In Norfolk, Gibbs, who testified later that he had nothing to do with the making of editorial policy, did not arouse either Sam Small or the board by this dream of enlarged political power. But Small was interested in public education. He had criticized Norfolk's penurious policies during the campaign. Now he began to peer at the state's school system as administered in Richmond.

The State Board of Education then was a three-man board: the governor, Charles T. O'Ferrall; the attorney general, R. Taylor Scott; and the superintendent of public instruction, John E. Massey—Small's old and personal enemy, the Parson himself. Its extensive powers included the selection of textbooks. The contracts for these ran into big figures. They created keen competition among publishers and sometimes aroused suspicions of skulduggery.

That precisely is what Small was suspicious of. On December 2, 15, 16, 20, and 21 the *Daily Pilot* grew increasingly critical. Prices

1. William DuBose Sheldon, *Populism in the Old Dominion: Virginia Farm Politics, 1885-1900* (Princeton, 1935), 108.

for school books were too high, it said. It was going to show why. It was going "to turn the light on the public school system of Virginia."

Then on Sunday, December 23, the *Daily Pilot* exploded. It published down the columns of its front page a long, detailed, and bitter article under the head, "Money by the Bundle." The article charged that before textbook contracts were signed in March, 1890, and again in March, 1894, Massey had been financially insolvent, but that in April of each of these years, after the contracts had been signed, he was conspicuously affluent.

It implied, if it did not charge outright, that Massey had been bribed by the winning publisher, the American Book Company, a corporation formed a few years earlier by the merger of five publishers and regularly called "the trust" by the *Daily Pilot*.

It implied that Governor O'Ferrall and Attorney General Scott were guilty at least of gross negligence.

The original "Money by the Bundle" attack did not identify its author. But it soon became known that the author was Richard E. Byrd, a lawyer of Winchester. He was the legal representative in Virginia of Ginn & Company, a textbook publisher which had bid for the contract in 1894 but lost out to the American Book Company.

Frequently mentioned in the article was J. W. Womack, of Charlottesville, the agent in Virginia of the American Book Company. The article charged that Womack paid Massey's expenses on a trip to Canada and otherwise had close financial relations with him.

"Money by the Bundle" was a sensation. From Tidewater to beyond the Blue Ridge news stories and editorials poured out of the Virginia press. Richmond bubbled with excitement. The governor was "very indignant." He pronounced the charge "maliciously false" so far as he was concerned, and he started formal investigation. Womack asserted that all the charges were false. A few days later the governor and the attorney-general issued a joint statement with further details and denials of improper action at every point. Massey denied everything and attacked Small in blistering words. Small replied with equal fury.

So for six days. Then on December 29 Massey announced that he would bring suit charging libel and demanding $50,000 in damages. He directed the suit against the Daily Pilot Publishing Company; against Small as managing editor; against all directors of the corporation, including well-known and eminent citizens and community leaders of Norfolk; and against Byrd, the lawyer, who wrote the text. The words that Massey held to be most damaging were these:

The adoption of the school books of the trust and the departure of Womack, agent for the company, was followed by an unusual wave of prosperity upon which the superintendent floated gleefully. We have proved that in January 1890, he was absolutely insolvent with judgments amounting to thousands of dollars outstanding against him. The trust books were adopted in the latter part of March. In April he was in possession of a large sum of money. . . .

We will now show that in 1894 as in 1890, immediately after the school contracts were signed, Massey, the bankrupt, came again into possession of a large sum of money. . . .

Where did you get that money, Mr. Massey? Verily every fourth year of Massey's superintendency has proven the year of the fatted kine.

Among much more was one charge that Massey, although lacking funds to do so earlier, had purchased a house in Charlottesville and paid $5,150 for it with money presumably from "the trust."

Massey contended that all these allegations could be interpreted only as meaning he had been bribed by the book company. To other newspapers he made a succession of statements, denying all charges and threatening in his suit to display the enormity of the offense against him. To these Small replied in kind. "We are ready and eager for the fray," the *Daily Pilot* said on January 7.

Small even gave his own legal muscles a workout, qualifying as a member of the Norfolk bar and appearing in several cases in Corporation Court before Judge Allan R. Hanckel, successor to Judge Brooke. He announced the opening of a law office at 8 Hill Street, the address of the *Daily Pilot*.

But beneath the surface all was not well within the *Daily Pilot* family. Small heard that some directors blamed him for not taking out an indemnity bond or other protection in event of a libel suit. Before publishing "Money by the Bundle" he had assured at least two directors that there was no reason to worry about its publication. In January he offered his resignation. But the board would have none of that. Rumors had reached the public, and the town was talking. As they waited for the trial the directors desired to present a solid front. They even announced on February 1 the presentation of a reclining chair to Small—an odd gift, it seems now, one that almost might have suggested a hint to calm down and take things easy—and a gold-headed cane to Zachary, secretary of the board.

A few days later, on February 13, the directors had more to read. The American Book Company published as advertisement a five-column statement in the *Virginian*, the *Public Ledger*, and the *Landmark*. The Byrd article in the *Daily Pilot* had called the publishing house "one of the greatest and most corrupt monopolies ever known in this country," and not only that but "a gigantic monopoly and monster," and, furthermore, "malodorous and merciless." In addition, the book company reminded, the *Daily Pilot* had called it "a scaly old boa constrictor and other names." Now its turn had come.

The advertisement described the *Daily Pilot* as having "servilely converted its columns into a common sewer, through which all the filth of these falsehoods is daily discharged." As for bribery or any other offense, it denied everything in voluminous detail; and as for "Money by the Bundle" itself, "it is known by us just where it was written and prepared and the agencies and processes by which its publication was secured." In the opinion of the *Virginian*, "the answer is very complete, and . . . meets with great clearness the charges which have been made."

On top of this, the governor and the attorney-general issued in pamphlet form the results of their investigations of school book contracts. They listed prices in Virginia and in other states to show that Virginia prices were not out of line. The *Landmark* published the statement in full and added for its weekly edition a three-column tabulation of book prices around the country. "We are glad to know, what we have not doubted, that our school officials are without blame," the *Landmark* summed up, "and have done their duty by conserving the interests of the people."

This was on February 20. The trial of the suit had been set for June. But the magnificent misjudgments of that period were not yet complete.

In March, Small crossed Chesapeake Bay to lecture on the Eastern Shore of Virginia. There he stayed in the home of the Rev. William C. Lindsay, in Bay View, and spoke in the church of which Lindsay was pastor. Small asked the minister to mail to the *Daily Pilot* any items of news that came to his attention. On March 29 a letter reached the *Daily Pilot* from Lindsay with several small news items enclosed. Enclosed also was a note addressed to Small. It read: "Dear Brother Small—I send you a few Eastern Shore notes. If they are of any interest, use them. I did not tell the latest scandal for I am not sure that it would be right to put it in print. I can tell you, however. You can do as you please about printing it. It is all O. K. though."

"The latest scandal," as sent thus by Lindsay to Small, fell first into the hands of one of the copy editors, Joe Martin. He considered it unfit to print. But his immediate superior, James A. Pugh, thought it would make "a corking story" and added that Small ought to be informed, especially because the attached note was addressed to him. Small read "the latest scandal," and directed that it be placed on the front page.[2]

The item which Lindsay sent was substantially the same as the news report which appeared in the *Daily Pilot* of March 30, 1895, in this form:

FORGOT HIS NOTES
Returning for Them,
He Found His Home Desecrated

Special to the Pilot

Bay View, Va., March 29—Rev. A. J. Reamy left his notes at home Sunday night when he went to church, and knowing that he could not do without them he returned home for them. On his arrival at home he found a son of Mr. Upshur Quinby in bed with his wife. A divorce suit will follow.

The "son" referred to was identified later as L. D. Treackle Quinby, a lawyer. Reamy was pastor of the Onancock Baptist Church.

If the *Daily Pilot* had set off an atomic explosion in Onancock, it could hardly have created greater surprise. When it became clear, as quickly it did, that no evidence was available to sustain the report of such a Sunday night liaison, Onancock gave way to anger.

On March 30, the day of publication, "a large meeting was held in the Masonic hall" in Onancock, the *Landmark* reported, "to denounce the slander and express indignation against the author and publisher of the report and sympathy for the persons assailed." The meeting adopted resolutions declaring the "wanton slanderers" deserved "the contempt and detestation of all truth-loving and high-minded men and women," and offered assistance to bring them to trial. For climax the meeting poured out into the street where "images representing the author of the report, the editor of the Pilot and a copy of the Pilot containing the article were burned in effigy." "Nothing," the *Landmark* added, "that has occurred here in many years has created such unbounded indignation."

The next day, a Sunday, Reamy and Quinby went to Norfolk. Reports circulated that they were looking for Small. Major Hum-

2. Martin reported these circumstances in the Newark, Delaware, *Post, circa* February, 1959, and confirmed the details in correspondence with Joseph E. Shank which began March 6, 1959.

phreys, a *Daily Pilot* director, called Mayor Pettit out of church to provide protection for Small, and instructions went to the police. But they were not needed. Reamy and Quinby did not come to Norfolk on Sunday morning to attack Small physically. They came to confer with legal counsel. They meant to bring suit and seek compensation.

In these circumstances Small began to retract and apologize. On March 31, the first issue after the publication of "FORGOT HIS NOTES," the *Daily Pilot* published under the head, "A FALSE REPORT," a statement that the report came "with such seeming certainty and reliable authority as to leave no question of its accuracy and general publicity on the Eastern Shore." But "the Pilot is assured that the scandal extant in Onancock in no wise involves the name, chastity or conduct of Mrs. Reamy and that the mention of her name in that connection by misinformed people was a gross and miserable error. We take the earliest occasion and the profoundest pleasure in correcting the publication and uttering our sincere regrets over the unfortunate mistake of our correspondent and the part which the Pilot was innocently made to play in the painful matter."

Although any kind of apology probably would have been inadequate to hold off an accounting, this one—with its implication that there was at least some kind of scandal in Onancock and that in printing such an unconfirmed report the *Daily Pilot* was innocent—was less than generous. Someone in the *Daily Pilot* organization must have realized as much. The next day it tried again. This time the head was "THE ONANCOCK AFFAIR—A Plain Statement of the Incidents Connected with the False Report." And this time the name of Lindsay was brought into the open:

> . . . So soon as the Pilot's managing editor [Small] had been apprised of the falsity of the report that had been sent to it, he promptly and fully made the most exhaustive amende honorable that was in the power of a fair and honest journal. The report of the matter that was printed on Saturday came to us on the evening boat from Cape Charles and was signed by the Rev. William C. Lindsay at Bay View. The editor of the Pilot had but recently lectured in this pastor's church and had been a guest in his home. It was most natural, therefore, for the report signed by the reverend gentleman and further privately endorsed, "It is all O. K." to be accepted in this office as trustworthy. The statement that the matter was generally known and that "a divorce suit will follow" sufficed to indicate that the alleged trouble had gone into full publicity in that community. Hence it found its way into our columns, just as 10,000 similar reports, both true and false, have gone

into the columns of the leading newspapers of America from time immemorial.

There could be no malice or evil intent in our action for all parties were strangers to us and the avouchment of the report was seemingly unimpeachable.

To this the *Pilot* added "MR. LINDSAY'S MANLY CARD." This long statement included Lindsay's telling that he sent the item

upon my thorough understanding that the matter was of common report in the community. . . . The circumstances as I reported them were reported to me by one of the most prominent men in the community. . . . Looking over the transaction now, I am amazed at myself for thus violating what had been the constant practice of my life, not to repeat such current rumors. . . . I sincerely mourn the miserable affair, and taking to myself all proper blame in the matter, state frankly that whatever I did . . . was without the slightest malice. . . . I stand ready to do everything in my power. . . . It will be a constant source of sorrow to me through my whole life.

Lindsay made this statement, he added, without "fear to myself of bodily harm or civil damages, nor is it an effort to avert either." The *Daily Pilot* reported that the Lindsay statement "was preceded also by efforts personally, and through ministerial friends, to atone for the unfortunate affair to the injured gentlemen, who were in the city. When Mr. Lindsay approached Mr. Reamy and Mr. Quinby on the public streets yesterday, for that purpose, they turned their backs on him and walked away." "The Pilot's part in the affair," the newspaper continued, "could not be misunderstood by rational men and we feel that with the above statement it can confidently rest its conduct in the calm and honest judgment of all reasonable people or a fair jury"—for Small knew that the issues would be fought in court.

There was no doubt about that. Reamy and his wife brought suit, charging libel, against the Pilot Publishing Company, Samuel W. Small, and the Rev. William C. Lindsay. They asked for $10,000 in damages.

So, within three months after its establishment, the *Daily Pilot* and its directing editor found themselves involved in one libel suit for $50,000 and within the second three months in another libel suit for $10,000. Neither of the sums sought for damages was small in 1895. But small or large any such cases were unusual. The *Public Ledger* could recall only three libel suits against Virginia newspapers in the past twenty-five years. And whatever the rarity of libel suits in general, these two suits clearly were serious matters. June, when both cases were set for hearing, would be a unique and critical testing time.

Small was already in deep trouble with his directors. The doubts that some of them felt after the filing of the "Money by the Bundle" suit in January multiplied with the doubts that more directors felt after the filing of the "FORGOT HIS NOTES" suit in March.

The break—probably the inevitable break—came on April 14, seven months and a few days after the newspaper and its managing editor, in the exultant aftermath of the 1894 election, began their joint career. The records do not show whether the directors demanded or Small proposed the severance, and it does not matter a great deal. The editorship would have been difficult, if not impossible, for either to continue.

News and editorial direction of the *Pilot* passed, after the end of Small, to the associate editor, James A. Pugh. He had come from Roanoke, after experience on two newspapers there, to join the *Pilot*'s staff when it assembled, and he had remained through its troubles.

To the last Small remained himself. Palm Sunday, two days before his editorship ended, the *Daily Pilot* declared in an editorial that if Jesus Christ came to Norfolk and asked people "to put away the evil that is being done to my people by the unbridled liquor traffic," the majority "before next Friday would drive Christ from the city and cover him with calumny—the modern substitute for the cross."

This lifted the *Virginian* to reproof. Under the head, "Abuse of a High Calling," it reported that "there is just and indignant protest in this community against the Palm Sunday comments of the Daily Pilot." It rebuked the *Daily Pilot* in these words: "The people of Norfolk, including 'ten thousand religionists,' are not perfect . . . but their accusers should be free themselves from all trace and stain of evil when passing a judgment that smacks of blasphemy." Both the judgment and the language of the *Daily Pilot* were, it said, "uncalled for."

The trial of the Reamy suit began on June 3 and ended the next afternoon. Interest was high, but drama was absent. The *Daily Pilot*'s confession of error had removed need for details of the published incident. Reamy on the stand called the publication "utterly false and without foundation in whole and in part," and no one testified otherwise.

Five witnesses, none of them from Onancock, did testify that they had heard rumors about Mrs. Reamy and Upshur before the publication. One witness, Charles Lankford, testified that he had told Reamy

that the publication was actually a favor because it exposed the falseness of the rumors, and that Reamy had replied, "Perhaps so, Brother
Lankford." But Reamy said he was speaking ironically. The defense
did not press the issue. Witnesses from Onancock had not heard rumors. They spoke well of Mrs. Reamy.

Small's testimony followed the line of his explanations. He insisted that the item had been handled in a normal manner, without
malice and with good reasons for believing it to be accurate. When
accuracy was found to be lacking, the *Daily Pilot* had made retractions
and corrections. He thought other newspapers would have published
the item.

But Murray of the *Landmark* testified that the item would not
have appeared "in any decent journal." Definitions and illustrations
of decency and indecency followed, including Murray's opinion that
the New York *Herald* was decent and the New York *World* was in-
decent. Glennan of the *Virginian* would not have published the item
"unless it related to parties at a distance" and then only after editing
the dispatch. Both editors admitted that newspapers sometimes published "disgusting material," as, for instance, in the Beecher-Tilton
case, reported in detail all over the country.

John Neely, a Norfolk lawyer, told the jury that when he agreed
to represent the Reamys he did not expect to collect "any respectable
judgment" from the *Daily Pilot*. The newspaper's lawyers leaped up
with objections to any suggestion that the *Daily Pilot* was insolvent.
Later, Neely referred to it as "Mr. Small's newspaper."

"That used to was," Small interrupted to say.

"Yes," Neely retorted quickly, "for if there is in Norfolk a better
specimen of neglected orphanage than the Pilot has been since you
left it, I have yet to see it."

The jury awarded $1,000 in damages. This was far short of the
demand, but it brought the Reamys a moral victory, darkened the
reputation of newspaper and editor, and cut sharply where the pain
hurt: in the bank account. It must have seemed a bad omen for the
Massey suit that would be heard in twenty days.

When the Massey suit began on June 24, the *Virginian* prophesied
confidently that it would be "the most sensational case tried in the
courts of this city in the last half-century and will be watched with
interest by news readers throughout the entire country." Judge R. R.
Prentis, of the Circuit Court, had moved to the larger courtroom of
the Corporation Court. But that was not large enough. For five weeks
the courtroom was jammed. Reporters sometimes had to crawl in and

out of windows. Their newspapers published every day from one to five columns of their reporting. Two Virginia governors, O'Ferrall, the incumbent, and McKinney, his predecessor, testified. The Virginia attorney general, members of the General Assembly, and state officials were witnesses. One witness came from as far away as the state of Washington (and then was not allowed to testify). The lawyers included artists in histrionics. Everyone knew of Massey, knew of Small, and rapidly was learning to know other fascinating characters.

In the fierce, humid heat of a Norfolk summer Parson Massey, then seventy-six years old, sat in the tightly packed mass "with," in the words of a *Public Ledger* reporter, "a mammoth palm leaf fan, which he used at intervals. In his other hand he held a handsome ebony cane with an immense and beautiful gold head. He wore, of course, his usual gold spectacles, and was attired in a black alpaca coat, white vest, dark pants, a standing collar and white tie."

Across the room sat his arch enemy, the leader of counsel for the defendants: John S. Wise, the many-sided Republican who had fought Massey toe-to-toe in the congressman-at-large election of 1882 and won, and had fought Fitzhugh Lee for the governorship in 1885 and lost. A lawyer of theatrical tendencies, he spent half his career in Virginia and half in New York, from which he had come for this trial, big of head, with a "tremendous chest" that made the "enormous belly seem natural," and with "the charm [which] made both seem unimportant."[3] He did not fail to bring also his vituperative tongue and his ruthlessness in attack on those he despised, high among whom was Parson Massey.

Arrayed with Wise were the James Elliott Heaths, senior and junior, as well as Byrd and Small. F. M. Whitehurst and the younger Lucien D. Starke represented two directors, John L. Roper and S. Q. Collins, respectively. Alfred P. Thom, the Norfolk lawyer of much legal talent and courtroom skill, John Neely, of the Reamys' counsel in the earlier suit, and Richard Walke were Massey's lawyers.

The initial thrust of the defendants was designed to show that Massey definitely had been bribed by the American Book Company, with Womack, the publisher's agent, as the principal figure in the payoff. In 1890 the New York *World* had published an article re-

3. The quotations are from "Very Well Rounded Republican: The Several Lives of John S. Wise," by Curtis Carroll Davis, in the *Virginia Magazine of History and Biography*, Vol. 71, No. 4 (Oct. 1963), 462.

flecting on Massey's handling of book contracts. He did not sue the *World*. The reason, his lawyers said, was that the *World* was too big and wealthy and he was too weak financially to grapple with the Pulitzer newspaper in battle royal. But when the defendants tried to prove that Womack, the publisher's agent, had used bribery in comparable circumstances in the state of Washington, Judge Prentis stymied them. He ruled out any evidence about the Washington affair —a bad blow, the defense thought.

Byrd, on the stand, told of his efforts to get the book contracts for his client, Ginn & Company. He lost out on all counts. Furious about these events, he began digging into schoolbook contract issues, aiming at a legislative investigation. He read the *World*'s 1890 charges, investigated more closely, did not like what he found or heard, and then learned that Small of the *Daily Pilot* was interested in the same subject. They conferred, and the publication of "Money by the Bundle" was arranged. Byrd received no pay for writing it.

But Byrd had to admit on cross-examination that some of his information was hearsay for which he could not vouch by personal knowledge; that Massey's financial explanations, though labored, brought out information which he had not possessed; and that, if he had to do it again, he would alter the article in some respects, though not in its main allegations.

Massey helped his own cause, but at a high price. In his five days on the stand the defense left no stone in his financial path unturned. He had to explain how before the Civil War he had bought "Ash Lawn," the six-hundred-acre estate of President Monroe near Charlottesville, for $32,500, and after the war owed $17,500 of the purchase price which a brother agreed to pay, with the brother's taking a deed in his own name while the Parson still lived in the shrine; how he was involved in a financial deal with a friend that went sour and forced him, in the Massey phraseology, to handle his cash thereafter "in a peculiar way"—that is, to keep much of it in a secret drawer; how he frequently charged the state for transportation costs while traveling free on railway passes; and how he had not returned for taxation money or credits due him. A long line of political foes reviled him as a man who could not be trusted, and who even had tried to bribe some of them, but this the Parson could counter with another line of witnesses who swore to his personal virtues—for the man had friends as well as enemies.

The defense could not pin down the bribery charge, as it knew it would have difficulty in doing. Wise had pointed out in his initial statement to the jury that "courts have held that these acts [of passing the money] are seldom seen of other men" and had to be established by bits of evidence. But Massey was adept at explaining. Mrs. Massey bought that other home in Charlottesville, he said—and she testified to this too—with money furnished her by two brothers from Alabama, who confirmed the statement, and with other money taken from the secret drawer, and who could show that she had not? The Parson never blinked, whatever the question (he was used to rough stuff from old days on the hustings), and Wise could not break him or beat him down.

But Wise could damage him, and that was what, when the bribery charge could not be made to stick, the strategy of the second line of defense called for. If Massey could not be proved a bribe-taker, then prove him to lack any character that could be damaged by the *Daily Pilot*'s making him out to be a bribe-taker. Nearly all the second half of the five weeks was devoted to tearing into his record. "You can't spoil a rotten egg," Wise thundered.

Beside this duel, Small shrank into a minor figure. He had heard criticism of schoolbook contracts and had published an article about them before meeting Byrd. He had "pruned" Byrd's article and did not consider it libelous. He kept on writing harshly of Massey because Massey said harsh things about him. No, he had not retracted anything or corrected any errors.

But Small was generous about an extrajudicial fight during the trial. K. Foster Murray, son of the *Landmark*'s editor, resenting something Small had written about his father, charged into him outside the courtroom with fists flying. Small joined in heartily. A policeman tried to stop the bout. Hugh Murray, another of the editorial family, resented the law's invasion of what he considered a private affair and attacked the policeman. When the battle wound up in court Small refused to prosecute anyone. Hugh Murray said he did not realize it was a policeman he interfered with. All three major participants were free to go back to the main arena.

Small testified that he had consulted with Gibbs about publishing "Money by the Bundle." But Gibbs could not remember any such consultation. Gibbs did remember well that at the instance of the directors he had gone northward before the trial to ask for help from Ginn & Company and other schoolbook publishers in fighting the Massey suit. All of them turned him down.

One of the witnesses who swore he would not believe Massey on oath was State Senator H. D. Flood, of Appomattox. Massey attrib-

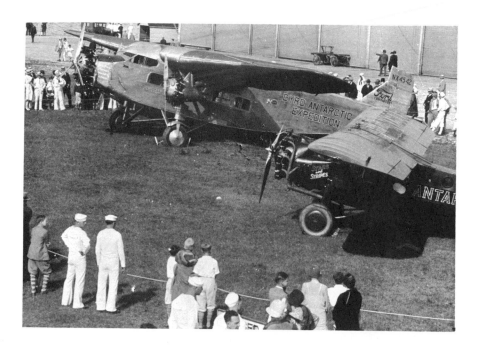

Hampton Boulevard was jammed as crowds flocked to the Norfolk Naval Base to see Commander Richard E. Byrd's expedition depart to establish Little America in the Antarctic in 1928.

Norfolk, 1934—Plume Street looking east from Granby toward Bank Street.

uted this lack of faith to old political enmity. In his testimony Flood said that Ginn & Company originally had asked him to represent it in Virginia. He suggested, however, that Ginn retain Byrd, who was his brother-in-law, and Colonel Tazewell Ellett, of Richmond, which it did. All these men were well known throughout Virginia, and their testimony heightened public interest across the state in what the Richmond *Dispatch* called "a war between book publishers around the shoulders of Mr. Massey."[4]

To newspaper men especially an interesting issue was whether directors of the publishing company could be held individually responsible for libelous publications by editors. In May the *Landmark* had spoken of the desirability of a clearer definition of how the law of libel applied, "especially as to the responsibility of directors and stockholders of a newspaper who may be sued for wrongs done by the editor who is in charge of their property as agent or manager."

Roper and Collins, of the directors, contended from the first that they could not be held responsible, not only because they had never attended a meeting of the directors but also because they had not participated in any decisions about the publication of "Money by the Bundle." Other directors made comparable pleas. Wise, in his opening statement, declared that members of the board were not responsible for the article. A condition of Small's managing editorship, he said, was freedom from interference in that editorship.

Counterarguments rested chiefly on the combination of earlier criticisms published before "Money by the Bundle," public notices that further charges were coming, and elaborate plans to publicize this article, including notices sent to public school officials and teachers and the printing of twenty-five thousand copies for broad distribution. If directors did not know, it was contended, they should have known what many others did know.

Roper, Collins, and J. W. Borum early were dropped from the list of defendants. Judge Prentis instructed the jury that "the mere fact that certain persons were stockholders or directors" was not sufficient to make them liable to the plaintiff. "The burden is on him [the plaintiff] to show that said defendants actually participated in composing, uttering or publishing libel." Massey's lawyers announced just before the case went to the jury that he sought no damages from eight directors but that he did from Luther Sheldon, president of the

4. Richard E. Byrd, legal representative of Ginn & Company, was the father of Harry Flood Byrd, governor, 1926-30, and United States senator, 1933-65; Eleanor Bolling Flood Byrd, sister of State Senator Flood, was his mother.

corporation, Zachary, secretary of the board, four other directors, and Gibbs, the business manager. All of these, the plaintiff held, participated in, or knew of, and could have stopped, the publication of "Money by the Bundle."

The lawyers' pleas to the jury lasted most of two days with the climax in Wise's arraignment of Massey and Thom's final defense of the Parson. No seats were empty when the stout Wise rose to speak. In the words of the *Virginian*, a "CYCLONE OF VITUPERATION" blasted off from his tongue. "Never in the courts of Norfolk has there been a severer denunciation of any man. . . . [Massey] was compared to all that is low and vile." Wise called him "a dirty worm. . . . I don't like him. I think he ought to have been in the penitentiary long ago." Looking straight into the eyes of the Parson, Wise shouted: "You are dirty from your head to your feet."

"The most bitter invective ever hurled at a litigant in any case ever tried in Norfolk," the *Landmark* pronounced the words of Wise. But in the calm that followed, Thom told the jury, "I know Captain Wise is sincere in his hatred. . . . But the time will come when he would give his right arm to unsay the things he said in this court yesterday. . . . [Massey is] the most outraged man I ever knew."

The jury ruled for Massey. It held that the *Daily Pilot* had libeled him. It assessed damages at $1,600—$100 for actual damages, $1,500 for punitive damages. It found the Pilot Publishing Company, Small, and Byrd guilty of the libel. It found all other defendants not guilty.

The date was July 27, 1895, the hour was 2:20 p.m., and the story was the *Public Ledger's*. It reported that no doubt existed from the beginning about Massey's getting damages. But the jurors, it said, varied all the way from $50,000 in damages to nothing at all, and the verdict obviously was a compromise.

Next day's morning newspapers could go into it more extensively. Massey told a *Landmark* reporter that he had been vindicated and was satisfied. A verdict for $1,600 probably was as good, he said, as a verdict for $50,000 so far as collecting was concerned. The *Landmark* concluded: "There was never a more stinging rebuke administered to a public journal than has been administered in this verdict to the Pilot for its effort to profit by a sensational publication founded on falsehood, and the incidental destruction of an old and distinguished man high in public life. This is a monumental warning to those who would follow in the path of such enterprise."

The *Virginian* thought the verdict "undoubtedly acquits Mr. Massey and the American Book Company of the charges that were uttered through the columns of the Pilot as to fraud and bribery." But "as to the injury to Mr. Massey's character, by the Pilot's publication of the charges, the jury's conclusion would lead to the opinion that they did not consider the damage very serious." The *Public Ledger* shifted the emphasis: "The verdict may be disappointing to Mr. Massey by reason of the small amount of the damages awarded, but he has the satisfaction of knowing that he has discomfited those who sought to destroy him. . . ."

The *Daily Pilot* itself joined this round-table discussion. It thought it had been impartial in reporting its own tortures, and it awarded the same star to the crowns of the *Virginian*, the *Public Ledger*, and the Portsmouth *Star*, "although it was well known that their sympathies were with the plaintiff, and that they did not approve the publication in the Pilot on which the suit was based. Their action seemed to us fair, dignified and in excellent taste."

But the *Landmark*, declared the *Daily Pilot*, was "in striking contrast. Its editor, the superintendent of public schools, is a subordinate of Mr. Massey. Yet he availed himself of every opportunity to prejudice the public, including the jury, against the defendants through the editorial columns of his paper. . . . The Landmark seems to think that the integrity of the Democratic party was involved in the Massey-Pilot suit. . . . We have not so understood the case."

These variations did not alter the impact of the Reamy and Massey suits and the double loss which the *Daily Pilot* and Small had suffered in reputation and money. Small was already out, and, as subsequent events showed, virtually done for as an editor in Norfolk. The *Daily Pilot* itself was *in extremis*. For a newspaper established in high hopes by moral reformers to be found guilty of serious libel twice in its first ten months, under circumstances that indicated irresponsible judgment and supervision, was a blow at its vitals. And though a total of $2,600 owed in damages may seem small on its face even for 1895, the costs of the trials lifted this figure far higher for a publishing company that owed in addition substantial sums spent in getting started.

On the third day after the Massey suit verdict the *Virginian* announced the denouement under this succinct head: "PILOT GOES UNDER." On the previous day (July 29) the publishing company had made a deed of assignment, listing debts of $14,530 to preferred creditors plus debts to others. The possibility of stockholders' recovering anything seemed slim. The court named former Judge James Elliott

Heath trustee. Publication continued while a new company was being organized.

August 4—a Sunday, when the *Daily Pilot* came out with eight pages, though not with enough advertising to justify eight pages—brought the announcement that the New Daily Pilot Publishing Company had bought the "name, chartered rights, good will and effects" from the trustee, but not assets of equipment and not anything else of substantial material value. For what it did buy the new company paid $200 plus the $1,000 Reamy judgment.

The new owners were some of the old owners: R. Y. Zachary, former secretary, now president; Ira B. White, vice president; J. W. Borum, secretary and general manager; Luther W. White, treasurer; and C. E. Verdier and T. C. White, all of whom were directors, and Frank Dusch, who was listed as a stockholder. W. W. Gibbs, who had been directing daily operations in editorial and news areas, was named managing editor—in effect, general manager.

Lacking primary equipment, the new owners sent Gibbs into northern markets for a press and stereotyping facilities. Meantime, the *New Daily Pilot* used the press of the *Evening News* (where Small had sought refuge) plus, as the *Pilot* reported, the electric motor of R. H. Dodson, of a short-lived newspaper called *The Rambler*. On September 14 a new Cox duplex press began turning out the *New Daily Pilot*, six columns per page. Supplementing the press were four new Mergenthaler typesetting machines operated by electric motors. This was modern material. The combination placed the newspaper in strong mechanical position and spurred other Norfolk newspapers to modernize their equipment.

To the public the *New Daily Pilot* presented a bold face and a jaunty air. Across the front page it ran on the first day a streamer: "The Daily Pilot Enters upon a New Era of Prosperity Today." A copyrighted article by Sam Jones on "Man's Social and Political Fads," with a picture of the evangelist, tied the newspaper to its past. So did its promise to wage "constant warfare upon the liquor traffic." But it came forward with an enlarged Associated Press news report, more pictures, and the Sunday School lesson for its Saturday edition.

An innovation was the records of the Norfolk Police Court "just as they are made up by Police Justice [J. J.] Burroughs," and "all requests for omission of convictions will be refused." A week later the *New Daily Pilot* had to explain this new policy at length in an editorial and to insist that the names of those convicted would not be suppressed. This kind of reporting had not been done in Norfolk.

Police court news was growing into a regular feature of many newspapers in Virginia and in other Southern states, often with humor, achieved or attempted, which built up the police justices into major personalities.

The *New Daily Pilot*'s new independence included disagreeing on occasion with Mayor Pettit, whom the earlier *Pilot* had endorsed with rapture. Issues came up in continuing police problems which led the newspaper to side with one of its own directors, Police Commissioner Verdier, rather than the mayor.

Small, who stepped out of *Daily Pilot* control on April 14, seemed determined at first to remain in Norfolk. He acquired control of the afternoon *News and Courier* and took charge on April 29. It had been established in 1890 by Calvin S. Blackwell and William W. Degge. When the latter was appointed postmaster, others came in: Charles W. Bennett, Benjamin Rowson, and Paul C. Degge. Still another Degge—John L.—was editor in 1894.

Small changed the name to the *Evening News.* But the venture did not satisfy him, and perhaps did not satisfy others. Besides, he needed money. By July his name as editor came down from the editorial masthead, and a group called the Evening News Associates took over, one of whom was Samuel W. Small, Jr. By September the *Evening News* was sold at auction to the old *News and Courier* group that owned it before Small arrived, and by October it was leased to Paul Degge and others. The Small era was over. Before he left Norfolk he and his wife made an assignment to John G. Tilton, trustee, "turning over all interest in the newspaper outfit known as the Evening News" for the benefit of creditors. That was the real end of the Small era. But not the last word from him.

For on October 27 the *Virginian* carried conspicuously on its front page a letter from Small declaring that he would return in the spring of 1896 to defeat in the city election of that year some officials who had disappointed him after being elected by his efforts—"social hoboes, religious hypocrites and political hogs," he called them. So to these words, with their flashes of the familiar fire:

> Stern necessity required that I resume my lecture tours in other states in order to recoup my losses of the past year and accumulate the means to relieve myself of indebtedness of an annoying character. Some so-called friends and open enemies in Norfolk have busied themselves abusing me, falsifying my intentions, and betraying their cowardly spirits by persecuting

my family.[5]. . . Their action toward me personally has passed the point of forgiveness and I propose to have a full reckoning with them. . . .

My ammunition chest is already getting crowded with the disreputable past and present records of some of the snake-fanged frauds whom I helped to foist upon the people of Norfolk and whom I will delight to force back into the dirty bogs that bred them. I thank God that I will be at home shortly to give to them personal and pointed notice of the opening of hostilities.

But these were words flung over Sam Small's shoulder. He did not return to Norfolk for the 1896 election, nor was he ever again a factor in the public life of Norfolk. In 1922, which was twenty-seven years after the fireworks of 1894 and 1895, he lectured in a Norfolk church. Both Norfolk and Small were different then, and neither revived the old wars. When he died in 1931 in Atlanta the *Virginian-Pilot* said (November 24) that he was "in many respects a different man. . . . Time had mellowed him. He viewed life more broadly and toler-antly." Almost to his eightieth year he wrote "pointedly and inter-estingly on the passing scene for the Atlanta Constitution. . . . The new issues which roused his passion were increasingly those of preju-dice and parochialism which continually have to be fought."

The *Pilot*, almost miraculously, began to take on permanence. It lost Gibbs in September. He left to work for a printing press com-pany. The prohibitionists of the board turned first to Borum and then to W. B. Wilder (originally from North Carolina, once editor of the Portsmouth *Times*, most recently with the Portsmouth *Star*) as general manager. They greatly needed an editor of distinction. By December, in the first of two major miracles, they had an editor of long experience, undoubted capacity, and considerable renown—Wil-liam C. Elam.

Fifty-nine years old in 1895, slight of figure, diffident in manner, thoroughly bearded, Elam had gone almost the whole round of news-paper experience in the Virginia of his times. Born in Fayetteville, North Carolina, in 1836, he studied law, wrote early for newspapers and magazines, made Fourth of July and anti-Know-Nothing speeches in his native state, and in 1860 was a Douglas elector. In the war he

---

5. Small had two sons, Samuel W. Small, Jr., and Robert Toombs Small. Both had successful careers in journalism. The former spent many years in Washington on the staff of the Associated Press. The latter was associated with David Lawrence in the Consolidated Feature Service.

was a lieutenant in the Fayetteville Light Infantry but shifted to an artillery unit from Ashland and thereafter was a Virginian.

After the war Elam plunged into the pugnacious journalism of Richmond, which was dedicated then to editorial polemics and the code of the duel. Elam had experience in both, fighting one duel with Colonel Thomas Smith, later a United States judge in New Mexico, and taking a wound, and fighting another—a widely reported duel— with Colonel Richard F. Beirne, of the Richmond *State*, and taking another wound from him. A threatened duel with C. O'B. Cowardin, of the Richmond *Dispatch*, was a *cause célèbre*, even though the law stopped it. Elam was not a killer (in one duel he even refused to fire at his man) so much as a victim of the times.

He broke loose from journalism from time to time, running for Congress from the Eighth District and losing to General W. H. F. Lee (son of General R. E. Lee), sitting in the House of Delegates, acting as secretary of the commonwealth, writing party platforms. But he always came back. The state really began to hear from him when as editor of the Richmond *Whig* he was the voice of Mahone in many campaigns and controversies in the readjuster wars. He got away from that editorship, founded a Republican newspaper in Harrisonburg, then swung around to the Democrats, where he stayed. With the Baltimore *Sun* he had intermittent connections, for the New York *Times* he reported the *Virginius* affair from Cuba, and eventually he took William Jennings Bryan and free silver to his bosom.

Whatever he did, wherever he was, he hit hard with emphatic and often dramatic writing. Norfolk editors of earlier years, though frequently disagreeing with him, admired him greatly. The *Landmark* in 1881 called him "a remarkable man in many respects, and the Readjuster Party will never have a more courageous or untiring champion."

Four years later the *Virginian* spoke of him as a "vigorous, earnest, finished journalist—perhaps the most forceful political writer in the state." Only a few weeks before the announcement of Elam's coming to Norfolk, William E. Cameron, writing a series of articles for the *Landmark*, spoke of Elam as having "no superior on this continent as a fertile, forceful and fearless writer." Cameron continued:

> I have known him to produce three columns of matter a day for months at a time on subjects requiring accuracy of knowledge, yet never lapsing into slovenliness of style nor lacking the tenacity of his grip. Mr. Elam, the mildest mannered of

men, was a warm partisan, and did not mince words when in the thick of a canvass. Although shortsighted to a painful degree, he was on the field more than once with persons who took umbrage at his editorial utterances. . . .

And many years later the historian of the readjuster movement, C. C. Pearson, wrote about the Elam of those years in these words:[6]

> With Elam the social note was ever prominent—"the Brokers" and the "Broker press," the "Scribe and Pharisee" parsons, the office-holding set who "generally train with the courthouse clique and always believe that money and position are stronger than the people." In lucid explanation of figures, often combined with unwarranted distortion of them, in effective reiteration of a leading idea in striking language, and in arousing suspicion of his adversaries' motives through insinuation, virulent personal attacks, and often deliberate misrepresentation, he was unexcelled. And for all such utterances of the Whig, though a recluse by habit and physically unfit, he held himself strictly accountable, according to the honor code of the "Bourbons" whom he so much affected to despise.

This was more the political editor "in the thick of a canvass" than the editor who had matured since readjuster days, though ever the fighter. Later generations would have called Elam a philosophical liberal. But he was so different from Sam Small, and people remembered so well his presence near the seat of readjuster power, that the *New Daily Pilot* felt obliged to explain what his presence in Norfolk, starting December 2, 1895, meant for a newspaper born of prohibition. On December 1, the newspaper said in words that suggest Elam may have had a pen in their preparation:

> Along the same lines upon which it has heretofore been so ably edited, the New Pilot will steadily pursue its course—slave to no party, abandoning nothing it has always advocated, advocating nothing it has heretofore opposed, independent in all things, neutral in nothing. Without regard to party it will continue to advocate what it believes to be good measures, good men and good government, and to oppose and reprobate the measures, the men and the government which it believes to be wrong and evil. If in doing this the Pilot shall assail men or measures of this or that party, it is those men and measures that are attacked, and not the party, except in so far as the spirit of independence and patriotism is invoked to an allegiance that transcends the claims of all parties.

6. Charles Chilton Pearson, *The Readjuster Movement in Virginia* (New Haven, Conn., 1917), pp. 113-14.

The dedication of the *New Daily Pilot* to the old spirit in which its predecessor had been founded was lessening. It retained the name of a prohibitionist newspaper and in a formal sense it supported national prohibitionist candidates, carrying their names at the top of its editorial columns in 1896. But it was throwing more of its weight in other directions, and its future lay elsewhere.

ELAM'S EDITORSHIP OF THE NEW DAILY PILOT BEGAN WHEN NORFOLK WAS warming up for the city election of 1896 that would continue or displace the prohibition-reform administration elected in 1894. Elam did not lack courage or candor. In his first week he cheered for President Cleveland's attitude toward the British government in the Venezuela affair but criticized Cleveland's rejection of free silver. To Governor O'Ferrall he gave praise for recommending election safeguards. But when the governor spoke well of the state's schoolbook contracts, the *Pilot* was blunt: "It has been incontestably proved and can be proved again that the book contracts put us to great disadvantage in many instances; nor has the verdict or judgment of any court even hinted to the contrary."

But it was Norfolk law enforcement issues early in 1896 that really brought Elam into action. Ed Miars, a Democratic political leader, operated a saloon at the corner of Princess Anne Road and Bank Street. It sat squarely on the Norfolk-Norfolk County line, the front door in the city, the bar itself in the county. On a Sunday night in April two city policemen were sent to investigate liquor selling. They found the front door (in the city) locked. They found the back door (in the county) wide open. Inside they found—in the *Pilot*'s words— "everything in full swing."

When the two policemen went into action, the Miars guards went into counteraction. They beat one policeman badly. In the grand jury investigation that followed, a witness was a mission school teacher. Miars saw him a few days later on the ferry wharf in Portsmouth, walked up to him, and without a word hit him on the jaw with a roundhouse right that knocked him unconscious. (This was the original report. In the trial Miars produced witnesses who said the teacher hit the first blow.) The *Pilot*'s news story pulled out all the stops: "Edward B. Miars, the notorious thug, cowardly ruffian, big brute, boisterous bully, dangerous desperado, tough dive keeper, low rum seller, ex-monkey house man, evil doer, terror to society, and defier of all law and order, is behind prison bars in Portsmouth jail, where he was committed yesterday . . . for ten days to await the result of his latest victim's injuries."

Editorially the *Pilot* proclaimed "A Reign of Terror," and specified:

> The worst feature of the matter is the aid and comfort that are openly and outrageously extended (under cover of law) to Miars and his gang and his allied bullies by the authorities of Norfolk county, including magistrates, grand jurors and the county court, all of these actively, unblushingly and zealously acting together to deliver Miars (especially) from the just grasp of the authorities of Norfolk—not that these county officers may themselves punish Miars, but that they may shield and deliver him, and keep him at large as a terror of all law-abiding people, and all who would put down lawless disorder. . . . As a certain kind of dogs are kept and bred for their ferocity, so these brutal roughs are kept, bred and encouraged by certain persons for special use in campaigns and elections. . . .

These words brought Elam into court on a charge of contempt. When he was tried, he fought fiercely. When he was found guilty, and fined $50.00, he kept on fighting fiercely. Miars had not been convicted of either the saloon or the assault charge. Said the *Pilot*: "There were no witnesses against him because the reign of terror still exists. Quiet ladies and gentlemen who saw Miars attack Morgan [the teacher] were afraid to testify against Miars. . . . A diligent court could have learned who these witnesses were and compelled their attendance. But so it goes. The man who created the reign of terror goes scot-free. . . . The editor who sought to have an end put to the reign of terror is fined for contempt."

In the municipal campaign the *Virginian*, the *Landmark*, and the *Public Ledger* reverted to their traditional Democratic allegiance, and the *Pilot*, still committed to those who had established it, found itself alone. When it defended its founders and slashed at the Democrats, it drew fire immediately from the *Virginian*. "Shall Norfolk," the *Pilot* asked, "fall back into the dark age of ring control, when everywhere the cities and the people are rising in their might against the old party hacks, heelers and hustlers?"

"No, sir, Mr. Editor of the Pilot," the *Virginian* retorted, "the people of Norfolk in the coming municipal election are going to wipe out of existence the sanctified ring that has outringed all rings that Norfolk has ever been inflicted with."

The Democrats swept back into power. They elected their candidate for mayor, Wyndham R. Mayo, former ship captain and a business man, and his associates, by large majorities and in hilarious spirit.

In the postelection calm the *Public Ledger,* ordinarily a quiet voice, rebuked the outspoken *Pilot,* though never mentioning it by name:

> A newspaper is a power, sometimes for good, sometimes for evil, according to the principles on which it is run. It may deceive people for a while by reckless assertions and irresponsible attacks, which many not assailed will read for a time, but in a well-balanced community it will have only a brief season in which to indulge in these malicious, undignified and unprofessional attacks. In its mission as teacher and guide it must first establish its character. This is especially true in a conservative state like Virginia, and it is vain to import brilliant writers and geniuses to overthrow this sentiment. . . . There is a well-defined opinion abroad that we are able to manage our own affairs without aid from professional agitators in whatever garb or disguise, and that character and responsibility are still desirable qualities to guide the individual and the body politic.

The *Pilot* came charging back, carrying the argument into a different area:

> There is not a word of truth in the Ledger's flings at us. It is easy to see what inspires these flings. The Pilot, as a newspaper in all its departments, having the news, and also an editor, has become a great success in this city of Norfolk where there are a great many people who want the news and also an editor in their daily journal. That the Ledger is lacking in these respects is not our fault, surely. And if our circulation is large and increasing, we cannot help it if that fact endangers the circulation and advertising patronage of the Ledger. We certainly have not sought to take the Ledger's place. We have imitated it in nothing, followed it in nothing, and now scorn the example, the mean and sordid self-seeking example, it has set in its malicious, undignified and unprofessional flings at us, and follow that of Uncle Toby when he put the fly out of the window: "Go on, Ledger! There is room for both of us in this world."

The *Pilot* continued to carry the names of the national prohibition candidates at its editorial masthead during the 1896 presidential campaign. But that was a further handicap when Bryan, McKinley, and the free silver debate had a corner on national attention. The *Pilot* supported Bryan so vigorously at the height of the campaign that its prohibition allegiance, if any existed then, was only nominal.

In its own organization managerial troubles increased. It had no real publisher or other top command. R. E. Turner came in as secretary and business manager in July of 1896, taking over duties which Gibbs at the start and Borum and Wilder later had carried out. Turner had been a printer in Norfolk, sometimes up, sometimes down, including periods with both the *Virginian* and the *Landmark*. Early in October he left the *Pilot* briefly when the Norfolk *Dispatch* began to appear as an afternoon newspaper, and R. H. Hart, with experience in Chattanooga and Knoxville, took over as business manager. In a week Turner was back.

These changes came near the time of the *Pilot's* moving from Hill Street to the south side of City Hall Avenue, opposite the Market House (later the Armory and Municipal Building), where it was in operation by November 3. But that did not affect its organic illness. Its chief hope now was a change in ownership, character, and purpose that would enable it to start over again as a distinctly different newspaper.

For that to come about, new ownership must be prepared to deal with formidable competition from two long-established morning newspapers in a city of forty thousand people flanked by another city (Portsmouth) of fifteen thousand. New ownership would have to provide capital requirements and meet operating costs when both had risen sharply and continued to head upward. Not many old-line newspaper men would care for that kind of assignment. Few of them had the resources. Something like a miracle would be needed.

Something like a miracle happened. On November 12, 1896, the *Public Ledger* reported that Albert H. Grandy and W. Thompson Barron had bought the *Pilot*. Two days later Barron's weekly *Journal of Commerce* reported that "talk prevalent for the past several days concerning a change in the ownership of the Pilot has been verified, that paper having, on November 11, been purchased by Messrs. A. H. Grandy, W. Thompson Barron, and others, Mr. Barron becoming general manager." Barron, who was associated with the *Landmark* in the reorganization of 1882, continued his publication of the *Journal of Commerce* and his management of the printing and bookbinding establishment of W. T. Barron & Co., 94 Roanoke Avenue. But more important was the role of Grandy. He had bought a majority of the stock; he had the money to operate with, and he had a special quality of leadership.

Not until a week later, however, did the *Pilot* itself make any mention of the change. It had waited because of "the absence of the editor," who, after the election, had gone away "for a little needed rest." But on November 19 it announced that "the former New Pilot Publishing Company has sold out the paper, the office, the machinery, good will and all thereto belonging to purchasers who have reorganized the company under the same name as follows: President, Albert H. Grandy; vice president, Thomas W. Shelton; treasurer, L. D. Starke, Jr.; secretary and manager, W. Thompson Barron; directors, Robert W. Shultice, together with the foregoing officers; superintendent [of mechanical operations], R. E. Turner. The editor, William C. Elam, will continue at the head of the paper."

Shelton was a young lawyer who a year earlier had been named city attorney. Shultice, also young, was treasurer of Barron's printing company. Starke, the third young man, a lawyer, was the son of the long-time member of the board of directors of the *Landmark* and twice its board president. All three were capable of giving support to Grandy and Barron, but their share holdings were very small. The retention of Elam as editor was more significant. It was evidence that Grandy wanted professionals for actual operation even though, as with Elam, they might be forthright personalities who would arouse some opposition in expressing strong opinions.

Grandy then was fifty-three years old. He had never had any connection with a newspaper and made no pretense to professional knowledge. Born in Camden County, North Carolina, across the line to the south of Norfolk, he moved with his parents to Norfolk when two years old, grew up there, and won a lieutenant's bar with the Eighth North Carolina Regiment in the Civil War. After the war he worked as bookkeeper and clerk with a wholesale grocery firm and then joined his family's successful firm of cotton merchants, C. W. Grandy & Co.

Grandy learned much about business and management. He liked other aspects of life too and showed initiative and leadership in the organization and establishment of Norfolk's first country club and was the first president. Newspapers fascinated him. He was confident that he could make money with a newspaper provided he could surround himself with men of capacity, experience, and zeal. He meant to do just that, and he had the executive ability to do it. He had strong convictions also that a newspaper had responsibilities peculiar to its nature and that meeting such responsibilities was necessary for its best development. In important respects he was Norfolk's first modern newspaper publisher.

Most of the *Pilot*'s initial statement followed the vogue of the times. Elam probably wrote it. In part it declared:

> The Jeffersonian principles of democracy in which our free institutions are founded and through which the liberty and prosperity of the country have had their only good and perfect development will be cherished and defended by the Pilot at all times, without partizanry, however, and without bitterness, the right of all men and all parties to their opinions being cheerfully recognized as a necessary part of the consent in which government alone can find a sure title. . . . The Pilot hopes to see the day when a Greater South will find here a Greater Norfolk cooperating and developing greatness and glory with the Pilot on deck to guide, to warn, to comfort, cheer and bless.

The next sentence got down to something different. It declared flatly that "the New Pilot now has ample means combined with experience and resolute business energy and will lack nothing to make it a first class newspaper." "Now has ample means" was something no earlier newspaper in Norfolk could say. The words marked the dividing line between the numerous small newspapers that could spring into being in the 1870's and 1880's, and earlier, because it cost little to do so, and, on the other hand, the machine-equipped newspapers under skilled management, which alone could compete with other machine-equipped newspapers under skilled management, that were pointing the way of the future.

How much Grandy and Barron paid for the *Pilot* is not disclosed in the known records. But the *Pilot*'s "ample means" did not come from the daily newspaper business. In overcrowded Norfolk, surpluses of this sort were difficult to build up. It was outside money. It came from other business activities and was invested in newspaper business. In that respect Grandy and his *Pilot* broke the pattern. Other newspapers in the Norfolk of that era, unable to accumulate surplus from their own operations, later followed this new pattern.

Kenton Murray, the *Landmark* editor and president of the corporation, died on December 29, 1895. He was only forty-five years old. "When the sad news that he was gone reached the office of the Landmark," that newspaper reported, "all its employees, of every kind, wept tears that testified to their affection and to his worth." Murray had been the principal editorial writer for the *Landmark* since Hope's death in 1887.

The directors elected Colonel Starke (the elder) as president, an office he had held earlier. They agreed that Nottingham should continue as the "responsible editor," which meant general manager, and authorized him to engage an editorial assistant at a salary of not more than $100 a month. Nottingham chose K. Foster Murray, son of the late editor. The directors elected the younger Murray to the board in October, 1897, raised his salary from $23.08 a week to $25.00 in July, 1899 (he was being called "associate editor" then), and after the death of Starke in March, 1902, elected him secretary and treasurer while Nottingham was being elected president.

These changes did not materially affect the policies or style of the *Landmark*. Nottingham was the supreme authority, subject only to the legal requirements of the corporation. His influence permeated the newspaper at all points. A story lingered for years that once, when tremendous news came in from the Spanish-American War, the editor in charge wrote a two-column head—a revolutionary change in the *Landmark*'s staid makeup ways—but the printers refused to set any head so drastic until they were sure that Nottingham approved. Kenton Murray's will named Nottingham as executor and directed that his stock should not be sold but should be retained and represented by the widow and by Foster Murray, the son, in a manner satisfactory to Nottingham. Other directors at this time were James Elliott Heath, C. A. Nash, James A. Kerr, and W. A. S. Taylor, all estimable citizens of Norfolk, but their holdings were minute beside those owned or controlled by Nottingham.

The *Evening News* had been unable to gain ground against the calm but relentlessly competitive *Public Ledger*, even though a dueling Richmond editor, Page McCarty, was brought in for a few months to succor the struggling newspaper. When R. H. Hart assumed command, he changed the name to the Norfolk *News*. But it could not go ahead, and in early October, 1896, Hart went to the *Pilot* as general manager. Before October 10 the Norfolk *News* gave up, and the *Public Ledger* was the only afternoon newspaper left in Norfolk.

This was a situation to excite newspaper men of the old school. Henry V. Vail, whom the town liked to call Pete, was such a man. He had been a *Public Ledger* reporter for ten years before an appointment as deputy city sergeant in the reform administration looked attractive to him. But now the Democrats were taking back the jobs. R. E. Turner was another such man to whom, in the managerial misery of the *Pilot* in that autumn of 1896, the opportunity was persuasive.

Vail and Turner joined hands and produced a new afternoon newspaper called *Norfolk Dispatch*, born November 7, 1896. Between them they knew something about reporting and printing, but not much about advertising and management. Neither had any money to speak of, nor did either pretend to.

The new capitalists saluted the town with entire frankness: "The purpose of the Norfolk Dispatch in entering the field of journalism is, briefly and plainly stated, to earn a living for its publishers and their families." The pledges that followed were conventional. But the Norfolk *Dispatch* had so little in physical equipment that every issue published was a triumph of the spirit.

This was in the old tradition, and the ghosts of many a venturesome printer must have cheered the enterprise. The *Dispatch* published four pages, with six columns to the page. Four columns of the front page carried local news, of which the big story on the first day was the paying of an election debt of a wheelbarrow ride from the Mansion House to the Atlantic Hotel. The fifth and sixth columns had short telegraphic items and a long European story clipped from the Baltimore *Sun*. There was no advertising on this page. Inside, editorials and advertising covered page two; market reports, transportation schedules, and miscellaneous items were on page three; and page four had advertising and two columns of general news. Miller, Rhoads & Company was the big advertiser of the day.

There was nothing very good, nothing very bad, and much that was very modest about this new newspaper. Its chief rival, the twenty-year-old afternoon *Public Ledger*, was still a four-page newspaper, but edited so competently and managed so carefully that it had survived many rivals. The *Virginian* regularly had been printing eight pages since 1890, more on some days and always on Sundays, and the *Pilot* was now following much the same schedule. The *Landmark* ran only four pages normally but was near the point of expansion. All Norfolk papers sold then for two cents.

The *Dispatch*'s old flatbed press and its single linotype machine, both badly worn, seemed pitiful equipment in comparison with that of others. Nor was the *Dispatch*'s manpower, in number or talent, impressive. Turner, scenting the possibilities of a revived *Pilot*, fled back to it almost before he had begun getting out the *Dispatch*, leaving Vail bereft of partners. But Vail kept on scratching, and found others who would join him, and presently the *Dispatch* was surprising readers with news about how landowners were trying to charge the city far more for additional watershed acres than the land was worth. Having achieved a scoop and wrought a public service, the *Dispatch* was almost embarrassed. "Now that the apologies are all in and the land is practically safe in the possession of the city at a reasonable price," it said, "it is well to forgive and forget the plot. The Dispatch has no chidings to administer and no harsh words to recall."

In one way and another the *Dispatch* continued to survive. In the over-newspapered cities of Norfolk and Portsmouth this was not only an impressive immediate accomplishment: it was also a historic fact. For the *Dispatch*, feeble though it may have seemed at first, was the last newspaper established in Norfolk that continued to survive (in merged form, like all other survivors) down to modern times. The *Virginian*, the *Landmark*, and the *Pilot* in the morning, the *Public Ledger* and the *Dispatch* in the afternoon—this was the lineup at the end of 1896. It was also the signal for years of hard competitive struggle.

In the same year Portsmouth had two afternoon newspapers: the *Evening Times*, whose ancestral lines ran back to 1873 and came down the years through the *Daily Enterprise*, the *Daily Times*, the *Enterprise-Times*, and the *Progress* to the *Evening Times* of that year; and, in competition with it, the *Star*, rising in 1894. Seven daily newspapers in the Norfolk-Portsmouth combination of less than sixty thousand population were in sharp contrast to four newspapers in Richmond, a city then nearing eighty-five thousand.

These newspaper changes were taking place during the year—almost during the very weeks—of a vivid presidential election. The rise of bimetallism found strong support among Democratic politicians in Virginia, notably from the oratorical Senator John W. Daniel and ultimately from the rising, conservative, business-minded Senator Thomas S. Martin, who had surprised many people by defeating Fitzhugh Lee in 1893. The *Pilot* championed free silver and thereby found itself once more alone among the newspapers of Norfolk. The *Virginian*, the *Landmark*, and the *Public Ledger* all distrusted the new panacea. In that respect they reflected strong sentiment among Second District Democrats.

Yet in that respect Lower Tidewater was at odds with Virginia Democrats as a whole. The Democratic state convention voted for the free coinage of silver at the ratio of sixteen to one, and only the Second District opposed the resolution. Of the twenty-four Virginia delegates to the national convention in Chicago all except three were for free silver. Those three dissenters were Glennan of the *Virginian*, J. F. West of Suffolk, and Carter Glass of Lynchburg. Virginia's Senator Daniel was the convention keynoter and shouted for free silver. That did not keep Glennan from opposing the free silver plank of the platform. But when Bryan was nominated new factors came into play.

The newspapers in Norfolk reported these events at great length and with color and excitement. They had done well by the earlier Republican National Convention, the *Virginian* devoting nine columns to it one day. For the Democratic convention the *Pilot* used its entire front page once and nearly as much every day, and so did the other newspapers. Bryan's "cross of gold" speech appeared in detail. "As if by the magic touch of a wand," the Associated Press report read, "delegation after delegation arose in solid phalanx and gave vent to the most enthusiastic demonstration in honor of the Nebraska orator. Everybody stood up, even the eastern men, who at first were disposed to remain in their seats. Deafening cheers rent the air."

But the Bryan-free silver victory threw the *Virginian*'s editorial writers, left at home while the editor was far away in Chicago, into a quandary. The *Virginian* had opposed all these developments. Yet it was Democratic. What to do now? At first, this:

> Bryan's nomination was a popular uprising. It was a revolution as to old leaders and old issues and is one of the most overwhelming surprises of the century. Up to his speech . . . he was looked upon as a merely remote possibility. The wonderful magic of his eloquence, however, captured the convention. . . . The victory was the most remarkable in the history of politics in the country, and it remains to be seen if this same great current of popularity will not carry him to the White House. . . . The platform is a radical one, yet it unquestionably represents the faith and views of the great mass of the Democracy. It plainly meets the issue. There is no straddle to it. The voter cannot fail to take one side or the other.

This appeared on July 11. On July 15, probably after Glennan had returned from Chicago, the *Virginian* tried again. A double-leaded editorial carried the head, "For Bryan and Sewall." It stressed the conviction that the Democratic convention was "unbossed" and explained that "there is greater danger to the country, its liberties, stability and credit by reason of the knowledge that the presidency is an office of barter and trade, than there is from a trial of a financial policy that may seriously injure the business of the country. The nation can never recuperate from the establishment of the one. The good sense of the people would speedily rescue it from the evil effects of the other. . . . The Virginian's position on the financial plank is well known, yet it does not hesitate to assert that there are two sides to the question."

By the end of the campaign the *Virginian* was "a sincere convert to the monetization of silver, and is in thorough accord with the Chicago platform. The conversion," it confessed, "was slow, but sure."

The *Public Ledger* had trouble, too. It disagreed with Bryan on money, but it would not turn anti-Democratic, and in the end it endorsed Bryan. It believed the party would return to what it called sound principles. The *Landmark's* anti-Bryan views were stronger. But it would not go Republican. The solution, it thought, was in the election of a Congress that would block the free silver program.

Norfolk voters were not so troubled. Bryan carried the city, though by less than two to one. The state vote was closer. Bryan's margin of victory was 20,000 in a vote of nearly 300,000. Gold Democrats in Virginia, with Governor O'Ferrall siding with them and former Governor Cameron campaigning for them, and some eminent Virginia Democrats refugeeing among them, polled only 2,200 votes.

But not even the 1896 campaign, for all that it gripped the country, could carry newspaper thoughts entirely away from their own problems and, for the long run, their own survival. Size was increasingly an issue, especially when some newspapers—the *Landmark*, the *Public Ledger*, and the *Dispatch*—were limited by their presses to four pages and therefore preached the virtues of compactness and the evils of multi-page editions, whereas the *Virginian* and the *Pilot* exploited their larger facilities. The *Public Ledger* reprinted in 1892 some reflections of the Petersburg *Index-Appeal* that "the tendency of newspapers in metropolitan centers is to such enormous proportions that readers scarcely get beyond a superficial knowledge of their contents gleaned from headlines." Full-column advertisements in the *Index-Appeal*, that newspaper said, were "not intended as profit-yielders but as space fillers." It thought that the *Public Ledger* "seems to sustain our view. . . . Big pages, big type, big advertisements . . . deceive only the ignorant and unthinking."

Five years later, in August, 1897, the Richmond *Times* commented that "in some respects it [the *Public Ledger*] is the most remarkable newspaper in the country. It has never grown an inch since it was born, but it always prints the news and is always clean and high-toned in its editorial content. . . ." That moved the *Public Ledger* to talk about itself:

> A great many people have suggested that the paper should be enlarged. To all such suggestions we have uniformly replied that nothing would give us greater pleasure than to enlarge the paper to meet the needs of the advertising public, but that we thought it much better to be in position to control our advertising space than for advertisers to dictate the prices they should pay. Scores of times we have been told by our advertisers that our prices were greater than the numerous dead ventures that have essayed to fill the afternoon field during the last 20 years. Our invariable reply has been that we did not regulate our prices by those established in other papers. . . . We have always held that quality rather than quantity should be considered in the makeup of a newspaper, and, so holding, we shall continue to give the latest local, state and general news in the same manner as before.

Another five years would pass before the *Public Ledger* abandoned this policy (in September, 1902) and bought a new press and other equipment that enabled it to go above four pages. It moved to new quarters in December, 1897, an event that would have caused Glennan's *Virginian* to publish a special edition. But the *Public Ledger* of Fiveash and Edwards was content to celebrate the change in these lines and no more: "The office of the Public Ledger has been removed from 36 Bank Street to 41 City Hall Avenue, opposite Armory hall, where in the future all business appertaining to the paper will be conducted."

This attitude was only a little more restrained than that of the *Landmark*. From 1890 its four pages had been printed on paper much larger than its contemporaries used. Not only were the pages deeper, but their nine columns were more than other newspapers had. The town, especially newspaper men, joshed that the *Landmark* was printed on "bed sheets" or "blanket sheets," and eventually the *Landmark* itself learned to like the terms. But a new Potter perfecting press, bought in 1897 for $3,160, lifted the *Landmark* into the more-than-four-pages group.

The *Dispatch* added its regret at seeing "some of the state papers enlarging in form and filling up much of the increased space with 'plate matter'. . . . Plate matter is prepared in some distant city and sent to all newspapers which use it without allowing them much opportunity for selection. The matter is often as suitable for Minnesota's

Norwegians as for Virginia merchants—and is alike unsuitable for either. . . ."

None of this deterred either the *Pilot* or the *Virginian*. The *Pilot* under Grandy was full of life. It even cheered for Norfolk and Portsmouth's seven-newspaper congestion. "So much more to the honor of Norfolk and Portsmouth," it sang. "And we trust they may all live and prosper." As for itself, it did not hesitate to run a streamer headline across all columns of its front page in March, 1897: "500 NEW SUBSCRIBERS ADDED LAST MONTH." In that same month, it announced that it would publish 12 pages daily. On a Sunday in April it had 16 pages, and a week later (aided by a real estate and building section) 24 pages. Two days later it ran a box on its front page listing its columns on April 23 as 144 against the *Virginian*'s 88 and the *Landmark*'s 36; and of its 144 columns 89 were in advertisements. In June it published a special summer resort section.

All this was strong competition for the *Virginian*. But that newspaper made the most of its opening of a two-story annex on Plume Street (which the perky *Dispatch* had reported six months earlier that the *Virginian* would build) for its news department, composing room, press and engine quarters, paper storage, and mailing areas. The business office remained at the corner of Main and Commerce Streets. The annex provided more space for a new Hoe press in particular, but for other departments too. As on Main Street, Glennan used first-floor space for stores rented to others.

And as always Glennan celebrated, this time in twenty pages. The principal head struck the keynote: "OUR NEW BUILDING—Elegant Establishment at Which the Virginian is Printed." And as always the special edition called the roll of employees, from managers, editors, and foremen down to "Master William W. Wellman," who brought in dispatches from Western Union, and to "Eddie and 'Double' King" of the mailing room. Nor did the *Virginian* forget its past. It was approaching its thirty-second anniversary, and as the dean of newspapers in Norfolk it liked to review and commend its attitudes and accomplishments.

These rivalries did not prevent Norfolk newspapers from uniting when, in April, 1897, the city councils, more to warn against journalistic independence than to enlarge municipal revenue, levied a license tax on newspapers, $100 a year for morning newspapers, $50.00 for afternoon newspapers, and $25.00 for other publications. The different levels of taxation reflected roughly the judgment in the late 1890's of the relative position of morning and afternoon newspapers.

This constitutionally dubious assumption of taxing authority brought the newspapers up fighting. They had assumed that the Virginia Bill of Rights shielded the press from governmental licensing which, in the hands of hostile government, obviously could destroy the press. They relied especially on George Mason's words in Article I, Section XII: "The freedom of the press is one of the great bulwarks of liberty, and can never be restrained but by despotic governments; and any citizen may speak, write and publish his sentiments on all subjects, being responsible for all abuse of that right."

In the long, hard, up-and-down fight that followed, the *Pilot* took the lead. It attacked again and again, with vigor as well as persistence, and often in headlong language. This was Grandy and Elam in action. The spirit was reflected in an editorial of May 29 called "The Press Muzzler" which declared that "if the free press of Virginia can be muzzled, nothing better adapted to that purpose can be discovered or applied than the license tax just imposed on the newspapers of Norfolk by an ordinance of our city councils."

Judge R. R. Prentis, of the Circuit Court, issued a temporary injunction in May of 1897 and made it permanent in December, holding that the city could not impose a license tax on any business or occupation not taxed by the state. This decision limited taxes on other businesses and occupations to such an extent that the city appealed.

In January of 1898 the Virginia Supreme Court of Appeals declared that "a tax imposed upon the business of publishing a newspaper is not an abridgement of the freedom of the press. The guarantees of the Constitution and the Bill of Rights in favor of the freedom of the press, freedom of speech and personal liberty were never intended to restrict the right of taxation. If these guarantees did restrict the right of taxation, the government would soon be insolvent and powerless to furnish the protection claimed." But the court added that the city had a right to impose such taxes "except only as may be limited by the laws of the state."

The last clause appeared to the newspapers to make an appeal unnecessary because it pointed to a removal of the danger by state legislation. Within a month the General Assembly approved, and Governor J. Hoge Tyler signed, a bill that took away from the city councils and county supervisors any right they may have had to require publishers to pay a license tax in order to publish a newspaper.

For practical purposes this was sufficient, and the satisfaction among newspapers of the state for the fight the Norfolk newspapers had led was strong. The protection of the state against efforts of local governments to impose a newspaper license has remained ever since, though broadened in language to include "operating or conducting any radio or television broadcasting station or service."

The *Landmark* of February 27, 1898, reporting Governor Tyler's signing the bill, wound up the hard fight with this item of news:

> An interesting little story attaches to the approval of the bill, which was taken to the governor by Mr. Bland [Delegate Charles T. Bland, of Portsmouth, who introduced the bill in the House]. The delegate bore in his hand, a very handsome pen sent him for the purpose by Mr. Albert H. Grandy, owner of the Norfolk Pilot, who drew the bill. The pen is a very handsome one with silver holder and pearl staff on which is engraved "Freedom of the Press." The governor said he would cherish the pen as a memento of the occasion.

Such evidence of the rise of the *Pilot* had even firmer basis than leadership in the license fight might suggest. The most intense newspaper competition in Norfolk was between the old, large, and seemingly solid *Virginian* and the new, vigorous, and ambitious *Pilot*. The *Landmark* operated on another level, going its individual way, imbuing its news reports and editorials with touches of the old Hope spirit and the new Nottingham practicality, less aggressive, a little old-fashioned, but tenacious, competent, much liked, and regularly though not brilliantly profitable.

The *Virginian* and the *Pilot* were the initiators, the pushers, the promoters, the better equipped to do things in bigger ways. But when each was determined to gain and hold the lead, no matter the cost, the rivalry of the two in a city that could not support this pace was a deadly affair. Both had undertaken expensive developments and were in debt.

Some evidence of strain appears to be suggested by the change in the legal status of the *Virginian*. Prior to September 4, 1897, Glennan's name—printed as he liked to limit it: M. Glennan—appeared regularly as owner at the editorial masthead. Thereafter the name came down. In October a charter for the Virginian Company established a corporate owner, and from October 23 the company's name appeared at the editorial masthead.

Glennan was president of the new company. James E. Allen, a brother-in-law, without newspaper experience, was vice president and treasurer. J. Arnold Dalby, a veteran newspaper man recently assistant editor of the *Virginian*, was secretary. All these were directors, and so were Marcellus Miller and Joseph M. Clark, who were not actively associated with the operation of the *Virginian* but were business men and friends of Glennan. The authorized capital stock of the company was not less than $5,000 or more than $25,000.

This move involved no change in the operating status of the newspaper. No new personality emerged. Glennan was still the chief executive and the chief editor. Some outside evidence suggests it was a protective step. A little later Glennan transferred nearly all his stock to his wife, Mary Elizabeth Keville Glennan. That he was under financial pressure seems plain. The costs of newspaper publishing had risen steeply. The expenditures for the *Virginian*'s recent annex, although falling technically on the newspaper, fell also on him as the owner. A few months later the *Virginian*'s debts were reported at $18,000.

Glennan may have been strained also by his large interest in the Gladstone Hotel, a four-story structure at East Main and Nebraska Streets, which had opened in 1891, but was undergoing managerial and leasing changes in 1897. A new home which Glennan began to build late in 1896 in the Ghent section of Norfolk may have added a financial burden. There is also the possibility that Glennan was not in good health.

Whatever the reasons, Glennan, still in his early fifties, was ready to merge with the *Pilot* on terms that placed the *Pilot* and Grandy on top in a corporate and controlling sense and relegated the *Virginian* and Glennan to second place—a hard and bitter blow, beyond question, for a man of Glennan's personal pride and his regard for successful accomplishment.

The circumstances testify also to the revolution Grandy and his associates had wrought with the *Pilot*. Within less than fifteen months after taking hold of a newspaper only a year and a half out of bankruptcy, and not in good repute, they were capable of playing the dominant role in a merger with the oldest and largest of the newspapers of Norfolk.

The stockholders of the two publishing companies agreed on March 24, 1898, to terms of consolidation effective on March 31—a document covering thirty pages in the minute book of the new corporation and including remarkable details. The new company was called the Virginian and Pilot Publishing Company, and the new newspaper was called the *Virginian and Pilot*. Eleven months later this name was changed (February 21, 1899) to *The Virginian-Pilot*. The name of the publishing company was not changed at this time. It had a capital stock of $30,000 and three hundred shares.

Of the 300 shares Grandy held 151, a majority in his own name. Starke had 14, Shelton and Shultice 4 each, and W. S. Wilkinson, bookkeeper and collector for the *Pilot*, 3 shares—a total of 176 shares. On the *Virginian* side Mrs. Glennan held 112 shares and Glennan himself had 3. Allen, Glennan's brother-in-law, had 4, as did D. F. Donovan, a Norfolk business man and a friend of Glennan. Marcellus Miller and Joseph M. Clark had one share each. The number of shares held by members of the old *Virginian* group thus was 124. This represented about 41 per cent of the whole, while the former *Pilot* stockholders held slightly above 58 per cent. Grandy's position obviously was commanding.

Officers elected for the first year were Grandy, president; Glennan, vice president; Wilkinson, treasurer; Allen, secretary. Besides Grandy, Glennan, and Allen, the directors were Starke, Shelton, Shultice, and Donovan. Of the seven directors four came from the *Pilot* side.

The numerous articles of agreement included broad principles of policy, such as a promise "to support measures and policy of the National Democratic party, in accordance with the National Democratic platform adopted at Chicago, 1896," thereby tying the new newspaper to Bryan and free silver, and another promise "to maintain absolute freedom and independence from all factions, cliques, rings, machines and bosses, and at all times to stand openly, vigorously and fiercely against all public wrongs of every nature," which suggests the mind and pen of Elam. One of the purposes agreed upon was "to have fewer elections, if possible." More specific details included these:

That the offices for the first year would be those of the old Pilot, City Hall Avenue.

That the directors would appoint Glennan manager of the new company with a salary of $2,500 and would continue him in this position for three years if his services were satisfactory.

That Keville Glennan, a son of Michael Glennan, would be employed when he left college "if M. Glennan should desire him to be so employed and the board of directors shall consent thereto."

That the *Virginian's* debt was recognized as being $18,000 and the *Pilot's* $12,000; that from $6,000 to $10,000 probably would be needed to meet operating expenses; and that this would be supplied as a loan by Grandy at 6 per cent interest if it could not be obtained by other borrowing.

That "should the private creditors of M. Glennan seek to set aside the transfer made by M. Glennan to the Virginian Company," the

Glennans would hold the new company "harmless and free from such claims."

That twenty-six employees of the old companies, listed by names and occupations, would be retained as employees of the new company. The list not only included Elam as editor but extended to a helper in stereotyping and two clerks in the mailing room. Roughly the division of old *Virginian* and old *Pilot* men retained was half and half. More of the mechanical men came from the *Virginian*. A good many employees must have been dropped.

The *Landmark*, which was almost certain to be affected more by the consolidation than other newspapers, greeted the news of the consolidation with a cheer. Its long-held views that Norfolk had too many newspapers, expressed repeatedly, notably in the middle 1880's, had received now a kind of proof. "The soundest business considerations induced the consolidation," it proclaimed the day after it went into effect. It continued:

> Experienced newspaper men wondered at the existence of three morning dailies in a field so small as this, and declared that such a state of affairs could not continue. Too many newspapers in a city are to the injury of all concerned. The papers themselves suffer and the public suffers in consequence, because the papers are not able to give the service that can be given when normal conditions prevail. It is decidedly in the interest of the newspaper-reading public of this section, as well as in the interest of the newspapers themselves, that there have ceased to be three morning newspapers in Norfolk. . . .
>
> Baltimore, a city of 600,000, has but four papers in all, morning and evening. Washington, with 250,000 population, has two morning and two evening papers. Richmond, with 100,000, has two morning and one evening daily, the State having discontinued publication. In New Orleans, whose population must be 300,000, there are only two morning and two evening papers.[1]

One part of the agreement between the *Pilot* and the *Virginian* was that no officer should receive any compensation for his services without the approval of the stockholders. At the start Grandy did not receive any salary as president. Relations between him and Glennan appear to have deteriorated during the first year. When the stockholders held their second meeting, February 21, 1899, a new bylaw proposed was that the rights and duties of the vice president—Glennan was being continued as vice president and was reelected as man-

1. The 1900 census credited Baltimore with a population of 508,957; Washington, 278,718; New Orleans, 287,104; Richmond, 85,050.

ager—should be "only such rights and duties as the general laws of the state confer upon the office of vice president of a joint stock company." No further explanation appears of a seeming attempt to restrain Glennan.

At the same meeting a resolution was offered but on Glennan's motion was laid over until another meeting that was scheduled for April, 1899. The resolution read:

> Whereas, Mr. A. H. Grandy has devoted a very large portion of his time and personal attention to the business of the Virginian & Pilot Publishing Company and largely to his judgment and work is due the success of the paper,
>
> And whereas he has been working for the paper a long time without any pay for his services because the company could not afford to pay him anything until now,
>
> Therefore, be it resolved that Mr. A. H. Grandy, in addition to his office as president, be and is hereby elected general manager of the Virginian & Pilot Publishing Company, and that he be paid a salary of $30 a week for the year commencing March 31, 1899, and ending March 31, 1900.

But if there was a Grandy-Glennan test in this resolution, it did not reach the testing ground. Glennan did not attend another meeting. He died March 3, 1899. The previous Sunday he suffered (in the *Virginian-Pilot*'s words) "an attack of vertigo" while attending mass at Sacred Heart Catholic Church and lingered only five days. He was fifty-five years old.

"Too much cannot be said of the indomitable spirit which carried Mr. Glennan to the front," the *Landmark* commented later. "As a boy, without resources or advantages, except his quick wit and his native energy, he determined to rise. That never-dying spark of ambition which has done so much for the world by lighting the way over hardships and obstacles in early life was in him." The *Public Ledger* pointed out correctly that "in newspaper circles especially will the absence of his familiar form and kindly nature be regretted."

The historical record sustains such judgments. For thirty-two years from the January day in 1867 when he took command of the barely breathing *Virginian* until his death in 1899 Glennan played a vital role in the newspaper drama of Norfolk, and of his state, and of his times. No one could follow the record of these pages without realizing often the importance of his influence, the humanity of his Irish nature, and the "indomitable spirit" to which his long-time rival paid just tribute.

In three days after Glennan's death Grandy was elected general manager as well as president, at a salary of $2,500 a year (the same as Glennan's had been as manager). Wilkinson's salary as treasurer went up at the same time from $900 to $1,200, and a month later Wilkinson was elected to the board for the place left vacant by Glennan's death. Whatever the old *Virginian* influence had amounted to in the personnel of command, it was weakening there, though much of it remained in the personality and spirit of the *Virginian-Pilot*.

The new *Virginian-Pilot* had done well in its first year—"a gratifying success," in its own words. The price of single copies had gone up to three cents but for a year's subscription remained at $5.00. It was publishing twelve pages regularly, seven columns to the page, and sixteen and twenty pages on Sundays, but no Monday edition. The *Landmark* held generally to eight pages, the *Public Ledger* and the *Dispatch* to four. The *Virginian-Pilot* was using more pictures and was experimenting in several directions, at the moment with a home-study course.

Its advertisement in the 1899 Norfolk Directory claimed that the *Virginian-Pilot*'s circulation exceeded that of all other daily newspapers in Norfolk combined; that its city circulation was 50 per cent larger than that of any other newspaper; that its out-of-town circulation was more than that of all other Norfolk daily newspapers combined; that it was carrying the largest amount of advertising and had the greatest number of advertisers in Virginia with the exception of the Sunday edition of one Richmond newspaper (not identified); and that it had the largest number of local news reporters among the Norfolk daily newspapers, nearly twice as many as any other.

Something beside their own efforts had helped Norfolk newspapers grow in more ways than in sheer size. The 1898 merger of the *Virginian* and the *Pilot* came at almost the same time as the explosion that sank the *Maine*. The Spanish-American War coincided with the first year of the *Virginian-Pilot*. Like all other American wars, it had immediate and large effects on Norfolk.

The war forced the Navy Yard in Portsmouth to increase sharply its work, including—for a single example—the fitting out of the collier *Merrimac* for Richmond Pearson Hobson to sink in his effort to block the channel from Santiago to the sea. When the Newport News Shipbuilding and Drydock Company launched the battleships *Kearsarge* and *Kentucky* a month before the declaration of war, tension was high and the watching crowd numbered twenty thousand. Schley's flying squadron waited on the alert in Hampton Roads until its orders came to sail out between the Virginia Capes for an engagement with destiny off Santiago. The Spanish admiral, Cervera, victim of that engagement, after being taken as a prisoner to Annapolis, was permitted to sail down Chesapeake Bay to Norfolk and especially to Portsmouth, where he visited wounded Spanish prisoners in the Naval Hospital there. Later he paid a second visit to the area.

Such events, close at hand, heightened the sense of intimacy with a war that was lifting emotions to heights not often reached. The newspapers discovered a demand for news, and a demand for getting news fast, that they had never before faced so long and so insistently. Yet the old habits and practices held on hard. At first it was not the older and larger newspapers but the new *Dispatch*, very eager to prove itself in crisis, that plunged into war reporting with the greatest enthusiasm.

After the *Dispatch* had beaten the town with news of Dewey's victory at Manila Bay, it proclaimed that this was not strange, for "the Dispatch has got the habit of being ahead," and further:

> This is precisely what happened yesterday morning when the Dispatch came out at 9 o'clock with as much of the news of the battle of Manila as was known at that time. Afterward another edition told the entire story in detail.
>
> No afternoon paper in Norfolk ever performed such a feat before. Until the Dispatch took its place among the institutions here afternoon newspapers had but one edition, and these were not made up and headlined after modern methods. Now the Dispatch has introduced methods which are being followed more or less correctly by all the Norfolk papers. . . .

Near the end of the war the *Landmark* could conclude that "few newspapers have made anything out of this war. Nearly all have lost." Businessmen had been cautious during the war. Publishing costs were up. The Associated Press had raised assessments 25 per cent. But in a war that has been called a newspapers' war, chiefly because of the newspaper exploitation by the Hearst-Pulitzer rivalry in New York, something had been learned about the virtues of speed. More than any other Norfolk newspaper, the brash young *Dispatch* had taught that lesson. It did not stop there. In a war full of tragic mistakes and incompetencies, when the current emphasis was on Spanish failures, the youthful *Dispatch* hit this high note:

"Let's not laugh at Spanish incompetency. Let's cure our own!"

THE GOOD QUALITIES OF THE ENTERPRISING AND CHEERFUL DISPATCH IN the afternoon could not overcome all the difficulties of its fragile economic structure and did not make it a threat to the *Virginian-Pilot*.

That newspaper, with nearly twice as much circulation as either ancestor had, could bid strongly for more advertising, and it got more. Its editors felt unleashed. In two years its stockholders raised Grandy's salary as general manager from $2,500 to $5,000, a big jump and a good salary in 1900. At the same meeting they raised Wilkinson, the treasurer, and Turner, the mechanical superintendent who that year became advertising manager too, from $1,200 to $1,500. When the younger Starke was elected secretary to succeed Allen, Glennan's brother-in-law, the Glennan influence continued to fade though Allen remained on the board.

In two more years the growth was even more conspicuous. The stockholders learned in April, 1902, that the company had not only paid the $30,000 debt with which it began business in 1898 but had accumulated $45,000 in surplus. They voted a 150 per cent stock dividend, raising the capital to $75,000, with 750 shares at a par of $100.

A year later (February, 1902) the stockholders voted to provide $30.00 monthly "in the nature of a pension" for James A. Pugh, who had "become incapacitated by reason of natural infirmities." Pugh had been associate editor of the *Pilot* and city editor of the *Virginian*. This is the first known instance in Norfolk of a newspaper pension.

The biggest publishing effort of the newspaper in those early years was its Twentieth Century Edition of June 8, 1900. It included the twelve pages of a normal edition plus a supplement of sixty-eight pages in eight sections. Twenty-five thousand copies were distributed "not only to every household in Norfolk and vicinity, but also," the *Virginian-Pilot* said, "to the Eastern Shore, Middle and Eastern North

Carolina and Southeastern Virginia, all over the United States and to many foreign countries."

This was the largest special edition that had ever been published in Norfolk. It told much about local and state governments, businesses of many kinds and the men who managed them, and Norfolk history. The population increase in the Norfolk, Portsmouth, and Berkley areas it put at 100 per cent during the past ten years, 200 per cent in the past twenty years. For itself the *Virginian-Pilot* described its Hoe double newspaper perfecting press, its five Mergenthaler linotype machines, "its full stereotyping plant," and other "paraphernalia . . . representing an outlay of $45,000."

The *Virginian-Pilot* was especially proud of a citation from *Printer's Ink*. That trade publication of good repute credited it with giving the best service in proportion to the price charged for advertising space among all newspapers east of the Mississippi River and south of the San Francisco-St. Louis-Cincinnati-Philadelphia line. *Printer's Ink* credited only one other newspaper, the Los Angeles *Times*, with doing better in the entire region south of this line.

But just when the *Virginian-Pilot* was getting on its feet in a period of much promise it lost its editor. Colonel Elam died on February 24, 1900, at the age of sixty-four. Never in robust health, weakened by heart attacks in recent years, he relented no whit in his characteristic pungency until his final three weeks. Then he went back to his old home in Louisa County and quietly died.

Though Elam's judgment might be challenged on occasion, the power and picturesqueness of his language excited readers. A special value for the *Virginian-Pilot* was the living proof which his strikingly different personality and philosophy offered that the Sam Small era belonged to a dead past. Elam kept up his vigorous advocacy almost to the last: for the popular election of United States senators, for primaries to nominate legislators, for Governor J. Hoge Tyler instead of Senator Thomas S. Martin for the Senate—and was beaten on all three counts. But Elam, independent of spirit and ahead of his time in many respects, was often on the losing side.

The choice of a new editor was distinctly unusual. To succeed this veteran of a thousand battles, steeped in Virginia politics, Grandy and his associates turned to a twenty-eight-year-old North Carolinian then with the Raleigh *News and Observer*, admired by those at close hand but just beginning to impress others at a distance.

This was Charles Pinckney Sapp. Born in Cabarrus County near Charlotte, he was an excellent student at Wake Forest College, where

Virginian-Pilot.
AND
THE NORFOLK LANDMARK.

VOL. LXI. NO. 2. NORFOLK, VA., WEDNESDAY, JANUARY 2, 1918. TEN PAGES. THREE CENTS PER COPY.

NORFOLK SWEPT BY GREATEST FIRE IN ITS HISTORY
PROPERTY WORTH $2,000,000 REDUCED TO ASHES

WEATHER FORECAST

Virginian-Pilot
AND
THE NORFOLK LANDMARK

NET CIRCULATION
Month of May
Average Daily, 50,152
Sunday, 50,444
No Duplication

VOL. CXXI. NO. 69 NORFOLK, VIRGINIA, MONDAY, JUNE 8, 1931 THREE CENTS PER COPY

$3,000,000 FIRE CHECKED

STORM LOSS $2,000,000

NORFOLK LEDGER-DISPATCH

HOME
★ EDITION ★

VOL. CXV.—No. 23 NORFOLK, VA., WEDNESDAY AFTERNOON, AUGUST 23, 1933 14 PAGES—PRICE THREE CENTS

THREE ARE ELECTROCUTED; ONE DROWNS

Mostly Fair
Gales Subside
High 43, Low 27
N, 15-25 m.p.h.
(Details, Page 2)

The Virginian-Pilot

Woman Wasn't
Left Alone;
Stork Arrived
By Telephone
(Page 45)

7th Year. No. 107 Telephone (Norfolk) MAdison 5-1411 Norfolk, Portsmouth, South Norfolk, Virginia, Thursday, March 8, 1962 60 Pages Price Five Cents

Waves break over concrete boardwalk at 15th Street beside wooden Virginia Beach Fishing Pier, end of which (right) has been severed by storm.

Storm Pounds Coast Into Ruins

Great fires, tropical hurricanes, Atlantic northeasters—natural disasters
through the years have supplied their share of both salt water
and printer's ink.

Norfolk's East Main Street, once famous among seafaring men the world over, is no more. The bars, tattoo parlors, and burlesque houses were leveled during the city's downtown redevelopment, and huge office buildings and an ultra-modern civic center have risen to replace them.

he wrote and spoke effectively, and briefly was a teacher in North Carolina and Kentucky. Politics must have excited him early. Certainly William Jennings Bryan did. Sapp made speeches for his hero in 1896. But the young man was not narrowly partisan. He knew well and admired the able Republican, Jeter C. Pritchard, who was elected a United States senator from North Carolina and later sat on the United States Circuit Court of Appeals. Tall, slender, dark of hair and eyes, very much in earnest, young Sapp had the look of a fighter.

Grandy brought Sapp to Norfolk in March of 1900, a few weeks after Elam's death. He consulted his stockholders about whether the company should pay a new editor as much as $4,000 a year, "the amount being so much in excess," as the report of the stockholders' meeting put it, "of the amount formerly paid by the company"—presumably to the older and better known Elam. Whether Sapp was hard to get or Grandy was especially anxious to get him is not clear. But $4,000 was more than most newspaper editors in Southern cities with less than fifty thousand population received in 1900. The stockholders advised Grandy to pay that amount if necessary, but the records do not show whether it was.

By April 1 Sapp was the editor. He went into action quickly, and the city learned that the *Virginian-Pilot* had another editor with strong convictions who would dig into public affairs persistently and write boldly. Within a few months he was deeply engaged in a controversy over telephone rates.

Norfolk still had two telephone companies, commonly held to be competitive: the Southern Bell, affiliated with the American Bell Telephone Company, which became the American Telephone and Telegraph Company, and the Southern States Telephone Company of Baltimore. Southern Bell startled Norfolk in August of 1900 by doubling its rates, office telephones going up from $30.00 to $60.00 a year and home phones from $18.00 to $36.00. Most Norfolk people had thought the city's franchises with the two companies prevented abrupt increase of this steepness.

When Southern States did not protest, the *Virginian-Pilot* did. It hammered away on such questions as whether Norfolk had any protection against extortionate rates, whether a virtual monopoly existed, and whether the councils would ever act. "Questions Southern Bell Has Not Answered," "Extortion by 'Phone Trust," and "Dodge of Dummy Competitor" were heads over *Virginian-Pilot* articles that pointed to the attitude and argument.

The city councils began to investigate, and the *Virginian-Pilot* began interviewing councilmen and recording their opinions. This count showed a majority in favor of stricter control of rates. But on the test twelve councilmen went the other way. The *Virginian-Pilot* immediately dubbed them "The Floppers." It published their names repeatedly and pushed them for explanations.

The president of the Common Council, J. Frank East, a "Flopper" in the newspaper's descriptive, warned Grandy that he would hold him personally responsible for "anything appearing in the columns of the Virginian-Pilot which reflects upon me in any respect whatsoever." But he received in reply a statement that "the Virginian-Pilot will criticise Mr. East's actions as a public official at any time it thinks the public interest demands it." And since Mr. East had denied giving an interview that appeared in the *Virginian-Pilot,* the newspaper countered with statements from W. S. Foote, city editor, Turner, the advertising director and mechanical superintendent, and Keville Glennan, the son of Michael, who now was a reporter, that all three had been present when Mr. East did give the interview.

In this controversy the whole *Virginian-Pilot* organization was involved. The newspaper announced that it was giving up its Southern Bell telephone connection. Trying to show the scope and depth of popular feeling, it sent reporters out to interview numerous citizens. Some citizens did not wish to comment, and when the reporters listed them as remaining silent, they complained. Grandy consulted the directors, although this would seem an issue to be settled without going to such a high appellate court. The directors agreed with the protesters, and thereafter their names were not printed. But the directors authorized Grandy, if the councils failed to act effectively in protecting the public, to call on business men for financial aid in compelling action through state courts, and to institute such proceedings.

But the time had not come. Southern Bell and Southern States continued as separate companies, presumably competitive, though not vigorously so, for another ten years until, in 1910, the two merged into one under a state regulatory system designed to prevent monopolistic abuses. The *Virginian-Pilot* remained much concerned about these matters.

Late 1900 brought another young man to Norfolk, not only as editor but as owner and publisher too. The *Dispatch* was managing to survive only because its investment, overhead, and operating costs were remarkably low. In 1897 it had moved to 99 Plume Street. In 1899, when a Negro newspaper, the *Daily Record,* left Norfolk for

Newport News after two years of publishing, the *Dispatch* set up an additional office on East Bute Street, near the homes of many Negroes, for the handling of news items, advertisements, and job printing orders from them—an unusual effort to attract business from a segment of the population on which other newspapers did not count heavily. But the *Dispatch*'s hard times continued.

The strain was so severe that Pete Vail cut his connection. A series of printers took up the command, including H. T. Plummer as treasurer and H. T. Hurtt as secretary and general manager. V. C. Dalby, at various times associated with the *Labor Advocate* and brother of an experienced newspaper man, J. Arnold Dalby, was advertising manager earlier. Charles I. Stengle was president at one time, and H. Morton Page secretary and general manager. The parade of doctors was evidence of the *Dispatch*'s anemia, and so was its appearance. Rumors about its future spread through Norfolk.

The *Virginian-Pilot* reported in September, 1900, that Norfolk Republicans were buying the newspaper. "Fake, pure and simple," the *Dispatch* declared that afternoon. But a sale of another sort was being negotiated.

"With today's issue the editorial and business management of the Norfolk Dispatch passes into new hands," the *Dispatch* announced on September 24. As sometimes happened in those years, odd though it seems, the *Dispatch* did not say whose were the new hands. A day later the Portsmouth *Star* gave a name to the new commander of the *Dispatch*, and a day after that (September 26) the *Dispatch* itself announced the name by the roundabout method of reprinting what the *Star* had published—thus, "Mr. James M. Thomson, formerly of Washington, D. C., has assumed charge of the Norfolk Dispatch. He will make many improvements in the plant. Mr. Thomson is a newspaper man of experience and will devote his best efforts to make the Dispatch a first-class publication. PORTSMOUTH STAR."

This introduction of Thomson did no justice to any of his attributes unless it was his modesty. He was a twenty-two-year-old youngster with little experience of any kind, but with a passion to edit and publish his own newspaper. He would like to write most of it too. Born near the Potomac River in Jefferson County, West Virginia, the son of a physician, he graduated from the Johns Hopkins University and studied law in an office in Harrisonburg in the Valley of Virginia. For six months he worked for the Washington *Post* and then decided that he must have a newspaper of his own. A circulation man of the *Post* suggested that Norfolk was the place to look for one.

The two went together. They found Hurtt and Plummer willing —even eager—to sell. But when the circulation man saw the Dispatch plant, he lost interest. Thomson held on. Years later[1] he said he paid $5.00 to Plummer and Hurtt for an option and undertook to pay the full price of $1,200 in one year. Plummer, who had been operating the linotype machine, left town the next day. Thomson recalled his own first look around: "I had some sense of sanitation and hired a colored man to clean up the tobacco juice and dirt in the composing room. We had an old flatbed press and printed a four-page paper at first, using the few columns of type from the one linotype and filling up with boiler plate [syndicated material that required no typesetting] and the advertising, which yielded a small revenue."

Total office sales of the *Dispatch* on the first day of the Thomson regime were (in Thomson's memory) 15 copies. The new business manager and editor opened a bank account, but he presented so little for deposit that after a few weeks the bank suggested he close the account. After that he paid employees and met bills with cash from his pocket. "The Old Dominion Paper Company, run by Robert Johnston, a very attractive man, sold me for cash sufficient newsprint for each day's operation when sent for by cart," Thomson remembered. The *Dispatch*'s Plume Street home had been rented from the *Virginian-Pilot*'s Grandy for $25.00 a month. "My landlord used to take an amused interest in talking with me and in following my gyrations with the *Dispatch*." His more immediate rival, the *Public Ledger*, "ran an excellent four-page paper. . . . Our personal relations were very pleasant, and I don't believe that at first they took my enterprise very seriously."

Inexperienced Thomson undoubtedly was. But some of those who did not take him seriously did not realize that he was essentially a practical man. Nor did his own refusal to take all things too seriously—he had a fine sense of humor—affect his own determination. There was a gaiety about him that was very attractive. He liked to stick a pin, not too deep, into the solemnities around him, and he could do so without offense. But he meant to do something with his newspaper, and in his pleasant and disarming way he did.

Thomson knew enough to produce better writing, editing, and makeup than his predecessors could present, and the *Dispatch* began to take on a more professional air. He knew he had to sell the newspaper against competition, and presently the *Dispatch* was on sale at six downtown locations. He knew he had to sell more advertising,

1. Interview with Joseph E. Shank, October 20, 1958.

and he tackled David Pender, then fighting hard to establish the grocery business which he built into the Pender pillar of Colonial Stores. Pender thought he could not afford to advertise. But when Thomson offered half a page in the *Dispatch* for $10.00, Pender tested it by giving five pounds of sugar to every customer who spent a dollar in the store. The device worked, and Thomson had a regular advertiser of importance. He believed the experiment had a long-range effect on both men.

Thomson knew he had to interest readers. So he plunged headlong into local subjects: water, streets, sidewalks, the appearance of the town. These were such old Norfolk problems that sometimes other newspapers forgot they too had once tackled them with ardor. "The condition of our streets, roadways and sidewalks is vile," the *Dispatch* announced with affable frankness. Few among its readers would fail to read more in order to see what under heaven the editor would say after that judgment. And once when a new filter plant had purified the drinking water, to the town's surprise and delight, the *Dispatch* commented thus:

> Only those who have imbibed the polluted waters of the James, such as our neighbors of Petersburg and Richmond, or those who have drunk from the filthy mud and offal of the Potomac and Delaware, as our neighbors of Washington and Philadelphia, or those who have suffered from the political jobbery of Ramapo water schemes, as have the citizens of New York, are in a position to thoroughly appreciate the benefit of the present supply of pure water which the people of Norfolk enjoy.

Many years later Thomson thought that the *Dispatch*'s reports of the shooting of President McKinley at the Pan-American Exposition in Buffalo (September 6, 1901) and of his condition during the days that followed marked a turning point in the newspaper's history. At the climax he himself was a patient in St. Vincent's Hospital, ill with typhoid fever. He remembered:

> Our small and enthusiastic force issued extras and sold additional copies . . . during the week that he lived. . . . Just about daylight one morning . . . I heard someone crying a Dispatch extra on Church Street. When the nurse came in she told me that McKinley was dead. Our boys had gotten the story by a lucky break and close attention to duty.
> Up to that time the Dispatch circulation had amounted to only several hundred copies daily. When I left the hospital and returned to the office, it had grown to about 1,500 because

of the interest in the McKinley news. That was the real beginning of our competition with the better afternoon newspaper,
the Public Ledger.

The season of the *Dispatch*'s rebirth coincided with the 1900 presidential election. A self-proclaimed Democrat, it felt bound to support
Bryan on his second try, though not with enthusiasm. It found comfort in the Baltimore *Sun*'s reasoning, which it quoted, that McKinley
must be opposed because of "the Republican policy of territorial expansion and the stupendous growth of the so-called trusts."

The *Dispatch* produced an election extra at 11:00 p.m. announcing
a McKinley victory on the basis of returns obtained "by Bell long
distance telephone." But while the other newspapers engaged in
postelection analyses, generally critical of Bryan's economic theories
but unhappy about McKinley's imperialism, the *Dispatch* was not
seriously perturbed. It summed up:

> The American nation has survived a greater blow than the
> re-election of McKinley. Always remember that if things don't
> suit you that you have another whack four years from now.
> The country will be here when all its present leaders and you,
> too, are gone. And it will still be the greatest republic on the
> face of the earth. Rejoice in the fact that you are one of
> 76,000,000 Americans and that your man put up a good fight
> whether he won or not.

Norfolk was as much upset by its own Second District confusions.
In 1896 the local count gave the victory to a Norfolk Democrat,
W. A. Young, over his Republican opponent, Dr. Richard A. Wise, of
Williamsburg. But the House held that the election was scandalously
crooked. It unseated Young in April, 1898, and put Wise in his place.

In November, 1898, the two met again, and again the local count
was in favor of Young. But again the House ruled, in March, 1900,
that the election was shot through with fraud. It heaved Young out
and restored Wise, though this time by a hair's breadth and perhaps
even with a touch of partisanship. The Republican speaker's vote was
necessary to break a tie and produce the 131 to 130 vote of expulsion.

The storms and furies of these events split the district Democrats.
When they met in convention in 1900 in Newport News to nominate
a candidate, the delegates cast fifty-nine ballots without agreement.
But on the sixtieth ballot, in a tense moment, the rising Norfolk politician, Jimmy Trehy, led enough Norfolk delegates to the support of
Harry L. Maynard, of Portsmouth, to put him over. Maynard had no
trouble beating Wise in November, by seventeen thousand to nine

thousand. Another result was the elevation of Trehy, who had been elected court clerk in 1896 and again in 1900, into a political manager of increasing prestige.

Not entirely by coincidence, the election manipulations of the Democratic hierarchy that led to congressional rebukes were matched by new evidence of the return—though the withdrawal had never been a rout—of the wicked ways and ineffective law enforcement that had made possible the municipal revolution of 1894. The reformers could not regain power. The old arrogance was back. The saloons and the town's underworld were breeding new troubles.

There was no great surprise, in November of 1900, when Church Lewis, a saloon operator, and Tom Fogarty, a blacksmith, arguing in the Lewis saloon at Princess Anne Road and Chapel Street, drew their pistols and began blazing away. Lewis was seriously wounded, Fogarty was killed.

"A perfectly legitimate product of conditions that obtain in this town," the *Virginian-Pilot* described the killing, "and the real wonder is that this sort of thing is not more frequent. Vile liquor, and too much of it, tells the story." And on to this:

> In no city in this country perhaps are there more liquor saloons where . . . meaner whiskey can be bought. The city has sown dives and is reaping crime, as was to be expected.
>
> Not as a matter of piety, but of cold business, brakes should be put upon this all-night dispensing of liquor that would take the hair off a dog's back. It is carried too far and it is doing the city harm. . . . Some of these saloons, where murderous jags are handed out for a nickel, should be shut up.

Three days later Councilman T. S. Southgate broke the news to the councils that the New York "Journal of Society," as the *Town Topics* of the variously celebrated Colonel William d'Alton Mann designated itself, had published a study of crime statistics that established Norfolk as "the wickedest city in the country."

"The wickedest"!

Savannah, Georgia, and Lexington, Kentucky, were high among the wicked, but Norfolk was pronounced supreme. In comparison, the historic metropolitan cesspools of crime and vice, as they had been heralded over the ages, were relatively pure.

The least Norfolk could do, Southgate argued, was to investigate. City Attorney J. G. Tilton protested against "dignifying *Town Topics* by notice of this kind," but in vain. The tides of the superlative were running against him. "Wicked" might have been taken in stride.

"As evil as Omaha" had been heard before. But "wickedest" demanded an answer. The councils handed the issue to the Board of Police Commissioners, who, they took care to say, "under our charter are held largely responsible for enforcement of the law."

In the excitement that followed this Gotham exposure, one of those who did not lose his head was the editor of the *Dispatch*. He did look warily toward the *Virginian-Pilot* in fear that it was "beginning to break out in spots. . . . the Dispatch is very much afraid that if a word of friendly warning and advice is not given in time, the city may be forced to undergo the horrors of another of those terrible crusades which that sheet occasionally perpetrates on a long-suffering public." As for its own views, the *Dispatch* continued:

> Of course it is preposterous to say that Norfolk is the wickedest city in this country. As a matter of fact the people who really constitute Norfolk are among the most conservative, God-fearing and best citizens of the republic. Likewise they are careless and blind to their own and their city's interests to a degree.
>
> Disgusted with the success of some charlatans who cloaked their work under a gospel hood and afterwards ran amuck under the guise of reform, many of the members of this class of people have lost all interest in the politics of their own city. The soil of Norfolk is particularly fertile for the growth of corruption, because the profits from corrupt dealing can be so great here. The large floating population of a busy commercial center seeks diversion among many lines which are not good. The seafaring element in the city is very large, and the reputation of a seaport town is proverbial.
>
> So, the good, honest and sleepy citizens of the city let things run along until conditions are just about as wide open in Norfolk as they ever get in any city. . . . such a thing as closing any but the front door of a saloon on Sunday has been out of the question for some time past in Norfolk. . . . Gambling places are open at all hours and to all comers. . . . As for the lower forms of vice they are rather bold in this city. . . . there are a number of sections of Norfolk where it is not safe for a stranger to be seen at night. The vicinity of Church Lewis' saloon is one of the few in which it is not safe for a prosperous-looking stranger to be seen in the day time.
>
> The responsibility for the existing state of affairs rests solely with the people of Norfolk.

While the Board of Police Commissioners continued to investigate, an unidentified Norfolkian wrote to *Town Topics* with details to embellish its own picture of the town. *Town Topics* printed this letter, and the *Public Ledger* reprinted it in January, 1901. It included such statements as these:

> Things are more wide open than in any western city of which I have heard lately. There are generally a dozen poker games going at night in a fashionable hotel here. On Main Street about 40 gambling houses are open day and night and some of these places are joints in name only, for they are palaces. Roulette and other refinements are found and the tiger can be bucked in every form. . . . It is no uncommon thing for policemen in uniform to be found going into these places, among which there is cutthroat competition. . . .
>
> The City Council took up your publication. There are some gay boys in that body. Rumor says that some of them are interested in the gambling dens and palaces. . . . Partly as a result of your publication a wave of reform, not incited by any popular outcry, however, has been sweeping the city government, and things are much better. . . . Everybody in Norfolk carries a pistol and everybody seems satisfied. In fact, the city is growing at a wonderful rate, and under clean government would become, in a short while, a dangerous rival of Baltimore.

Among those who carried a pistol for a few months was Thomson himself. On arriving at Norfolk he found (as he recalled much later) so many men carrying pistols that he thought it was obligatory for him to follow the social custom. But in a few months he gave up his gun. He thought his temper was too quick, and he had rather be killed than kill. Thereafter he grew increasingly critical. In June of 1901 the *Dispatch* burst out:

> This reign of terror caused by pistol carriers should cease at once. . . . When a negro commits an offense the full penalty of the law is inflicted. The other day one was sentenced to 10 years in the penitentiary for drawing a pistol on an officer. The Dispatch makes no objection to this. The punishment is harsh but the crime was a serious one.
>
> On the other hand, three white men who have killed their man during the past year have been allowed to go free in Norfolk. The killings may all have been justifiable, accidental and permissible. . . . The pistol-carrying habit is the cause of many murders. It is a senseless, cowardly habit.

But Thomson found his resolution difficult to carry out. In April, 1902, a few days before a municipal election, the *Dispatch* published a series of articles, two of them under the heads, "Orgies Run Full Blast" and "Policy Playing Rife in Norfolk." One of the articles referred to N. B. Joynes, familiar to political and sporting circles, as having been nicknamed Boney Joynes because of the rolling of the bones in a room above his Church Street saloon. He was the well known Napoleon Bonaparte Joynes.

Infuriated by the reference, Joynes and his brother, W. L. Joynes, stalked into the *Dispatch* office, asked for Thomson, and inquired why he had let the reference stand. With that the war began. Fighting flowed out of the editor's private office, brought in the composing room foreman, the chief pressman, and two Joynes allies (Boney denied this later), and spread out into the street. Blacked eyes, lost teeth, swollen cheeks, injured shoulders, smashed hands, twisted necks, and numerous bruises were the chief wounds. The *Dispatch* offices looked like a battlefield—as indeed they were—on the day after the battle. Two Joyneses were convicted and fined.

This time Thomson considered that he did have reason to carry a pistol. Because he heard that Boney had threatened "to return and kill the whole Dispatch force from editor to office boy," he obtained pistol permits for himself and four men of the *Dispatch* staff. (Joynes denied any intention of going back.)

When the Board of Police Commissioners finished in March of 1901 its investigation of "the wickedest city in the country," it reported that *Town Topics'* conclusions rested on inaccuracies in relating population and arrests. With unmistakable pleasure the board included a New York *Herald* charge that for many crimes in New York the police did not bother to make arrests.

In short, the board concluded, Norfolk would be considered free of crime if its police made no arrests at all. "The fact that the number of arrests in Norfolk is large enough to attract attention is a tribute to the vigilance and efficiency of the police." Thus the board found itself deserving of the highest praise rather than the opposite kind of superlative. But the melody lingered on.

For in important aspects of law enforcement the Norfolk of the early 1900's was much like the Norfolk of the early 1890's—the pre-Sam Small days. Major issues in the mayoralty elections of 1900, 1902, 1904, 1908 (after the term had been lengthened to four years), and 1912 rose out of conflicts of reform elements and the professional political leadership, generally called "the ring," and its followers. But neither side produced an Old Si or a Parson Massey.

The chief personality was Dr. James G. Riddick, a physician who held the office of mayor so many of the dozen years that it could be called the Riddick Era. His champions apotheosized him at the start as a man of character, which he was. He quickly learned about politics, and sometimes he had support from one group of professionals, sometimes from a competing group. The newspapers split from election to election, but generally Riddick had the respect of most of them.

The era's chief political managers were the normally antagonistic but sometimes allied chieftains, W. W. Dey, the Billy Dey of those years, who was a Riddick supporter before some other politicians learned to be, and Jimmy Trehy, who sometimes worked in association with James E. Prince and sometimes did not. Trehy fought Riddick, favored Riddick, and fought Riddick again. Norfolk prohibitionists of the early 1900's had less influence than a decade earlier. But all over Virginia prohibitionists were rising in numbers and demands, because dissatisfaction with liquor problems was making more converts. Shrewdly practical and ruthless political leaders had not risen from their ranks, but they would.

Whatever the degree of Norfolk's wickedness it did not rest on addiction to the crime of lynching. The decades after the Civil War show many instances of violence and, in the early postwar years, clashes between whites and Negroes. But the files of Norfolk newspapers for the 1870's report few mob actions in the Southern states of the kind commonly identified as lynching. The number increased in the 1880's and rose sharply in the 1890's. As it did so, and because murdering by a mob often was dramatically brutal, sadistic, and agonizing, the reports themselves were dramatic and ran to great length.

In the editorial eye some of these lynchings seemed justified, generally on the ground that the victim was guilty and, in the rough estimates of the times, that justice was being done. But over the years the supposition that lynching was justified for this reason began to change—slowly, irregularly, and in varying degrees, depending on many factors.

When a mob forced its way into the Bedford jail in western Virginia in May, 1885, and lynched Hairston Terry (who almost certainly was insane), Norfolk's respected John Goode, a former congressman and newly appointed solicitor general of the United States, wrote to the family in words which the *Public Ledger* printed: "I will not trust myself to characterize the conduct of the misguided men who, under cover of darkness, took the unarmed and helpless boy from the custody of the law and hanged him from a tree like a dog." Thomas Whitehead, editor of the Lynchburg *Advance*, demanded the punishment of the "murderers," as he called them, but received a warning himself to keep quiet or he would get the same treatment. The Norfolk newspapers did not comment, but the lynching was big news and was so treated. The *Landmark's* headline was "SWIFT JUSTICE."

Nor did newspapers in Norfolk comment in November of the same year when a mob hanged a Negro in adjacent Princess Anne County. Four years later, in 1889, after a mob hanged a Negro accused of attacking a white woman in Accomack County on the Eastern Shore, the *Virginian's* headline was "DESERVEDLY LYNCHED." The *Landmark* added that "the public approves of the lynching." The following year a *Landmark* report of a lynching in Winton, North Carolina, was printed in this form:

> Kinch Freeman, the murderer of N. B. Adkins and mother, was found hanging in his cell at Winton, N.C., after 250 masked men had forced their way into the jail.
>
> He was a noted scoundrel and deserved all he received. There is no clue as to who the lynchers were. Everybody is rejoicing at Freeman's death.

But broader tragedies on a bigger stage could produce different judgments. In September of 1893 Roanoke police jailed a Negro on charge of robbing and beating a white woman. When a mob threatened to attack the jail, Mayor Henry S. Trout called for militia for additional protection. In the confrontation of mob and militia, shooting began, and the mayor was hit. When the militia fired, five men were killed, many were wounded, and eventually the death list rose to nine. The mob dispersed.

But the war was not won. Police had taken the prisoner away from the jail for safety's sake. As they brought him back at 5:00 a.m., members of the mob waylaid them and wrested the prisoner away (having been informed by police of the opportunity, a grand jury charged).

This time members of the mob shot their man and hanged him. They went for the mayor, but he had gone to Lynchburg for medical treatment. They tried to bury their victim in the mayor's front yard, but a minister dissuaded them. So they dragged the body to a river bank, built a bonfire, and cremated it.

This was tremendous news, and the reaction was tremendous. To the *Public Ledger,* "those who attacked the jail were altogether in the wrong. It was the duty of the civil authorities to protect the prisoner." To the *Virginian,* "the terrible tragedy" in Roanoke was "a great calamity, awful in its nature and consequences." It sought to analyze and interpret:

> It is asserted . . . that it has been the lax execution of the laws . . . and inefficient city officials who extended favors to the offending classes and lawbreakers . . . in order to secure their help for political advance that was at the bottom of the purpose of the people of Roanoke to take the execution of the laws into their own hands, a determination in which they succeeded in a manner and with an emphasis that was simply horrible.

The *Landmark* lifted the issues to a higher level:

> Lynching, which sometimes appears to be justifiable as a swift retribution for admitted crimes of the grossest and most brutal character, is always and under every condition brutal and cowardly. It cannot be condoned. It must be condemned, and all who participate in it should be punished for crime. It is much more probable that an innocent man may be lynched by an excited crowd than that a guilty man will escape through the imperfections and delays of the law. Life, property and liberty are in danger wherever lynching is tolerated.

The gradual turn toward reasoning about lynchings *per se*, attempting to understand them and searching for what to do about them, continued conspicuously after an especially cruel mob murder in October, 1895, in Coal City, Tennessee. Editorially the *Pilot* reflected:

> In every state of the union there is now going on a serious discussion of the ways and means to prevent lynching. In order to correct the evil, it is necessary to first diagnose the case and find the exact cause.
>
> Unquestionably, in our judgment, the root of the lynching evil is to be found in the law's delay—the possibility of wearing out a case in court by continuances and technicalities until the public has well nigh forgotten the circumstances of the crime, or the principal witnesses have died or removed beyond the reach of the court, and the red-handed murderer or brutish rapist goes unwhipped of justice, or escapes with light punishment.
>
> There are occasions of crime when an outraged sentiment cannot constrain or control itself, but these are fortunately very rare. The great majority of lynchings occur solely because the people fear that the fiend will be able to evade adequate punishment in the courts and here is where the work of reform must commence—at the very fountain head of the peoples' discontent and want of confidence.

Slow recognition by newspaper editors and government officials of the evils of mob power did not bring about a quick moral revolution.

Though progress was visible in time, the mob spirit could control a whole community, as it did in March, 1900, in Greensville County in Southside Virginia, seventy-five miles west of Norfolk.

The victim "deserved to die; that nobody denies," the *Virginian-Pilot* declared. "But did the community of Emporia and the State of Virginia deserve a thousand citizens should soil their hands with his butchery?"

Three years later the *Virginian-Pilot* published over several days extracts from speeches at the conference on lynch law held in Chautauqua, N. Y. John Temple Graves, the Atlanta editor and orator, thought that "the remedy for lynching must be the elimination of the crime"—that is, attacks by black men on white women—and therefore, he said, the black and white races must be kept apart. A line of other speakers did more justice to a complex subject than Graves' incomplete diagnosis did. Discussions were detailed and thoughtful. The *Virginian-Pilot* brought much of this to the attention of its readers.

The turn of the century was marked by state actions throughout the South to impose more rigid segregation (for instance, Virginia's statute requiring segregated seating on railway trains was adopted in 1900) and to take away by constitutional and legislative devices much of the voting right which Negroes had enjoyed since their emancipation. In Virginia this movement came to a head in the constitutional convention of 1901-02.

When newspapers in Virginia began in the early 1890's to discuss the holding of a constitutional convention to supplant the Underwood constitution of carpetbagger days, they added other reasons. One strong argument—especially the *Landmark*'s—was to cut governmental expense. Too many officeholders, the *Landmark* contended, too many judges, too many prosecuting attorneys, too many fees to enrich officials. Better education was another reason. A fair election law was another. But Democratic politicians argued that honest elections could be attained only when Negro voting was restricted.

In the end, the attack on Negro voting rose to first place. That in turn was a major reason why Virginia Republicans opposed holding any constitutional convention at all, and *that* in turn made the convention a Democratic cause and decreed that the new constitution would necessarily be a Democratic document.

The rising Democratic sentiment was further disclosed by State Senator Carter Glass (later representative in Congress, secretary of the treasury, and United States senator). While speaking on the additional issue of whether a new constitution, when written, should be submitted to a popular vote, Glass brought the Democratic state convention in Norfolk in 1901 to its feet by declaring, in the *Dispatch's* account, that "the new constitution should not be submitted for the sanction of 140,000 Negroes in Virginia."

In January of that year the Richmond *Times* said frankly that the constitutional convention was being called "mainly for the purpose of making such changes in the suffrage as shall take away the possibility of Negro rule in any section, and the fear of it." A year earlier (May, 1900) the Democratic state convention adopted a grandfather resolution declaring that "in framing a new constitution, no effort should be made to disfranchise any citizen of Virginia who had the right to vote in 1861, nor the descendant of any such person. . . ."

Alone among the Norfolk newspapers (and almost among all Democratic newspapers in Virgina) the *Pilot* and later the *Virginian-Pilot* under Elam opposed holding any convention. All essential reforms, Elam insisted, could be attained by amendment or by legislation. He feared the Pandora possibilities of conventions—"they are always revolutionary in character, if not in purpose." He argued that

> disfranchisement is not necessary. We have neither Negro rule nor imminent danger of it in Virginia. If we had either, nobody would more strenuously advocate disfranchisement than the Virginian-Pilot. But nowhere, not even in those States where the Negro has been disfranchised by constitutional amendment, is white rule more firmly established than here in Virginia. Nowhere is the Negro more completely subordinated, or more completely disarmed of all power to do harm. There is not the slightest chance that the negro or his party can gain ascendancy in Virginia under present conditions. Every intelligent man knows that. . . . As a party measure, disfranchisement is political imbecility.

But the *Virginian-Pilot* was arguing against the political tides. The convention wrote the poll tax as a prerequisite for voting into the constitution. It required that three years' payments be made six months in advance of an election to qualify in this respect for voting—the same requirement and procedures that were standing sixty-five years later in state elections and almost as long in federal elections before dying under Supreme Court decisions.

No one seriously attempted to conceal the purpose, and Carter Glass, spearhead of the movement for the poll tax, speaking to the point in the final debate, proclaimed the purpose in his exchange with the Henry County delegate, A. L. Pedigo, a Republican. The words are historic:[2]

> Mr. Glass. Mr. President. . . . there stands out the uncontroverted fact that the article of suffrage which the convention will today adopt does not necessarily deprive a single white man of the ballot, but will inevitably cut from the existing electorate four-fifths of the Negro voters. (Applause) That was the purpose of this convention; that will be the achievement. . . .
>
> Mr. Pedigo. Will it not be done by fraud and discrimination?
>
> Mr. Glass. By fraud, no; by discrimination, yes. But it will be discrimination within the law, and not in violation of the law. Discrimination! Why that is exactly what we propose, that, exactly, is what this convention was elected for—to discriminate to the very extremity of the permissible action under the limitations of the Federal Constitution, with a view to the elimination of every Negro who can be gotten rid of, legally, without materially impairing the numerical strength of the white electorate. . . .

The age of segregation had begun.

2. *Report of the Proceedings and Debates of the Constitutional Convention, State of Virginia, Held in the City of Richmond, June 12, 1901, to June 26, 1902*—Richmond, Virginia, 1906. The *Virginia-Pilot* published a detailed account of this debate by Harold Sugg, March 1, 1964.

IN THE STIFFENING COMPETITION AMONG THE NEWSPAPERS IN NORFOLK the *Dispatch*'s Thomson was not content to sit still with his meager printing plant and his small staff. The *Dispatch* was better than it had ever been. But it could not, within any foreseeable time, accumulate enough funds from its own earnings to buy badly needed equipment and to build up a working force to match its rivals, and it might not even survive. Thomson would have to look to other sources.

This did not prove to be difficult. Thomson took charge of the *Dispatch* in September, 1900. In December he sold half interest to Peter Wright, general manager of the Norfolk Railway & Light Company. With the proceeds he set about immediately to make up his shortages.

Wright was born in Scotland and educated there as an electrical engineer. He worked in Philadelphia with the United Gas Improvement Company and in Orange, New Jersey, before arriving in Norfolk in 1898. There he was president of the Norfolk Electric Company when it was sold in June, 1899, to a group of Richmond and Baltimore capitalists for $700,000. This was one of five companies subsequently consolidated into Norfolk Railway & Light.

Five months after buying an interest in the *Dispatch* Wright resigned his public utility general managership in Norfolk, and Mayor C. Brooks Johnston resigned as mayor and stepped in as Wright's successor. Wright was thirty-seven years old. He had made some money out of his American operations. His purchase of half of the *Dispatch* had the look of a personal investment, not an investment made in his name by the public utility of which he was general manager.

The corporation changed its name from the Norfolk Dispatch Publishing Company to the Dispatch Publishing Company. Wright had general supervision of the business department. Thomson's name came down from the editorial masthead, but he continued as manager and editor and directed daily operations. He quickly bought a new linotype machine and other mechanical equipment. The *Dispatch* moved from 99 Plume Street to larger quarters at 91 Roanoke Avenue—that long-time Fleet Street and Park Row of Norfolk. It changed from six columns to seven and soon was publishing six pages instead of four. It enlarged its staff. But outside capital, not the profits of daily newspapers in the Norfolk of that time, enabled these steps to be taken.

No one in Norfolk had more reason to measure these changes by the *Dispatch* than its afternoon rival, the *Public Ledger*. The new *Dispatch* was a new and formidable threat to its own long-dominant position. Would its old policies and methods enable it to hold on? Could it match the new means and the enlarged facilities of its competitor? The town watched, and inevitably rumors began to spread.

In September, 1901, the *Virginian-Pilot* published a report, "given general credence upon the streets of Norfolk yesterday," that the *Public Ledger* "has been or is about to be bought by the Williams syndicate to be used as the official organ of that combine in this city. . . . It has been known that the Williams people [the financial house of John L. Williams & Sons, of Richmond] desired to secure a mouthpiece here for their policy and have made several overtures toward that end. . . . [They] control the gas and electric power supply, and have at present the only street car lines. They have the Seaboard Air Line, the Portsmouth gas works and it is hard to tell what else. For this reason, it seems they have come to the conclusion that they must have a newspaper to blow their horn through."

The next day the *Public Ledger* said "there is no truth in it." But the evidence of sharper competition increased. On April 23, 1901, the *Dispatch* had cut its price to one cent a copy from two cents and to six cents a week from ten cents. Three weeks later, the *Dispatch*, feeling chipper now, congratulated the *Public Ledger* on going to seven columns and on being "as large as the Dispatch." It was careful to add that the *Public Ledger* was not carrying as much advertising. In July the *Dispatch* went to six pages and was clearly larger than the *Public Ledger*.

A year later the *Public Ledger* became a penny paper again, joining the *Dispatch* at that price with a characteristic announcement: "PUBLIC LEDGER ONE CENT—On March 9, 1880, the Public Ledger, after being published almost four years as a one-cent paper, advanced the price to two cents, in consequence of the increased cost of white paper. On Monday, June 2, the price of the paper will be reduced to what it was in the early days—one cent a copy, six cents a week, 25 cents a month delivered."

But the *Public Ledger* had more important news on that May 31, 1902. The long reign of Walter A. Edwards and Joseph G. Fiveash as sole owners had ended. They organized a stock company in which each bought approximately one-third of the shares. Both became officers and directors. The Smithfield planter and packer, Pembroke Decatur Gwaltney, had bought a substantial interest, probably one third, for which he was reported to have paid about $13,000.

Gwaltney's son-in-law, John E. Maxwell, an experienced news and editorial man, was already a member of the *Public Ledger* staff. Gwaltney did not participate actively in routine operations. He left that to the professionals. But for the third time, following Grandy's investment in the *Pilot* and Wright's investment in the *Dispatch*, outside money came to the aid of a Norfolk newspaper that needed it.

Edwards was president, Fiveash vice president, and Maxwell secretary and treasurer of the new Public Ledger Publishing Company that took control on June 2, 1902. Three other Norfolk citizens were elected to the board of directors: Nathaniel Beaman, a banker; M. T. Cooke, a real estate man and, for a brief period, a member of the General Assembly; and T. Phil Williamson, bookkeeper of the *Public Ledger*.

The new *Public Ledger*'s initial announcement told also that "the new company will immediately make arrangements for the purchase of a large and fast press and other machinery in order that the business of the paper may be extended in a direction that has not hitherto been possible." Policy would not be changed, "except"—and there is no mistaking the emphasis—"except that with enlarged capital and some accessions to the force, it is expected to place the paper abreast of the times and keep it so."

The new press went into operation September 1. On that day the *Public Ledger* printed six pages instead of the four to which it had held since its first appearance on August 3, 1876. New subscriptions, lured by the reduced prices, poured in, and new agents were put to work in Portsmouth and Berkley to get more. In Norfolk facilities for subscribing were established in a dozen stores. The conservatively edited *Public Ledger*'s heads grew bigger and blacker. It continued to emphasize local news on the top of its front page. Telegraph news generally was below the break of the page. Page two also carried local news. Berkley news was on page three, editorials on page four, miscellaneous news on page five, Portsmouth news on page six. In January of 1903 the *Public Ledger* went to two editions daily, the first published at 3:00 p.m. for Portsmouth and Berkley, the second at 4:00 p.m. for Norfolk.

The *Dispatch* stood up under this barrage of innovations from its long quiescent rival. It even proclaimed that on a November day of 1902 it had published forty-three columns of advertising (out of a total of eighty-four columns) against thirty-seven columns in the *Virginian-Pilot,* the same number in the *Landmark,* and twenty-six in the *Public Ledger.*

Claims were never a novelty. The *Virginian-Pilot* announced that its March, 1902, circulation was 11,088 daily and 12,263 on Sundays— "by far the largest in Norfolk." No other newspaper challenged these figures directly, but in November, 1902, the *Dispatch* declared it had a larger circulation inside Norfolk than any other newspaper. In the following April the *Dispatch* announced 7,775 circulation inside the city. Neither the *Landmark* nor the *Public Ledger* offered definite figures during this period, but the latter reported a gain of 2,000 within a few months after its new press went into operation.

The succession of changes made it easier for more rumors to spread. In February of 1903 the *Virginian-Pilot* reported that the *Dispatch* and the *Public Ledger* were engaged in merger negotiations. The two afternoon newspapers let that pass in silence. But in April a publication called the *National Gazette* reported that a charter had been granted to the Ledger Dispatch Publishing Company, with an authorized capital of $200,000, and with Wright as president and Maxwell as secretary.

This forced the *Public Ledger* into confession. It explained that in June, 1902, a *Dispatch* representative, later identified as Wright, had approached the *Public Ledger* with proposals to buy, sell, or consolidate. The *Public Ledger* declined to buy the *Dispatch* or to consolidate. It listened to proposals to sell to the *Dispatch.* Negotiations reached an agreement on a price. But the *Public Ledger* said that Wright failed to come up with the money, and that the negotiations, which had continued into 1903, ended. "During the negotiations the intending purchasers obtained a charter which has not been used," it said.

The need for public explanation of this kind appears to have irritated the *Public Ledger.* In August, 1903, it turned on the *Virginian-*

Pilot and the *Landmark* and bluntly demanded of these two: "Why not consolidate?" It cited reasons that it thought logical.

Neither of Norfolk's two morning newspapers, the *Public Ledger* argued, was able to provide adequate Washington coverage or other desirable services for its readers, but a consolidated morning newspaper might be able to do so. "Norfolk newspapers have frequently had to rely upon the Richmond Dispatch for news from the national capital," the *Public Ledger* insisted. A consolidation might give Norfolk a morning newspaper equal to the Richmond *Dispatch* or the Atlanta *Constitution*.

To this public proposal the *Virginian-Pilot* replied in a jesting spirit and with a designation of the *Public Ledger* as "Aunt Arabella." If the *Public Ledger* had exercised due diligence, the *Virginian-Pilot* said, it would have understood that

> the Virginian-Pilot is not what is known as an eligible party. It is, so to speak, already a staid couple, and respect for the law of the land would prevent it from becoming a bigamist.
>
> In the second place, it has just suffered the pain of being compelled to observe Aunt Arabella, late in life, sitting up and taking notice. A few months ago Aunt Arabella donned her crispest furbelows, gave an extra twist to her corkscrew curls, daintily hoisted her best poplin skirt and ambled down the street to make "goo-goo" eyes at that young scamp known as the Norfolk Dispatch.
>
> Being a properly reared rascal, the Dispatch hawed and smirked, was "dee-lighted," but said nothing. But Aunt Arabella, in a moment of pique, confided the story to the public.
>
> We are both pained and surprised that the dear old lady, with the best intentions in the world, should have, as it were, butted in and hung out her shingle as a matrimonial agent. But the Virginian-Pilot, for statutory reasons, cannot fall in with Aunt Arabella's well meant plans.
>
> That being said, the Virginian-Pilot desires to add, with due emphasis, that, whatever Aunt Arabella may say, it does not and does not have to rely upon any other newspaper whatever for news from the national capital.

To the *Public Ledger* this did not seem as amusing as it was meant to be. Its editor did not like the implication that the *Public Ledger* had been a suppliant. "As a matter of fact," the *Public Ledger*'s reply stated categorically, "the Public Ledger has never endeavored to acquire any other newspaper. Had the Virginian-Pilot known the inside story of the negotiations of Mr. Peter Wright for the purchase of the Public Ledger, it would never have made that erroneous statement."

With that the *Public Ledger* told again of the *Dispatch*'s 1902-3 attempts to buy it. But the news was in the last paragraph:

> This is all there is to the Virginian-Pilot's "goo-goo" eyes statement, but now a word about the opposition of the Virginian-Pilot to becoming a bigamist . . . To this we have only to say that the management of the Virginian-Pilot in 1898 made three distinct requests to the management of the Public Ledger for a conference with a view to merging the Ledger with the Virginian-Pilot, but all three invitations were declined. We think that if the Virginian-Pilot will make inquiry in newspaper circles in this city, it will ascertain that similar invitations were extended to other newspapers here in 1898 and again in 1903.

This version would greatly enlarge Grandy's ambitions and consolidation goals both in 1898, the year the *Pilot* merged with the *Virginian*, and in 1903, when the *Dispatch* was seeking to buy the *Public Ledger*. It would lift Grandy's goals in 1898 to a morning-afternoon combination and may have included the same objective in 1903, although in 1903 Grandy may have had his eyes on the *Landmark*—which, in a sense, would be anticipating history. The *Public Ledger*'s words strengthen other evidence that the period was a restless one of change, reorganization, and consolidation.

In this fresh, Twentieth Century spirit the energizing forces within the newspapers in Norfolk were further stimulated by the aggressiveness of two editors, one still deep in his twenties, the other just touching his thirties: Thomson of the *Dispatch* and Sapp of the *Virginian-Pilot*. Impatient with inadequacies and defects, determined on improvement, these editors were taking new looks at nearly everything. They were bent on a better world, starting with Norfolk.

Thomson was the more graceful writer, with wit and a delicate sense of humor. He could make the *Dispatch* move fast when the news was hot or when time was a factor, and when aroused he could hit hard. Sapp hit hard nearly always. His humor was broader than Thomson's, and he was more positive. Often he joined other editors in the southeastern states in their half serious, half jocular exchanges of views on social oddities, changing habits, pompous politicians, and bad Southern poets. But at heart Sapp was a crusader, impatient with slow-moving government, adamant against official derelictions, strong for personal rights.

Thomson was still new in Norfolk when in December, 1900, he tangled with the Portsmouth *Star*, then as always jealous of Portsmouth's position and prestige. The *Star* had charged that "Newport News is claiming every ship which enters the capes as a Newport News ship, and is claiming the Norfolk Navy Yard"—located in Portsmouth, but so named by the United States Navy—"likewise as an adjunct of Newport News." The *Star* concluded:

> It is truly bad enough to have the benefit derived from the fact that the Navy Yard is situated in Portsmouth stolen from us by Norfolk, but when the lusty infant shipyard town, Newport News, which, during its brief career has proved so adept at stealing things, undertakes to rifle our prestige chest, it is too much, and everybody over this way who knows anything about the high-handed business is mad.

Completely unabashed, the *Dispatch* replied:

> Ah, Sister Portsmouth! The very idea of the great city across the Elizabeth [River], Norfolk, stealing anything from you! Is not and should not all that you have be ours? Is not everything that we have yours?
> Are not our interests one, common and identical? . . . Does not the Star know that when the average Portsmouth man dreams of paradise a vision of Norfolk pictures itself in his mind? . . . Why, then, these bitter words, Oh contemporary? You must not mind Newport News and the things she says. Remember that your big brother across the way will take care of you and see that you lose no prestige.

Three years later the subject came up again (as it had done for decades, as it would do for many more). This time the Portsmouth *Star* was fuming because the *Virginian-Pilot* had referred to Norfolk as "the deepwater terminal for the big transcontinental trunk line"—the Seaboard Air Line, which had its terminal in Portsmouth. The *Star* said that the *Virginian-Pilot* has "taken the Navy Yard over to Norfolk, also the naval hospital. . . . Missing punishment for this wrong, why should it hesitate to go the whole hog and lift the Seaboard Air Line. . . . However, the meek shall inherit the earth. . . ."

How did the *Virginian-Pilot* deal in 1903 with the same kind of complaint which the *Dispatch* faced—and laughed off—in 1900? Thus:

> The Virginian-Pilot very frankly confesses that it never thinks of this community in terms of three cities, but always of one. Norfolk, Portsmouth and Berkley all look alike to it . . . it cannot attain to that acme of provincialism that would enable it to see any conflict of interest among the three cities. It hopes sincerely that the time is near when they shall be one in name as well as in fact. . . . It uses, so to speak, the name of the senior member of the firm and goes ahead.

A joint committee trying then to unite the cities could not produce unity. Nor did consolidation efforts in 1905, nor those of 1908, nor others in 1909 and 1910. The pride of a city living adjacent to a larger city—separated only by the river between them—was constantly stimulated by the *Star* under Trugien in early years and Hamilton in later years. Though newspapers in Norfolk favored the municipal consolidation principle they tended to leave Portsmouth's decision to Portsmouth people. A half-century later cooperation in many activities had greatly increased, but the governmental walls between Norfolk and Portsmouth remained. Norfolk annexed Berkley in 1906.

In January of 1901 the *Dispatch* returned to a favorite theme, inspired this time by events in Newport News. The Rev. Dr. Charles H. Parkhurst, of New York, a much quoted preacher of the times, had been imported for evangelical meetings there. He announced from a Newport News pulpit that "in proportion to population yours is the vilest and wickedest city in the entire country." This amused Thomson, and he commented with delight:

> To offset the sensational publications of Town Topics, the literary representative of New York holiness and virtue, Newport News . . . obtained for her own vilification and abuse the foremost clerical representative of New York righteousness. . . . In his sermons there is no necessity for facts. All that is needed so far as he is concerned is the concentration of a certain amount of humanity in any given area. Parkhurst then knows that there is wickedness.
>
> New York, the wickedest city in the world, is being cleansed by Croker, the Tammany boss. Newport News, the wickedest city in the world, is being purified by Parkhurst. And Norfolk, whose laurels of vice have been torn from her brow, is being completely regenerated as the result of the crusade of that highly virtuous, moral and dignified publication, Town Topics. Thus, the world grows better.

Between the two of them, Thomson and Sapp filled the early 1900's with pointed criticism of the condition of streets in Norfolk and of highways everywhere, of Bible kissing by court witnesses (deplorably unsanitary, they pointed out), of the advantages of drinking cups over dippers, of the nakedness of the police wagon with no top to cover victims en route to jail or hospital, of the hatchet-wielding of Carrie Nation, and of Negro citizenship, which both newspapers distrusted and disliked.

The *Virginian-Pilot* would be the one to argue for the right to criticize judges. It lost a $2,000 libel suit to City Attorney J. G.

Tilton in December, 1902, and did not seem upset, but successfully withstood libel suits for $15,000 from three councilmen whom it had charged in 1903 with selling goods to the city contrary to law. When Peter Wright bought several ice-making plants in Lower Tidewater Virginia, the *Virginian-Pilot* thundered, "Is It a Trust?" It reproved Virginia corporations which were resisting the new State Corporation Commission, ordained by the state's new constitution for their regulation. It discovered that seventy-nine of one hundred signatures on a petition for a conduit franchise were faked: the names of persons who did not exist or had not given permission for the use of their names—a series of discoveries in which the *Dispatch* enthusiastically joined.

In the midst of these vigorous years the *Virginian-Pilot* suffered a tragic and a heavy loss. Grandy, its publisher, died suddenly—August 5, 1903, in Lake Placid, N. Y. He was sixty years old and had been a publisher only seven years. But within those seven years he had regenerated an almost defunct *Pilot*, had merged with the largest of Norfolk newspapers, the *Virginian*, and had led the *Virginian-Pilot* into a period of journalistic and economic growth and financial success, and had done so in a period of hard competition.

Grandy brought sound, enlightened business methods to a journalistic business that often had been managed as journalism but not as business. His financial resources were important, but he had more than money. His own staff liked him unaffectedly. Editors had his backing. Reporters knew he was interested in their work, how they did it and the adventures they had. He understood a newspaper's role in the life around it and a newspaper's responsibilities. In an editorial surely written by Sapp the *Virginian-Pilot* spoke of him in these words: "[He] stood as ready to champion courageously, aggressively and with no thought of personal interest the rights of the humblest citizen as to maintain his own. That was his idea of his duty as the owner and manager of a public journal. . . . His closest friend could not warp him from his support of the right as he saw it, nor silence him in the face of wrong as he felt it."

The *Landmark* called Grandy "remarkable in having won a distinguished position in a laborious and difficult profession, which he entered after passing the meridian of life." The *Public Ledger* credited him with finding "his greatest pleasure when championing the cause of the general public as against the encroachments of corporate or individual greed. He did this regardless of the enemies it might make for him." To the *Dispatch* he was "a man who has fought the people's battles, who has dared to stand forth fearlessly for what is right regardless of the powers that be, regardless of the personal, financial, political and social influences which may be brought to bear upon him. . . ."

The Richmond *Times-Dispatch* thought of Grandy as "bold and aggressive and those who opposed him in a discussion were sure to get blow for blow;" and the Petersburg *Index-Appeal* noted a significant quality: ". . . it was a display of nerve as well as sound judgment when he made [actually, retained] Colonel Elam the principal editorial writer in the face of a political record that would have staggered a publisher of less discernment and grit. . . . And then again . . . Mr. Grandy discovered in Mr. Sapp, a young man comparatively unknown to fame, an editorial writer worthy to succeed Colonel Elam. . . . [Grandy] seemed to possess those qualities which enabled him to select the right man and see that everything is done."

One thing Grandy did not do: he did not provide for a successor. Before he left for Lake Placid he had given to L. D. Starke, Jr., the company secretary, his power of attorney. But at the December directors' meeting after his death Hugh C. Davis, a Norfolk lawyer who represented the Grandy interests, presided. At the annual stockholders' meeting in April, 1904, Davis represented 395 of the company's 750 shares. Other stockholders who had been associated with Grandy were Starke with 25 shares; Shelton, 10; Wilkinson, 8; Charles Sharp, a lawyer elected to the board to succeed D. F. Donovan, 2.5; and Shultice, 2—a total of 442.5 shares.

The Glennan interest, deriving from the *Virginian*, consisted of 297.5 shares plus 10 in the name of James E. Allen, brother-in-law of Michael Glennan—a total of 307.5 shares. The Grandy control elected from its own ranks six of seven directors: Davis, Starke, Shelton, Wilkinson, Sharp, and Shultice, the other director being Allen. But it had no normal plan for the executive direction of the *Virginian-Pilot*.

In this dilemma the controlling interest abandoned the presidency as such and set up executive direction by committee. It designated the executive committee of the directors as chief administrator. Starke was chairman of this committee. Davis and Shultice were the other members. Shultice resigned in 1904, and C. W. Grandy, brother of the late publisher and proxy for his widow, was elected a director and placed on the executive committee. Davis was a lawyer of firmness and ability, but he was a man of the deeply conservative spirit, not so much an initiator as a preserver, and therefore not like the late publisher.

Though Starke was nearer the chief executive than any other one man, the salary of $1,500 voted him in 1904—or the $1,700 of 1907, or the $2,000 of 1909, or the $2,500 of 1910—did not suggest that stockholders or directors wished to emphasize any such status. Grandy's salary had been $5,000. Not until 1911 was the concept of a presidency restored. Starke then was elected to that office as well as chairman of the executive committee. Meantime, and during important and well-nigh decisive years (as will become apparent), a committee of three—a committee of which one member had limited newspaper experience and of which two members had virtually none at all—was the chief executive.

No comparable dilemma had faced the *Landmark* when its president, the elder Lucien D. Starke, then seventy-six years old and senior member of the Norfolk bar, died on February 21, 1902. He had never exercised the chief executive duties. Those duties devolved upon the secretary and treasurer, S. S. Nottingham, Jr. After Starke's death the bylaws were changed, and Nottingham was elected president in name as well as in fact.

K. Foster Murray, editor and a large stockholder, was elected secretary and treasurer and was designated second in command. Other directors then were James E. Heath, C. A. Nash, and James A. Kerr. In June Wallace W. Starke, son of the *Landmark*'s late president and brother of the *Virginian-Pilot*'s executive committee chairman, was elected to the board.

The gusto of Grandy's *Virginian-Pilot* had showed up particularly in its reporting of the most notorious murder the region had known in decades. When nineteen-year-old Nell Cropsey disappeared on a night in November, 1901, from her home in Elizabeth City, across the North Carolina line from Norfolk, the *Virginian-Pilot* fought for fifteen months not to let North Carolina newspapers—or Baltimore or New York newspapers, which followed the story with keen interest—get the better of it in territory it regarded as its own.

Nell had quarreled with her close friend, perhaps her suitor, James E. Wilcox. When he went one night to her home beside the Pasquotank River, she would not speak to him. When he asked her to come out on the front porch with him, she followed in silence. No one saw her thereafter except Wilcox. He said he left her there.

The search for the girl gripped eastern America. For five weeks of intensive effort, involving bloodhounds and confused by crackpots and fantastic rumors, it led nowhere. Then Nell's body was found in the river. The coroner held that she had been killed by a blow on her head. Wilcox was charged with murder.

The trial in March of 1902 was full of mystery and excitement. Circumstantial evidence was the chief reliance of the prosecution. Wilcox did not testify, and his air of aloofness, earlier and in court, irritated spectators so much that when his lawyer began to argue to the jury they walked out of the court room. The verdict was guilty. The sentence was death.

When the jury handed in its verdict, the hour was late on a Saturday night. But the *Virginian-Pilot* was ready to pull out all the stops. Its story and its headlines drenched the entire upper five-sixths of the front page. A two-line streamer, heavily staggered, topped the array of type, followed by an inverted pyramid, and two single lines, all streaming across the full width of the page with the language of Victorian melodrama, thus:

AMID OIL LIGHTS' FLICKERING SHADOWS "JIM" WILCOX HEARS THAT HE MUST DIE.

FOUND GUILTY IN THE FIRST DEGREE BY A JURY OF HIS PEERS.
Judge Jones Immediately Pronounces Sentence.
Seals the Prisoner's Doom.
Wilcox Stolidly Indifferent to the End

END OF THE FAMOUS CROPSEY MURDER TRIAL, WHICH HAS ATTRACTED THE ATTENTION OF THE COUNTRY
It Is Thought the Case Will be Appealed at Once.

The story began with this paragraph in fourteen-point type running from one side of the page to the other: " 'Guilty of murder in the first degree,' said the jury to Jim Wilcox. He stood up and heard his doom fearlessly. His nerve of steel did not forsake him. It was 10:10 o'clock."

Only Wilcox's face, in a single-column cut, broke the cataract of type.

The North Carolina Supreme Court would not let the verdict stand. Too much reliance on circumstantial evidence, it found; too much spectator conduct that could prejudice the jury. A second trial, this one in Hertford instead of Elizabeth City, produced in January, 1903, a verdict of guilt and a sentence of twenty years. "WILCOX SAVES HIS NECK" was the *Virginian-Pilot's* top headline.

In the summer of 1903—a year that made the expression especially ironical—the *Virginian-Pilot's* editor wrote about "The Airship Folly" with supreme confidence that "aerial navigation is an interesting fad" but "there is not the smallest probability that it will ever become anything more. . . . It will never be able to compete successfully with the methods of travel on land and water."

Three months later (August 9, 1903) the *Virginian-Pilot's* headline on the big story of the day was:

LANGLEY AIRSHIP FLIES TO THE BOTTOM OF THE RIVER

The story was a serious attempt to do justice to the testing of S. P. Langley's flying machine. It should have been. The breakthrough was coming up fast. Only four months later Wilbur and Orville Wright made their first flights, December 17, at Kill Devil Hill near Kitty Hawk on the Outer Banks of North Carolina, then a singularly remote and isolated region eighty miles to the south of Norfolk but much farther removed in time and convenience by any means of public transportation.

That event set the stage on which the *Virginian-Pilot* achieved the most historic scoop of a century of Norfolk newspaper publication. With full awareness of what it was going after, with a good bit of luck, with some uncertainties still standing as to how all that was printed was procured, with a fantastic degree of error in detail but with the heaviest emphasis placed squarely on the vital fact—with all this in the background and in the story itself, the *Virginian-Pilot* of December 18, 1903, reported for the world the arrival of the aviation age.

It did so at a moment when the world, for the most part, was not ready to accept such a report. Most newspapers to which a condensation of what the *Virginian-Pilot* printed was offered by telegraphic query regarded it as beyond the bounds of credibility or not important enough for them to publish, and turned it down.

Of the twenty-one newspapers to which the story was offered, sixteen did not care to see it. Five asked that it be sent to them. They were the New York *American*, the Chicago *Record-Herald*, the Philadelphia *Record*, the Cincinnati *Enquirer*, and the Washington *Post*.

Of these five, three—the Chicago *Record-Herald*,[1] the Philadelphia *Record*, and the Washington *Post*—did not publish the story on December 18. Two newspapers did. They were the New York *American* and the Cincinnati *Enquirer*. Both put it on the front page.

The *Virginian-Pilot* published the story with a big bang. It used a thirty-six-point two-line staggered streamer, in italicized capitals, across all seven columns of its front page:

FLYING MACHINE SOARS 3 MILES IN TEETH OF HIGH WIND OVER
SAND HILLS AND WAVES AT KITTY HAWK ON CAROLINA COAST

Down the right-hand column ran a series of five subheads, the first in the boldest and biggest type (forty-eight point), the others smaller:

NO BALLOON
ATTACHED
TO IT

THREE YEARS OF HARD, SECRET
WORK BY TWO OHIO BROTHERS
CROWNED WITH SUCCESS

ACCOMPLISHED WHAT
LANGLEY FAILED AT

WITH MAN AS PASSENGER HUGE
MACHINE FLEW LIKE BIRD
UNDER PERFECT CONTROL

BOX KITE PRINCIPLE
WITH TWO PROPELLERS

Down the remainder of the seventh column, the story itself:

The problem of aerial navigation without the use of a balloon has been solved at last.

Over the sand hills of the North Carolina coast yesterday, near Kitty Hawk, two Ohio men proved that they could soar through the air in a flying machine of their own construction, with power to steer it and speed it on its way.

This, too, in the face of a wind blowing at the registered velocity of 21 miles an hour.

1. The Chicago newspaper to which the story was sent may have been the *Inter-Ocean*, but it did not publish on December 18 a story of the flights.

Like a monster bird the invention hovered over the breakers and circled over the rolling sand hills at the command of its navigators and, after soaring for three miles, it gracefully descended to the earth again and rested lightly on the spot selected by the man in the car as a suitable landing space.

While the United States government has been spending thousands of dollars in an effort to make practicable the idea of Professor Langley of the Smithsonian Institution, Wilbur and Orville Wright, brothers, natives of Dayton, Ohio, have quietly, even secretly, perfected their invention and put it to a successful test.

They are not yet ready that the world should know the methods they have adopted in conquering the air, but the Virginian-Pilot is able to state authentically the nature of their invention, its principle and its chief dimensions.

The idea of a box kite has been adhered to strictly in the basic formation of the flying machine.

The huge framework of light timbers, 33 feet wide, five feet deep and five feet across the top forms the machine proper. This is covered with a tough but light canvas.

In the center and suspended just below the bottom plane, is the small gasoline engine which furnishes the motive power for the propelling and elevating wheels.

There are two six-bladed propellers, one arranged just below the center of the frame, so gauged as to exert an upward force when in motion, and the other extends horizontally to the rear from the center of the car, furnishing the forward impetus.

Protruding from the center of the car is a huge fan-shaped rudder of canvas, stretched upon a frame of wood. This rudder is controlled by the navigator and may be moved to each side, raised or lowered.

Wilbur Wright, the chief inventor of the machine, sat in the operator's car and when all was ready his brother unfastened the catch which held the invention at the top of the slope.

The big box began to move, slowly at first, acquiring velocity as it went, and when half way down the 100 feet the engine was started.

The propeller in the rear immediately began to revolve at a high rate of speed, and when the end of the incline was reached the machine shot out into space without a perceptible fall.

By this time the elevating propeller was also in motion, and, keeping its altitude, the machine slowly began to go higher and higher until it finally soared 60 feet above the ground.

All this time the machine headed into a 21-mile wind.

The little crowd of fisher folk and coast guards, who had been watching the construction of the machine since September 1 with unconcealed curiosity were amazed.

"It is a success," declared Orville Wright to the crowd on the beach after the first mile had been covered.

But the inventor waited. Not until he had accomplished three miles, putting the machine through all sorts of maneuvers en route, was he satisfied.

The errors in this account are numerous. No flight on December 17 was three miles long (the longest was 852 feet). None was over water. None was witnessed by a "crowd" unless the five Outer Bankers who were the only persons present beside the two Wrights could be so described. Wilbur did not make the first flight; Orville did. He did not sit in a car but lay prone. Instead of being thirty-three feet wide and five feet "deep," the wings were slightly above forty feet long and six feet apart. The flights were against a twenty-one mile wind, however, and there were two propellers.

The errors distressed the Wrights, but they were distressed in the first instance by any *Virginian-Pilot* report at all. They understood the importance of what they had done, and they realized the story would have to be told. But Dayton, not Norfolk, was where they wanted the story to emanate from.

On the day of their triumph, accordingly, after eating luncheon, the brothers walked the four or five miles to Kitty Hawk to send a telegram to their father in Dayton. The Outer Banks had no commercial telegraph or telephone line. A message could go only by the telegraph line operated by the United States Weather Bureau or by the telephone line of the Life Saving Service (later the Coast Guard). Both connected in Norfolk with commercial lines.

Orville Wright wrote the message and handed it to the Kitty Hawk operator, Joseph J. Dosher. It read:

SUCCESS FOUR FLIGHTS THURSDAY MORNING ALL AGAINST
TWENTYONE MILE WIND STARTED FROM LEVEL WITH ENGINE
POWER ALONE AVERAGE SPEED THROUGH AIR THIRTYONE
MILES LONGEST FLIGHT FIFTYNINE SECONDS INFORM
PRESS HOME CHRISTMAS

Dosher established contact with Norfolk almost instantaneously (so the Wrights remembered) and sent the message promptly. The time was about 3 o'clock. When Dosher had finished, he turned around and told the Wrights that the Norfolk operator, Charles J. Grant, had asked whether he could inform a newspaper friend in Norfolk. What about it? The Wrights' answer was an emphatic no!

Dosher tapped that answer to Grant. But the Wrights believed later that Grant did leak out their message.

When the message reached Dayton about 5 o'clock, another Wright brother, Lorin, wrote out the substance of it and carried it for national distribution—though not until the family had finished the evening meal—to the Dayton correspondent of the Associated Press, Frank Tunison, a telegraph editor of the Dayton *Journal*. He scorned it:

"Fifty-seven seconds, heh? If it had been fifty-seven minutes, it might have been a news item."

(An error in transmission had changed the fifty-nine seconds in Orville's message to fifty-seven as recorded in Dayton.)

By that time the *Virginian-Pilot* knew that the Wrights had flown, was trying to develop the story, and certainly was going to publish it. What each of three *Virginian-Pilot* men knew and did that day, and when, are questions that left a legacy of uncertainty and romantic tradition as well as of accomplishment. The three were:

1. Keville Glennan, the twenty-three-year-old city editor, son of the late Michael Glennan, *Virginian* proprietor and editor, brought up in the newspaper tradition, competitive and aggressive, later managing editor of the *Virginian-Pilot* and still later of the not-yet-established *Ledger-Dispatch*.

2. Harry P. Moore, a twenty-year-old circulation department assistant who worked principally in the mailing room. Ultimately he rose to be marine affairs reporter of the *Virginian-Pilot* and worked in that capacity for many years. Already he was Norfolk correspondent for several out-of-town newspapers. It was he who queried other newspapers and sent stories to the five that asked for them.

3. Edward O. Dean, a reporter (later a reporter of the New York *Times*), one of whose daily assignments was the Norfolk Weather Bureau office. This brought him in touch with more than weather reports. Other news might come up by wire from the long line of the Outer Banks to Cape Hatteras and beyond—ships in distress along that dangerous coast, or the gossip that enriched the telegraphic talk of operators who, with fingers on the key, were as human as anyone else.

On December 17 Dean went to the Weather Bureau as usual. The time (he thought years later) was about 5:00 p.m. There he heard something that jerked him to attention. Word had come up the line that the Wright brothers had flown that morning in their crazy machine. It was bare news, no details. Dean jumped fast. He took the tip straight to his city editor.[2]

Glennan, as well as Dean, knew the tip was precious. He knew that the necessity of making the most of it was compelling. He was excited. So was Dean. They were both young, and they could not sit still. But they did not tell anyone else in the news room.

Dean's account long afterward—Moore agreed with this, Glennan did not—is that while he and Glennan were talking about what to do next, young Moore walked up to the city desk and asked:

"Have you got the story of those fellows flying down in Carolina? They're brothers named Wright, and one of them flew three miles and landed safely. I have it all."

This shocked Dean. He thought he had the story. Yet here came a young chap, not even a reporter, hardly more than a boy, declaring blithely that he had the whole works in his hand.

Glennan remembered the sequence of events differently. He gave full credit to Dean's being the first to bring the news to the city desk—"that's the finish line in news races," he liked to say. He knew that he had to find out more, and he was determined at the same time that his primary competitor, the *Landmark*, would not learn of his tip from anything he or any other *Virginian-Pilot* man did.

He himself was night correspondent of the Associated Press in Norfolk and therefore obligated to supply it with all news worthy of wider distribution originating within thirty miles of Norfolk. But eighty miles was beyond the range of his responsibility to the AP. Fearing that if big city newspapers received an Associated Press report they might call their Norfolk correspondents for more details and that their Norfolk correspondents might be *Landmark* reporters, he told the AP nothing. For the same reason Glennan participated with Moore in the selection of newspapers to which Moore, in his own private venture, later sent queries, and he checked the list carefully.

Glennan said years afterwards that at the 5:00 p.m. stage he had not seen Moore and did not know that Moore had any information until about 7:00 p.m. Meantime, he sent Dean back to the Weather Bureau in search of more information. He himself telephoned two Life Saver friends from whom during the past summer he had twice heard about the Wrights' earlier experiments. They too had heard of the day's flights, but they knew nothing more. Could they get more? They would try.

2. Dean's subsequent accounts did not disclose who gave him the tip. The Wrights thought it came from J. Frank Newsome, office manager.

Whether one of these two Life Savers, Nelson Holmes, did get more information for Glennan (the other, Edgar Chadwick, said he did not) is only one of the uncertainties. Glennan thought Holmes did. Glennan thought he tried to reach the city desk by telephone. The newspaper used two buildings then, and Norfolk had two competitive telephone companies. Mistakes in calling the *Virginian-Pilot*, Glennan said, were frequent. He suspected that Moore answered a phone call and took a message designed for Glennan from Holmes and thus learned of the flight.

But Moore said he received information by a private telegram delivered to him in person by Grant, the Norfolk operator. It read (said Moore in one account later): "Wrights flew in motor-driven machine 11:20." Thus alerted, Moore telephoned a friend at the Norfolk Weather Bureau. What had he heard? "At last the nuts have flown," the word came back.

Moore was reticent about the identity of the sender of the personal message which he said he received. His newspaper associates assumed that he was protecting the source of his information. Eventually, but long after, he said the message came from A. D. Etheridge and J. T. Daniels, Life Savers, who were two of the five spectators of the flights. He would never concede that Grant, the telegraph operator, gave him information from the Wrights. He had traveled on the Outer Banks, he insisted, and had friends in the Kitty Hawk region. He had asked them, he said, to let him know if anything came of the Wrights' experiments. They had already told him, he continued, something of the Wrights' machine.

In the long decades that followed, when aviation, slowly at first, swiftly in time, was growing beyond anyone's imagination in 1903, and the fame of those who were in at the birth began to grow too, Moore matured into the newsroom oracle of the Wrights' flights. Dean had always been modest about his role, and, besides, he had left Norfolk. For a quarter-century Glennan did not make any point of clarifying how the story was handled, and for a time he dropped out of newspaper work. So it was Moore who wrote the anniversary stories and the personal recollections, it was Moore who was appealed to on disputed issues. Not all of the results were alike; sometimes they seemed contradictory, and they did not always include other *Virginian-Pilot* men. Moore was reluctant to admit that Dean played any part worth mentioning, and he did not do much better by Glennan.

But whether Moore got information by Grant's passing along to him details of the Wrights' telegram, as the Wrights believed, or by taking a telephone call for Glennan, as Glennan suspected, or by personal message from eyewitnesses, as he said, he did produce information. Much of it was inexplicably inaccurate, but Glennan used it.

The production of the story was far more than a one-man *tour de force*. Glennan made that abundantly clear in a letter he wrote to the editor of the *Virginian-Pilot* in 1928, the twenty-fifth anniversary, when the congressional monument was dedicated on the Outer Banks. For that event Moore wrote an advance story of the historic happenings in 1903. On top of his story an italicized editorial note was placed to identify Moore with his subject. In this note appeared the statement that Moore had "scooped the world."

This was too much for Glennan, at that time not a member of the newspaper's staff though still a stockholder. He wrote a letter to the editor of the *Virginian-Pilot*, published December 22, in which he said: "For the purpose of keeping the record straight, I would like to inform you that the credit for the magnificent 'beat' which the Virginian-Pilot scored on that occasion does not belong to any individual man—no one person 'scooped the world.'" Glennan continued with some events of the day of the flights and then summed up in these words: "So I took the Weather Bureau confirmation of the flight that Dean had first given me, the array of details that Moore had gathered, and the knowledge I had of what the Wrights had been aiming at, and from this material I wrote the first story that was ever printed of man's actual conquest of the air."

More than sixty years have not produced a better summary. It defines and pays tribute to the roles of Dean and Moore, and it suggests as a byproduct how a news staff ought to cooperate. That Glennan himself wrote the story is not in doubt. He wrote the major headline too, and probably the subheads. He did not leave in doubt where much of the story came from or that at its heart, if not in most of its details, it was correct. Orville Wright said later, after he had mellowed, that "it was an amazing piece of work. Though 99 per cent wrong, it did contain one fact that was correct. There had been a flight."

Not only that: Orville Wright could have added with full justice that there had been also a newspaper report of that flight which, in the peculiar and frustrating circumstances that prevailed, any other news staff would have been taxed to better, and no other did. In intelligent appraisal of the meaning of the news, in ingenuity in breaking unnatural concealment, in courage in going all out on a story judged to be tremendous—and how time has confirmed that judgment!—and in an odd but effective sort of united effort, the news story is a classic. It deserves more recognition from American journalism than it has yet received.[3]

3. Keville Glennan's letter to the editor of the *Virginian-Pilot* in 1928 was the first important challenge to the popular assumption in Norfolk that Harry P. Moore was preeminently responsible—almost solely responsible—for obtaining and even writing the published news story of the Wrights' first flights. The day after Glennan's letter appeared, the *Virginian-Pilot* published on its front page a box with the word "Publisher" in the signatory position, though the name of Lucien D. Starke, Jr., who then was publisher in effect, was not included. "Publisher" said that "Mr. Glennan's description of the event is entirely correct." He regretted "any erroneous impression that the anniversary articles might have created."

This unusual official judgment did not deter Moore, or, in fact, others who had lined up in the *cause célèbre* which the whole affair had grown to be within the newspaper organization. Public interest in the uncertainties was always much less. Moore rallied to his support retired newsroom veterans of the 1903 era. They praised his role, and, since they were calling on their memories of events a quarter-century behind them, they added a few new errors.

Dean's recollections of the events are in *Editor and Publisher*, August 6, 1927. Outside investigators like Mark Sullivan in his "America Finding Herself," *Our Times, 1900-1925* (Charles Scribner's Sons, New York, 1936), II, and the Associated Press in its examination on the fiftieth anniversary (December, 1953), all added information, analysis, and sometimes fresh errors. Fred C. Kelly's authorized biography, *The Wright Brothers* (Harcourt, Brace and Company, New York, 1943), has excellent detail and generally is accurate; and the present account owes much to this attempt to reconstruct a tangled tale. Kelly does not deal with the roles of Dean and Glennan. The writer also owes much to Robert Mason, editor of the *Virginian-Pilot*, 1962——, for his "When Flying Was News," in the *Virginian-Pilot* of December 17, 1950, and for his notes about his investigation. Mason interviewed Glennan, Moore, Kelly, and others. He had talked with men in Norfolk and along the Outer Banks who had connections with the events of 1903, and he was familiar with the documents. His weighing of the evidence at varied points is probably the best to be found.—L.C.

18 · SLOVER AND THE
LEDGER-DISPATCH

ON A DAY EARLY IN 1900 A TALL, STRAIGHT YOUNG MAN, WITH EYES THAT could look through you and a suggestion about him of his east Tennessee background, walked into the office of Joseph Bryan, owner, publisher, and editor of the morning Richmond *Times*. Bryan was the principal newspaper personality of Richmond, a man of means, social standing, and dignity, important in many respects in the life of the capital. But if he seemed formidable to this twenty-eight-year-old advertising salesman for a New York trade journal whose territory included Virginia, the young man did not show it.

When the two came to the point, the visitor was frank. He had come to ask Bryan for enough money to buy a newspaper in Norfolk.

Bryan was astonished. "I don't know you very well," he said. He had never seen the young man before and probably had never heard of him.

The young man (as he said much later) did not really expect to get the money, "but I knew he wouldn't forget me." Now he went a step further. If he could not buy a newspaper for himself, he would like to sell advertising for the *Times*.

Bryan shook his head. The *Times* had no vacancy for an advertising salesman. But that did not stop the young man either. H e told Bryan that he would sell advertising for the *Times* on a commission basis and in soliciting would avoid present advertisers altogether.

This time he won, and in more ways than either man foresaw. Working in an unfamiliar city, the young man sold so much advertising that in half a year his commissions were larger than the salaries of other advertising solicitors, and of the editor and of the general manager of the *Times* as well. The word spread abroad. It reached down the Virginia Peninsula to Newport News.

There the *Morning Herald* and the *Evening Times* had been established in April of 1900 in competition with the older morning *Daily Press.* In six months the new newspapers were in distress. The owners turned to the young man in Richmond with a proposition: he could have half interest in the *Evening Times* if he would pull it out of the red in a year. He leaped at the opportunity.

Thus Samuel L. Slover came to Virginia, and thus in October of 1900 he came within sight, across Hampton Roads, of Norfolk, his goal in the first instance and still his goal.

Slover cut the *Evening Times'* price to a penny a paper. He poured energy into the news department so that in reporting sometimes the *Times* jumped ahead of other newspapers. He built up circulation until the *Times* claimed to have the largest in Newport News. He sold advertising. He provided vigorous, intelligent management at all points.

A year later (December, 1901) the *Times* and the *Herald* merged into the *Evening Times-Herald* (later the *Times-Herald*) with Slover as publisher and controlling figure. (In Norfolk the *Landmark* commented that "wise business judgment undoubtedly dictated the action.") He was still under thirty years of age. He was deeply in debt. But he had one of the two newspapers in Newport News, and he was on his way.

No magic had enabled young Slover to move fast once he had started. He was born March 23, 1873, in Anderson County in eastern Tennessee where his father was clerk and master of the chancery court. After going to school in Clinton, he spent a year at the University of Tennessee. But he sought more action. He worked in real estate, helped his father as a deputy, campaigned for a Republican legislative candidate, and acquired a small newspaper, the Clinton *Gazette.* Of the *Gazette* he liked to say later that he was "sole owner and publisher for ninety days, the longest period for which a bank in those days would accept a note." He went to the Knoxville *Journal* as an advertising salesman. By 1893, when he was twenty, he was its business manager. The morning *Journal* was struggling hopelessly against the afternoon *Tribune.*

The crisis arrived in 1895. In that year Slover reported to the directors that he had made substantial improvements in operations, so that "today advertisers who have business to place give it first to the Journal and then consider the Tribune." But the *Journal*'s debt was above $36,000, much of which he had inherited; and he warned that the desperate battle—

has caused me, aside from worry and annoyance, loss of character and credit, and I admit to you that I feel it keenly, and cannot and will not continue business further under the circumstances because the people who are not on the inside do not know the reason for my refusing to pay my obligations promptly and meeting bills and accounts. All this has worked very seriously to my disadvantage . . . there can be only one result if this indebtedness is not relieved. . . .[1]

The indebtedness was not relieved, and the *Journal* was merged with the *Tribune*. The merged newspaper did better—a fact that Slover noted well. Although there is no indication that he was responsible legally for the *Journal's* debt, he thought he had a moral obligation, and he knew the newspaper owed some of the money to friends who had trusted him. He shouldered the payment of $36,400. With great effort and after many years, he paid it in full. The whole experience made a powerful impression on him, and he never forgot any detail of it.

The New York adventure in 1899 was brief; coming to Virginia was permanent. So, within human limitations, was Slover's association with Harvey Laird Wilson, whom in 1902 he brought to Newport News as editor of the *Times-Herald*.

Wilson was fifteen years older and had broader experience. Born in Boydton, Virginia, he grew up in Baltimore and attended school there. He went to North Dakota to work in the territorial government, then to Norfolk with a lumber company, and in 1891, when he was thirty-three, to Richmond as a reporter of the *Times*.

Reporting carried Wilson into many parts of Virginia and to Washington as the *Times's* correspondent there. A big, handsome man, he had a capacity for getting along with people, knew hundreds of them well, and was a striking figure in any company. His writing attracted attention. Sometimes it had a deep strain of sentiment. On Christmas Eve, 1894, he wrote from Washington an article for the *Times* entitled "There Is No News Tonight" which began with " 'Tis the night before Christmas and from the neighboring church the grand hymn, ' 'Tis the Birthday of the King,' comes up from the rehearsing choir and reaches the office of The Times with its sacred melody. There is no news tonight. . . ." Paragraph after paragraph continued the refrain, each beginning with "There is no news tonight," and so to the climax:

1. Slover kept a copy of his written report to the directors in a personal scrapbook as long as he lived.

There is no news tonight, for this is the only day in the year when the bugle-call of duty is lost in the discordant notes of the tin horn in the hands of the boy; lost in the labor of love as the altar is built in our homes and lost in the laughter of Joy as he gilds the shrine for the passing of the holy day.

'Tis the mistletoe, the evergreen and the holly whose banners are hung above the people today, and while the flag of the country floats dearest for such days, there is no news tonight for " 'Tis the Birthday of the King."

For years "There Is No News Tonight" appeared in the Christmas edition of many a Virginia newspaper beside Francis P. Church's "Is There a Santa Claus?" from the New York *Sun* and the first twenty verses of the second chapter of the Gospel according to St. Luke.

From Washington, Wilson returned to Richmond, made a new reputation as city editor of the *Evening Leader,* and in 1899 established the afternoon *News.* But that was sold the next year to John L. Williams & Sons, the financial house, and Wilson, after remaining for a while as associate editor, joined Slover in Newport News in an association that continued until his death in 1917. The two became close friends and worked together with understanding and confidence. They quickly built the *Times-Herald* into a profitable newspaper.

But the goal was still Norfolk. Its forty-six thousand population alongside Portsmouth's seventeen thousand was more attractive than Newport News' nineteen thousand. Thomson, who had bought the *Dispatch* at almost the same time that Slover was reaching Newport News, recalled long afterward that Slover approached him in 1902 or 1903, "offering to buy in with me and help me run the paper"—the *Dispatch.* Thomson was doing well and did not encourage this proposal. The *Dispatch* seemed out of the reach of Slover and Wilson. They turned their attention to the *Public Ledger.*

The attempted rehabilitation of the *Public Ledger* in 1902 when it broke out of its managerial conservatism had not brought conspicuous success. By 1903 the owners were willing to sell to the *Dispatch* and would have done so if Peter Wright had found the money for the agreed price. The *Public Ledger* trailed the three other newspapers in volume of advertising. Gwaltney, the new part-owner, was not playing an active role. Fiveash was not in good health. Edwards had mechanical skills but less executive ambition and capacity. The *Public Ledger* was ripe for a proposition. By 1904 Slover and Wilson were actively negotiating. By January of 1905 they had their Norfolk newspaper.

The *Dispatch*—eager and alert in those years, and deeply interested in this transaction—broke the news on January 26. It reported erroneously that the purchasers were a syndicate with which—these were the first names mentioned—Nathaniel Beaman, president of the National Bank of Commerce of Norfolk, and W. J. Payne, president of the Newport News and Old Point Railway and Electric Power Company, and president also of the Norfolk and Atlantic Terminal Company, were connected. Alvah H. Martin, the Norfolk County political leader and bank president, was "mentioned in connection" with the new company.

Slover and Wilson, the *Dispatch* continued, were believed to "have been prominent in organizing the new company." Slover would be president, Wilson vice president, it said; and the directors would be Beaman, Payne, Slover, Wilson, and W. H. Kellogg, the latter a Newport News banker. The price was reported to be $50,000, "part in cash and part in bonds, to be issued against the paper's property." The *Dispatch* added this paragraph: "The purchase of the Public Ledger is being made, it is understood, because certain political and financial interests have been dissatisfied at not having a voice for their views on matters affecting financial and political interests which they represent."

This suggestion probably rose out of the *Dispatch*'s belief that Beaman, Payne, and Martin were important figures in the deal. They were not. It was the worst error in a generally inaccurate report, and the new owners had to correct it. They turned to the *Landmark* with information that made the *Landmark*'s story the next day (January 27, 1905) virtually an official statement. It announced in its first paragraph that Slover and Wilson were "the purchasers." The price was "estimated" at "about $50,000." Slover and Wilson would come to Norfolk to live, but would continue "in the active management of the Times-Herald" in Newport News. The remainder was left to a Slover-Wilson letter "which the Landmark has been requested to publish." This read:

> To the Editor of the Landmark:
> The statement published this afternoon [in the *Dispatch*] to the effect that the Public Ledger has been purchased by Messrs. Beaman, Payne and Martin is untrue.
> The capital stock of the Public Ledger has been purchased by us, and the paper will be consolidated with the Times-Herald, our paper in Newport News, and they both in the future will be published by us.
> It is true that Mr. Beaman for some time has had a small interest in the Public Ledger, which he retains. It is also true

that Mr. Payne has an interest in the Times-Herald, with us, which he will continue to hold.

It is a purely business enterprise with a view to profit only, and has not the slightest bearing or connection with the political aspirations of any man or body.

We believe that Norfolk offers a good field for a progressive and up-to-date newspaper, which we will endeavor to supply.

S. L. Slover
Harvey L. Wilson

In the Norfolk of 1905 "a view to profit only" meant a struggle. Slover and Wilson had little money for this kind of war. Slover was carrying much of the Knoxville *Journal*'s debt. He had not finished paying for the *Times-Herald* in Newport News. He and Wilson had to scratch hard to make their initial payments for the *Public Ledger*, and they assumed heavy obligations. Norfolk banks, with unhappy experience behind them, rated newspapers low as credit risks and were wary about going in deep now. But Beaman and Martin, who was president of the Merchants and Planters Bank, with whom Slover had conferred during negotiations, helped in the financial arrangements. Bonds had to be issued. Nothing about the deal was easy.

Long afterwards, Slover liked to recall that in the thick of the bargaining Wilson committed the buyers to pay $5,000 more than Slover thought was necessary. When all was over and they had their newspaper, Slover suggested that the moment called for champagne.

"Isn't that a little rich?" Wilson asked.

"Not for a man who can give away $5,000," Slover replied.

The first issue of the *Public Ledger* under its new ownership, now called the Norfolk-Newport News Publishing Company, appeared on February 9, 1905. A day earlier the *Landmark* carried a two-column advertisement under the head:

"The Public Ledger, the paper you have always read, tomorrow, under new management."

It continued:

> After an honorable and successful record of 30 years, representing all that is clean and wholesome in journalism, the Public Ledger will begin tomorrow the publication of the full Associated Press report, without doubt the greatest news gathering organization in the world, thus placing Norfolk on an afternoon basis with the largest cities of the country.
>
> There will be no departure from its time-honored policies of the past. It will adhere to its recognized conservatism, Democracy, independence and reliability.

Nothing will be overlooked that will make it a progressive newspaper in every sense of the word. The efficient staff of the old Ledger has been greatly enlarged in every department.

The next morning, on the day when the new *Public Ledger* would first appear, the *Landmark* carried a second two-column advertisement. It was headed: "SEE THE NEW OLD PUBLIC LEDGER TODAY," and the first paragraph read: "Greater Norfolk steps into the front rank as an afternoon newspaper field and the Public Ledger receives over a direct leased wire into its building and disseminates the full day service of the Associated Press." Praise for that news-gathering institution followed, along with the reminder that "the very best service to be had costs money" [in this instance about $6,000 a year] and the promise that "such service this section shall have."

"The new management," the advertisement continued, "believes that the prosperous, largely populated Tidewater Virginia wants and will support an afternoon newspaper of the first class. The Public Ledger will be such a paper. Look at it today. One cent a copy. Delivered everywhere for six cents a week. Mailed anywhere for 25 cents a month, $3 a year. A valuable souvenir will be given today to every news boy who comes to this office."

The new *Public Ledger* might say "there will be no departure from the time-honored policies of the past." But it was a much changed newspaper—aggressive, assertive, determined. Slover's name went to the top of the editorial masthead as president and manager, Wilson's as vice president and editor. The old slogan, "Independent on All Subjects" remained fast. (The *Public Ledger* had liked slogans. Two others it had used were "All the News That Is Known to Be True" and "A Newspaper That Is Read in the Home.") The naming of P. T. Marshall as business manager of the *Times-Herald* and of Robert E. Golden as editor of the *Times-Herald* in Newport News was more evidence that Slover and Wilson were concentrating on Norfolk. New typesetting equipment was ordered, more correspondents in Tidewater Virginia and North Carolina were being sought, and larger quarters than those at 41 City Hall Avenue were promised.

In a week the Public Ledger claimed a gain of sixteen hundred subscribers; in two weeks, three thousand—a remarkable increase. Within a few days more it had published a "night special" to report that the new coal-carrying railroad, soon to be named the Virginian Railway, which Henry H. Rogers was building from West Virginia mines to deepwater, would locate its terminal in Norfolk.

The *Virginian-Pilot* had paid its first tribute, after the announcement of the purchase, to the old *Public Ledger,* "our next door neighbor" on Plume Street. It was warm in its farewell:

> Under the editorship and management of Messrs. Edwards and Fiveash the Ledger has been a clean newspaper, as far as possible free from the sensational. It has won its way to the heart of the people by reason of the fact that it was accurate, forceful and unusually correct in whatever appeared in its columns. In this day of kept newspapers that respond to the pulling of strings not in the public interest such a newspaper will be sadly missed in this community. Certainly it can be said that the new proprietors find ready to their hand a policy that would be hard to improve upon. To the new company, we wish all the success that may be earned.

These references to the new owners were more restrained than the *Landmark*'s greeting on February 10, the day after the new *Public Ledger* had appeared: "Messrs. Slover and Wilson are both newspapermen of long experience, and Mr. Wilson has an established reputation as a brilliant editorial writer. We cordially welcome them to this field. The first edition of the Ledger under their management presents a lively and attractive appearance." The next day the *Virginian-Pilot* added its own "cordial welcome" to Slover and Wilson: "They will hereafter form a part of the congenial newspaper community of Norfolk. They are both newspapermen of long experience and will unquestionably add a sparkle to the newspaper business of our community."

Morning competitors found it easier to be correct. The real test was between Thomson and his afternoon *Dispatch* and Slover and Wilson and their afternoon *Public Ledger.* The *Dispatch* had gone ahead of the old *Public Ledger* because of its youthfulness, alertness, and modern spirit. Now it was under challenge from fresh competition that no one could call old-fashioned. The *Public Ledger*'s emphasis on advertising and on effective management reflected a man who could contribute more in these areas than newspapers in Norfolk had ever known.

The very times were right for such capabilities. Growing cities were producing more circulation that in turn required more machines. Higher costs were making industrial institutions out of personal organs, and partisanship was declining as independent journalism continued to rise. Larger yields from advertising were a necessity, and newspapers lacking good management did not survive. The old *Public Ledger,* for all its personal appeal to readers who liked its simple ways, represented the past; the new *Public Ledger* represented the future.

The new *Public Ledger* and the *Dispatch* went to war immediately. It was a time of anxiety for Thomson because he saw the *Ledger* rising. It was a time of anxiety for Slover because he was stretched close to the limit. Once when he sought a loan of $500 for the *Ledger*, a Norfolk bank turned him down. More than once, when a payroll had to be met, he pawned his gold watch. Sometimes he had to ask employees to be patient. On occasion a friend came to his aid with a one-man loan. Charles H. Consolvo, the hotel operator, did. So did Martin. At first he had thought the young publisher "extravagant"; later he learned to admire him. He had good reason: the new ways of the new owners were paying off.

The dramatic advertising gains of the new *Ledger* are suggested in the following comparisons, based on the first Tuesday after Slover and Wilson took hold and a Tuesday four months later, Tuesday being generally a stable day in advertising volume:

Date	Newspaper	Pages	Total Columns	Columns of Advertising
2-14-05	*Public Ledger*	8	56	17
	Dispatch	8	56	24
	Landmark	8	56	26
	Virginian-Pilot	12	84	42
6-13-05	*Public Ledger*	12	84	46
	Dispatch	12	84	47
	Landmark	10	70	32
	Virginian-Pilot	12	84	42

The fight to gain this ground brought an army of weapons into operation. For circulation the *Public Ledger* organized contests and gave prizes to people who had brought in the most new subscribers. It published more social news, more brides' pictures, more about sports, more church and lodge news, more real estate news (including an article on "How to Build a Comfortable House for $960"), all at a time when it also was calling attention to its broadened Associated Press reports.

It proclaimed its results so persistently that the *Dispatch* invited merchants to check the paid circulation of Norfolk newspapers and offered a full page for the findings. The *Virginian-Pilot* endorsed this strongly. The *Dispatch* was claiming thirteen thousand circulation when the *Ledger* put its own at eleven thousand.

Hard fighting developed in classified advertising, limited then largely to employment or workers wanted. The *Ledger* went after this business hard. It advertised its own advantages, ran sample advertisements free, offered bargain rates for new advertisers, held out other inducements. Soon it was counting 150 daily want ads whereas early in 1905 it had been publishing only 30.

The *Virginian-Pilot* was caught up in this struggle and increased its own efforts to get readers and patronage. Both it and the *Landmark* were publishing a page and more of social news with pictures, on Sundays. When the *Public Ledger* announced that it had subscribers in sixty-five towns around Norfolk—something new for an afternoon newspaper, it said—the *Virginian-Pilot* announced that its country edition, called the Norfolk *Journal of Commerce and Twice-a-Week Virginian-Pilot*, published on Tuesdays and Fridays, was going into thirty-three counties in Virginia and North Carolina.

Editorially the *Public Ledger* pumped hard for Norfolk growth in all ways but especially through the merging of Norfolk, Portsmouth, and Berkley into one city, or the adoption of a borough system like New York's. This was a theme that always attracted new editors, so natural did it seem. "Within the next few years," the *Ledger* declared in April of 1905, "Norfolk will be the largest city in Virginia." Richmond would remain the capital, the *Ledger* admitted, but "Norfolk will be to her what Baltimore is to Annapolis, Philadelphia is to Harrisburg, Chicago to Springfield, or New York City to Albany." The Richmond *Times-Dispatch* noted Norfolk's "fixed determination to become the largest city in Virginia" but did not seem disturbed. More than half a century had to pass by first.

At the end of its first year the *Public Ledger* claimed that its circulation was up from 3,500 for the six months before February, 1905, to nearly 10,000 for the same period in 1906; that its display advertisements had risen in the same period from 62,000 to 131,000; that its classified (want) advertisements had multiplied by better than four—from 5,700 to 26,000—and were now the most numerous in Virginia.

Thomson was hard put to it to fight off this hammering competition, the like of which he had never encountered before. His health was not good, and he was a very young man who had been under a heavy strain. He may well have been despondent. In this mood he went one night in early 1906 to a Norfolk theater, thinking more about where to get the money to fight his war than about the drama on the stage. Looking around, he saw in the audience his arch-newspaper rival, Slover, accompanied by a young lady, both of whom seemed to be enjoying themselves immensely. Slover was in high humor, apparently without a care in the world, the very spirit of assurance and confidence.

Looking closer, Thomson saw that Slover's companion was Fay Martin, daughter of the Alvah H. Martins—the Martin with substantial means of his own and with strong political, banking, and financial connections. Thomson reflected: Can I beat that combination? Am I fighting a losing fight and increasing my losses? Should I settle the issue by selling out, at a good price, before a bad situation grows worse?

At that moment, said Thomson many years later,[2] he decided. (Slover and Miss Martin were married on October 28, 1909.)

On April 18, 1906, fourteen months after Slover and Wilson had bought the *Public Ledger*, that newspaper and the *Dispatch* announced that "this field is not sufficient to take financial care of the two large afternoon papers." Accordingly, "the interests of the Public Ledger and the Norfolk Dispatch have been merged, with a division of securities satisfactory to both papers." The new newspaper was the *Norfolk Ledger-Dispatch*.

To make the decision unmistakably plain, the announcements said also that the *Ledger-Dispatch* "will be conducted by the present management of the Public Ledger, Mr. Peter Wright and Mr. James M. Thomson having decided to retire from the newspaper business for the present."

Wright retired from newspaper business entirely. Thomson, who could not keep out of it long, waited a year, part of which he spent in Norfolk, recovering his physical strength. Then he bought the afternoon New Orleans *Item*. Taking with him Marshall Ballard, his *Dispatch* managing editor, and Franklin S. Cook, his *Dispatch* advertising manager, he began a long and successful career in New Orleans that reached a climax, in an editorial sense, in his persistent fight against the Huey Long regime. (Cook soon returned to Norfolk.)

The new *Ledger-Dispatch* found sympathetic understanding from the *Landmark*. That newspaper agreed with "the views expressed by both the Ledger and the Dispatch in their explanation that there is not a living in this city for two up-to-date afternoon dailies. . . . There is a field for one up-to-date afternoon newspaper and the Ledger-Dispatch begins its career with an opportunity and the facilities at hand." But the situation was more historic than the *Landmark* could see.

2. Interview with Joseph E. Shank, October 20, 1958.

For the first time since the rebirth of newspapers after the Civil War—a few days in 1896 excepted—Norfolk had only one afternoon newspaper. The *Ledger-Dispatch* would be the only continuing afternoon newspaper in Norfolk for the next sixty years, before the end of which it acquired the Portsmouth *Star* and changed its own name to the *Ledger-Star*. Two attempts would be made to establish other afternoon newspapers, but the first ended in forty-five days and the second in two and a half years.

Contemplating these developments Norfolk people must have asked themselves—indeed, the *Landmark* in particular, which always welcomed the lessening of newspapers in Norfolk, must have asked itself—whether the survival of only one newspaper in the afternoon pointed to a day when Norfolk would have only one newspaper in the morning. Morning newspapers had a longer tradition and in medium-sized cities generally had greater strength and influence than afternoon newspapers. But the period was one of deep changes, and what was happening in the afternoon demanded serious attention from those interested in the morning. The eventual picture was not complete.

The desirable position of the *Ledger-Dispatch*, however, was clear. It now had the combined circulation of the *Public Ledger* and the *Dispatch*. When it had eliminated duplicates it reported figures from eighteen thousand to nearly twenty-one thousand and began to post them every day in its right dog-ear—the upper right-hand corner of the front page. Its circulation was substantially larger than that of the *Virginian-Pilot* or the *Landmark*. It could argue more persuasively about its values for advertisers.

The *Ledger-Dispatch* used at first both the *Public Ledger* quarters on City Hall Avenue and the *Dispatch* building on Plume Street. When the lease for the City Hall Avenue property ran out late in 1906, it began moving all facilities to Plume Street. By March of 1907 it was located entirely at 102 and 104 Plume, on the north side, almost opposite the Post Office of that era—later, the City Hall. It had added another deck to its Hoe press, which now could roll out twenty-four thousand papers an hour if the edition ran no more than sixteen pages, or twelve thousand an hour of editions with twenty to thirty-two pages.

Classified advertisements were still breaking records, the 323 of a day in March of 1907 being more than any other Virginia newspaper had ever carried. In a new contract with printers in that March the *Ledger-Dispatch* raised the rate of pay from $17.00 weekly to $19.00.

The increase on morning newspapers was from $19.00 to $20.00.

In May of 1907, the *Ledger-Dispatch* dropped forever the penny-a-paper charge with which the *Public Ledger* had begun operations three decades earlier and to which it returned (following the *Dispatch*) in its final years. The formal explanation cited a 25 per cent increase in white paper, a 100 per cent increase in metal for type and stereotyping, and increases in wages and in other directions. And so, "these being the facts, it has become necessary to advance the price of the paper from six cents to 10 cents a week, delivered to the homes, and from one cent to two cents on the streets, effective May 1. . . . In every city of importance in the South where the full Associated Press dispatches are taken," the *Ledger-Dispatch* added, "the price now adopted . . . prevails."

An immediate effect was a drop in circulation from above twenty-one thousand in March of 1907 to sixteen thousand in September—this in a big summer in Norfolk, the summer of the Jamestown Exposition. But the figure was larger than the *Virginian-Pilot* or the *Landmark* claimed, and eventually it climbed upward again.

The *Ledger-Dispatch* was now in a position—with improved quarters and equipment, with printers' wages settled for a time, and with an increase in circulation receipts—to begin to prosper, and it did. It established itself solidly not with outside capital such as the *Virginian-Pilot*, the *Dispatch*, and the *Public Ledger* had obtained, but by its own developing resources and its own administrative efficiency. It did so without any surrender of its constitutional duties. It was printing the news and expressing opinions freely. In the offices of the *Virginian-Pilot* and the *Landmark* some hard thinking must have been going on.

The *Virginian-Pilot* had problems of its own. It suffered a grave loss when its young editor, Charles Pinckney Sapp, died in August of 1905. He was only thirty-three years old, and he had been editor, following the much older Elam, only five years. He had never been physically robust in Norfolk. But within these five years he had risen swiftly into a figure of recognized force. His grappling with tough subjects, his emphatic views, his sharp expression made people read him.

Sapp often reflected the thinking of his time. He saw little hope for Negro development, he regarded the poll tax barrier to voting as a wise check, and he distrusted political independence—the party was the thing. The *Virginian-Pilot*'s slogan of that period, "True to the

Democratic Party in Victory or Defeat," had been hoisted to the masthead before his arrival, but Sapp thoroughly personified it:

> We know nothing more illogical, ridiculous and absurd than the egotistical Pharisaism of the mugwump [he wrote in 1903]. He is cocksure that the country leans for support upon his broad and manly shoulder, and he never loses an opportunity of saying so. No street corner stand for him when he is enlightening the world upon that point, either! A nice housetop location and megaphone are indispensable. . . . He is the balance of power, the voice of civil virtue. He is the essence of wisdom and patriotism. He is the whole hog!
>
> Now see here! What has your mugwump, your party turncoat, ever done for this country of ours? . . . It is the party man who has borne the heat and burden . . . while his mugwump fellow citizen was making the welkin ring with his futile complaints. . . .

Josephus Daniels, of the Raleigh *News and Observer*, sent to the *Virginian-Pilot* a tribute that described Sapp as a scholar well trained in political economy, a follower of Jefferson, and one "deeply read in fundamentals." The *Landmark*, which correctly placed him "in the anti-conservatism school in his convictions," thought "he could have conducted with distinction the editorial department of any newspaper in the country whose policy suited his principles." The *Dispatch* said his reputation "went for beyond the borders of the state and aided in gaining for his paper a strong and unique position among the newspapers of the South."

Sapp's death forced a major decision on the *Virginian-Pilot*'s executive committee, then still the newspaper's chief executive. Temporarily it put John Wise Kelly in the editor's chair. A thoughtful and able member of the news staff (and of the Wise family, of the Eastern Shore, that produced some individualistic and capable men), he did well in uncertain circumstances. If allowed more opportunity he might have made a wider reputation for himself. But the *Virginian-Pilot* was setting its sights high.

Eight months later, on April 21, 1906, the newspaper announced that William E. Cameron, the *Virginian*'s editor of forty years earlier, Virginia's Readjuster governor in 1882-86, often a controversial figure but always a respected figure in the life of the state, had "accepted a position on its editorial staff and will assume his new duties today. . . ." Kelly, the announcement said, "will be associated with Colonel Cameron in the conduct of the editorial department."

The wording appeared to avoid the title of editor. Sixty-three years old, Cameron had not been in newspaper work for many years, did not know the Norfolk and Lower Tidewater of 1906 intimately, and did not take on duties which in that period often were under the editor's jurisdiction—command of the news department, for instance. Regard for Kelly's position as associate may have been a factor. But whatever the niceties, Cameron universally was called editor, and in time the *Virginian-Pilot* itself recognized his real status.

Cameron had a widely ranging and often dramatic career.[3] After his nine months as editor of the *Virginian,* in 1866 he returned to Petersburg for work with the *Index*, later the *Progress*, and then went to the Richmond *Enquirer*. The governorship must have been a hard time for him. His natural associates were among the established families, but his political principles had carried him into the Mahone camp. Socially he was almost ostracized in Richmond. In the end he won respect because of his own virtues. He began to gain new popularity when, like other important lieutenants, he broke with Mahone after the latter had gone all-out Republican and even more all-out as a political boss. Thereafter he fought Mahone at every chance and with slashing attacks.

 By 1890 Cameron was back among the Democrats. He lived briefly in Florida, practiced law in Petersburg (he had a good name as a constitutional lawyer), and wrote often on historical and political subjects. The *Landmark* published many of his articles. During the World's Columbian Exposition in Chicago in 1893 he spent much time on its jury for awards in the fine arts and as exposition historian. In the constitutional convention of 1901-2, in which he carried weight, he was chairman of the committee on the executive department and a member of the committees on the judiciary and final revision. He had become something of a grand old man.

But when he entered the Democratic primary for congressman from the Fourth District in 1904, he soon found it wiser to withdraw. He had been a Gold Democrat in 1896, and under him the *Virginian-Pilot*'s editorial page would be more conservative—or perhaps less liberal. In some ways the new editor belonged more to the last half of the Nineteenth Century than to the new times into which the *Virginian-Pilot* was advancing.

But though much of his fame was behind him, Cameron was a striking personality. He knew well the Virginia of his times, in large part through personal participation in the thick of its struggles. Nor-

3. Chapter 3 has details of Cameron's early life; Chapter 5, of his duel with R. W. Hughes; and Chapter 11, of his Readjuster years.

folk not only respected him but was fond of him. At the Virginia Club, where he lived and drank his whiskey neat, he could talk vividly of the Crater and of Appomattox, both of which he had seen and felt firsthand, along with much else. His "erect, soldierly figure, handsome and dignified" (in Tazewell H. Lamb's words), and the vandyke beard and the mustache, both white, made him a marked man, but it was the broad sweep of his mind and the sense of history that his listeners felt most.

When Cameron reached Norfolk in April of 1906 he moved into a newspaper building which had been finished a few months earlier. The first newspaper printed there appeared on the fortieth anniversary of the *Virginian-Pilot*: November 21, 1905. This was the building on Tazewell Street, on the south side, between Granby and Boush Streets, near the site of the historic Tazewell home. It had three stories and a basement for storing newsprint, and in time a building in its rear, abutting Brooke Avenue, met increased space demands.

The *Virginian-Pilot* celebrated the move with a special edition on December 10 of thirty-eight pages, of which fourteen were devoted to a plant that was unique in a city where most newspaper buildings had been remodeled quarters. The *Virginian-Pilot* had left two buildings, used simultaneously, one on the south side of City Hall Avenue, east of the Arcade, the other on the south side of Plume Street, adjacent to the Post Office of that era. A year's subscription cost $5.00; a month's (by mail), fifty cents; a week's, ten cents, and a single copy was three cents. The *Landmark* had the same schedule of prices. Neither newspaper had begun Monday publishing. The *Virginian-Pilot* had more of a modern air. But the *Landmark* could delight many readers with its characteristic flings at life around it.

In early 1903 the Boston architect who was designing the new public library on West Freemason Street planned to adorn the frieze with the names of such world figures as Homer and Vergil, Horace, Cicero, and Sophocles, Shakespeare and Milton, Cervantes and Schiller, Dante and Moliere, and then, turning to America, listed a group of New Englanders. He included no sign of a Southerner.

The *Landmark* demanded to know why this startling omission. Why not Poe? Why not James Barron Hope—Poe "at any rate," and Hope if the Boston architect was "inclined to do the graceful thing." For Hope was "the greatest poet Virginia ever produced," and "it would be particularly fitting for his name to find a place upon the public library of Norfolk, the city with which his memory is most closely linked." And, indeed, why not Father Abram J. Ryan, the

Confederate priest-poet who was intimately associated with Norfolk?

When the *Landmark*'s first shots seemed to fall short, it fired again, asking how the architect had allowed Homer and Vergil to slip in among this list of so many Northerners when Walt Whitman and Harriet Beecher Stowe were available. In the end the *Landmark* scored. Poe was allowed to enter.

The *Landmark* did not like Henry James either. When the transplanted novelist was visiting the United States in June of 1905, he spoke from a Bryn Mawr platform about the "black eruptions of type, which roar like maniacs breaking loose" in American newspapers. That brought the *Landmark* up with a recent magazine article by James, which it called a "linguistic nightmare." It quoted a paragraph from the article and then pronounced judgment on James: "No man who writes like that could hold a job on a newspaper three days. It comes with poor grace from the author of such sentences as we have quoted—and they are sentences fully representative of his style— to criticize 'newspaper English.' Mr. James should go back to his puzzle-making."

Poe, Hope, Father Ryan, and Henry James had their moments, but from 1900 through 1907 the Jamestown Exposition was most often in the news columns and rarely absent from editorial thinking of the Norfolk newspapers—especially, at the start, of Thomson's *Dispatch.*

The Association for the Preservation of Virginia Antiquities gave in 1900 institutional endorsement to celebrating in 1907 the three-hundredth anniversary of the first permanent English settlement in America. But the lag that followed and the assumption of some Virginians that the celebration would be in the state capital prepared the way for Thomson's *Dispatch* to jar Tidewater Virginia into action. The *Dispatch* published on February 4, 1901, the following frank comment:

> There should, of course, be a fitting celebration in Virginia of the 300th anniversary of the settlement at Jamestown. The importance of this event is beyond question. . . . Out of the small settlement grew the great colony of Virginia, and Virginia made the Union.
>
> A great exposition of some kind should be held. Norfolk is undoubtedly the proper place for the holding of this celebration. . . . Norfolk is today the center of the most populous portion of Virginia, and every historical, business and sentimental reason can be adduced in favor of the celebration taking place here rather than in Richmond. . . .
>
> Richmond knows the value of expositions of this kind, and

is more than anxious to have it settled some years in advance that she shall have in hand the celebration. But there is no particular reason why she should be allowed to coolly walk off with everything of this kind.

Norfolk should have the celebration, and all that she has to do is to make public her claims and let her intentions in the matter be known.

From that moment the *Dispatch* was the foremost champion of the movement for a Norfolk site for the celebration. In August it was asserting that "the exposition belongs in the Tidewater section and it is going to he held here." In September the *Dispatch* was urging support from Newport News for a Tidewater location. In the same week the *Dispatch* denied the accuracy and reasoning of statements in the Richmond *Dispatch* that the idea of an exposition originated in Richmond and *therefore* the exposition should be held in Richmond. The Norfolk *Dispatch* declared:

> This is incorrect. The Norfolk Dispatch must sacrifice its modesty in the interest of historical truth and confess that the idea of an exposition to celebrate the settlement at Jamestown originated in its own sanctum. Likewise, the idea of a naval demonstration in Hampton Roads was first given publication by the Dispatch, and, so far as the paper knows, was original with it.
>
> Norfolk is the principal city of Tidewater Virginia and as a city whose history is almost contemporaneous with Jamestown would naturally be expected to take the lead in such a celebration. Newport News, which is the nearest Tidewater city to Jamestown, would naturally cooperate to the utmost extent in the holding of an exposition on Hampton Roads.
>
> Richmond has absolutely no claim to the celebration except her location on the James River.

On September 19 of 1901 the *Dispatch* was delighted that the Norfolk City Councils had given support, "adopting the Dispatch scheme for the Jamestown exposition and asking the entire Tidewater section to cooperate." After that, but with agonizing slowness and always with laborious efforts, the prospect brightened.

In 1902 a company was formed. Fitzhugh Lee, the former governor and the most popular man in Virginia, was elected president, and an initial $300,000 issue of stock was put on the market. The decision was made to locate an international exposition on a mile-long frontage at Sewells Point overlooking Hampton Roads, approximately equidistant from Norfolk, Portsmouth, Newport News, Hampton, and Old Point. In 1903 the Virginia House of Delegates shocked

Lower Tidewater by refusing to appropriate $200,000. But Norfolk descended on the legislators like an army, and the House reconsidered and approved. So did the Senate.

The year ended with a desperate crisis. The Jamestown Exposition Company's charter required that $1,000,000 be subscribed in capital stock during 1903. On December 31, in the final hours, total subscriptions still lacked $40,000 of reaching the mark. In a public meeting of hallelujah emotionalism in Norfolk the total crept up, thousand by thousand, hundred by hundred. In an electric moment, with clocks nearing midnight, the final triumphant dollar marched historically into the pot. The deed was done.

But not the final deed. Congress was a tough nut. Speaker Joseph G. Cannon fought any substantial financial aid—too many expositions, he grumbled; many congressmen were indifferent. Norfolk was challenged as being too far from Jamestown. Other expositions were standing in line, hat in hand. Time dragged out disastrously and almost fatally. Congress delayed until June of 1906 for an exposition that was scheduled to open in April of 1907. It was doomed to be unready.

At home management difficulties multiplied. Fitzhugh Lee died while drumming up business in New England for the exposition, and two thousand Norfolk citizens rode to Richmond to mourn at his funeral. The *Virginian-Pilot* needed ten columns to report the obsequies. Harry St. George Tucker succeeded Lee, and the *Landmark* published his picture—a rare act for that newspaper. But Tucker had to take up the leadership in midstream. David Lowenberg, a Norfolk business man, was director general. For appealing to state legislatures to participate Cameron was the choice with the title of commissioner general. "The work suits him admirably," the *Public Ledger* pronounced in an editorial full of praise for Cameron.

Logistical problems mounted. Road-building proved to be a major difficulty. Piers had to be constructed for handling supplies for exposition buildings. Water problems were perplexing (old Norfolk would have understood). Worst of all, work on the great Federal government pier, elaborate and highly decorative, at the heart of the exposition design, seemed never to start, and, when it did, seemed never to pick up speed. All construction dragged. Money was forever on the point of running out.

There were a few cheerful signs. President Roosevelt gave much encouragement. Twenty-two states built state buildings. International cooperation in the naval review was excellent. The Navy and the

Army came forward systematically and on time. Hotel construction in Norfolk was, for a city of not many more than fifty thousand people, remarkably extensive and generally satisfactory.

But on April 26, when President Roosevelt arrived to open the exposition, much was not completed, and the embarrassment was acute. Only a fifth of the electric lights could be turned on. The Warpath (for recreation) was far from ready. Construction on the government pier had churned up the ground in the middle of the exposition into mud. Not until September was this central feature dedicated. For five months it handicapped the whole show.

Visitors were critical of these conditions. They began to talk. Reports by out-of-town newspapermen stressed the raw state of things, and attendance fell far below expectations, aided by the policy of closed doors on Sundays—a local moral sentiment, which Congress wrote into its financial measures. Of the 2,988,437 attendance in the final audit only 1,480,908 represented paid attendance.

The newspapers in Norfolk rallied to clarify, to explain, to defend, to challenge error, and to rebuke newspaper sinners—in Baltimore, Washington, and Richmond especially. They had celebrated the opening with special editions, the *Public Ledger* and the *Virginian-Pilot* with thirty-two pages, the *Landmark* with twenty. Now, as the coldest June in thirty-seven years turned into an abnormally hot July the editors labored hard to overcome adverse reactions and to convince a reluctant world that daily the exposition was growing better—as in fact it was.

Under these pressures organizational weaknesses in exposition management grew worse. The board of governors—more than a hundred strong, named to represent local governments rather than to bring experience or to provide direction—was always a cumbersome body, often split factionally. A new management expert with large powers, J. M. Barr, recently president of the Seaboard Air Line, was brought in for rescue operations. When he cut operating expenses, new animosities flared up. A feud among official entertainers, involving President Tucker, developed. In the final weeks, when Barr gave up, Alvah H. Martin, of Norfolk, took financial command. The financial problems, however, were insoluble.

Yet by September, when the exposition was at its best, it was architecturally, scenically, educationally, and entertainingly superior and in some respects unique. "From a spectacular point of view," the official historian wrote later (C. R. Keiley, son of Anthony M. Keiley, first editor of the *Virginian*, and himself a later editorial writer of the

Landmark), "perhaps the great naval participation was the most important Exposition feature. Our magnificent Atlantic Squadron, which acted as a host for the monster ironclads of Austria, Argentina, Chile, England, France, Germany, Holland, Italy, Japan, Norway, and Sweden . . . for a considerable period was concentrated in Hampton Roads."

"THE EXPOSITION IS MAGNIFICENT—Come and See It," the *Landmark* cried in the last six weeks over an appeal which, though a partly salvage effort, was full of truth too:

> It would take a hardened cynic to contemplate without enthusiasm the beautiful buildings, with their brilliantly varied styles of architecture, their charming arrangement, their instructive and interesting exhibits, and the substantiality of construction which distinguishes these buildings from those of any other fair.
>
> The beauty of the location is beyond description. Here in Tidewater Virginia we have grown so used to the magnificence of Hampton Roads that we do not fully appreciate it. To the visitor looking upon the majestic marine roadstead for the first time, the impression of grandeur and beauty is overwhelming. There is no other such exposition site in the world.

Let that be the final word on an enterprise not blessed by fortune. Within a week after the exposition closed it was placed in receivership. Nearly ten years would pass before the final disposition of the land. But the 1917 purchaser was a government leading a nation in a recently started war and accepting as fact what the United States Navy had long understood: that the Hampton Roads area was indispensable for naval base purposes in a world struggle and would be indispensable thereafter for innumerable naval purposes.

THE RISE OF THE LEDGER-DISPATCH UNDER SLOVER'S MANAGEMENT AND Wilson's editorship exerted new pressures on both morning newspapers but especially on the *Landmark*. After the reorganization of the *Landmark* following the death of James Barron Hope in 1887, its outstanding stock, with a par value of $100, varied from sixty-eight to seventy-four shares, of which Nottingham, president and manager, and K. Foster Murray, editor (son of the earlier editor, Kenton C. Murray), held nearly all. Other directors generally held one share each. There were never more than six of these, and by mid-1910 the company had bought all their shares. Nottingham then held thirty-eight shares, Murray had thirty-two.

In May of 1910 the company paid $450 for the share of W. W. Starke and $600 for the share of C. A. Nash. The meager reports of the minute book of stockholders' and directors' meetings suggest a paper value then nearer $851, though the available information does not assure this figure. Company resources were put above $74,000 at the end of 1906, above $86,000 at the end of 1907 (the year of the Jamestown Exposition), above $85,000 for 1908, and almost as much at the end of 1909. "Excess of earnings over expenses" for these four years was, in round numbers, $13,000, $14,000, $4,000, and just under $4,000, respectively.

In dividends the *Landmark* was paying 6 per cent in the late 1880's and 8 and 9 per cent in the early 1890's, with a $20.00 extra for 1892. In the late 1890's dividends dropped back to 6 per cent, but they rose sharply from 1900 and for the next nine years varied from 12 to 16 per cent, and in one year (1901) rose to 20 per cent. The percentage of the dividends was based on the par value of the stock.

The *Landmark*'s principal owners were long inured to depending on careful administration and on special news and editorial quality.

Under that policy they had profited moderately before the arrival of the new kind of competition that faced them now. Nottingham was fifty-eight years old in 1910, and Murray much younger. Their record is ample proof that they would not give up easily. But the offer they received, just at this time, must have been unusually attractive. A striking change in the *Landmark*'s history had come.

On June 2, 1910, Nottingham and Murray sold all the stock in the Norfolk Landmark Publishing Company to Charles S. Abell, grandson of Arunah S. Abell, founder of the Baltimore *Sun*, and himself a member during the past fifteen years of the staff of the *Sun*, in which he held a stock interest.

Abell assumed "personal management" of the *Landmark* that day. Nottingham and Murray remained with him, Nottingham as secretary and treasurer, Murray as editor. One share of stock was transferred to Nottingham so that he could qualify as a director. For the same purpose another share went to John T. Morris, long a Baltimore *Sun* reporter and city editor, later a police commissioner in Baltimore, and at this time a practicing lawyer there. Abell was the only other director.

The *Landmark* of Abell made a conventional announcement but added an unconventional one by saying that "the Landmark's policy shall be that of the Baltimore Sun as declared in the editorial in the first edition of that newspaper, May 17, 1837," in these words:

> We shall strive to render it a channel of useful information to every citizen in every department of society, whether literary, professional, mercantile, manufacturing or miscellaneous. . . . We shall give no place to religious controversy nor political discussions of merely partisan character. On political principles and questions involving the interest or honor of the whole country it will be free, firm and temperate. Our object will be the common good without regard to that of sex, factions, or parties, and for this object we shall labor without fear or partiality.

The borrowing of these words for his Norfolk venture suggests how close Abell felt to his Baltimore *Sun* background even though the sale of a majority of the *Sun* stock six months earlier, in January, 1910, had the effect of removing him from its highest position. His father was George W. Abell, who had succeeded the first Abell as publisher and editor and made a notable record. Historians of the *Sun* credited George W. Abell with being "the possessor of a sound newspaper heart," who "could not be reached," whom "no social, business, religious or political influence . . . could divert from a course he had once taken."[1]

Born in 1876, Charles S. Abell entered the *Sun* office in 1894 at the age of eighteen and worked for the next fifteen years in the business and editorial departments. He was elected a director in 1898, one of four, and later he was secretary. Eventually, after the second-generation Abells had died, differences arose among the grandsons. Charles dissented frequently from policies of the presidency under a cousin, Walter W. Abell. When the latter declined reelection, Charles as vice president became the chief executive. For nine months (April, 1909-January, 1910) he presided over a prosperous operation. But other members of the family and their trustees joined in selling stock to Charles H. Grasty and electing him president and editor, and Charles resigned. He retained his holding in the *Sun*.

At thirty-four, after fifteen years' experience with an excellent newspaper, with money in his bank account and income from his *Sun* stock, it was natural—almost inevitable—that Charles S. Abell should look around for a newspaper. The *Landmark* was a challenge which, at that moment in his life, he seized with the determination to make a success whatever the odds against him.

The newspapers in Norfolk gave Abell a friendly greeting. The *Virginian-Pilot* called him "a gentleman who will be welcomed as representing in himself and by inheritance the best traditions of southern journalism," and it added: "For three generations the Abells have made the Baltimore Sun as near a Virginia newspaper as one published elsewhere could be. . . . Mr. Abell makes his advent as neither an alien nor a stranger." The *Ledger-Dispatch* noted that the new publisher was "still interested in the Baltimore Sun" and concluded that "its well known policy of conservatism is a guarantee of the future policy of the Landmark along the lines it has so well established." After a compliment to Nottingham as "not only the best known, but assuredly the most admired of the newspaper fraternity in Virginia," and to Murray, "able and talented . . . the literary excellence of its [the *Landmark*'s] editorials will remain undiminished" under him, the *Ledger-Dispatch* extended a "hearty welcome to the new management."

"The new management" plunged into improvement. Within less than two weeks it rented two Mergenthaler linotype machines (Model

1. The quotations are from Gerald W. Johnson, Frank R. Kent, H. L. Mencken, and Hamilton Owens, *The Sunpapers of Baltimore* (New York: Alfred A. Knopf, 1937).

5, at $550 yearly, and Model 4, Double Magazine, at $725 yearly).
Fourteen months later it bought both for $1,000 in cash and $4,475 in
twelve monthly notes. The *Landmark* blossomed out in new type,
looking fresh and clean, and drawing compliments around town. It
quickly established its own photoengraving plant, the first modern
facility of the kind in Norfolk. It put a full-time news photographer
to work, the first in Norfolk (though other men were using cameras
for the newspapers), and began publishing a page of pictures in a
Sunday magazine.

Far more startling, within two months the *Landmark*—after prep-
arations in warlike secrecy—published on August 1, 1910, a Monday
morning edition, the first since the *Virginian* began publishing Sundays, but not on Mondays, in 1874. So surprised were the other newspapers that they sent emissaries to the *Landmark* to inquire: Are you
experimenting? Or is this a permanent policy? Permanent, Abell assured them. Back they hustled to their own offices. The next day the
Virginian-Pilot announced that it too would publish on Mondays.

This was no light decision. Publishing costs were now measured by
seven days, not six days. Yet the price by the week remained the same,
and the advertising revenue on Monday, not ordinarily a big advertising day, rarely made up the difference. The change definitely increased costs. But it brought slower paced publishing into line with
modern and permanent practices.

All these moves spelled outgo. For income Abell went after circulation with four pages of colored comics on Sundays, contests in
which the prizes were trips to Europe, and a sharpening and expanding
of local news in all departments. He brought a Baltimore *Sun* man
in as managing editor, Frederick Julien Bailey, who soon was elected
vice president, a newly established office, and also a director of the
corporation. A new slogan appeared on the front page: "It's all here
and it's all true"—distinctly different from the selectivity principle of
Nottingham and Murray.

So strong was the Baltimore *Sun* heritage that the *Landmark* began to shift the cream of its local news to the back page. That was
a hallmark of the *Sun* (and in the middle 1960's still was). Thereafter it was *Landmark* policy and eventually the policy for decades of
its successor newspaper. At that time other Norfolk newspapers placed
most of their local news on pages one, two, and three.

In advertising Abell carried his attack most conspicuously—though
he hardly stopped there—to the classified front. The big growth of
the *Ledger-Dispatch* in such advertising was a direct challenge. But

by December, 1910, the *Ledger-Dispatch* was still far ahead with a page of classified advertisements to the four columns each in the *Virginian-Pilot* and the *Landmark*. Abell's new *Landmark* was fighting formidable opponents.

Particularly conspicuous was the *Landmark*'s exploitation of the local news-feature story for Sundays. Better facilities for pictures helped to add the power of illustrations to such stories as "Norfolk Show Horses," "Ghent Bridge Twenty Years Ago and Today," and "Woman's Club of Norfolk," now adorned with 180 members. Other newspapers had published such feature stories for years, but the *Landmark* reporters and photographers, turned loose almost for the first time, raked Norfolk and Tidewater history.

They celebrated, among much else, the lightships off the coast, the Civil War anniversaries, the Dismal Swamp in springtime, the disappeared volunteer firemen, the Navy Yard in all aspects, famous Virginia resorts, the powder supply at St. Julien's Creek, Chincoteague's pony-penning, Yorktown's glories, the Myers House in Norfolk, Suffolk's peanuts, battleship building in Newport News, the Norfolk Cotton Exchange, the romance and tragedies of the Ripraps where Fort Wool stood in the harbor, the education of Negroes in Hampton Institute, Smithfield's hams, winter homes on the North Carolina coast, and "Norfolk's Quaint Laws of 100 Years Ago."

The *Landmark* went further and invented subjects. "What Norfolk Needs Most" ran for many days as citizen after citizen filed his prescription. "How I Earned My First Dollar" brought out more citizens. When ministers were asked to answer, "What Do You Consider the Most Effective Hymn?" the winner turned out, after many days, to be "Lead, Kindly Light."

These devices stimulated the other newspapers. The *Virginian-Pilot* reexamined Fort Henry, rehonored Maury, recalled old Memorial Days, and recelebrated "Norfolk's Great Water Passenger Traffic." The *Ledger-Dispatch* depicted, on the one hand, the "Early History of Freemasonry in Virginia" and, on the other hand, "200,000 Norfolk as It Will Be in the Coming Years," and much in between. "Norfolk's Beautiful Homes" was a hit. The *Ledger-Dispatch* stretched that series through a long line of columned fronts, towered-corner residences of recent years, riverbank houses, and a few genuinely ancient homes still standing.

It is doubtful whether another period produced such a glut of local history as that which, in 1910 and 1911, these reporters and photographers and editors dug up and wrote and illustrated and published.

Editorially the new *Landmark* changed less. Six months after Abell's purchase, Murray, the editor who stayed on, resigned (November, 1910). He gave up newspaper work for a time but came back as Washington correspondent of the *Virginian-Pilot*. Charles Russel Keiley, the son of the *Virginian*'s first editor, familiar with the Norfolk scene after writing and editing the *Blue Book of the Jamestown Ter-Centennial Exposition*, took over the *Landmark*'s editorial page. He had been trained in Europe as well as the United States to be a mining engineer, but his health required a change, and he had worked for several newspapers.

Associates admired Keiley. Tazewell H. Lamb, the city editor of that period, wrote later[2] that Keiley "was given a free hand and demonstrated why he had been known in New York as one of Mr. Dana's 'bright young men' "—as many of Charles A. Dana's associates on the New York *Sun* were called. Lamb thought his paragraphs (those epigrammatic and theoretically witty comments of two or three lines that were popular then and later) were "brilliant" and called him a "master of the apt phrase."

And he was master of the blunt phrase too. Lamb told of the politician who stormed into the *Landmark* offices with a demand that the newspaper publish his denial of something it had written about him. "If you insist, I'll call you a liar in ten-point," Keiley informed the politician, ten-point being bigger type than the *Landmark* ordinarily used. "The politician hadn't the foggiest notion of what a liar in ten-point might be," Lamb continued, "but it sounded bad, so he withdrew his protest in the face of this dire threat."

When interest rose in a better form of government for Norfolk, the *Landmark* produced studies of how the new commission form was succeeding in Houston, Dallas, Memphis, and Berkeley, California. When Navy Yard improvements did not lead to a battleship construction contract, the *Landmark*, in December, 1910, and later, urged Virginians to "stir up their congressmen;" when two battleships were to be built somewhere, it urged Norfolk and Portsmouth to go after one of them. Racetrack betting at the Jamestown Jockey Club drew repeated rebukes and drew arguments in rejoinder too. To the *Landmark* the argument of community benefit was especially unimpressive. "Reno reaps a reward from its divorce mill," it said, "and Monte Carlo garners bushels of ducats from its casino," but it marked down their repu-

2. In a letter to Harry P. Moore, *circa* April, 1961, from which Joseph E. Shank took notes.

tations as undesirable, "and neither of them does the thing that can make them consistently prosperous—produce."

The charges in the Democratic senatorial primary of September, 1911, when Senators Martin and Swanson beat off the efforts of Representatives William A. Jones and Carter Glass to supplant them, disturbed the *Landmark* more than other Norfolk newspapers. Jones enlivened that campaign with quotations from letters relating to Martin's handling of railroad contributions for politicians in earlier campaigns, the so-called "yellow dog fund," a term Virginia politicians had borrowed from the New York insurance scandals. The *Landmark* criticized Martin and then gave him space to reply. It was not favorably impressed by his statement.

Evidence to sustain the charges did not impress the state. The *Ledger-Dispatch* in particular defended Martin, and voters sustained him. But J. Taylor Ellyson, the Democratic state chairman, had felt it necessary to declare that "everyone in politics then knows that from the time John S. Barbour was elected Democratic state chairman in 1883 until the adoption of the new constitution [of 1901-2] we were accustomed to collect campaign funds from railroads and other corporations" in order to maintain white supremacy. The demands for such funds were much less after the adoption of the poll tax requirement for voting. Though the 1911 Democratic primary seemed to stir the state with its debate, the vote in neither contest reached ninety-seven thousand. The *Landmark* felt that it could "not conscientiously congratulate Mr. Martin."

But for all its efforts the *Landmark* could not cut deeply into the position of either the *Virginian-Pilot* or the *Ledger-Dispatch*. Abell and his staff were producing a livelier newspaper, but they did not add sufficiently to circulation or advertising. They were publishing a more expensive newspaper without adding materially to revenue. In the counting room the news was not good.

Abell could not doubt that hard fact after the stockholders' annual meeting in January, 1911. Reports for ten months ending December 31, 1910, which included his own first six months, showed that for the first time since the corporation was chartered "excess of earnings over expenses" had turned into "excess of expenses over earnings." The expenses that mounted with Abell's attempt to enlarge and improve the *Landmark* had produced a deficits "excess" of $13,611.07.

That must have been a bad time for Abell. But he did not hesitate long. At some moment during 1911, probably well into the second half, he determined to cut the loss short. He went straight to the *Virginian-Pilot*. Would that newspaper be interested in an arrangement to merge the *Landmark* with the *Virginian-Pilot*?

There was no doubt of the answer. The history of newspaper publishing in Norfolk in the forty-six years since 1865, and most vividly in the second half of this period, had been one long story of newspaper consolidation. The economics of publishing was ending the multiple-newspaper era. It had forced (as it was forcing all over the United States) the consolidation of competing newspapers. No newspaper voice had been so insistent as the *Landmark* itself in pointing out that there were too many newspapers in Norfolk.

The *Landmark* made the first announcement on Saturday, December 30, 1911: "On January 1 [of 1912] the good will and business of The Norfolk Landmark will be merged with that of the Virginian-Pilot, and the two papers, as one publication, will appear under the name of the Virginian-Pilot, with the notation, 'The Norfolk Landmark.' . . . The present owners of this paper will acquire a stock holding interest" in the Virginian and Pilot Publishing Company. The *Landmark* submitted the case to popular judgment in these words:

> An aggressive and liberal policy of expenditure by The Norfolk Landmark has demonstrated that Norfolk could not, at least for the present, support two morning papers, which, in the volume and accuracy of the news and the manner and promptness of its service, would prove worthy of the city.
> When the owners of the Virginian-Pilot were approached it was found that they fully shared this opinion but their attachment to the interests of the city and the commanding position which they had established for their paper in the community was such that they desired to maintain the same, and, accordingly, a consolidation of interests suggested by this paper has been, after serious deliberation, successfully concluded. . . .
> [Also] it was concluded that the real welfare of Norfolk and its citizens would be best served by one morning newspaper that would combine the work of both in a united effort to upbuild and promote the best traditions and interests of Norfolk . . . the best interests alike of a newspaper and of the community in which it exists, and exercises its influence are never at odds, but ever identical. . . .

The *Ledger-Dispatch* said frankly that "since the present owner purchased the paper and enlarged its facilities, adding a Monday morning paper and colored supplements on Sunday, it is understood that The Landmark has been operated at a considerable loss, and the merger is believed to have been the logical sequence."

Financial arrangements showed increasingly sophisticated corporate management. The Virginian and Pilot Publishing Company increased its stock from 750 to 5,000 shares. It declared a dividend to old stockholders of 3,100 shares, so that they then held 3,850 shares, leaving 1,150 shares not assigned to them.

These 1,150 shares of stock, 23 per cent of the total issue of the enlarged company, went to Abell for the *Landmark*. At a par value of $100 a share they would represent a valuation of $115,000 for the *Landmark*, not including such assets as cash, book accounts, and other specified property. The enlarged company paid the rent for the *Landmark's* Main Street quarters and sought to lease the building to others.

The old *Virginian-Pilot* stockholders established the G. and G. Corporation (taking the initials from Grandy and Glennan) to hold their property, including cash, bonds, notes, open accounts, and real estate, for their benefit. The G. and G. Corporation leased the Tazewell Street plant to the enlarged company for continued publishing operations.

The division of the new shares among the old stockholders was based on their relative holdings in the 750-share Virginian and Pilot Publishing Company. Of the pre-1912 capital stock the Grandy group held above 58 per cent of the shares; the Glennan group, above 41 per cent. But in the enlarged capital stock of 5,000 shares the entry of the Abell holding of 23 per cent had the effect of reducing the combined Grandy proportion to a little above 45 per cent of the whole, and the combined Glennan share to approximately 30 per cent.

Abell played no major part in the management of the merged newspaper other than as a director. He decided to learn more about circulation. Characteristically, he went to the Philadelphia *Public Ledger* because it was a successful newspaper and because his grandfather had been one of three men to establish it in 1836, a year before moving to Baltimore to establish the *Sun*. But after studying circulation techniques there Abell turned aside for railroad work in the West and in Washington and was in the Army during the first World War.

In 1919 he was back in Norfolk. He reorganized the *Virginian-Pilot's* circulation department and remained five years in the business department—"an officer without portfolio," in his words. In 1925 he was business manager of the Washington *Post*, but resigned after a year. He died in 1953 at the age of seventy-six. His son, William S. Abell, a Washington lawyer, was for many years a valuable member of the board of directors of the newspapers in Norfolk.

The name chosen for the merged newspaper was cumbersome. At

the front-page masthead the words "Virginian-Pilot" appeared in the normal position in the familiar type. Below and in much smaller type were the words "and The Norfolk Landmark." But the *Landmark*'s name looked like the tail of a kite. People tended to call the newspaper "the *Virginian-Pilot*." A frequently used term was "the *Pilot*," and still is.

The newspaper made profits from the start. In July of 1912 the directors declared a 2 per cent dividend on earnings for the first six months of the new operation. Early in 1913 they declared another 2 per cent dividend for the second half of the year—in all, since the dividends were based on the par value of the $500,000 capital stock, a total of $20,000.

Before the merger the *Virginian-Pilot* had been paying 10 per cent annually on its capital stock of $75,000, or a dividend of $7,500, and in 1911 it paid an extra 5 per cent, lifting the total to $11,250 for that year. The *Landmark*'s premerger dividends varied from 12 to 16 per cent, but that was on a capital of only about $7,000 and in dollars would not have lifted the total of the two separate newspapers to a sum as large as that which the merged newspaper began paying.

The gain was not surprising. The new status of the *Virginian-Pilot and the Norfolk Landmark* was unusually favorable. It was not only the sole morning newspaper: it had now gone ahead of the *Ledger-Dispatch* in circulation. In that respect it was the top newspaper in town.

Three months before the merger, in October, 1911, the American Association of Advertisers, which had begun checking the circulation of some newspapers, credited the *Virginian-Pilot* with a circulation of 16,992. The *Landmark* did not submit to external checking and almost never disclosed its circulation. The nearest *Ledger-Dispatch* figure was in April, 1911. It showed 17,821. The *Ledger-Dispatch* had gone ahead of the *Virginian-Pilot* when the *Public Ledger* bought the *Dispatch* in 1906.

Whatever the *Landmark*'s circulation was, the merged circulation included duplicates. But in November, 1913, the morning newspaper was showing 22,692 and was ahead of its afternoon competitor. By May of 1914 the *Virginian-Pilot and The Norfolk Landmark* could report 25,798 for a weekly average and 31,722 for Sunday. Almost simultaneously, in April, 1914, the *Ledger-Dispatch* reported a six-months average of 20,372 for its six-day publication.

Both newspapers benefited in circulation by the heightened interest in Mexican disorders and dangers. The Veracruz incident sent ships of the Atlantic Fleet steaming out of Hampton Roads. One day that April when the news was hot the *Ledger-Dispatch* sold 41,600 copies; in three days, 113,595, a record. With the onset of the World War in August, 1914, all circulation rose, especially the *Ledger-Dispatch's*. Like other afternoon newspapers in America, it could receive much war news from European theaters in time for publication on the day of the events, and it gained. It continued to have vigorous circulation soliciting from a management that would never be content with second place.

In circulation and in all other aspects of newspapers—their virtues and their failings—the *Ledger-Dispatch* and the *Virginian-Pilot* inevitably were pitted against each other. The end of the multi-newspaper age had arrived, the beginning of the two-newspaper age was at hand. The two were starting twenty years of direct rivalry on a new plane. They were starting more than fifty years of competition in their primary newspaper sense. They would bring all their resources to bear on this struggle. They would do so in a city that, more than nearly any other American city, would feel the impact of the international age that was just ahead.

Elsewhere in Norfolk another newspaper had begun to breathe, so quietly at first that few people heard it, though in time they would. In 1910, P. B. Young, a Negro editor and all-round newspaperman, took command of a fraternal lodge's newspaper, reduced its name to the *Journal and Guide*, and began to demonstrate what could be done with a Negro weekly. It had a circulation of five hundred then; it had fifty-five thousand later, spread over several states. Its news was almost entirely about Negroes, and its editorial columns discussed intelligently their affairs and rights. Other Norfolk newspapers respected it, and in time the *Journal and Guide* and its editors won many distinctions.

Julian Street, of *Collier's Weekly*, probably the best known national magazine reporter and feature writer of his time, came to town late in 1916 and shocked Norfolk by announcing that he had never heard of Matthew Fontaine Maury, "The Pathfinder of the Seas." Even worse, Street said he had asked school boys who Maury was and they had not heard of him either.

That set the newspapers off into long protests and examinations, chiefly of the way history was being taught. And that led to the suspicion that Maury was unheard of in Street and schoolboy circles because, in the words of the *Virginian-Pilot*, he was "a Virginian, a

Southerner and a Confederate," and therefore did not get into the history books. The editor cited recent evidence:

> The pupils of one of our Norfolk schools took part in a spectacular drama supposed to portray the genesis of our country. The first act pictured the voyage and discovery of a new country by Columbus. The second presented the landing of the pilgrims at Plymouth Rock. This is Virginia, which was settled prior to the coming of the Puritan colony to New England. Virginia already had a representative government and an elective legislature when the Mayflower anchored off the then wilderness of Massachusetts.

Much must have been forgiven Street when his article on Norfolk appeared that December in *Collier's*. Street described Richmond as "the Boston of Virginia and Norfolk as its New York." He thought that from the tops of tall buildings Norfolk looked like a miniature New York: the Elizabeth River as the East River, Portsmouth as Brooklyn, Newport News as Jersey City and Hoboken, and Willoughby Spit as Sandy Hook. He described the spending population as being larger than the native population, just like New York, and he kept right on: "Norfolk, in short, likes the things New York likes. It likes tall office buildings and dotes on signs of commercial activity by day and social activity at night. Business and population grow in Richmond, but you don't feel them growing as you do in Norfolk. You feel that Richmond business men already have money, whereas in Norfolk there is less old wealth and more scrambling for new dollars."

Did the town blink over that characterization!

One of those who was scrambling for new dollars early in 1912 was Thomas H. Gilliam, Jr., a year and a half out of a Norfolk high school and determined to be a *Ledger-Dispatch* reporter.[3] He approached the editor and saw "a most frightening man—big, gruff, very evidently annoyed that I had broken in on whatever . . . he was doing, and brutally frank about it . . . almost without looking at me from his position, hunched over a big desk with a two-inch pad of newsprint copy paper and the greatest collection of short pencils I have ever laid my eyes on, he sort of snorted out the advice that I had better get the idea out of my head—or, anyhow, find something else to do than worry him with it. He wanted me to get out of there and let him alone, and he told me so." The sitter for this portrait was Harvey Laird Wilson.

And when young Tom Gilliam eventually wangled a place for

3. Letter from Thomas H. Gilliam, Jr. to Joseph E. Shank, April 16, 1961.

himself as a cub reporter by proposing to work for a month without pay, he looked around at his working quarters:

> The city room looked as though . . . [it had been] designed by Rube Goldberg in one of his most delirious hours—especially the lighting. From a string of two wires running around the wooden ceiling, drop lights fell down in one direction only to be led by strings to another direction so as to let the light bulbs hover over an assortment of antiquated typewriter desks and tables ranged along two walls . . . one [table] was piled high with copies of newspapers from a wide geographical area— "exchanges," we called them, I learned later. The other table held just a clutter of copy paper and odds and ends, including overcoats in winter, an umbrella or two nearly always and almost anything else you could imagine that could be thrown on a table, except hats. Hats were never taken off in the office apparently by anybody, except Henry Perkins, who was city editor, and Eddie Holmes, who was telegraph editor.
>
> The city editor's desk was out in the middle of the floor . . . a big old-fashioned roll-top thing. The telegraph editor's desk was closer to the windows on a sort of line with that of the city editor. The Associated Press telegrapher had a table with his typewriter and old-fashioned telegrapher's instrument— just a simple open "key" thing—along the wall facing the telegraph editor's desk. . . . The atmosphere of that city room was damaging to the romantic notions of a youngster looking to newspaper work as a career. . . .

Here Henry Perkins presided in his quiet, professional way, already an experienced city editor in Richmond when he came to Norfolk in 1906, overwhelmed by work and harassed every minute, but forever unexcited, never raising his voice, and capable of doing anything—most beloved of all *Ledger-Dispatch* men for nearly half a century. Here "Old Man Hamilton," as young Gilliam thought of Richard Hamilton, wrote about deaths and funerals and the news of churches. His son, Norman R. Hamilton, wrote about business, real estate, and federal government activities, but soon he would be appointed collector of customs and eventually would own the Portsmouth *Star* and go to Congress.

Walter Virnelson was the city hall reporter and wrote the news of the courts. Tom Gilliam soon was handling police and fire news, and Virnelson and he "covered sports as a sort of side line"—local sports, while Eddie Holmes and the AP wire took care of the rest. Frank Wing and Hugh Steele were "in-and-outers," and "each of us was always subject to some sort of special assignment almost every day.

Even on the dullest days there wasn't much time between 8 a.m. and 5:30 p.m."

In a year or so, when Gilliam was feeling his oats and thought he was entitled to $18.00 a week but could not get it, he left for a $20.00 job with the Savannah *Morning News*. But he came back to the *Ledger-Dispatch* before he departed permanently, an exile in an advertising career that led to an N. W. Ayer & Son vice presidency. His heart never left Norfolk. Though he was a *Ledger-Dispatch* reporter in early Slover years, W. O. Saunders' heart probably never was in Norfolk. The independence, courage, earthiness, and confidence that flowered later in his own Elizabeth City *Independent* were apparent in his brief career in Norfolk but necessarily found less opportunity for growth under the stricter management of a larger newspaper. "We could never understand each other," Saunders said of Slover.

When Tazewell H. Lamb came to Norfolk, originally from Elizabeth City across the Tar Heel border but most recently from El Paso, he worked first with the *Ledger-Dispatch* and knew Gilliam's colleagues. Then he moved over to "a copy desk job" with the *Landmark* where Eddie Holmes was at that time, and Bruce Salley, who was sent to Kitty Hawk in 1908. Lamb thought the *Landmark* well named because "you knew where to find it and the *noblesse oblige* spirit of Mr. Nottingham reached from front office to press room. Typical: Interrupted as he stood at the bar, he said to an obnoxious individual: 'You will excuse me, I am having a drink with a gentleman'."

But newspaper men had restless feet, and presently Lamb was with the *Virginian-Pilot* when Keville Glennan was city editor and Harry Moore was "a reporter who scored beats invariably anywhere along the coast from Cape Henry to Cape Hatteras." Then Lamb was away from Norfolk for a year or so on lesser enterprises until Starke brought him back as managing editor of the merged *Virginian-Pilot*. Years later he recalled that

> Harry Moore was my assistant. Sam Potts was telegraph editor. Asa Biggs was sports editor—and very good. Later he went to the Baltimore Sun and was in charge of the cable desk when he died. . . . Bob Glass was our ace political news writer. He went on to become editor of the Lynchburg News, owned by his uncle, Carter Glass, United States senator. Keville Glennan was Sunday editor, brilliant but unpredictable. Bessy Chamberlaine was society editor. R. E. Turner was business

manager. And "Billy" Wilkinson, genial treasurer, generally helpful to everybody on the payroll foundered in a financial storm.

These were the scenes, these were the news men who worked in them, and this was the way they talked.

These were also witnesses to the coming of prohibition in Virginia and the first World War at almost the same time. The approach of prohibition long had been visible. But it was not until the early 1900's that the Virginia Anti-Saloon League began to make extensive gains in countryside and small towns by local option votes. It was not until the Rev. James Cannon, Jr., took command of the Anti-Saloon League with his driving energy, astute sense of organization, and political ruthlessness that the dry movement marched to legislative triumph.

By 1908 the prohibitionists had dried up much of Virginia piecemeal. The shrewder among them doubted their ability yet to sweep the state. But they had sufficient political power to bring about in 1909 a rapprochement of the prohibitionists led by Cannon and the state Democratic organization led by Senator Martin for the election of William Hodges Mann, a prohibitionist, as governor over Harry St. George Tucker, whom Norfolk had known well as president of the Jamestown Exposition.

This embracing by regular politicians and dry politicians was commonly believed to guarantee for Martin's followers who favored liquor that the prohibitionists would not press for a referendum on statewide prohibition during the four years of the Mann administration— a referendum which prohibitionists were doubtful of winning then. The arrangement was believed to benefit prohibitionists by giving them a favorable governor and more time to build up a larger following. Mann won over Tucker, though only by 5,078 votes, and the big issue was in fact postponed.

The oasis character of the larger cities continued to be a constant challenge to the prohibitionists. Cannon could boast in April, 1910, that in less than a decade 3,000 saloons in Virginia had been cut to 850; 800 distilleries had declined to nearer 50; Lynchburg, Danville, Charlottesville, Fredericksburg, Winchester, Staunton, Clifton Forge, Radford, and Suffolk "refuse to license saloons, and in Bristol and Roanoke they exist by a small purchased majority." But Cannon doubtless knew, because the *Landmark* published it in December, 1909, that liquor dealers in Norfolk alone were shipping into nearby dry Virginia and North Carolina areas from ten to twelve carloads of liquor every day.

The Mann governorship ran out early in 1914, and the massive drive for all-state prohibition, with Cannon in the leading armored car, pushed easily through the House of Delegates and battered to a tie vote in the Senate. When J. Taylor Ellyson, the lieutenant governor, voted with the prohibitionists, they had their enabling act for a referendum. In September of 1914, in the referendum thus ordained, Virginians voted by 94,251 to 63,886 for state prohibition—only 158,000 votes in a state of 2,000,000 population—and the victory was complete.

Virtually all of this had run counter to newspaper thinking in Norfolk. Back in November of 1902 the *Dispatch* had warned that "the women are organizing and begging their friends to vote for the suppression of the liquor traffic . . . the plea of a mother, a wife or a sweetheart will not go unheeded." "Prohibition is a mistake," the *Landmark* thought early in 1903. "It creates conditions worse than it essays to rectify. . . . People generally are not prohibitionists. . . . But they prefer any other extreme to that of letting the law be flagrantly and impudently violated by dealers in liquor." In the following June the *Virginian-Pilot* called it "a sad commentary upon the politics of our cities that the greatest single political power is the saloon."

When Judge William Hodges Mann, the prohibitionist, was being boomed for the attorney generalship in May of 1903, the *Virginian-Pilot* was troubled by the prospect that, if elected, he would strengthen the concept of state action against liquor rather than local option. "We have seen with deep concern the Democratic legislatures of Virginia and North Carolina make asses of themselves by agitating an issue that by all Democratic theories and principles should be left to . . . local self government," it said. ". . . A pretty disagreeable experience will follow, in both states, before the sleeping dog the legislators wantonly kicked goes back to sleep."

By 1908 the *Virginian-Pilot* felt stronger than ever about prohibition *vs.* local option. It declared in December that:

> The Virginian-Pilot, while favoring local option, is opposed to prohibition by legislative enactment and makes no bones about declaring that opposition.
>
> If prohibition ever prohibits it must be where the predominant sentiment of the people in any given locality favors the abolition of the saloon, and thereby gives notice to local officials that enforcement of the law will be required at their hands. . . .

The experience of Georgia and Alabama with state prohibition is but proving a repetition of Maine and Kansas and every other state which has tried it. This solution of the liquor traffic question won't work. That's all there is to it.

But by the time of the referendum in September of 1914 West Virginia as well as North Carolina had gone dry, President Wilson had announced that no alcoholic drink of any kind would be served in the White House, Navy Secretary Daniels had ruled out wine on naval vessels, and the advance of national prohibition in many parts of the country had gone further down the road. Only a handful of cities and only a quarter of the counties of Virginia had withstood the pressures to close out liquor sales. The result was not seriously in doubt.

Just before the referendum the *Virginian-Pilot*, in words that almost surely were written by Cameron, said sadly but thoughtfully:

> The controversy has developed a bitterness of spirit not conducive to the moral, spiritual, social or political health of the community. . . .
> It is more in sorrow than in anger that we have seen the contention in Virginia over the most efficacious method of legislating to minimize the curse of intemperance in drink assume the shape of a religious propaganda and the thunders of the pulpit called into requisition to denounce as impious the earnest convictions of thousands of Virginians whose only offense has been they cannot view statewide prohibition as others would have them see it.
> Whatever the result at the polls may be, the ill effects of the campaign of intolerance and proscription will linger as a blight on the kindly forbearance with which Virginians have heretofore agreed to disagree on public topics. . . .

The *Ledger-Dispatch*, looking at a vote that carried seventy-six of one hundred counties and all cities except Norfolk, Richmond, Alexandria, and Williamsburg, did not believe that "enforcement of the law is going to work any disaster to the state, and that the abolition of saloons in many localities will result in inestimable good cannot be questioned." Advocates, doubters, and opponents of prohibition all had much to learn.

In contrast to the paced arrival of prohibition in Virginia the European war—as it seemed limited then to American minds—exploded in the same summer of 1914 in a series of streamers across the front pages, including these, alternately, in the *Ledger-Dispatch* and the *Virginian-Pilot*:

Austria-Hungary Declares War on Serbs	(July 28)
Austria Ready to Declare War on Russia	(July 31)
European War Certain, French Diplomats Say	(August 1)
Germany Declares War Against Russia	(August 2)
German Armies March into Russia and France	(August 5)
War Declared Between Germany and England	(August 5)

President Wilson's pleas for neutrality and such assurances as the *Ledger-Dispatch*'s that "it is highly unlikely the war will last as long as six months" (because it could not be financed or supplied with munitions) helped most Americans to keep the fighting at a distance. But in Norfolk that grew more difficult in March of 1915 when *Prinz Eitel Friedrich*, the German liner converted into a raider, steamed into Hampton Roads, seven months out of Chinese waters, carrying 80 passengers and 247 seamen from ships she had sunk. British and French naval vessels guarded the Virginia Capes against her departure. They did not prevent *Kron Prinz Wilhelm*, drab and dirty looking after months of raiding, short of food and fuel, her crew riddled with beriberi, from seeking internment a month later, as *Prinz Eitel Friedrich* had done. Both fell under the control of the recent *Ledger-Dispatch* reporter, Norman R. Hamilton, now collector of customs, whose handling of unfamiliar duties drew praise from his old colleagues.

A more puzzling problem arrived a year later when *Appam* sailed into the harbor. A German prize crew from the raider *Moewe*, which had captured her off the African coast, was in charge of this former British passenger ship, now loaded with prisoners. Lawyers began a long fight over ownership, but *Appam* joined the other interned ships.

Deutschland excited the newspapers even more. When this submarine slid between the Capes on a dark night in July, 1916, carrying chemicals, dyestuffs, and mail, but no sign of a weapon, she was classified as an unarmed merchant vessel. A tug had waited two weeks for her arrival, and Harry P. Moore and Marcus Richter, *Virginian-Pilot* reporters, knew the tug was up to something. But they could not verify their suspicions and so could not persuade editors to print what they had. The tug escorted *Deutschland* up Chesapeake Bay to Baltimore, where the submarine was a sensation. Three and a half weeks later she was at sea again. Her real cargo was propaganda.

Wilson's appeal for an end to killing noncombatants and his steps to protect Americans from submarine attacks were characterized by the *Virginian-Pilot* as "firmness, calm courage and wise restraint" which "should go far to inspire the people with confidence in whatever developments may arise." But it could not understand "what ails the British Navy" and reported hints of "friction in high places."

When Bryan resigned as secretary of state in the aftermath of the *Lusitania* sinking the *Virginian-Pilot* sharply rejected his attitude. "The people are behind President Wilson . . . in his determination to uphold the dignity and honor of the nation." And when, in June of 1916, Wilson called preparedness "the imperative duty of the hour," Norfolk responded four days later with a preparedness parade which the *Virginian-Pilot* reported in a page of pictures.

The port was buzzing with new and larger activities. Western horses for France were being loaded on ships at Pinners Point (the contract called for 132,000 of them). The naval collier, *Cyclops*, which later would disappear mysteriously, claimed a record in coal deliveries to naval vessels out of Hampton Roads. Navy Secretary Daniels visited overcrowded St. Helena in Berkley, where the receiving ships were training seamen, and twenty-five thousand people greeted him. The Navy's need of much larger facilities increased its efforts to acquire the Jamestown Exposition grounds. Secretary Daniels and members of the House Naval Affairs Committee inspected the exposition site late in 1916. The *Virginian-Pilot* reported that "practically every member of the committee" favored the area "for use as an aviation station, submarine and torpedo base without parallel."

When war came in April of 1917 the Senate accepted Senator Martin's item in a military appropriations bill for $1,400,000 for the purchase of the exposition grounds and some adjacent acreage and for $1,600,000 for preliminary work on a base there. Senators were moved especially by Martin's report that naval recruits were being sent home for lack of a place to put them. The House balked at first. Not until President Wilson himself appealed for fast action did it approve the appropriation.

But on June 15 the President signed the appropriation bill, and on June 28 the transaction was completed. On July 4 construction of the initial barracks began. On October 12 fourteen hundred bluejackets marched from St. Helena to the raw construction area for the formal ceremonies. There Rear Admiral A. C. Dillingham delivered the training station to Captain J. H. Dayton and pronounced the historic words: "The Base has begun to function." Seventeen hundred recruits per week were scheduled to arrive until the total reached 10,000.

Long before—as early as February—an antisubmarine net had closed the door to any armed *Deutschland* that might try to slip into Hampton Roads. The spy hunts had begun, inflation was taking hold and biting harder, the *Ledger-Dispatch* was calling for people to raise their own vegetables and was offering a gold medal and cash prizes for a thrift essay contest, the names of volunteers for the armed forces were being published daily in the newspapers, but the draft caused more talk, and the Liberty Loans and Red Cross drives were on their way.

Issues of censorship in a Justice Department bill had arisen and had drawn an immediate and strong protest from the *Virginian-Pilot*. Cameron had not forgotten his principles. He put his pen to work in the old, oracular style for a *Virginian-Pilot* editorial:

> When it comes to the point that the people or the press, which is their most zealous and faithful champion, shall be subject to pains and penalties inflicted by some Jack in office, or some shoulder-strapped centurion, for pointing out blunders in the civil or military prosecution of the war, then the United States will be wearing the collar of a tyranny which no autocracy in Europe dares impose on the populace or journalism. . . . God forbid it! . . . Full provision against seditious publications and those giving aid and comfort to the enemy should be made, but the fundamental rights of the people must not be invaded. . . .

Work on Langley Field on the lower Peninsula for a great air base had begun in the preceding February. Work in expanding and modernizing the long-established Navy Yard in Portsmouth had been going on for months, and would increase and continue unceasingly. But the planting of the Navy on the Hampton Roads site where the Jamestown Exposition had sparkled in its completed beauty was, more than anything else in that era and ever since, the recognition of the values of the passage between the Virginia Capes and of the riches inside—the bays, the roadsteads, the rivers, the surrounding complexes of land and cities and railroads and people—for utilization for national defense in war or in peace. Nothing of greater importance had come into the life of Norfolk since it was established as a town two hundred and thirty years earlier.

20 · WAR YEARS AND CITY MANAGER GOVERNMENT

WHEN THE UNITED STATES ENTERED THE FIRST WORLD WAR, BOTH THE *Ledger-Dispatch* and its chief owners, Slover and Wilson, were in a strong position. The *Ledger-Dispatch* had been the only afternoon newspaper in Norfolk for eleven years. For the first five it had a larger circulation and a larger advertising volume than any other Norfolk newspaper. When the *Virginian-Pilot* and the *Landmark* combined and went ahead in circulation in 1912, the *Ledger-Dispatch* was not so far behind as to be hurt significantly.

In April, 1916, the Audit Bureau of Circulations—a national organization with crews of its own for examining newspaper circulation objectively—credited the *Ledger-Dispatch* with a six-day average of 30,754. In the same month this auditing body credited the *Virginian-Pilot* (plus the *Landmark*) with 25,005 for the six weekdays and 32,514 on Sunday. The two newspapers argued over technicalities of circulation counting, but the *Ledger-Dispatch* obviously had climbed back to the *Virginian-Pilot's* level and on a six-day basis was slightly higher.

In June, 1918, the Richmond *News-Leader* proclaimed that it had the largest circulation in Virginia, 46,028, but the *Ledger-Dispatch* challenged the claim. Its own circulation, it said, was 47,301. The war had lifted the circulations of nearly all newspapers. But the *Ledger-Dispatch* was doing better than growing with the times.

With this circulation the *Ledger-Dispatch* could increase its volume of advertising, from which the greater part of the newspaper's revenue came. The *Virginian-Pilot's* larger Sunday edition was an important asset, but on other days the *Ledger-Dispatch* was ahead. It had established strong roots.

Not even the bad fire of March 19, 1913, from which the damage was estimated at first as between $50,000 and $80,000, really hurt the newspaper. The insurance protection was good. Six weeks earlier the *Ledger-Dispatch* had announced its lease of the Carpenter block, so called, on the south side of Plume Street, between Concord Street and Martin's Lane, and also a vacant lot in the rear where it planned to build a structure for the mechanical work. The *Ledger-Dispatch* was still occupying the old *Dispatch* quarters and adjoining buildings on the north side of Plume Street a little to the east, and the move would be across the street but within the same block.

The fire hastened the move. Temporarily the *Ledger-Dispatch* used *Virginian-Pilot* facilities, but fast patching enabled it to utilize old burned quarters. Another eight months were necessary to convert the Carpenter building to newspaper purposes, chiefly concentrated on the second floor and to the rear. First floor space was rented to a dozen outside businesses. By November of 1913 the new home was ready for occupancy, and by New Year's Day the *Ledger-Dispatch* celebrated with a big descriptive edition. Here it remained, gradually enlarging the quarters and absorbing the first floor space, for the next twenty-four years until it moved in 1937 into the Brambleton Avenue structure where it has been ever since.

Organizationally the *Ledger-Dispatch* had built solidly too. Slover and Wilson were schooled and experienced. The division of responsibility between the two was well understood. They worked together smoothly, each with respect for the other.

Wilson's bringing in Henry Perkins from Richmond in 1906 had given him a competent back-up man. Late in 1907 Slover engaged as stenographer, on the recommendation of a friend, a nineteen-year-old Pennsylvanian, Paul S. Huber. Born in Chambersburg, Huber graduated from high school there and went to Chicago to work for a coal company. Eighteen months later the company transferred him to Cumberland, Maryland. He did not know anything about newspaper publishing, but he was intelligent, and he learned fast. In two years his name was on the editorial masthead as secretary of the corporation. He was well started on a career that lasted thirty-eight years in Norfolk and carried him to the presidency of the Ledger-Dispatch Corporation and to stock ownership in it and in other newspapers in which Slover was interested.

A week after Huber went to work in January of 1908, Franklin S. Cook returned from New Orleans after five months as advertising manager of the *Item* under his old Norfolk *Dispatch* publisher and editor, James M. Thomson. He joined the *Ledger-Dispatch* organization as advertising manager. The next year Slover brought in from the Chicago *Daily News*, published in a city where circulation was a fighting word, young Norman N. Hill to be circulation manager.

Huber in business management, Perkins in news and editorial duties, Cook in advertising, Hill in circulation—all these hitched their fortunes to the *Ledger-Dispatch*'s in its first three years, all were young and eager, all remained with the newspaper throughout their careers, all were strongly influenced by Slover's leadership, and all were pillars in the newspaper's development.

In 1907, the year after the *Public Ledger* bought the *Dispatch*, Slover joined his friend Alvah H. Martin in buying the afternoon Portsmouth *Star* from Paul C. Trugien. A. McK. Griggs, earlier a reporter of the *Virginian* and a correspondent for out-of-town newspapers, and at this time the *Star*'s city editor, was one of the purchasing group. He was made editor and continued in that capacity until 1926.

Martin, not Slover, was the moving force in this transaction. He was the leader of the unique fusion of political forces that controlled Norfolk County (a separate governmental entity, not connected with the city of Norfolk). Democrats, all the way from the county to the state organization, often tried to recapture the county, but rarely succeeded in any substantial degree. The *Star* was a sharp and persistent critic of the fusion regime and, in Martin's opinion, was unfair and unjust. A practical man and a direct actionist, he determined to remove this thorn by buying the newspaper.

Political purposes would not have moved Slover to join in buying a newspaper, but loyalty to a friend—always a powerful characteristic of his—would. The *Star* was not a large newspaper then, and the price for it probably was low. But Slover was struggling with debt problems of his own, and the financial arrangements necessarily rested chiefly on Martin. Slover thereafter kept in managerial touch, giving the *Star* supervision, though the day-by-day operation remained in Portsmouth.

In December of 1916 these owners of the Portsmouth *Star* sold a one-third interest to Norman R. Hamilton, the former *Ledger-Dispatch* reporter and more recently collector of customs in Norfolk. Hamilton took on the duties of publisher, Griggs remained editor. Two years later Martin died, and in 1924 Hamilton bought the remaining two-thirds, paying—he said much later—$50,000. He assumed the editorial duties too. Over the years he developed the *Star* substantially.

Changes had been made, meantime, in Newport News. In 1909, four years after Slover and Wilson bought the *Public Ledger* and moved to Norfolk, they sold their *Times-Herald* in Newport News to Walter S. Copeland. He had worked in Norfolk as a *Virginian* reporter in the early 1880's. When J. Richard Lewellen went to Danville to publish the *Register*, Copeland joined him and acquired an interest in the *Register*. In the 1890's he was associated with Richmond newspapers and later was editor of the Richmond *Times-Dispatch*. Professionally and personally he was well known in Virginia and much admired. Slover and Wilson brought him to Newport News to edit their newspaper before he organized the company that bought it.

The sale confirmed still further that Slover and Wilson had settled on Norfolk as the base of their operations. "The Ledger-Dispatch will continue as at present," that newspaper said in announcing the sale in Newport News. It added, characteristically, that it was not affected by the sale "except in the benefit it derives from the proceeds." One benefit was the wiping out of whatever remained of the debt that Slover and Wilson had incurred when they began publishing in Newport News.

In April of 1914, the *Ledger-Dispatch* reported that its outstanding capital stock was $125,000, with a par value of $100 a share, of which Slover's holding was put at $50,300 and Wilson's at $50,200. The remaining $24,500 was divided among Martin; Nathaniel Beaman, the banker in Norfolk; Frank W. Darling, of Hampton; and George May, another friend and business man. All four had aided Slover and Wilson in financing newspaper purchases. The Slover-Wilson control was based on more than 80 per cent of the outstanding stock.

By 1917—in some instances earlier—Slover was able to strengthen his position in other ways. The improved position of the *Ledger-Dispatch* over the last decade had enabled the newspaper to pay the remainder of the debt incurred by the *Public Ledger*'s purchase of the *Dispatch* in 1906 and most of the bonds issued in 1905 when Slover and Wilson bought the *Public Ledger* from Edwards, Fiveash, and Gwaltney. On top of these achievements Slover completed his payment of the $36,400, owed by the Knoxville *Journal* in the 1890's, which he had voluntarily assumed after his years of business management. It had taken him nearly twenty years to lift the last of his burden of heavy weight and special meaning. He counted the day of final payment a day of triumph.

And then, at this moment of visible accomplishment and new opportunity, a hard blow fell. Wilson died suddenly on May 6, 1917, still short of his fifty-ninth birthday—editor of the *Ledger-Dispatch*, supervisor of its news, writer of its editorials, vice president, and, from Slover's personal point of view, his principal partner, his closest business associate, his best friend.

Slover almost never wrote for publication, then or later, but he was too moved not to express his emotion. The article at the head of the editorial columns the next day—more his cry of anguish and his testimony of affection than an editorial—carried the head of "My Partner" and the name of "S. L. Slover" at the end. It read:

> Harvey L. Wilson, my partner for over 15 years, is dead. He was a grand partner, friend and companion. It was not always smooth sailing for us, but he was always there when things were threatening. There was something reassuring in his strong voice and personality. He looked after the news and editorials, while I the business end. We talked everything over, often many times. He never criticised me for mistakes. My mistakes were his mistakes. When we had made a good deal, he was glad, when we lost, well—that is where he was great. He never complained and said why did you not do it differently. He took his full measure of the loss and blame, even though it was all my fault. We have prospered together, but who could help it with such a partner as Wilson?

To the *Virginian-Pilot*, Wilson was "able, progressive, unceasing in an effort to promote the welfare of his city and state and combined in marked measure force with grace of diction. Personally he was bighearted, whole-souled, amiable to a degree and generous to a fault— an altogether lovable character."

Across Hampton Roads the Newport News *Daily Press* said Wilson "not only . . . knew how to write but what to write and what not to write. His judgment was almost unerring, and he had a wide discretion in handling the news, in the selection of editorial topics, and in writing the right thing at the right time in the right way. In both humor and caustic sarcasm he was a past master, and in that particular line of work he had no equal in Virginia with the possible exception of Alfred B. Williams.[1]

The Hampton *Monitor* really let itself go. In its view Wilson had "such a genius for the newspaper . . . as 'Blind Tom' had for music, Edison for invention, Gibson for art, and Caruso for song"—a piquant combination of comparisons, but a sentiment that is unmistakable.

---

1. Alfred B. Williams was at various times, from 1900 to 1918, editor or editorial writer of the Richmond *News, News Leader, Virginian,* and *Evening Journal,* and of the Roanoke *Times.* In the judgment of many newspaper men of that era he stood higher as an editorial writer than any other Virginian.

The Portsmouth *Star* added the discerning judgment that "no man will ever be able to fully appraise how much of Norfolk's growth in the past decade and a half has been due to the splendid work of this forceful writer, who believed so intensely in the future of this entire section of the South that he compelled others to share his conviction. His work for Tidewater Virginia, through the columns of his newspaper, is a lasting monument to his public services."

Slover, still moved by Wilson's death, gathered all the editorial comment and biographical details that had been published and added samples of Wilson's earlier writing, including the often republished "There Is No News Tonight," and a few of his poems and had these printed in a leather-bound booklet of twenty-one pages entitled "In Memoriam—Harvey Laird Wilson—1858-1917."

Wilson's contribution to newspapers in Norfolk (and earlier in Newport News) had the timeless combination of working strength, journalistic judgment, and productivity in his own efforts and in stimulating others. These were invaluable qualities for the struggling years. His editorial efforts were nowhere so persistent as in his striving for growth, commercial development, the utilization of natural resources, and integrity and intelligence in government. Wilson often hammered away, as he did on January 1, 1913, at problems like Norfolk's needs. In that New Year editorial he listed them thus:

An unlimited supply of good water.

Extension of the Belt Line Railroad to the Norfolk side of the Elizabeth River.

Consolidation of Norfolk and Portsmouth.

Municipally owned docks and warehouses.

A new and larger dry dock in the Navy Yard in Portsmouth.

Construction of "the greatest hospital in the world—on the site of the present Marine Hospital across from Norfolk."

An immigration station for Norfolk.

A hundred more factory whistles.

A united business body to make these and other efforts more effective, including a traffic bureau to help Norfolk grow into a distributing city for manufactures of all kinds.

Three weeks later twenty-five business men met in F. S. Royster's office to consider the organization of a chamber of commerce. At a dinner in April more than five hundred business men celebrated the establishment of this institution. Before April ended membership rose above fifteen hundred. Not all the *Ledger-Dispatch*'s goals which

Wilson was trumpeting were so quickly attained. If he were alive, some would still be on his list.

Slover and Wilson had agreed that the control of the stock of whichever partner died first would be vested in the other. In time Slover bought all of Wilson's interest, but the transaction extended over several years. As late as October, 1923, the *Ledger-Dispatch*'s owners were recorded in a published statement of ownership as Slover, Mrs. Junius F. Lynch (Mrs. Wilson's name after remarriage), and Nathaniel Beaman. Slover acquired Beaman's stock, a distinctly minority holding, by an agreement made in January, 1926, with the administrators of the Beaman estate. The price was $31,800 for 150 shares, or $212 a share. Earlier Slover had acquired the minority holdings of Martin, Darling, and May. In his own words later, "In February, 1926, I purchased the last outstanding share of stock in the publishing company and thus became the sole owner of the Norfolk Ledger-Dispatch."

To fill the editor's chair Slover turned to Richmond. On June 30, 1917, the *Ledger-Dispatch* announced that "Douglas Gordon, formerly of the Richmond Times-Dispatch, will next week become associated with the Ledger-Dispatch and assume charge of this paper's editorial columns."

Wilson had been responsible for both news and editorials, as Fiveash had been for the *Public Ledger* and Thomson for the *Dispatch*. But Gordon was editor in the sense of being the newspaper's spokesman and the director of the editorial page where its views and convictions were set forth. Though he might be called on for advice and counsel from time to time, especially on big issues, he had no responsibility for the news.

This was Cameron's role with the *Virginian-Pilot*, as it had been Sapp's (though Elam had broader authority), and it would be the role of Cameron's successor and of *his* successor. None of these editors was in charge of the news. Their advice about news was sought on special occasions, but they concentrated on the editorial page. But for the *Ledger-Dispatch* Gordon's coming marked a change. The effect was to accentuate the position of the managing editor (who then was Perkins) without lowering the position of the editor. The managing editor had charge of the main flow of the news, of background and supplemental writing, and of entertainment features—comics, for instance. The work of the old editors had grown too big and had to be divided or reorganized in one way or another.

Gordon, then forty years old, was a Richmond native, a University of Virginia graduate, a licensed lawyer, and a newspaper writer in special fields. He had practiced law in Richmond, but he had other interests, especially music and the theater, and in time they were more important to him than law. He wrote about both for the Richmond *Times-Dispatch* with a style and with opinions that attracted attention. He reviewed books too and showed respect for the language, its niceties and proprieties. All that he did suggested a certain elegance and grace, and he became a figure in the life of the town. For several years he was a member of the Richmond Board of Police Commissioners, an advisory responsibility that brought him into contact with municipal government. When he began editorial writing for the *Times-Dispatch* he could bring important knowledge into play. He found an excellent opportunity in a Norfolk that was plunging deep into war.

The war possessed Norfolk as wars always did—destroying it in the American Revolution, paralyzing its port and shattering its economy in 1812, isolating and blighting it by military occupation for three years in the Civil War. This time war came rushing in with demands for growth far beyond anything Norfolk had dreamed of.

The Navy must have training facilities, depots, and housekeeping establishments on the Jamestown Exposition grounds and on hundreds of additional acres. It must have four miles of bulkhead and thirty-five-foot channels right now; six-story warehouses for supplies for the fleets; miles of streets, miles of railroads; piers thrust into the Elizabeth River four times the length of a football field; buildings to house everything from messes and laundries to mines and machine shops—all in a hurry.

In the Navy Yard in Portsmouth "the most complicated piece of mass concrete construction ever built in this country" was set forty feet deep beside the water to dry-dock the biggest battleships. All around it the Navy Yard turned modern, spread farther, grew by thousands of employees. The largest naval hospital facilities on the Atlantic Coast almost inundated the white columns of the old, historic Naval Hospital in Portsmouth.

The port mushroomed. Shipments from Norfolk of under $10,000,000 in 1914 doubled in 1915, and that figure doubled in 1916 and kept going up; Newport News's shipments jumped 1,400 per cent in a single year. The coal that the Chesapeake & Ohio rolled into Newport News, and the Norfolk & Western and the Virginian rolled into Norfolk, was dumped into the ships of the world. When America's railroads staggered under continental loads, Norfolk's coal turned swiftly by sea to keep furnaces burning in the Northeast. In one year domestic tonnage going out between the Virginia Capes—chiefly coal—leaped from 290,000 to 5,525,000. And when supplies for Europe piled high on New York's docks and piers shippers turned to Hampton Roads' waterside facilities.

By early 1918 the Army planned on the Elizabeth River near Sewells Point what the *Virginian-Pilot* called "the greatest army depot in the United States . . . the greatest terminals in America." Estimated to cost $16,000,000 when the work began in April of 1918, they cost $30,000,000 before completed in 1919.

These developments demanded manpower far beyond the capacity of a city of 67,000 population in 1910 and 115,000 in 1920, or, together with Portsmouth, 100,000 in 1910 and 170,000 in 1920. Nor could nearby regions fill the needs. Government and contractors combined to pull in tens of thousands of laborers from as far away as the Rocky Mountain states. Their sheer numbers in a community poorly prepared for such a mass of humanity created major housing problems, strained local supply sources to the crippling point, overwhelmed public utilities, and enlarged the army of camp followers that already was a formidable force. The population of Norfolk doubled. The perplexities of living multiplied.

Dr. F. C. Steinmetz, rector of the dignified Christ Episcopal Church, startled the town in May of 1918 by proclaiming that "immoral indulgences" were rendering a third of certain groups of the armed forces in Norfolk "incapable of properly serving their country." "One Hundred Sailor Boys" signed a statement quickly published in the *Virginian-Pilot* denying the worst of the allegations. But police reported arrest figures, and the *Virginian-Pilot* summed up:

> The number of such women arrested in the city within the last eight or ten weeks totals, we are told, over 500, a large percentage of them being girls under the age of 18 and a still larger percentage having been found infected with communicable diseases.
> Because protection of the public health and public morals demands that they be held somewhere and because there is no other place to hold them, they are herded into the city jail in plain violation of a state statute and the ordinary dictates of humanity.

Venereal disease clinics later struggled with such problems.

Government-built villages began to spring up—not all of them completed before the war ended, and therefore abandoned—to provide living quarters for the new population that had overrun the old cities: Cradock and Truxtun near Portsmouth, Glenwood near the Naval Base, Hilton Village on the Peninsula where ship construction, the dispatch of war supplies to Europe, and the flow of troops outward-bound dominated life.

The mounting pressures on public utility systems not built for such loads led to breakdowns that reached a climax in the autumn of 1918. Boiler troubles created a gas famine; power plant repairs deprived home owners of electricity at the height of the year's classic influenza epidemic; street cars that were sitting dead on their tracks came to life, rolled three blocks, and died again; business plants that began operations after two weeks of inactivity had to shut down again; power for the Naval Base and the Army Base was reduced at one time by 50 per cent. Even when wheels turned again, civilians were asked to use no power for three and a half hours each afternoon.

The newspapers exploded with anger. It is inconceivable, the *Virginian-Pilot* declared, "that Norfolk and its people should be helpless in the face of conditions absolutely insufferable." To the *Ledger-Dispatch* it seemed that "Norfolk's patience with the local traction company and allied companies long ago passed the breaking point." It handed down this verdict: "In every respect the company's service to the public has failed. Physical equipment began to deteriorate long before the war and the company failed to keep its properties up. . . . The fact is that Norfolk has the worst power, light and street car facilities anywhere in the east and that these facilities are operated by nonresident owners."

But when the Norfolk government considered municipal ownership, the *Ledger-Dispatch* advised caution. "Norfolk is in a mood to try almost anything that is suggested," it admitted, but "because of its desperate mood it behooves Norfolk to consider very carefully every suggestion that is made . . . before it adopts any radical plan." The city did try to negotiate. It could have bought the gas plant, but the electric power facilities were not for sale.

The strain of the war, the deficiencies in transportation, and the profiteering of some merchants inflamed the sailor-civilian relationship. Halloween celebrations in 1918 degenerated into downtown disorders in which a policeman was killed. On New Year's Eve rioting smashed store windows, killed one sailor, and wounded others. A Marine Corps detachment was called out to clear the streets with the butts of rifles. Navy Secretary Daniels ordered an investigation, and city and naval authorities went into serious conference. One result was the establishment of a Navy Shore Patrol for downtown streets, an institution of high value and later a permanent asset.

"Why Dislike Norfolk?" the *Ledger-Dispatch* asked as it tried to reason about problems in wartime living:

> . . . we hear on all sides that enlisted men in particular dislike Norfolk, and when inquiry is made the reasons will not stand investigation.
>
> The cause most frequently given is discrimination against men in uniform. To a limited extent that charge is justified. How limited . . . is shown by the fact that the Navy's intelligence department . . . has judged it proper to proceed against only about half a dozen firms in a year.
>
> As to lack of transportation, it is a mistake to say that Norfolk people have got used to their own low grade street car service. They have not, and they are as indignant about it as any man in the Navy. . . .
>
> The city was unprepared to take care of abnormal crowds, and hasn't been able even yet to meet the demands made upon it. Is it fair for the men of the Navy to blame Norfolk for conditions under which Norfolk's own people are suffering and chafing and protesting?
>
> If the men will analyze their feelings they will find that they "dislike Norfolk" simply because there is not enough for them to do, not enough amusement, not enough excitement of various sorts. . . . neither Norfolk nor any other community of like size can attempt or pretend to compete as an amusement center with the larger cities.

Norfolk newspapers would repeat such arguments down the decades. But among Navy men the reputation of the town suffered more than twenty-five years, primarily because of the number of people, in uniform and out of uniform, who were squeezed into it by national needs in 1917 and 1918.

Wartime newspaper circulation rose sharply. A single day of high-powered news could lift the sales high—like the *Ledger-Dispatch*'s more than fifty thousand on July 21, 1917, the day when the first draft numbers were drawn. The much larger population and the public interest in war news consistently pushed the totals higher and higher. Late in 1918 the *Ledger-Dispatch* was well up in the forty thousands and near the end of the year was close to fifty thousand. The *Virginian-Pilot* was not far behind on week days and generally ahead on Sundays of the *Ledger-Dispatch*'s week-day peak.

But white paper (the term used then more frequently than newsprint) grew scarce and cost far more, and other costs rose fast. The

Ledger-Dispatch first and then the *Virginian-Pilot* raised their prices in April, 1918, both going from ten cents a week (carrier-delivered) to twelve cents, and from $5.00 a year to $6.00. Both held to their single-copy price of two cents. Both offered the same reasons.

Higher paper and ink costs, said the *Ledger-Dispatch*, added $50,000 a year to its outgo. The *Virginian-Pilot*, noting that it had held to ten cents a week and $5.00 a year for more than half a century, although the newspaper was much larger and was published seven days a week instead of six, declared that "within the last three years every item of expense entering into the makeup of a newspaper has increased from 25 to 100 per cent." For white paper it was paying $40,000 a year more than it had paid in 1915. Its labor costs were up by $20,000.

Seven months later, in November, both newspapers lifted their prices again, and for the same reasons. This time the *Ledger-Dispatch* went from two to three cents a single copy; from twelve to fifteen cents a week of six days (home delivered); and from $6.00 a year to $7.00. The *Virginian-Pilot* adopted these figures three weeks later. Its publishing costs for seven days a week obviously were more than the *Ledger-Dispatch*'s for six days.

Both newspapers' staffs were stripped to the bone. The war drained off employees, and replacements were hard to find. Women reporters had increased opportunities, and some of them did well—Margaret Davis of the *Virginian-Pilot*, for one. Paper shortages cut back the number of pages, and a ten-page newspaper was no longer unusual. But the few experienced men in command always carried heavier burdens.

For the *Virginian-Pilot* newsroom this meant primarily Keville Glennan, Harry P. Moore, and Sam T. Potts (telegraph editor, later sports editor), whom companions among the typewriters called "Governor." Until he left in October of 1917 Robert Glass was the political and city hall reporter.

In the *Ledger-Dispatch* newsroom Henry Perkins as chief news editor and E. M. Holmes as telegraph editor were the backbone of a depleted staff. For part of the war years they had the aid of Winder R. Harris, who came to Norfolk in 1917 to be city editor of the *Virginian-Pilot* but moved over to daytime work.

Harris, born in Raleigh, North Carolina, had worked for newspapers in Spartanburg, South Carolina, in Charlotte and Raleigh, and in Newport News. He left Norfolk in 1918 for national and international reporting for Universal Service, generally from Washington but also from political conventions and campaign trains, and once from abroad. He returned in the middle 1920's as managing editor of the *Virginian-Pilot*. Powerfully built, forceful in personality, with gifts as a conversationalist and public speaker, he did not let his enforced use of a cane from early age deter him for an instant in aggressive pursuit of news.

These veterans and their makeshift staffs had to cover, under exceptionally harsh and unfamiliar conditions, the worst fire that anyone could remember in Norfolk: the burning on January 1, 1918, of the 340-room Monticello Hotel and adjoining buildings.

That winter of 1917-18 was one of exceptional cold. For the week of the fire the temperature held below the freezing point every day. On the day before the fire it sank to nine degrees above zero—very rare for Norfolk. Just before 4:00 a.m. on New Year's Day, with the thermometer standing about twelve degrees, flames were discovered in a building next to the hotel. From that moment the struggle against fire in freezing weather continued more than twenty-four hours. With icicles hanging from hats and clothes, firemen had to attack sheets of ice as well as flames. Three of them died. Portsmouth and Suffolk fire departments and naval contingents joined the long, frigid battle.

Extra editions loaded with pictures came pounding off the presses. When the *Virginian-Pilot* gathered itself, it presented on the following morning a two-line, ninety-six point streamer reading:

NORFOLK SWEPT BY GREATEST FIRE IN ITS HISTORY
PROPERTY WORTH $2,000,000 REDUCED TO ASHES

Except for four short items the entire front page was all fire reporting: the overall story under a two-column head over columns six and seven, with emphasis on suspicions of incendiarism; the financial losses and insurance under a two-column head over columns one and two; and between them, on columns three, four, and five, a ten-inch-deep picture of smoke billowing from the hotel and firemen attacking with hose and water. Below the break of the page ran stories about injuries to firemen and the one death at that time, about the imposition of martial law, about twelve arrests in the police investigation of arson possibilities, and summaries and sidebars.

The main lead made little effort for verbal pyrotechnics. This was a moment for sobriety. The story began calmly, in the classical style, with heavy emphasis on suspicions that reflected the wartime atmosphere:

The most disastrous and the most stubbornly fought confla-
gration that has ever visited Norfolk, made up of three separate
fires, each of independent origin, destroyed four Granby Street
buildings yesterday, entailing a property loss of more than two
million dollars, a toll of one dead and 17 or more injured more
or less by exposure and falling bricks and timbers.

While neither Major C. G. Kizer [the police chief] nor
[Fire] Chief R. F. McLaughlin would make a direct charge
that the fires were of incendiary origin, both indicated that ap-
pearances pointed to something other than coincidence, and
the prevailing opinion throughout the city last night was that
there had been an effort, probably organized, to destroy the
business section of the city.

Students of journalism might wonder where the fire was, but students of humanity would understand that no one in Norfolk that
morning, and few of those elsewhere who would read the *Virginian-
Pilot*'s story, lacked that information. The difference in style and
spirit, in both headlines and stories, between the 1918 fire and the
1902 jury's verdict in the Jim Wilcox trial in Elizabeth City is marked.
Victorianism belonged to the past.

Yet hardships in a city weighted down by war did not hold back—
and may have pushed ahead—the most revolutionary turnaround in
city government in Norfolk's two and one-third centuries of community life.

City government in Norfolk rested on a ward system of nominations and elections for an absurdly large bicameral council. Nominations and elections rested in turn on controls in the hands of local
branches of national and state political parties whose principles and
policies had little or no relation to most of the requirements of municipal government.

"It would be difficult," the Bureau of Municipal Research found
in November of 1917, "to devise a form of government better fitted for
shifting responsibility than the present government of Norfolk. Its
complexity tends, moreover, to cumbersome procedure, red tape,
waste motion, duplication, unnecessary expense and curtailment of
service." Furthermore, the report added, the city government provided inequitable representation of the electorate.

Few of the many pre-Twentieth Century attempts to improve this
government seriously attacked the size of its legislative body. Norfolk had had large councils since it became a city in 1845, two councils of thirty-seven freeholders then, and tradition held hard. All of
these were representatives of wards, not of the city as a whole. When

the city created new wards, as it did after annexations, the size of the councils automatically increased. In 1902 there were forty-three councilmen; in 1904 there were forty-six, and in that year the candidates for these offices numbered eighty-four. The 1906 charter provided for fifty-three councilmen, of whom thirty-three were members of the Common Council and twenty of the Board of Aldermen, the new name for the old Select Council, members of which were elected by councilmen from their own membership.

After the annexation of Huntersville, part of Villa Heights, and Lambert's Point in 1911, the number rose to sixty-four, which palpably was ridiculous. Even the professional Democratic politicians who had been reveling in sheer numbers—democratic government, they called it—knew this was getting out of hand. James E. Prince, one of their leaders, proposed a reduction of the wards from ten to four. By 1914 the number of the city's legislators was down to forty, and in 1916 to twenty-five—"a political trick to stave off reform," reformers charged.

Thinking turned toward the commission form of government that had gained popularity after Galveston had resorted to it in the emergency of its 1900 flood. This form placed both legislative and executive powers in the hands of (generally) three commissioners. But when Norfolk adopted in 1906 a board of control consisting of three elected members, it imposed this board on top of its massive council and its mayor, who was armed with a veto, instead of substituting it for both. The combination was a contradiction in terms and in fact.

Twenty-seven citizens accepted Mayor Riddick's invitation in November of 1911 to confer on these matters. They sought immediately to enlarge the group to a hundred. D. S. Burwell and John B. Jenkins were early leaders in this organizing, but there were many others: J. H. Cofer, H. H. Rumble, G. W. Perryman, H. G. Barbee among them. Barbee was the head of a group that had been championing a commission form of government. In broad objectives they were all united, and they had full support from the newspapers.

In the last month of its existence as an individual newspaper (December, 1911) the *Landmark* commented that "it is not charged that the local councils are controlled by graft, but that the present ward system invites logrolling." A month later, in January of 1912, the *Virginian-Pilot* was continuing the argument:

> The main trouble with municipal government in the United States is that politics usurps the first place in the choice of pub-

lic officials who should be elected with prime reference to their character and business qualifications.

A commission form of government, patterned generally after that which has worked so successfully in other cities, notably in Galveston, would, in our judgment, be far preferable to the clumsy and costly aggregation of ill-balanced wheels and drivers which the Virginia constitution imposes on its civic corporations. But the electorate should address itself to the formation of the commission with the same care that a capitalist would exercise in the selection of the superintendent in his factory or custodian of his money.

Two months later, in March of 1912, the *Virginian-Pilot* said that "as to the desirability of redistricting the city with a view to cutting down the size of the council there is no room for a difference of opinion." The next day the *Ledger-Dispatch* carried this point further:

> Not in years has public sentiment in Norfolk been more completely centered on a subject than it is today on the need of redistricting this city and the substitution of a smaller and more responsible council in place of the numerous and unwieldly body that now prevails. The minimum council and board of aldermen should be provided. We at one time advocated four wards, but if enumeration means delay, then let us have two wards. Now is the time to make the change, and the people want action.

In the June, 1912, election the reform movement could not prevent the Democratic candidate for mayor, W. R. Mayo, from defeating the independent Riddick. But the campaign had been one of education and insistence that (in the words of the *Virginian-Pilot*) mixing party politics with city government was an absurdity; if party regularity were the proper test of fitness for the mayoralty neither candidate "would have the slightest claim to consideration on the score of loyalty to the party's behest"; and "in selecting administrators for the business of a city no question should be raised whether the applicant is a Democrat, a Republican or a mugwump."

During 1914 and 1915 these ideas won increasing credence. At the same time thinking about governmental forms showed a marked swing away from the commission form and toward the even newer council-and-manager form that had come out of Staunton a few years earlier. The ideas had more popularity among top business and professional men, however, than among voters in general. A referendum in August of 1915 failed to produce a strong enough demand for change.

Portsmouth did better. Three months later a referendum there went strongly for the city manager form of government. In September of 1916 a newly elected council of five, chosen at large, took office. In December T. Z. Shertzer came in as the first city manager, followed in August of 1917 by W. B. Bates.

These positive actions spurred the Norfolk movement. In June of 1917 Norfolk voted by a wide margin to have a new charter written for another referendum to approve or disapprove. A commission of nine with Tazewell Taylor as chairman and with R. W. Peatross, H. H. Rumble, John E. Burke, C. H. Hix, Albert L. Roper, Hugh L. Butler, John S. Jenkins, and W. Taylor Ham as members, and with H. B. G. Galt as a substitute, prepared this charter. The interest grew intense. Both newspapers were fighting hard for charter approval. Not even the war—with American troops beginning to embark for Europe and with developments in France and Russia pointing to a long struggle—could distract attention from this governmental climax.

The vote in November, 1917, was decisive: 3,403 for the new charter; 1,222 against. The General Assembly had to approve, but that was soon assured. The voters had to select a council of five, but the new mood was so strong that when Mayor Mayo was elected as a councilman he stepped aside in order to give the new government a clean slate of advocates of its ideas. The new Council, when formally established, had to find a city manager, on whom this kind of government could stand or fall. But this turned out to be one of the easy decisions of the times. The Council chose Charles E. Ashburner.

Ashburner was probably the best known of the new breed of city managers. He was then in Springfield, Ohio. Earlier, beginning in 1908, he had been in Staunton, Virginia, where, under the title of general manager, he had been the first in the country to perform city management duties. Before that he had been a division engineer of the Chesapeake & Ohio Railway. To his new duties he could bring a professional engineering background, executive ability, and an understanding of the nature of public office. He had a good council with which to work—Albert L. Roper, who was chosen president of the council and ex officio mayor, J. Watts Martin, Hugh L. Butler, C. E. Herbert, and I. Walke Truxtun—and he needed every ounce of help he could get. Substituting modern municipal government for the form of government Norfolk had inherited—and had allowed to degenerate for more than fifty years—could not possibly be easy.

But it was the vote of November 20, 1917, and all that was embodied in the change that became effective in 1918, that created the opportunity. Of the role of the *Ledger-Dispatch* and the *Virginian-*

Pilot in that achievement, the campaign manager of the citizens' movement, J. H. Cofer, said that "without such splendid work by them I believe success would have been impossible."

In the forty-nine years of its experience the city manager government of Norfolk has had its unimpressive hours. It has required continued understanding, and sometimes reminders, of the principles of its organization. It has needed renewals of spiritual power and always superior personal capacity. But the new sense of professionalism that came with trained men as city managers, the new thinking about the whole city instead of its wards, the new freedom from old political party controls, the new authority and responsibility in policy making by small councils—all these, with the new realization that Norfolk was growing into a first-class city and deserved better than second-class government, brought a new type of citizen-leadership into office and, for the most part, has insisted upon it ever since.

21 · OUT OF WAR AND INTO PROSPERITY

WHEN THE ARMISTICE SIGNALED THE END OF FRANTIC BUILDING AND OVER-
time pay in Norfolk, war workers began to drift away. Newspaper
circulation declined. The *Ledger-Dispatch*, still holding first place,
lost two thousand in the first six weeks. But the construction that
everyone could see, the powerful stimulation of the Navy, the elevation of the port to a new level of utilization and activity, and the
larger residual population seemed then to guarantee a brilliant future.

"To Norfolk," the *Virginian-Pilot* said on January 1, "1919 offers
the chance of realizing its greatest dream, the winning of a proper
share of the world's commerce. Military activities have already
brought to this harbor a larger share of the world's traffic. . . . The
new year places continued prosperity within the reach of the city. . . ."

Material gains from the war, the *Ledger-Dispatch* said at the same
time, "have been due in large part to the fact that the great advantages" of Norfolk as a port "were quickly recognized by the government and were promptly utilized, so that her resources were given
advertisements within less than two years which many years of normal
trade and commerce could not have spread abroad." The mood of
the times showed up in such words as the *Ledger-Dispatch*'s estimates
of Norfolk's population:

> Within the last 12 months its population is estimated to
> have increased by more than 80,000 making the number of per-
> sons living in this city itself, as of July 1, 1918, more than
> 186,000, or including Portsmouth, which is a part of the com-
> munity, 250,000, while its estimated shopping population is
> more than 675,000.
>
> Its national importance as a community—apart from its posi-
> tion as a war center, a position recognized by the government's
> expenditure of some $200,000,000 of funds within or near the
> city limits—may be realized from the fact that it is now the sec-
> ond port in the United States.

This was going strong—as events turned out, much too strong—for a city of 67,452 population in 1910 and a population in adjoining Portsmouth and South Norfolk, and across Hampton Roads in Newport News and Hampton, of under 80,000 at the last census. It was a time of exultation. "Build, Build, Build!" the *Ledger-Dispatch* proclaimed as the slogan for 1919.

But scarcity of goods and sharply increased demands forced prices upward. Living costs shot higher. Old salaries could not meet new conditions. Surprise, anger, and defensive steps showed up beside the new gusto. Trade unions demanded better wages. Strikes that would not have been called while the nation was at war marked the first year of peace, nationally and in Norfolk.

The Norfolk police were hard pressed financially and won the support of the *Ledger-Dispatch* for better pay. But when the *Virginian-Pilot* published in August of 1919 the names of 225 policemen who had joined a union affiliated with the American Federation of Labor, the new director of public safety, retired Rear Admiral A. C. Dillingham, "practically demanded" that the union be disbanded. It was. The men voted fifty-eight to five to surrender their union charter and to maintain only a benevolent and mutual cooperative.

The *Virginian-Pilot* thought "the policemen have chosen wisely," and the *Ledger-Dispatch* renewed its suggestion that they did in fact deserve higher pay. The council agreed to a 25 per cent increase.

Dillingham's handling of Norfolk's police problem came in the August that preceded Governor Calvin Coolidge's September actions in the Boston police strike. Dillingham was widely praised and often called on by admirers for interpretation of his policy—in Washington, among other cities. "Boston's experience with her police strike," the *Ledger-Dispatch* said later, "vindicates the position taken by Admiral Dillingham, a position in which he was strongly supported by the rest of the city government. . . . We feel justified in commending to other cities that may have to deal with a police crisis—the Norfolk plan."

In such an era, when ambitions never attained seemed within reach, the standing issue of Norfolk-Portsmouth consolidation inevitably received fresh consideration. Many earlier efforts that did not succeed and the failure as recently as 1910 calmed Norfolk enthusiasm only temporarily. By 1915 the Norfolk Chamber of Commerce and the Municipal Board of Control began an active campaign. "In Union There Is Strength," the *Virginian-Pilot* cried in full support. But conferences and mass meetings led only to disagreement.

Two years later the *Ledger-Dispatch* thought that "now is the time to extend the boundary lines and make Norfolk the greatest city in Virginia" by uniting Norfolk, South Norfolk, and Portsmouth. But "Greater Norfolk" did not appeal to Portsmouth. City Manager Ashburner had been in office only ten days in 1918 when he called for another attempt at consolidation. His new voice had no greater success. Yet in 1920 the two cities were conferring again; although nothing came of that effort Councilman S. Heth Tyler had hardly been chosen president of the Norfolk Council in 1924, and in effect mayor, before he was pleading for the governmental unity of the two cities that physically were so close together.

If it was not the city manager or the mayor of Norfolk who was speaking to the consolidation idea, it was the Norfolk newspapers. On this issue they were as consistent, decade after decade, as they were unsuccessful. The two cities could agree on unity in a chamber of commerce, a port traffic commission, a Hampton Roads port commission. But governmental unity involved tougher political and financial issues and more of pride and face than the adjoining cities could settle then.

Nor could newspapers control the swing of economic forces. Construction in Norfolk for the twelve months ending June 30, 1919, set a record. But the summer of 1919 brought such higher prices that Ashburner appointed in August a commission, one member of which was the *Virginian-Pilot*'s Keville Glennan, to investigate local food costs.

"When granulated sugar that sold for five cents a pound costs a quarter of a dollar," the *Virginian-Pilot* complained in May of 1920, "and Irish potatoes sell by weight for the same price as apples and grapefruit, the exact percentage of increase in the cost of existence over pre-war days becomes a matter of purely academic interest." But there was nothing academic about that newspaper's further protest:

> The cost of living in Norfolk is . . . so high that we are ashamed to talk about it in the presence of visitors looking for sites to establish new industries. . . . this city must deplore the statistics just made public by the Federal Department of Labor, showing Detroit and Norfolk standing at the head of a list of 14 cities in point of increase of living costs from December, 1914, to December, 1919, with jumps of 108 and 107 per cent, respectively.
> The economy movement that began a few weeks ago with a slowing down of real estate speculation . . . has squeezed considerable water out of the city's inflated values. It must con-

tinue until the Federal government can no longer advertise to the United States that it costs 10 to 18 per cent more to live in Norfolk than it does in Boston or Philadelphia.

Nationally a downward movement was gaining momentum. In the same May of 1920, the *Virginian-Pilot* pointed out that:

> From coast to coast the country is in the midst of a price-cutting wave that is without parallel in the history of the present generation. There is being dumped on the market a vast accumulation of goods, chiefly wearing apparel, at prices 10 to 50 per cent lower than the general price level in effect when a prophetic voice from Tampa called upon the nation to put on overalls. There is a mad scramble to turn heavy stocks into money. The public had demonstrated its power to boycott against watered prices.

Eighteen months later, in October, 1921, the *Ledger-Dispatch* declared bluntly that "some call it reaction, some call it one thing or another, but everybody knows the nation is in a slump. But even as we have survived the panics, just so will we recover from the slump."

That was easier for the country than for Norfolk. The city was highly vulnerable to these postwar pressures and strains. It faced the difficulties of a boomtown from which suddenly the boom had faded. Real estate speculation had stretched many accounts tight. The loss of new population was heavy. The decline in Federal activity was sharp. The shipping of the port dwindled. While the country recovered from postwar economic gyrations and was finding a normal growth, Norfolk was finding itself too weakened to join fully in the nation's climb. It was suffering a depression of its own.

The loss of circulation, which both newspapers felt after the armistice, continued in the early 1920's. In March of 1921 they spread their rivalry in the public columns in a series of claims and charges that led to the *Ledger-Dispatch*'s making a $5,000 "challenge" to the *Virginian-Pilot*. The latter had reported on March 11 its own circulation figures as 33,181 daily and 38,114 on Sundays. It asked the *Ledger-Dispatch* to publish figures authenticated by the Audit Bureau of Circulations for a period preceding September, 1920. The *Ledger-Dispatch* did so. For that period it reported its circulation as 36,001 (average net paid), and, it added, the *Virginian-Pilot*'s for the same period was 31,498.

But, the *Ledger-Dispatch* declared, "this is ancient history." For the first nine days of the March in which the two newspapers were disputing, its figure was 43,868—a remarkable jump indeed. Furthermore—and now came the challenge—the *Ledger-Dispatch*'s principal edition, not to speak of its other editions, consisted of more copies than the *Virginian-Pilot*'s several editions combined, and here was the money to back the statement!

Historically the significant fact was that in 1920 and 1921 both newspapers were well below their war-time circulation totals. Both reflected the post-war slump in Norfolk.

The newsprint shortage that followed shortly after the war forced the newspapers into severe rationing. By April, 1920, the *Ledger-Dispatch* had to discontinue its early edition and drastically curtail advertisers' calls for space. Its pages were limited to eighteen, and on one day in April it omitted forty-five columns of advertising. It could only note that conditions were bad in Washington, Baltimore, and other cities, including New York, where the *Tribune* made the historic appeal: "Don't Buy the Tribune—Borrow It." The *Virginian-Pilot* did not go that far, but the number of its pages was cut on one day to twelve. Yet a little earlier it had found enough newsprint to publish a ninety-four-page edition on Sunday, December 14, 1919.

Three years passed before the *Ledger-Dispatch* came close to that figure. Its Greater Norfolk-Hampton Roads Edition of January 1, 1923, had eighty-eight pages. The New Year was not the only inspiration. Norfolk had just annexed twenty square miles of land of Norfolk County. These residential areas were thought to include 31,000 people and their annexation raised the hope that the enlarged Norfolk would show 150,000 population in 1930. It had shown 115,777 in 1920, up from 67,452 in 1910. Portsmouth's figures were 33,190 in 1910; 54,387 in 1920; and 45,704 in 1930. But the Norfolk dream broke badly on a 1930 census of 129,710.

Yet both newspapers were showing vitality and progress. The *Ledger-Dispatch* installed a new and bigger Scott press in May, 1919, capable of printing seventy-two thousand thirty-two-page newspapers in an hour, and remodeled its Plume Street building to provide more office space. It was using the news reports of the Associated Press and the International News Service, and in November, 1923, added those of the United Press. Webster's cartoon appeared on the editorial page, and the Ring Lardner column on a sports page, and there was a long line of other features. The comic strips were gathered on one page now where Bringing Up Father, Polly and Her Pals, and Barney Google presided over a flock of friends.

The *Virginian-Pilot* had an advantage in its Sunday assortment of colored comics. The Gumps, Mutt and Jeff, Tillie the Toiler, and all others, went into exile during the paper shortage, but the newspaper welcomed them back in January, 1923. It was trying to exploit magazine-type features, like Ludendorff's narrative of the German war effort and Rear Admiral William S. Sims' articles on American naval operations in the war. Telegraphic news dominated the first of seven sections on Sunday, local news the second, society news the third, Virginia and North Carolina news the fourth, magazine features the fifth and sixth, and Portsmouth news the seventh.

The most striking change in this postwar period was in the editorship of the *Virginian-Pilot*. Cameron was seventy-seven years old in 1919, though he lived until 1927. The *Virginian-Pilot*'s announcement of September 2, 1919, said:

> Not to take effect at once, but so soon as the necessary arrangements can be perfected, former Governor Cameron will be relieved at his own request of active management of and direct responsibility for the editorial department. . . . He feels that advanced age and increasing physical infirmities call for a lightening of burdens which would tax to the utmost the vigor of a younger man; and the management has regretfully acceded to his wish, recognizing so much to be due to many years of capable and faithful service.

"The management" of the *Virginian-Pilot* was led then by Lucien D. Starke, Jr. He faced an important responsibility in finding a successor to Cameron. John Wise Kelly, often called co-editor and associated with Cameron since his arrival in 1906, had been forced by poor health to retire. Malvern H. Tillitt, a native of North Carolina, came up from the newsroom to fill his place, but Starke's choice for the top post was bold and imaginative. He had learned of the work of a thirty-one-year-old political reporter and assistant city editor of the Richmond *Times-Dispatch*, well known to associates there, to other Virginia newspapermen and to men in commanding positions in Richmond, though less known to the state at large and to Norfolk. He was the man—Louis Isaac Jaffé. He would be the *Virginian-Pilot*'s editor for the next thiry years, the longest editorship in the *Virginian-Pilot*'s history and one of unique distinction.

At the moment Jaffé was in Paris where six months earlier he had exchanged the uniform of a lieutenant in the American Expeditionary Force for a uniform of the American Red Cross. Born in Detroit, he had moved with his family to Durham, North Carolina, when he was twelve years old. In Trinity College (the core of the later Duke University) he attained high academic standing and won a local reputa-

tion by his writing and editing for the college newspaper and magazine. After graduation in 1911 young Jaffé worked for a few months
for the afternoon *Sun* in Durham, but before the year was out he was
a reporter for the Richmond *Times-Dispatch*. In the state capital he
had a newspaperman's education in the government, politics, traditions, and spirit of Virginia.

The first World War took Jaffé to France as a lieutenant. In Paris
in March of 1919 he went to see Henry W. Anderson, a Richmond
lawyer of eminence who soon became head of the American Red Cross
Commission to the Balkan States, then war-ridden and generally deso-
late areas. Anderson's interest in public affairs and politics (he was
Republican candidate for governor in 1921 and later state chairman)
had brought the two men together in Richmond. He asked Jaffé to
investigate how efficiently Red Cross activities in the Balkan countries
were being conducted.

As soon as he could obtain his Army discharge in France, Jaffé
left on a four-month tour in remote, often primitive, and tragically
blighted regions. On the completion of his reports in July, he worked
with the American Red Cross news service in Paris until he returned
home. The whole experience had a permanent effect on a young man
of unusually humane instincts, intellectual curiosity, and understanding of foreign peoples. Forever afterward he would show interest in
European affairs, sympathy for suffering, and anger at injustice.

These characteristics and other positive qualities began to show
themselves as soon as Jaffé took command of the editorial page in
November, 1919. Tillitt continued as associate editor until October,
1922, but Jaffé was attracted by the work in the *Ledger-Dispatch* newsroom, notably in his writing about business, of John Newton Aiken,
whom he had known in Trinity College. Aiken was one of several
World War veterans who joined the *Ledger-Dispatch* staff in 1919
and 1920. He joined Jaffé as associate editor early in 1923 and quickly proved his worth. The two produced an editorial page that commanded wide attention and gained national recognition.

Jaffé had strict professional standards and a high regard for quality. His range of interests was broad, and he wrote in colorful language and with vigor and courage. When he could get away from
public issues, he wrote with warmth and grace, and he was not afraid
of humor. "The 'Stars' in Their Curses" was his headline for comment on an acrimonious debate between the Winchester *Star* of the
conservatively minded Harry F. Byrd and the Portsmouth *Star* of the
(then) liberal Norman R. Hamilton.

Under Jaffé the editorial page grew more cosmopolitan. The times were with him, for the war had made Americans conscious of other lands and other peoples, and the fight over the League of Nations was stimulating public discussion of such subjects. He would know from hard reading the background of a French foreign minister's fresh statement and could reach intelligently for its purpose, meaning, and impact. He could do the same with a flare-up in the Near East, with a Swiss theologian's doctrines, or with a Russian dancer's interpretations.

Jaffé tried to make the editorial page reflect more of what he called "the older preoccupations of civilized people." In March of 1926 he wrote that

> The charmed phrase of the hour is "great Virginia asset." We hear it said of our apples and our oysters, of our tobacco and of our coal, and of the great harbor at Hampton Roads . . . seldom, in the literature of our chambers of commerce, is it expanded to include those state assets that feed the mind and nourish the spirit. . . . We take due and satisfied public account, and properly, of a new cigarette factory at Richmond, or a new cement factory at Norfolk, but no account do we take of a comparable enterprise in the field of literature . . . the establishment, for example, of a magazine like the Virginia Quarterly Review.

At the moment that publication from the University of Virginia was celebrating its first anniversary. The *Virginian-Pilot*'s citation was typical. During the 1920's Jaffé brought in for the Sunday editorial page a column on books, "The Literary Lantern," written for a time by Howard Mumford Jones, of the University of North Carolina (who went on to a distinguished Harvard University career as professor, critic, and author). A column of modern poetry clipped from magazines began to appear beside it. By special arrangements articles in the Baltimore *Evening Sun* by H. L. Mencken and the column of Franklin P. Adams ("F. P. A.") of the New York *Tribune* and later of the New York *World* became *Virginian-Pilot* features.

The editor sought to develop his own book reviewers. He found one in a young Marine Corps officer stationed in Norfolk, John W. Thomason, who wrote for the *Virginian-Pilot* before his book with his sketches of Marines in the first World War, *Fix Bayonets!*, caught the national eye. Toward the end of the 1920's Stringfellow Barr, then a history professor of the University of Virginia, later leader of the St. John's College experiment, wrote editorials during vacation periods and in emergencies. So, a little later, did Phillips Russell of the faculty of the University of North Carolina at Chapel Hill.

These interests were additions to, never substitutes for, the consideration of public affairs in Norfolk, Virginia, and the nation. Nor did these or anything else lessen the gravity with which the editor went about editing. After he had gone over the copy of an associate with his black pencil, a rewritten editorial might emerge. He would never tolerate shoddiness. The subject had to be absorbed, the attitude toward it had to be made clear, and the conclusion had to be to the point.

The two newspapers joined their strength to attack many abuses: Virginia's fee system, for one, by which public officials were paid, often in extravagant amounts, from the fees levied by their offices; the tight and profitable monopoly of the Virginia Pilots Association, with its virtual father-to-son membership and its control of a public service without being itself under effective regulation; and always the rising illegalities of prohibition enforcement.

They stood together in defense of the city manager government in a city that was still carrying the weight of decades of bad government and was still harassed—but not captured—by old political forces. Under more youthful editors the newspapers were showing a modern sense of fairness toward the Negro population in education, opportunity, and legal rights. The *Virginian-Pilot* was darkly suspicious of the Ku Klux Klan when it emerged in the robes and masks of the post-Civil War organization but with broader prejudices against minorities. As the character of the Klan movement grew clear, the newspaper grew sharply and persistently critical of its spirit and its works.

In the same spirit the *Virginian-Pilot* began a never ceasing campaign against lynching, prevailingly a crime of the Southern states and predominantly a crime against Negroes. Jaffé made comprehensive and minute examinations of numerous lynchings with two main objectives: public enlightenment as to the true nature of mob murders and public education in the necessity for orderly constitutional processes in dealing with persons charged with crime. Lynching itself he regarded as a particularly horrible manifestation of man's nature. "Lynching goes unpunished in Virginia," he wrote in December, 1927, "because, deny it as one will, it commands a certain social sanction. An unwritten code is invoked to give the color of social necessity to a crime which is plainly destructive of guarantees which have been regarded as inviolate in Anglo-Saxon thinking and jurisprudence since Runnymede."

Bringing the issues more closely to possible remedies, Jaffé concluded that more was needed than local control and less should be asked than Federal action. "To the Virginian-Pilot," he wrote, "it seems more and more clear that there will be no adequate grappling with this form of savagery until the punishment of lynchers is made a primary obligation of the State, and legislation is enacted to that end."

The *Virginian-Pilot* turned especially to Governor Byrd. It quoted the words of North Carolina's Governor Angus W. McLean: "The only way to suppress lynching is to let those who engage in it understand that they will be punished, and punished severely." The editor asserted that "the incoming Governor [of Virginia] can render no higher service to the cause of law and order than by ordering the adoption of the same strong-arm methods that have enabled the State authorities of North Carolina to deal effectively with every attempt at mob violence."

Jaffé made this appeal even more direct when, after a particularly abhorrent lynching that involved both Kentucky and Virginia, he wrote in a personal letter to Governor Byrd: "I hope you will find a means of forcing a showdown on this outrage—in the name of Virginia and in the name of decency." He himself believed strongly in the necessity "to single out lynching for the special and effective condemnation that was early in the present century directed against dueling."

Governor Byrd requested Jaffé to outline his ideas about anti-lynching legislation, and he did so. The governor, already troubled by the crime and seeking means to deal effectively with it, took the case to the General Assembly. Some changes, none of major consequence, were made there in the Byrd recommendations, but the governor's purpose and strength, in addition to the inherent virtues of his recommendations, were strong enough to push the bill through both houses. He signed the bill on March 14, 1928.

This legislation designated lynching and mobs by name and description, declared participation equivalent to committing a comparable crime as an individual, and made members of mobs civilly liable. It fixed responsibility for apprehension and prosecution more definitely on the attorney for the commonwealth, aided by the state's attorney general or other prosecutors designated by the governor, who was authorized to spend such sums as he deemed necessary for these purposes. All told, this was a powerful battery of law. Since its adoption there has never been a lynching in Virginia.

About Jaffé's role in this enactment Governor Byrd subsequently wrote: "Mr. Jaffé's editorials over a long period in advocacy of making the punishment of lynchers a state responsibility, supplemented by his personal representations to me, had more to do than any other single outside urging in convincing me that I should make one of my major recommendations the passage of a drastic anti-lynching law providing that lynching be a state offense."[1]

There was no surprise, in the light of this record, in the *Virginian-Pilot*'s reaction to the vicious lynching in Houston, Texas, in June of 1928 that shocked the United States and world opinion. At the moment Houston was under brilliant spotlights. The Democratic National Convention—it was the convention that would nominate New York's Governor Alfred E. Smith—was assembling after the rare choice of a Southern city as convention site. Hundreds of reporters from across the United States and from foreign countries were on the ground. Much Southern sentiment, still impregnated with reverence for prohibition, in name at least, and opposed to Al Smith because of his religion, was at odds with the remainder of the country. A good deal had been printed about Houston's responsibility as host. Yet now Houston was dramatically presented as the setting for the most conspicious lynching of the year.

On June 22, 1928, the day after the report of the lynching, the *Virginian-Pilot* published an editorial written by Jaffé under the head, "An Unspeakable Act of Savagery." The words were taken from the first sentence: that Houston

> is disgraced by an unspeakable act of savagery. There is no other way to describe the performance of the eight armed men who yanked Robert Powell, 24-year-old Negro, from a hospital cot on which he lay with a bullet in his stomach, and hanged him from a tree just outside the city. Powell was under the charge of killing a detective in a shooting match from which he himself emerged with an apparently mortal wound. In the event of his recovery, he was headed for the courts. But to this Texas mob, neither Death nor Justice was an acceptable arbiter. Nothing would satisfy them but a loathsome act of murder carried out against a human being while he lay in agony with a bullet in his entrails.

The editorial noted the unusual extent to which official Houston had been "stirred by this foul thing laid on its doorstep just when

1. A statement sent to Columbia University in support of the nomination of Jaffé for a Pulitzer Prize; John M. Hohenberg, *The Pulitzer Prize Story* (New York: Columbia University Press, 1959).

it was most anxious to show itself to the world at its cleanest": a grand jury ordered to drop all other business to investigate the lynching, $10,000 from the city to speed it on its way, a reward by the state, a detail of Texas Rangers to aid investigations. "If the perseverance of the authorities is in keeping with their initial burst of energy," the editorial said, "one or more of the group that bravely did to death a crippled man lying on a hospital cot, may see the inside of the Texas penitentiary."

But the meaning of the deed itself could not be washed away so easily. It required further examination:

> The year that saw four months pass without a single lynching has now accumulated five of them. Five lynchings in six months represent a proportional reduction in savagery from last year's record of 16 lynchings in 12 months, but the year is only half gone and no one may be too confident. We have come a long way from the dark days of 1892 when America celebrated the 400th year of its discovery with 255 lynchings, but we have not yet arrived at that social abhorrence of this crime that must precede its practical extinction. When eight presumably decent and rational beings can gain the consent of their conscience to rob a hospital bed for the purpose of executing summary vengeance, and when, as was the case a few days ago in Louisiana, two Negroes are torn from their guards and lynched because they were brothers of another Negro who was accused of murder, it must be recognized that the rise and fall of the lynching curve is governed by racial passions that remain still to be brought under civilized control.

In the following May of 1929, Jaffé received the Pulitzer Prize in journalism for distinguished editorial writing in 1928—the first award of any Pulitzer Prize in journalism, and the highest award of any kind that had been made to a Virginia newspaperman. The text of the official certificate includes the statement that Jaffé "has been awarded The Pulitzer Prize in Journalism for his editorial entitled 'An Unspeakable Act of Savagery,' in the 'Norfolk Virginian-Pilot,' an editorial which is typical of a series of articles on the lynching evil and in successful advocacy of legislation to prevent it."

The award was thus in significant degree a recognition of a policy long held and persistently championed. It was a tribute to the *Virginian-Pilot* for such editorial distinction. But preeminently it was a tribute to the editor and to the man himself. For the words written about the crime in Houston reflected the very essence of Louis Jaffé.

Though the *Virginian-Pilot's* antilynching convictions brought it special recognition, the *Ledger-Dispatch* understood the mob spirit and the racial prejudice inherent in most lynchings in the South. It challenged both. But in their attitude toward another major issue of the 1920's the two newspapers wound up on opposite sides. This divergence came at the climax of decades of effort to make good roads out of bad ones—chiefly, how to pay for them.

In 1872 the original *Virginian* denounced Virginia roads as "shocking to gods and men and fishcarts." In the 1890's a country reader complained that if a Norfolk merchant gave him a wagon-load of silver dollars he could not transport them home over roads he would have to use. The *Landmark* paraphrased Goldsmith with "Ill fares the land, to hastening ills a prey,/Where mud accumulates and roads decay," and then added: "All roads lead to Rome except bad roads, and they lead to revolution." But this revolution took its time.

By the middle 1890's advocates of good roads were holding conventions and adopting resolutions, one approving a plan to raise as much as $230,000 for "permanent improvements" of Virginia roads. Toll highways began to flourish, but they were so bad that the Norfolk County *Democrat* said "the collection of toll for their use [was] little better than highway robbery." Philosophical principles interfered so strongly that in 1904 the *Dispatch* declared "there is no reason in the world why either the state or national government should appropriate money for country roads."

But in 1906 the *Public Ledger* thought that "aside from those subjects that have a moral side, as education and . . . state asylums, Virginia cannot spend any part of her revenue to better advantage than on the establishment of the highway commission, extending aid to good roads in the Commonwealth." (Governor McKinney thought in the 1890's that a state system would be unconstitutional.) In 1910 Alvah H. Martin gave "his personal check for $21,000 to Colonel Walter H. Taylor, who held the stock in escrow, and is now the absolute owner of Cottage Toll Road that leads from Chapel Street to Ocean View." Martin was offering it to Norfolk County at the price he paid for it, after which (or so it was hoped) the road would be "a free boulevard."

By 1913 the Tidewater Automobile Association was in business, and the *Virginian-Pilot* was suggesting routes for an ideal Sunday automobile tour and was calling for comfort stations. In November, 1915, the *Ledger-Dispatch* reported that "the toll roads and bridges in Norfolk City and Norfolk County are now the property of the city and county"—all, that is, except the Campostella Bridge: it was making so much money that its owners would not sell. The route for the Norfolk-Virginia Beach highway was being surveyed in 1916, a year when there were twenty-five hundred automobiles in Norfolk. But when Congress provided $85,000,000 for road building in the next five years, the *Virginian-Pilot* commented, a little sourly but realistically: "Hardly a drop in the bucket." Besides, it did not like such action by Congress: "The states could and would take care of the problem by and of themselves."

In 1918 the state was taking responsibilities seriously enough to plan a state system, and the issue was bonds vs. pay-as-you-go. The day of Waterloo had arrived.

In that year the General Assembly began amending the Virginia constitution so the state could issue bonds for state highway construction. But by 1922 this widely approved authorization was encountering the opposition of half the legislators, notably that of a youthful, pink-cheeked apple-grower, newspaper editor, and state senator, Harry F. Byrd.

Byrd objected to placing "a bond burden" upon the people. He argued that roads built with bonds would wear out before the bonds were paid for. Especially he could not forget the state's long struggle in the post-Civil War decades with the pre-Civil War debt.[2] This struck home. Byrd's family had so little money then that he had to go to work in his teens. The thought of debt, the cost of debt, the fear of debt disturbed him deeply.

In March of 1923 Governor Trinkle's message to the General Assembly seemed to the *Virginian-Pilot* "a closely reasoned abandonment of bonding in favor of pay-as-you-go," an "about-face" that "is complete and appears to be final." But to the *Ledger-Dispatch* it was proof that the governor had been "taken bodily into the pay-as-you-go camp." The program included a gasoline tax for building roads immediately and a November referendum on a $50,000,000 bond issue.

The *Virginian-Pilot* thought that "a pay-as-you-go plan placing a larger share of the burden on the general taxpayer would probably finance the road program more economically than . . . if the whole enterprise were financed with bonds." To the *Ledger-Dispatch* the "half-baked road building provisions" were indicating "the quality of statesmanship, intelligence . . . and courage which has caused, and is causing, the Old Dominion to limp along near the end of the procession of states. . . . We are not without hope that Virginia will emerge from her hidebound complacency and self-satisfaction

2. Described in Chapter 11, "The Unmanageable Debt."

some day; but such a record as the legislature has just written does not encourage the hope."

The first of the major Byrd victories was now about to dazzle Virginia. Pay-as-you-go carried the state—though not Norfolk and not Portsmouth—by nearly thirty-five thousand votes. "Pay-as-you-go" was the slogan that bit and caught hold. It held on for most of the next forty years, not only in road building where its control of expenditures by the state government long was absolute, but as an attitude toward all governmental expenditures and toward life itself. At the height of its influence it was economic and political dogma, and Virginians who doubted the universal virtues attributed to it were economically, politically, and even socially a little suspect.

And whatever the effect on the rate of road building (in the 1960's complaint of slow progress was louder than ever before), pay-as-you-go was a powerful factor in building the career of Byrd. Two years later he was elected governor, largely because of his success in leading the pay-as-you-go fight. He was on his way, and he went far.

In 1923 a change of importance left the *Ledger-Dispatch* without an editor. Douglas Gordon was not in normal health, and Slover thought his editorial work was suffering. A change for a time might be better, he concluded, and Gordon agreed. The *Ledger-Dispatch* announced on July 2 that Gordon had "connected himself with the Richmond Times-Dispatch and hereafter will make his home in Richmond." The newspaper's opinion of Gordon was not in doubt. "He leaves," it said, "with the heartfelt good wishes of the Ledger-Dispatch management and staff."

The title of editor was held in reserve against a day when, obviously, the *Ledger-Dispatch* hoped Gordon would return. Meantime, as in many another emergency, Perkins took charge, assisted principally by Goodridge W. Lineweaver from the city desk and aided by occasional writing by several men in the news room. Robert B. Tunstall, a Norfolk lawyer, with an interest in public affairs and a distinctive style, wrote many editorials. Gerald W. Johnson, then a professor of journalism at the University of North Carolina, earlier associate editor of the Greensboro *Daily News*, later an editorial writer for the Baltimore *Evening Sun* and the *Sun*, and an essayist, critic, and historian, wrote editorials in summer months. So did William B. Smith, later editor of the Roanoke *World-News*.

Gordon was away four and a half years, during which he became associate editor and then editor of the Richmond *Times-Dispatch*. When he returned in January, 1928, the delight of the *Ledger-Dis-*

patch was unconcealed. Its leading editorial on December 24, 1927, said:

> It is with pleasure that the Ledger-Dispatch presents its readers with a Chrismas gift in the shape of the announcement that Douglas Gordon is shortly to be transferred from the editorship of the Richmond Times-Dispatch to resume a similar position with the Norfolk Ledger-Dispatch. . . . His brilliant editorial work for the Ledger-Dispatch from 1917 to 1923, when he resigned to return to his native city of Richmond to re-associate himself with the Times-Dispatch, won him thousands of admirers. As for friends, their name is legion, and they are restricted to no particular locality. A man of rare personal charm, a logical thinker, a writer of graceful yet forceful English, Mr. Gordon is an acquisition to Norfolk and Tidewater, the value of which it is difficult to overestimate. . . .

The editorial quoted complimentary remarks from the *Times-Dispatch*, the Richmond *News Leader*, and the Lynchburg *News*. The *Virginian-Pilot* called Gordon's return "good news. . . . He knows his Tidewater and his state and nation. He writes with charm, with urbanity and, when needed, with downright hate. There are in these times, as there have been in all times, things to cherish and exalt and things to condemn and attack. Mr. Gordon brings to the discharge of these necessary editorial offices fairness, discrimination and a liberal outlook. His return to the Tidewater publishing field is one of the happy developments of the new year."

Gordon continued as editor for the next sixteen years until his death in 1944.

Whether the editorial pages agreed or disagreed in the 1920's, the rivalry of the newsrooms never ran down: in their handling of the big national news of Wilson and the League of Nations, Hughes and the disarmament conference, Harding and Teapot Dome, the Leo Frank lynching, the Scopes trial, the Loeb and Leopold agonies, and the transoceanic flights.

So it was with such Norfolk news as the attempted hijacking on a Christmas morning in Hampton Roads of the Japanese ship *Kaisho Maru* to get the ship's liquor and the killing of two sailors who resisted; the burning in Norfolk of the dirigible *Roma*; the international Schneider Cup races that circled Hampton Roads; the abduction in Princess Anne County of the Catholic priest, the Rev. Vincent Warren, by a masked mob armed with pistols; the Billy Sunday sermons,

U. S. AND JAPAN AT WAR

Norfolk Virginian-Pilot

Vol. CLXIII. No. 69 — Norfolk, Virginia, Monday, December 8, 1941 — Three Cents the Copy

Japan Attacks Hawaii And Philippines

Norfolk Stunned By News; Japanese Seized

Japs Lay Claim To Sinking Three U.S. Warships

NORFOLK LEDGER-DISPATCH

HOME EDITION

VOL. CXXVI.—NO. 139 — NORFOLK, VA., MONDAY AFTERNOON, DECEMBER 8, 1941 — 22 PAGES—PRICE THREE CENTS

CONGRESS DRAFTS DECLARATION OF WAR AS U. S. ANNOUNCES 3,000 CASUALTIES

2 Battleships, Carrier Listed As Destroyed

Domei Boasts 60 Per Cent of Hawaiian U. S. Strength Shattered

Tokyo, Tuesday, Dec. 9 —

White House Announces Two Battleships Destroyed In Pearl Harbor Attack

Large Number of Planes Also Reported Destroyed, Washington Announces, But U. S. Forces Account for Several Japanese

Norfolk Virginian-Pilot

Vol. CLXXVII. No. 38 — Norfolk, Virginia, Tuesday, May 8, 1945 — Five Cents the Copy

V-E Proclamation Today

Nazis Surrender In Czechoslovakia

SECOND EXTRA

NORFOLK LEDGER-DISPATCH

SECOND EXTRA

VOL CXXXIV.—NO. 38 — NORFOLK, VA., TUESDAY AFTERNOON, AUGUST 14, 1945 — PRICE FIVE CENTS

WAR OVER

Japan Surrenders Unconditionally

From Pearl Harbor to V-J Day, Norfolk's newspapers told the story of World War II in page-one headlines.

The announcement of Japan's surrender in World War II triggered the wildest celebration in Norfolk's history. Sailors snake-danced in the streets, waving copies of the *Ledger-Dispatch*'s war-end extra.

the marathon dancers, and the marriages of the Berkley-born darling of the camera men, Peggy Hopkins Joyce.

And so it was too in the era of Jack Johnson, Willard, Dempsey, Carpentier, Firpo, and Tunney and of the apotheosis of the World Series scoreboards that choked Plume Street for the *Ledger-Dispatch* and Brooke Avenue, and eventually the City Auditorium for the *Virginian-Pilot*.

The end of the war had brought reporters and desk men trooping home from the armed forces, and newcomers joined the depleted staffs. Besides Aiken and Lineweaver (from the Valley of Virginia), the *Ledger-Dispatch*'s newcomers included Edward G. Maxwell (son of the *Public Ledger*'s John E. Maxwell), who later went to the Baltimore *Sun*; Thomas A. Hanes, from Alabama, an aggressive and resourceful personality who knew Norfolk when he wore a Navy uniform and came in as sports editor (succeeding "Tom Jones," who was really Jay Lewis); Joseph E. Shank, another Valley of Virginia man who filled most of the newsroom positions and always was at the heart of operations there; and Charles Day, who wrote Edgar Guest-type verse that led in 1940 to his designation by the General Assembly as poet laureate of Virginia.

Another Alabamian, Ellis Loveless, who had gone from the Portsmouth *Star* to the Navy, came to the advertising department and rose to be head of it and a vice president and a director of the corporation. Still another Navy man, William S. Davis, from Pennsylvania, directed classified advertising.

Henry Perkins, on being named associate editor during Gordon's absence, was endowed with a private office, "for the first time in his life, and I think he liked that," Tom Gilliam remembered. But Perkins could not be confined to one room, whatever his title. E. H. Millen, a New York *Times* man, had been made managing editor, but when he left in a year or two to join the Curtis magazines in Philadelphia, Perkins was in command again.

A personality of the period, with an unusual schedule, was James Donaldson. At heart he was a circus man. To the satisfaction of both, he worked for several years with the publicity staff of Barnum & Bailey from April to October and with the *Ledger-Dispatch* from October to April, migrating to the lions and the clowns and then migrating back again to the typewriters and the high jinks of the news room. He must have been a competent man indeed.

The Paris peace conference sent the *Virginian-Pilot*'s managing editor, Keville Glennan, streaking across the Atlantic under a commission to report the conference for a group of newspapers, including his own. He resigned in 1921 for "purely personal" reasons after twenty-nine years with the *Virginian-Pilot*. Earlier in that year, in February, the *Virginian-Pilot* began collecting its big local news on the back page and continued to do so until the 1950's—a distinctive style of makeup that the *Landmark* under Abell had used in the 1910-12 period. In quick succession Glennan went to newspapers in Newark, Rochester, and Washington before returning to Norfolk in 1923. This time he was news editor of the *Ledger-Dispatch*.

T. M. Byrne, the city editor, succeeded Glennan briefly in the *Virginian-Pilot* news command, and R. W. Simpson, of the Associated Press staff in Washington, well known in Virginia and North Carolina, followed for another brief period before going to the Tampa *Tribune*. The turnover ended when Winder R. Harris came back from Washington in 1925 and began a sixteen-year tenure lasting to 1941 when he was elected to Congress—a dominant managing editor and a popular citizen.

Virginian-Pilot reporters looked to a city desk presided over by W. H. Jenkins, Jr., until 1924, and by John Spencer until 1941, when he succeeded Harris as managing editor—a long-time Associated Press man with experience in Washington. Joseph A. Leslie, Jr., who had started out with his family's weekly in Tazewell, Virginia, and worked for Bishop Cannon's Richmond *Virginian* before going to Newport News, crossed Hampton Roads in November, 1919, for a long career in Norfolk. He quickly proved to be fast, accurate, and intelligent in reporting city government and political news, and anything else that needed to be done. Under the name of Josephus Bush he wrote a weekly column that paralleled the news with humor and imagination and grew into a widely read Monday morning feature. In time he was associate editor and editor of the *Ledger-Dispatch*. He had covered sessions of the General Assembly, and so had Frank S. Pace, who was systematic and precise, and eventually would be production manager.

The long line of *Virginian-Pilot* reporters and desk men of the 1920's included Spencer R. McCullough, who made a good name in later years as a national reporter of the St. Louis *Post-Dispatch*; R. K. T. Larson, who held every position in the newsroom that a man could hold; W. E. Debnam, who, after a hitch with the *Ledger-Dispatch*, established a Norfolk weekly, the *News Index*, that helped develop sentiment for clearing out the city's slums, and then was a North Carolina radio celebrity; Robert Murray, a police reporter believed to be well acquainted with every member of the Norfolk force (later a Baltimore *Sun* man); and a historian of the newsroom, Arch W. Jarrell, a Kansan in Virginia.

Jarrell thought of Glennan as "an excellent newspaper man with a pixyish sense of humor when he had sampled the bootleg liquor of those mad days."[3] He recalled that Harry Moore, when day city editor, "invariably greeted us with a 'Happy New Year,' winter and summer." He remembered William Carney, the telegraph editor, "who was also a member of the Sinn Fein and an ardent supporter of the Irish revolution," and Oland Russell, who later was in Warsaw, "and I received a heartbroken letter from him after that city had been bombed to pieces in World War II."

Jarrell remembered, too, the assignment he had in 1922 of covering the legislative session in Richmond, and how "I quickly formed a triumvirate with Junius Fishburn of the Roanoke Times and Bob Glass of the Lynchburg News . . . we scored many good scoops over the Richmond papers, thanks to such good friends as the young state senator from Winchester, Harry F. Byrd."

But chiefly, it is easy to assume, Jarrell remembered the morning in July of 1922 when he and Robert Murray joined a posse of some five hundred men and boys who were scouring the countryside near Norfolk for a man named Chambers who was charged with killing two Federal prohibition agents. He wrote:

> He was found in a copse of woods near Forest Lawn cemetery on Ocean View boulevard . . . . Somehow I had obtained a .32 caliber pistol. . . . About 5 o'clock in the morning Chambers backed out of the woods not far from where Murray and I were standing. I fired the pistol at about the time 499 others began shooting, and Chambers was soon riddled with bullets.
>
> Murray, in his story, related the pistol episode, and intimated that my bullet was one of the lethal ones. I received threatening letters and telephone calls, although my accuracy with firearms is so bad that jackrabbits sit and sneer at me as I come up to them. The autopsy, however, uncovered no .32 bullets in the body of Chambers.

This was the newsroom in which Miss Bessy Chamberlaine began earlier her long career as society editor. The *Virginian-Pilot* never had a reporter or editor who tried harder to beat the *Ledger-Dispatch.* Miss Bessy was the embodiment of inherited and inherent elegance. She knew the family lines of Norfolk as some people know their

3. In a personal communication from Jarrell to Shank, April 10, 1961.

Bible. By her very presence, as well as by her need for someone to tell her how to spell, she commanded attention and dignity even in rough newsroom moments.

The *Ledger-Dispatch*'s Mrs. Stella Upshur could write feature stories and food columns and handle other news while keeping up with the weddings, the births, the teas, the germans, and the marriages, and when, under the name of Beatrice Fairfax, she gave advice to the lovelorn, she was a prize. For some twenty years she averaged twenty answers a day to letter-writers. But on that subject let Arch Jarrell have the last word: "I left Norfolk with many happy memories of my two years. I also left my fraternity pin with a blond named Celestine, who declined to return it to me, saying it would be a nice souvenir."

The two newspapers in Norfolk were growing up. The staffs were much larger and had more varied backgrounds. They had better education too. They were more experienced and more professional. It is not surprising that the two challenges in the early 1920's from new newspapers ended in failures.

The Norfolk *Tribune,* published afternoons and Sunday mornings, appeared on October 8, 1920, from quarters at 141 West City Hall Avenue. It used mechanical equipment from the Richmond *Virginian* when that journal of the prohibitionists gave up in the previous May after ten years of efforts to combine dry propaganda with news. J. Peter Holland was president of the *Tribune*'s publishing corporation, and W. W. Holland was secretary and treasurer, both with nearby Southampton County backgrounds.

Forty-five days later the *Tribune* ceased publication and closed its doors. The Newport News *Times-Herald* pronounced judgment: "It was one of the most remarkable experiments in Virginia journalism. . . . It can be accounted for only on the theory that there are still in the world sane men who fancy that newspapering is a freak and a frolic instead of a normal orderly business."

The other competitor had the opposite background. The Norfolk *Post,* an afternoon newspaper, began publication June 1, 1921, from quarters at 112-116 West City Hall Avenue, an enlargement of the *Tribune* offices. It was established by the Scripps-McRae newspaper chain which changed its name to Scripps-Howard in 1922.

Of this organization of generally vigorous, independent, and professionally competent newspapers, the *Post* was number 24. Its first edition came rolling off its press "dressed up," said the *Virginian-Pilot*, "in the Scripps-McRae afternoon best—tabloid news articles, capsule editorials, pictures, cartoons, rhymes, questions and answers, simplified spelling, 'n everything." The *Virginian-Pilot* noted especially the *Post*'s declaration that "fair and square competition will be its rule of conduct." Good, said the *Virginian-Pilot*; the *Post* "will receive that kind of competition from papers already in the field, for that is the only kind of competition the spirit of Norfolk will tolerate. To emulate the Post's own economy of words, Go to it!"

The *Ledger-Dispatch*, once again the chief target, did its greeting duty, concluding with "whatever may be the faults and shortcomings of Norfolk and its tributary territory, narrowness and provincialism are not to be numbered among them. Wherefore . . . the Norfolk Post is warmly received and its confidence in the future of Norfolk and its opportunities is cordially recognized." But the *Ledger-Dispatch* knew well that Scripps-McRae newspapers, though different from those Norfolk had known, often had been successful elsewhere. It did not take the *Post* lightly.

The *Post*'s style included sharp and critical journalism—for instance, news and editorial attacks on bad conditions in the city jail, an old target and one that was standing much later too. The *Post* concentrated on a few news subjects and exploited them. Pages were few, rarely more than eight or ten; stories were brief; headlines were big and bold; entertainment features were numerous. In its way it was bright and vigorous.

Still the *Post* could not make substantial headway. Most of its principal personalities were sent in by the chain. Frank S. Newell was business manager throughout its career, but the succession of editors—Max B. Cook, W. N. Burkhardt, and J. M. Shields—pointed to unhappiness. Two *Ledger-Dispatch* men joined the *Post*. But nobody could lift circulation above 10,000. On the other hand, the *Ledger-Dispatch* had 41,514 a few days before the *Post* began to publish; it had 40,164 two months later, and had 41,661 two and a half years later.

After these two and a half years, Scripps-Howard leaders, among whom Roy W. Howard had risen high, decided to give up the *Post*. Or perhaps they could buy the *Ledger-Dispatch*? Could they? Roy Howard carried the inquiry to Slover. Would he sell? And at what price?

Slover had no wish to sell. He did not like the competition of the *Post*, but the *Ledger-Dispatch* was doing well. He gave Howard no encouragement. Howard pushed persistently and hard, and eventually Slover named a figure that he himself thought was so high as to be beyond any danger of being accepted. Immediately Howard snapped him up. "We'll buy at that price," he said. The legal details were handed to lawyers.

When word of these developments seeped through to *Ledger-Dispatch* officials, editors, and other workers, gloom descended. A rumor spread that the Scripps-Howard people were sending to Norfolk a contingent of managers and editors, and the gloom grew stygian. Half the staff feared it was on the way out. The Plume Street building's rooms, corridors, and closets witnessed a never ending series of conferences.

Slover, meantime, was himself growing unhappier by the hour. He could not let the deal go through.

The lawyers had bogged down, and Slover had no difficulty cutting short their negotiations. He admired Howard's attitude and behavior, and in the windup he offered to buy any of the *Post*'s equipment for which the *Ledger-Dispatch* had need. But Howard said no. "You didn't ask us to come in," he said. "We'll take our own losses," and Slover admired him the more.

The *Post*'s announcement was frank. It had begun publication, it said, "on the assumption that there was an opportunity in Norfolk for a second evening newspaper. It is apparent to the owners of the Post that their entry into Norfolk was premature." And so, after February 2, 1924, the *Post* published no more. About this the *Ledger-Dispatch* commented:

> . . . When such an organization of experienced and able newspaper men, with almost unlimited capital, as the Scripps-Howard Newspaper Syndicate is recognized to have, takes this view [that "their entry into Norfolk was premature"], it must be accepted as conclusive. . . . The Ledger-Dispatch, itself a consolidation of the old Public Ledger and the Norfolk Dispatch, realizes a responsibility that now rests upon it as the only afternoon paper in Norfolk. It promises to endeavor to live up to it.
>
> Perhaps it may be of interest to emphasize the tendency in late years toward fewer papers and better papers rather than more papers.
>
> It is only necessary here in Virginia, at least, to call attention to the preponderance of hyphenated names of newspapers, the results of mergers and discontinuances, and the consequent loss of much effort and capital. Our morning contemporary, the Virginian-Pilot, the Richmond Times-Dispatch, the Richmond News Leader, the Roanoke World-News, the Newport News Times-Herald are Virginia examples, and so on throughout the United States. . . .

Alongside these formal actions was the celebration of the men of the *Ledger-Dispatch*. They gave a dinner to honor Slover and to afford themselves a setting to roar out their delight. It was a night to remember. They even produced a newspaper for the occasion named in high glee *The Post Mortem*. Knowing that the owner was fond of shooting from the blinds on the nearby coast, they produced one story under the head, "Ferocious Duck Attacks Norfolk Sportsman—S. L. Slover Has Narrow Escape" and another under "Tremors Felt in Portsmouth." The business editor reported "Market Tone Steady" and told why:

> Following a period of uncertainty and irregularity, due to bear activities during the early part of the week, bullish advices from the front [reported] that bear raiders had been repulsed shortly after Wednesday's call [and] the financial outlook assumed a brighter aspect. Industrials came more in evidence Thursday and with the declaration of dividends Friday [the newspaper's payday] the week closed strong.

Undoubtedly Slover learned something about gratitude that night.

THE ISSUE OF WHETHER SLOVER WOULD SELL THE *Ledger-Dispatch* IN 1924 to the Scripps-Howard chain rose a year after the climax of the series of newspaper investments outside Norfolk that placed him (after being in control much earlier of the Newport News *Times-Herald*) in control not only of the *Ledger-Dispatch* but also of the Portsmouth *Star,* the Petersburgh *Progress-Index,* and the Richmond *Times-Dispatch* and *Evening Dispatch.*

This was a series of ownerships and managerial operations for which there is no parallel in Virginia history. It aroused much curiosity, especially among other newspapers and politicians, and in banking and business circles. Was this a Slover chain? Would these newspapers be operated collectively? Did the man who controlled them plan—as some conspicuous heads of newspaper chains in the United States had done—to unite their influence and use it for political purposes? What was Slover's goal?

When Slover and Harvey Wilson bought the Norfolk *Public Ledger* in 1905, they were reported to have political purposes. They felt the need to correct that report, and they did so in these words: the purchase "is a purely business enterprise with a view to profit only." Slover knew he could not earn profit unless he had something genuine and desirable to sell. He liked to do a good job all the way through. But essentially he was a business man.

His success in the newspaper business attracted the attention of other businesses. Early in his Norfolk residence he was elected a director of the bank that became the National Bank of Commerce and later the Virginia National Bank. When his father-in-law, Alvah H. Martin, died in 1918, Slover was asked to take over the presidency of the relatively small Merchants and Planters Bank, located in Berkley, of which Martin had been president. He did so, and later he was chairman of its board. In this instance he thought he had a personal and family responsibility.

In time Slover was elected a director of the Norfolk & Western Railway and of the Newport News Shipbuilding and Dry Dock Company, and had other outside responsibilities and could have had more. But there was never any doubt that his first interest was newspaper publication.

Slover did not acquire control of newspapers for any outside ambition or goal. He had no idea of creating a newspaper chain, and he did not create one. The newspapers he was interested in were never secondary to something else in which he was interested more. Primarily and always he was a newspaper publisher with all that that implies.

The Slover interest in the Portsmouth *Star* for seventeen years began (as noted earlier) with his sense of loyalty to Martin. After Martin died, the owners completed the sale to Hamilton in 1924. Hamilton had small resources then and was paying the purchase price for many years.

The Petersburg purchase also was the result of a personal plea. In 1919 William Edward Harris was owner and editor of the morning Petersburg *Index-Appeal*, which he acquired in 1910. He had worked for the original Norfolk *Virginian*, later for the Charleston, West Virginia, *Gazette*, and still later was Washington correspondent for several newspapers, including the *Ledger-Dispatch*. News and editorial management interested him more than business management. In Petersburg he was badly overworked and needed relief and assistance. He and his wife, friends of the Slover family, appealed to Slover to devise a better arrangement.

The time was not convenient. Slover had lost his partner, Wilson, in 1917, had just taken over the presidency of the Merchants and Planters Bank in South Norfolk, and was heavily engaged in adjusting the *Ledger-Dispatch* to postwar strains. Somewhat reluctantly, he set about seeing what he could do. He was confident that if the *Index-Appeal* and the afternoon Petersburg *Progress* could be united, they could establish a sounder business basis than either then had. As a first step he submitted to Harris a proposal by which he himself would acquire an interest in the *Index-Appeal* and take over the business operation. Harris was attracted. "The feature which appealed to me," he wrote Slover on July 30, 1919, "was my being relieved of every connection with the business office. I really wished to make some arrangement of that sort and can think of no man I had rather have it with than yourself."

Slover found the owners of the *Progress* willing to sell, perhaps in part because they knew that the *Index-Appeal* would offer more formidable competition. He wrote to Harris on October 4, 1919:

> I have arranged to acquire the entire capital stock of the Petersburg Progress Publishing Company, and have personally obligated myself to pay therefor. It is my purpose to consolidate this company with the Index-Appeal Publishing Company by forming a new corporation which shall take over from you and me jointly the stock of the Index-Appeal Publishing Company, and from me that of the Progress Publishing Company.

In 1920 the Petersburg Publishing Company was established to publish both newspapers, with Harris as editor of both. On February 6, 1922, the *Progress-Index*, formed by the consolidation as originally planned, began publishing. With Harris as editor Slover continued as president of the corporation until 1928. He sold his interest then to two Norfolk friends, Frederick Lewis, who was associated with Slover in several transactions, and Paul S. Huber, later president of the Ledger-Dispatch Corporation.

The Richmond *Times-Dispatch* investment involved its associate, the smaller *Evening Dispatch*. Ownership earlier had been concentrated in the Bryan family, of which Joseph Bryan was the chief figure. After his death the heirs sold two-thirds of the stock to two brothers, J. O. and T. S. Winston, of New York and Virginia. The other third was held by the Hasbrook interests, represented at first by C. L. Hasbrook and later by C. P. Hasbrook, who in 1923 was publisher and manager.

On August 11, 1923, Slover and Frederick Lewis, of Norfolk, completed negotiations for the Winstons' holdings. Each bought approximately one-third of the stock of the corporation, but Slover and Lewis had a trust agreement providing that Slover would vote the Lewis stock for the next twenty-five years. Lewis was a Pennsylvanian with considerable resources of his own in oil and other interests. He had moved to Norfolk and there became a friend of Slover and an admirer of his business sagacity. He knew little about newspaper publishing then and was quite willing for Slover to vote his newly acquired stock. His purchase of an interest in the Petersburg *Progress-Index* from Slover came later. In 1930 he bought a substantial interest, as will appear, in the *Ledger-Dispatch*.

In Norfolk, Portsmouth, and Petersburg the newspapers in which

Slover was interested were afternoon newspapers. Although the Richmond *Times-Dispatch* seemed to him to have unusual opportunities in its own right (he was much less impressed by the smaller *Evening Dispatch*), he was the more attracted because it was a morning newspaper. He thought then that morning newspapers had larger possibilities than afternoon newspapers and that the trend was in their direction. Hasbrook remained in command of daily operations in Richmond. In time, Huber, Franklin Cook, and Norman Hill, of the *Ledger-Dispatch* organization, bought some of the *Times-Dispatch* stock.

The Associated Press's report of the purchase of the *Times-Dispatch* appeared on Sunday, August 12. It included a statement that "there will be no combination of Mr. Slover's newspaper properties." But Slover, after he had returned to Norfolk, thought something more should be said. The newspapers of August 13 published what he had in mind. Two-thirds of the statement consisted of happily expressed tributes to Richmond as a city and to the *Times-Dispatch*, which he said "has come to be recognized as the leading newspaper of the state." The final paragraph was in these words:

> In the matter of policies, the chief business of the newspaper is to publish news—accurately, completely and fairly. This we shall unceasingly endeavor to do. Editorially, the usefulness of the papers will be maintained best by preserving complete independence on all public questions with scrupulous fairness to all sides. The Dispatch papers, along with my other newspaper properties, are Democratic newspapers in a Democratic state, but they are not servants of party or faction.

There was still something more to say, and the Newport News *Times-Herald* (which Slover had united) said it in words almost surely written by its editor, W. S. Copeland, early associate and friend of Slover:

> It is an interesting turnabout that S. L. Slover, who entered the field of Virginia journalism as a member of the advertising staff of the [Richmond] Times, should now have become the chief owner of that distinguished newspaper property. . . .
>
> Mr. Slover has never pushed himself. Indeed he has rather shrunk from publicity, but he has distinguished himself through his successful newspaper in Norfolk, and is recognized to be one of the ablest publishers in the South. . . . It is a wonderful achievement for a comparatively young man who entered the field less than 25 years ago as an obscure employee. . . .

By the time of the Richmond purchase Slover was being called "Colonel" more frequently than by any other designation. Governor

Westmoreland Davis (1918-22) appointed him a colonel on his staff, and the title stuck. Probably the appointment was one reason why, in earlier speculation as to what he would do with his newspaper properties, the Richmond *Journal* reported that Colonel Slover would support Davis in his 1922 race against Senator Claude A. Swanson for the United States Senate, which Swanson won. The *Ledger-Dispatch* did support Davis. So did the *Virginian-Pilot*. But there were real reasons. Davis was one politician who did not bend the knee to Bishop Cannon. The editors of both Norfolk newspapers liked that attitude. It had been an important reason for their support of Davis when he ran for governor in 1917.

The most significant election campaign of the decade, however, was the 1925 contest for the gubernatorial nomination between Byrd and G. Walter Mapp, an Eastern Shoreman with a strong prohibition record but respected by antiprohibitionists. Since Byrd was "historically dry," prohibition did not play a major role. But because Byrd had been a regular of the controlling Democratic wing led by Senator Martin and had held the state Democratic chairmanship until he became a candidate, the contest did have the effect, as the *Ledger-Dispatch* pointed out, of tearing apart the state Democratic organization and the Anti-Saloon League from their perennially embarrassing but politically useful embrace. The dominant issues came from elsewhere, rising chiefly out of Virginia's postwar growth, which by 1925 included Norfolk's growth too, and out of the need to reform the state's old-fashioned government, its out-of-date taxation system, and its sprawling bureaucracy. The *Ledger-Dispatch* supported neither candidate.

The *Virginian-Pilot* had stood by Byrd's side in the pay-as-you-go road fight two years earlier. But when it asked the question, "Will the election of Mr. Byrd or Mr. Mapp more surely make for reform of the obnoxious fee system, for taking the state school system out of politics, for condensing the overstaffed departments of government, for bringing about that tax equalization which business men hold to be the most badly needed reform of all?", it answered that Mapp was the choice, and it urged his election.

The state had other ideas. It elected Byrd by a big majority. When his inaugural address and his messages to the General Assembly in early 1926 disclosed a dynamic series of reforms, the *Virginian-Pilot* was greatly pleased. It emphatically agreed with nearly all of Byrd's program for the equalization of tax assessments, the reorganization of state government, the cutting and consolidation among the state's more than a hundred boards and commissions, and the reduction of state officials to be voted into office from ten to three—the governor, the lieutenant governor, and the attorney general. Of all this the *Virginian-Pilot* said:

> The outstanding political development in Virginia today is the shelving of the ideas of the old Democratic machine in favor of ideas drawn from the world of business. That is the salient characteristic of Governor Byrd's short ballot program. It flies directly in the face of the old party doctrine which favored more offices for the faithful and longer ballots for the people.
>
> We don't know how Governor Byrd graduated into this attitude from the chairmanship of the state Democratic party, but there he is. What he proposes today is anathema to every test of partisan politics and by every application of the principle that to the victor belong the spoils. . . .

When Byrd won legislative approval of his proposals virtually without change, the *Virginian-Pilot* declared "the legislature of 1926, led by a governor armed with an axe and the courage to use it," addressed itself to the Byrd program with "historic results." Its record, the newspaper said, was "distinguished."

That year marked the fiftieth anniversary of the *Ledger-Dispatch's* ancestor, the *Public Ledger* of Lewellen, Edwards, and Fiveash. The special edition of August 3, 1926, reviewed in detail the history of the *Public Ledger* and of the *Dispatch*. The principal story was written by William S. Meacham, then a *Ledger-Dispatch* reporter, later editor of the Danville *Register*, associate editor of the Richmond *Times-Dispatch* and later of the *Virginian-Pilot*, and eventually the latter newspaper's editorial page editor.

The *Ledger-Dispatch* had 150 employees then. Its circulation was above forty-three thousand, slightly higher than the *Virginian-Pilot's*. Its first edition was on the streets at 11:00 a.m. The Portsmouth edition came out at 2:00 p.m., the main city edition at 3:00, and the final at 5 o'clock. Huber had risen to vice president and general manager. Miss Ethel Dozier, a notable personality in business operations, was secretary. The whole operation, from the top managerial posts through all departments, was vigorous and alert.

The *Ledger-Dispatch* responded fast to new ideas and sought to exploit them. Early in 1926 it was testing the potentials of the new radio broadcasting station in Norfolk, WTAR, and had its own studio in its Plume Street building. There, by arrangement with WTAR, Tom Hanes in sports, and D. C. Carr, James Streetman, Joe Shank, and W. E. Debnam in news, were broadcasting.

Amateur broadcasting in Norfolk began five years earlier. The Hampton Roads Radio Association arranged for the City Band to broadcast on October 21, 1921, from police headquarters. It was heard distinctly, and with surprise, in Lafayette Park. Amateurs struggled with their own improvised receiving sets in those years, swearing over static and trying to induce the Navy to keep its wireless operations from interfering. By May of 1923 the *Ledger-Dispatch* had begun the publication of a column of "Radio Broadcasting News." That year it arranged with a Portsmouth amateur, Dr. C. T. Mercer, to broadcast local election returns from his own station. Late in 1923, WTAR was born, taking over from H. B. Bennett's amateur station, W3GY, and began regular commercial broadcasting. Bennett and Jack Light of the Reliance Electric Company had been building sets, and Light became first manager of WTAR in its operations in the Reliance building on Harrington Street. In 1929 H. B. Goodridge bought the station, and in 1932 the *Ledger-Dispatch* bought it from Goodridge. The price was $15,000.

The *Ledger-Dispatch*'s early interest in radio and its relations with WTAR were in keeping with the newspaper's policy of stimulating and associating itself with many activities which it thought would interest the public. For years it gave prizes for the best photographs of babies or young children. When flying was new it sponsored an aviation show. It sponsored a community Christmas tree in 1921 and an empty stocking fund. It initiated contests for the best statements of "What Norfolk Needs Most." In summer months it appealed for a milk fund for the King's Daughters' operations. It conducted cooking schools (very popular) and organized marbles tournaments and spelling contests. It ran a contest for a slogan for itself, but that backfired. The winning slogan ("Truth, Justice and Public Service") turned out to be the slogan of a New York newspaper.

In 1924 the *Ledger-Dispatch* even sponsored an Adam and Eve experiment to see if a modern married couple could survive for a week in a modern Garden of Eden (in an area near Cape Henry that later became Seashore State Park) in the clothes they wore—no living equipment, no food, no tools, no contact with "civilization" (except a daily visit from reporters and photographers). Within two days after the announcement of the experiment fifty-one couples sought to be the guinea pigs.

There must have been criticism, for editorially the *Ledger-Dispatch* assured readers that its Adam and Eve had intended to get married in any event. Only the weather refused to cooperate. November at the Virginia Capes can be capricious. Reporters and photographers found the couple one day beside a fire, shivering in short sleeves but determined to prove their adaptability to a coastal Eden even in winter's first blast. When they returned to Norfolk for an appearance on a theater's stage, they were almost mobbed.

But the *Ledger-Dispatch* could be pleased by other developments. It liked the economic picture at the end of 1925 and called it the best year since the World War. The *Virginian-Pilot* agreed in two New Year editorials, one national, one local, with these conclusions:

> The year 1925 has been marked in America by an unusually high degree of business activity. It has been a year of record-breaking building construction, of enormous sales of new automobiles, of tremendous shipments of merchandise over the country's railroads, of exceptional real estate booms, not only in Florida but in many other localities, and finally of an unparalleled outburst of speculation on the New York Stock Exchange. Farmers . . . have more to spend than in any year since 1919. . . . Labor has been able to find almost continual employment at substantial wages. Despite the activity there seems to have been no dangerous inflation of credit.

The "high degree of business activity" in the nation was plain enough. But the "no danger of credit inflation" is more difficult forty years later to set beside the "exceptional real estate booms" and the "unparalleled outburst of speculation on the New York Stock Exchange" than it was then. The local summary, with its historical background, stands up better;

> From 1920 through 1924 Norfolk had a succession of lean business years, during which the city felt the impact and after-effects of post-war deflation. The curtailment of business activity was particularly marked in the years 1921 and 1922. During 1923 and 1924 there was no perceptible movement backward, but neither was there any notable movement forward. With 1925 came evidence that the turn had been reached. Business indices in the 12 months ended yesterday pointed toward increasing activity more consistently than at any time in five years.

It was a period of road construction for the swelling automobile traffic; of structural building, notably in Virginia Beach where the new Cavalier Hotel and the improving Princess Anne Club set important standards; of much effort to capitalize on advantages of port and rails and resorts; of new recognition of the meaning of state parks, whether in the mountains where the Shenandoah National

Park was a stimulant, or on the coast, where people were thinking of the Seashore State Park; of a fresh awareness of the exceptional historic sites of Virginia; and of the birth of the city's symphony orchestra, the establishment of its community fund, the growth of its hospitals, and the improvement of its public schools.

The newspapers were of powerful assistance to the city manager government when it came under the fire of Democratic partisans hot to get their hands on the controls. The editors fought the Democratic City Committee's 1928 attempt to amend the city charter so political parties could nominate councilmen in party primaries, a proposal that lost in a referendum by ten thousand to three thousand. They fought the 1930 effort of the Democratic floor leader of the House of Delegates, Ashton Dovell (not of Norfolk), to make the same partisan change.

At the height of this fight Dovell referred to "the Republican press of Norfolk" only to have the *Ledger-Dispatch* tell him that the words were "merely the snap and snarl of one who has been flicked on the raw with the whip of truth." The *Virginian-Pilot* warned that if the Dovell bill became law the newspaper, "although historically Democratic in its origins, outlook and allegiance," would "not have the slightest hesitancy in using all the influence it possesses to help defeat candidates for the council nominated in a Democratic primary foisted on this community without the voters' consent in every case where a better qualified candidate is offered by the Republican party or under independent auspices." The Dovell move was beaten.

But in the national wars among the Democrats in 1924 and 1928 the *Virginian-Pilot* and the *Ledger-Dispatch* could not fare as well. They sweated through the long convention of 1924 with the conviction that Carter Glass was the best of the candidates. They had much admiration for Governor Al Smith's administrative capacity, progressive outlook, and conviction that prohibition could never prohibit. They disliked William G. McAdoo's association with professional drys and his willing acceptance of support from the Ku Klux Klan. The Klan then was near the peak of its power in Virginia, including the Norfolk area, where a July 4 meeting before a burning cross was reported to have drawn a crowd of thirty thousand people.

When, after 103 ballots in New York's Madison Square Garden, the Democrats compromised on John W. Davis, the *Virginian-Pilot* thought he would make "a distinguished President," but it was not optimistic about his winning. The *Ledger-Dispatch* was deeply concerned about activities of klansmen. "Any organization, whether

Ku Klux or not, which raises the standard of racial or religious belief as a test of fitness for public office," it said, "does violence to the
spirit of American institutions and must be condemned by all who
believe in American ideals."

Both newspapers were angry about the corruption in the Harding
administration. After Coolidge-led Republicans won the 1924 election by a wide margin, the *Virginian-Pilot* was convinced that "the
least deserving administration of fifty years of American history has
received another four-year lease of power."

Four years later the *Ledger-Dispatch* and the *Virginian-Pilot* were
strong for Al Smith from start to finish. Both newspapers were fully
aware of the political enmity to Smith's views on liquor and the widespread opposition to a Roman Catholic in the White House. Both
newspapers fought persistently against heavy odds with no thought of
silencing their views because in that year theirs were not popular
views. The number of Southern newspapers that publicly supported
Smith was very small. Most of the Virginia press, nearly all of it
Democratic before and afterwards, dealt cautiously, if at all, with the
furies of the campaign. State Democratic leaders, for the most part,
hid in cyclone cellars. But the Norfolk newspapers fought it out to
the last inch at a time when the danger of doing so was personal and
economic.

The *Virginian-Pilot* especially, under Jaffé as editor, conducted
a long, detailed, never ending defense of Smith. It made a minute
examination of every charge brought against Smith in order to show
its error or venom: his Roman Catholicism, his views on prohibition,
his Tammany associations, his Fulton Fish Market upbringing, his
manner of speech, his very pronunciation, and the issues of his
wife's appearance, manners, social graces, clothes, and whether Al
Smith's election would mean, as was publicly charged, putting a
Jiggs and a Maggie into the White House.

These careful examinations extended to the assumptions of cleri-
cal politicians that only they could speak for "the moral and religious
forces" of Virginia, or the South, or the United States. The *Virginian-
Pilot* returned again and again to such assumptions to uncover their
arrogance and the falseness of their pretense. Jaffé threw himself
into this editorial campaign with great determination, persistence,
and skill. All told, it was probably the finest example of editorial
political fighting in his career.

In the end the newspapers in Norfolk were overwhelmed. The
anti-Smith vote carried Norfolk by 8,300 to 5,800. It carried Ports-

mouth by 3,400 to 2,500. It carried the Second Congressional District for the Republican candidate, Menalcus Lankford, by 18,000 to 14,000. It carried the state by 164,000 to 140,000—the first time the Virginia electoral vote had ever gone to a Republican. But on the two dominating campaign issues of religious freedom and the control of liquor, time has shown the soundness of the newspapers' positions.

In the years preceding 1929 newspapers in Norfolk did not exhibit more financial and economic prescience than many others did. The good business year of 1925 was followed by a better business year in 1926. The *Virginian-Pilot*'s New Year editorial thought 1927 would equal 1926 and cited local developments as reasons for thinking so. Locally it was right.

But speculation in real estate in Norfolk had gone beyond reason, and prices weakened in 1929. A respected house dealing in real estate mortgages, Guaranty Title and Trust Company, closed its doors in June. The town was shocked, and confidence was badly shaken. Still, if this was a warning of the great depression, or even of the stock market crashes of October that led the way down the national spiral, it was not so interpreted by wise men in Norfolk.

The emotionalism of stock market operations by the summer of 1929 had carried prices to heights which the country never before had seen. Warning halts and declines began to appear, but public excitement was so high that recoveries were quick and advances were resumed. September increased the signs for those who could read them. By mid-October the dam began to burst.

The *Virginian-Pilot*'s business page of Saturday, October 19, published the Associated Press summary of New York Stock Exchange operations that marked a major crack. The single-column head over market events of Friday the 18th was in these words:

SHARP REACTION
IN STOCK MARKET

Utilities Break Wide Open and
General List Takes Precipi-
tate Tumble

The AP report in the issue of Sunday the twentieth, covering the abbreviated stock exchange session of Saturday the nineteenth, carried news of the widening of the crack. The volume of trading was "the second largest Saturday turnover in market history." At times the ticker was an hour and a half late in reporting transactions and prices.

Monday the twenty-first began with "a wild rush of selling." But the AP lead in the *Virginian-Pilot* report that was published on the morning of Tuesday the twenty-second placed the emphasis elsewhere. The first sentence read: "Powerful banking support was thrown into the stock market today [Monday the twenty-first] to check what threatened to become one of the most nerve-wracking declines of recent financial history." That "support" halted the trend for a day.

But the lull was deceptive. On Wednesday the twenty-third the market broke wide open. The *Virginian-Pilot's* news editors for the first time in that October judged the news to be front-page-must. They held its presentation on the twenty-fourth to a one-column head topping the fourth of the page's eight columns; the story ran over to page three. The words of the head went beyond anything previously printed:

STOCK EXCHANGE
IS THROWN INTO
NEAR PANIC BY
SLUMP IN PRICES

———

Wholly Unexpected Avalanche
of Selling Sweeps Over
Market Carrying Scores of
Issues Down From $10 to
$96 Per Share

———

Brokers' Offices
Scenes of Disorders

———

Trading in Last Hour of Day
Maintained at $50,000-
000 Per Minute Pace; Quo-
tations on Ticker Fall More
Than 90 Minutes Behind

Worse was coming, and nothing now could stop it. October 24 was the Black Thursday of that historic autumn. The furious flow of selling that had swept the market downward was more dangerous than the banking leadership of lower Manhattan—Morgan, Chase, National City, Guaranty Trust, and their allies—thought they could permit. At the climax of the day's operations they sent Richard Whitney striding across the floor of the stock exchange with his dramatic bid of 205 for twenty-five thousand shares of United States Steel. The stock could have been bought for 193½. But Whitney was not buying steel as such, though armed by the banks to do so. He was signaling that the banks were trying within their considerable means to come to the rescue. For a brief time the signal was heard, and the gesture, with selected buying of other stocks by the banks, slowed the runaway. The Federal government itself began to organize controls.

The *Virginian-Pilot*, trying to cram all this news into headlines on October 25, went to a three-column, three-line head over columns six, seven, and eight of page one—a dark, massive head proclaiming:

BANKERS' STATEMENT CHECKS
HEADLONG, PANICKY PLUNGE OF
STOCK TO RECORD LOW LEVELS

Three series of subheads hung from this black ceiling of type. Down column eight ran the major story of the day:

Era of Avid Speculation
Comes to Climax in Most
Terrifying Stampede of Sell-
ing Ever Experienced on
New York Exchange

Total Sales Reach
12,894,650 Shares

Sickening Drop of Prices Halted After Financiers Express
Confidence in Business Outlook; Wild Confusion Pre-
vails on Floor

Down column six ran the human story: the public reaction to this terrifying day, the people and how they behaved, what they did, in what spirit and mood they watched and interpreted. The subheads over this story balanced in type and length the subheads down column eight. Between these two, in column seven, was a photograph of Thomas W. Lamont, of J. P. Morgan and Company, a leader in the effort to dam the flood. Over the picture of Lamont was one word:

OPTIMISTIC

Beneath this picture was a Washington story with the extraordinary head:

FEDERAL OFFICIALS

UNPERTURBED OVER

DECLINE IN STOCK

If Federal officials in reality were not perturbed, they were almost the only people in the United States who were not. But to strike this note seemed to Washington to be governmental duty. President Hoover himself issued a statement designed to reassure. As the market slowed a bit, the country may have agreed that he was right in saying that "the fundamental business of the country, that is, production and distribution of commodities, is on a sound and prosperous basis." At the moment the new fear had hit stock market prices only.

For another day the *Virginian-Pilot*'s news editors kept the story on the front page. On Saturday, October 26, in recounting the events of the day before, the top of the main head, single-column, was this:

STOCK EXCHANGE
MEMBER HOUSES
SURVIVE DRASTIC
BREAK IN PRICES

But on the twenty-seventh the story was off the front page and back on the market page.

Events would not let it stay there. The worst of all was yet to come. Saturday's relative steadiness and Sunday's calm were delusions. Monday's and Tuesday's tidal waves of selling forced the *Virginian-Pilot* of Tuesday the twenty-ninth to return to a front-page, four-line, single-column head at the top of column eight ("Stock Market / Prices Dive / Down Again at / Alarming Rate"). On Wednesday the thirtieth the newspaper resorted to a two-column, two-line head over columns seven and eight. This one rested on a new hope: "Stampede Checked by Buying / Orders in Record Market." But the "Turnover of 16,410,000 Shares" that "Sets New Mark" was a record that still stands. By this time every recourse for reviving confidence was working at high speed, including the announcement of the entry of the elder John D. Rockefeller into stock market buy-

ing (accompanied by a picture of his ancient lineaments) as a re-
storative catalyst.

Perhaps the devices helped. Perhaps the market temporarily was
spent. And perhaps the closing of the New York Stock Exchange
("To Allow Brokers/To Balance Books") for Friday and Saturday at
the end of October made it easier for the storm to blow out.

Two months later, by the end of the year, the newspapers of Norfolk were not publicly admitting grave concern. The *Ledger-Dispatch*
published fifty-six pages, including an eight-page rotogravure section,
for its year-end edition on December 31; the *Virginian-Pilot*'s New
Year edition was sixty pages. The *Ledger-Dispatch* reported that its
average circulation for the last week of 1929 was 48,309. The *Virginian-Pilot* announced its circulation as 46,087 daily and 47,483 on
Sunday. It reflected on recent events:

> Business . . . embarks on the New Year with a certain wari-
> ness that was born of the stock market collapse, and which the
> presidential pulmotor has not yet succeeded in entirely elim-
> inating. Perhaps it is just as well that the business year opens
> with the accent on caution. The country has passed through a
> disturbing experience, and, everything considered, has kept its
> head remarkably well. . . . The prevailing view is one of con-
> fidence tempered with caution.

The persisting and seemingly irresistible downward drag of 1930,
1931, and 1932 had not yet become clear. But 1930 began to teach its
lessons. The *Ledger-Dispatch*'s year-end edition was less than half the
size of the previous year's. Circulation was holding up, advertising
was slacking off. Locally, however, "the most impressive and illuminat-
ing features of the reviews of 1930 and forecasts for 1931 printed in the
Ledger-Dispatch today are the spirit of optimism that prevails as to
the future and the reflection that the major payrolls upon which this
community prevails arise from sources that are not involved in any
possible curtailment during 1931, while there are evidences of expansion in shipping facilities and other factors that lend confidence to
the future." The next day's *Virginian-Pilot* took a broader and more
sober look:

> If there is one development which marks this date as de-
> cidedly different from the corresponding date a year ago, it is
> the substitution of rational thinking for the combination of
> surprise, perplexity and uncertainty which marked the last
> months of 1929 and the first months of 1930. Unwillingness to
> face the facts continued well into the past year. President

Hoover, for instance, is seen now as being wholly unjustified in saying last March that the worst would be over in 60 days. . . .

The business structure which goes through such a process is far cleaner, sounder and stronger than it could have been otherwise. . . . The uncertainty of a year ago is matched by uncertainty today. But it is a different kind of uncertainty. . . . [It included confidence, however, of "the turn of the tide."]

These solemn events of the early 1930's were falling upon two newspapers of which the high commands and ownerships were undergoing deep and extensive changes.

On December 24, 1929, the *Ledger-Dispatch* published on its front page a statement two columns wide and nearly twelve inches deep under the head, "To the Friends and Readers of the Norfolk Ledger-Dispatch." At the bottom was the name of "S. L. Slover." It began in a quiet, reminiscent mood:

On January 1, 1905, just twenty-five years ago, my partner, the late Harvey L. Wilson, and I purchased from Messrs. Five-ash and Edwards the old Norfolk Public Ledger. In April, 1906, we acquired also the Norfolk Dispatch and consolidated the two under the name of the Norfolk Ledger-Dispatch. As partners having equal authority, Mr. Wilson as editor and I as business manager, we continued to publish together the Norfolk Ledger-Dispatch until Mr. Wilson's death, on May 6, 1917. Under the terms of a contract between us, I then became vested with the control of his interest as well as mine in the property, later acquiring his entire interest. And in February, 1926, I purchased the last outstanding share of stock in the publishing company and thus became the sole owner of the Norfolk Ledger-Dispatch.

Then came the heart of Slover's announcement:

For a number of years I have been considering the matter of offering large participation in the ownership of the Ledger-Dispatch to my associates in newspaper work, who have contributed heavily to the success of both the Norfolk Ledger-Dispatch and the Richmond Times-Dispatch. I am now in position to carry out my long-held purpose.

Accordingly, I have disposed, as of January 1, 1930, of the controlling interest in the Norfolk Ledger-Dispatch to a company headed by P. S. Huber, as president, and including as its officers and stockholders: Frederick Lewis, Henry D. Perkins, Douglas Gordon, F. S. Cook, N. N. Hill, C. E. Boggs, Roy W. Nagle and others. Most of these have been associated with me in the publication of the Ledger-Dispatch for more than twenty years, and some of them for nearly twenty-five years.

Huber was then vice president and general manager. Lewis was Slover's associate in control of the *Times-Dispatch* and was principal owner of the Petersburg *Progress-Index*. Gordon was editor of the *Ledger-Dispatch*. Perkins had been city and managing editor from early *Ledger-Dispatch* days. Cook was the long-time advertising manager. Hill was circulation manager. Boggs was in charge of the press and stereotyping departments. Nagle was superintendent of the composing room.

Slover retained 16 per cent of the stock in the new corporation. He explained his relationship to the newspaper under its new organization in these words:

> I am retaining a substantial minority interest in the Ledger-Dispatch, as well as all of my interest in the Richmond Times-Dispatch, and shall continue, as chairman of the board of the Ledger-Dispatch, to perform such executive and advisory duties as I have heretofore performed, not differing greatly in the future from those in the past save for a certain lightening of the responsibility imposed by them.

In further explanation of what he was doing, Slover said:

> This newspaper has never been a personal organ. To the contrary, its policies have been and are the result of the closest cooperation and thought on the part of those responsible for them, who have held themselves charged with the duty of advancing the interests of this community, this section and this state. In passing the control and management of the paper to this group, I am firm in the conviction, and assure the public, that its policies will in no wise be changed.
>
> The organization which assumes control, the result of years of development, has been and is a source of great pride to me.
>
> Aside from their undoubted ability to publish a good newspaper, the men who compose it are all interested in this community, are all residents, and all taxpayers. . . .
>
> Whatever measure of success has come to the Ledger-Dispatch has been due in considerable degree to the fact that its personal ownership has been all but denied, certainly ignored, and that, instead, a feeling that the paper belonged to the community and was published in its interest has permeated its entire organization. That feeling, shared by all of us, has been so strong that it has impelled me to refuse many tempting offers from outside interests to purchase the property, in order that I might fulfill what I conceived to be my duty to safeguard its ownership in home people.

A long editorial printed the same day, headed "Associates' Appreciation of Mr. Slover's Action," written by Gordon and speaking for other new stockholders, included the statements that Slover acted "at a financial sacrifice to himself," and "at a heavy pecuniary sacrifice." It said that what he did "would be regarded by participants in nearly every other newspaper sale as quixotic"; and that the transaction "is literally unique in the history of American journalism—if, indeed, it is not without a precise parallel in the history of American business."

As to other newspapers in which Slover and his associates were interested then—Slover and Lewis substantially in the Richmond *Times-Dispatch*, and other *Ledger-Dispatch* men in the same newspaper in less degree, and Lewis and Huber in the Petersburg *Progress-Index*—the editorial said that "anything resembling a chain of newspapers is carefully and consistently avoided; but there is a certain community of interest among them which strengthens each of the papers affected."

The *Virginian-Pilot* thought that the passage of the *Ledger-Dispatch*'s controlling interest to experienced Norfolk newspapermen "is a matter for general satisfaction to people of the community." *Editor and Publisher*, a national weekly dealing with newspapers, declared:

> We know of no instance parallel to the action of Samuel LeRoy Slover in disposing of his controlling interest in the very profitable Norfolk (Va.) Ledger-Dispatch to a new company made up of employees of the newspaper. It is a new way of solving the much-discussed problem of employee profit-sharing. It is one of the finest tributes an American publisher has ever paid to a loyal and able staff. Fortunate, these men. But more fortunate, the retiring publisher. . . .

Slover was fifty-six years old at this time and (in the opinion of the *Ledger-Dispatch*'s editor) "at the height of his striking mental powers" and "in robust health." He lived another thirty years. As events turned out, though he lessened his daily work, he was not able for many years to avoid heavy responsibilities.

The arrangements of the sale provided that the "associates," led by Lewis and Huber, would buy the *Ledger-Dispatch* from Slover for $2,500,000. They would pay for it with (1) $500,000 in cash; (2) the assumption of first mortgage bonds of the Ledger-Dispatch Corporation amounting to $340,000 held by Mrs. Mary S. Lynch, widow of Slover's earlier partner, Harvey L. Wilson; and (3) a new issue of $1,500,000 six per cent bonds of the corporation on which payment would begin in three years and be completed in twenty years.

The remainder of the purchase price, amounting to $160,000, was represented by the 16 per cent of the capital stock held by Slover of the new company to be organized by Lewis, Huber, and their associates.

The new capital stock consisted of 10,000 shares. On the basis of the purchase price of $2,500,000, exclusive of the bond debt that was assumed ($340,000 plus $1,500,000, or $1,840,000), the book value of the 10,000 shares of stock would be $66.00 a share. In those days Slover used to say in good humor that he sold out "for 60 cents on the dollar." In at least one instance an "associate" received a few shares of stock as a gift from him.

Many of the new stockholders lacked means of their own to pay in cash for the stock they bought. To most of these Slover made loans, varying from $1,525 to $25,000, to assist them in their purchases, holding as security for these loans the shares of stock belonging to the borrowers. Ultimately the corporation paid for the bond issues out of corporation earnings, and the new stockholders paid for their stock out of dividends.

The new Ledger-Dispatch Corporation organized with Slover as chairman, Huber as president and general manager, and Frederick Lewis as secretary and treasurer. Huber and Lewis had bought 3,360 shares apiece, or 33.6 per cent each. Together with Slover's 16 per cent, these holdings reached 83.2 per cent of the capital stock and left 16.8 per cent for other shareholders.

Cook and Hill took 5 per cent each. The remaining 6.8 per cent (680) shares were divided in varying amounts among Gordon, Perkins, Boggs, Nagle, and "the others" mentioned by Slover but not identified by him. These latter were Loveless, Lineweaver, Ernest H. Smith, Henry S. Lewis, George P. Church, Mrs. L. E. Evans, and Gladys M. Berry. Their holdings necessarily were small.

For the success of the whole arrangement much depended on the newspaper's continuing to be profitable. In 1929 the *Ledger-Dispatch* was showing excellent earning capacity and had done so for years. With the economy of the country, including the economy of Norfolk, going down hill throughout 1930, 1931, and 1932, the question of the ultimate effect on earnings grew more serious year by year. When the $90,000 interest requirement for the $1,500,000 bond issue grew burdensome, Slover reduced the rate of interest from 6 to 3 per cent.

But the newspaper's operation stood up well. For the "associates" the opportunity to buy the stock of a closely held and profitable enterprise with which they were associated and the form of payment made available to them were unusual and were welcomed. For the most part they—and their families—held tightly to their share of the *Ledger-Dispatch*.

In top management the *Virginian-Pilot* of the 1920's was a different sort of newspaper. Its chief executive was Lucien D. Starke, Jr., chairman of the executive committee after Grandy's death in 1903 and president from 1911. Robert E. Turner, the veteran who began as a printer and worked since the early 1880's with the *Landmark*, the *Evening Telegram*, the *Dispatch*, and the *Pilot*, as mechanical superintendent, advertising manager, and business manager, was general manager. But in 1931 he was sixty-eight years old and not in good health. W. S. Wilkinson, originally a bookkeeper, had been treasurer since 1898, secretary since 1921, and a long-time director.

The directors, in addition to Starke and Wilkinson, both of whose stock holdings were small, included John F. Marshall and later L. R. Sargent, former naval officers who had married daughters of Albert H. Grandy, representing the Grandy interest inherited from the *Pilot*; Keville Glennan or his brother, William S. Glennan, a business man who lived in New York, representing the Michael Glennan interest from the original *Virginian*; and Charles S. Abell, representing the *Landmark* interest. None of these groups held a majority of the stock.

Starke had come into the Virginian-Pilot organization as a lawyer for Grandy. He continued his practice even after he was elected, in effect, publisher. Ultimately he devoted all his time to the newspaper, but through January, 1925, meetings of stockholders and directors were held in his law office. He had been the chief negotiator for Grandy in buying the *Pilot*, and for the *Pilot* when it merged with the *Virginian* in 1898, and for the *Virginian-Pilot* when it merged with the *Landmark* in 1912. The designation of "architect-in-chief of the modern *Virginian-Pilot*," which the directors gave him later, had much merit. But in the practicalities of daily administration he encountered unusually skilled, experienced, and aggressive competition from the *Ledger-Dispatch*, and some of his directors lacked thorough journalistic skills or extensive financial experience.

There was one sharp disagreement among them. In January, 1923, they approved a resolution for a ten-year contract with Starke "for his continued services as directing head or publisher" at a salary of $8,500. Keville Glennan voted no. He put into the record a statement that "I do not believe, as shown by the audits, that the paper is being efficiently or economically managed. With a President, a general manager, and assistant general manager, an advertising manager, and a circulation manager, together with a treasurer to attend to its financial

affairs, drawing salaries that total more than 25% of the company's
profits for the past year, I am opposed to spending more money on
the present management, especially when income from advertising and
circulation shows a decrease and the operating expenses show increase."

Glennan found no support for this view. The date came after the
slow business years of Norfolk's postwar depression. *Virginian-Pilot*
dividends voted during the 1920's, after being on an annual basis of
4 per cent of the par value of the five thousand shares of stock before
and during the first World War, rose in 1922 to 5½ per cent. For the
next two years they were 6 per cent, then 6½ per cent in 1925, 7 per
cent for the next three years, 9 per cent in 1929, and 11 per cent in
1930. They reached a high point of 13½ per cent in 1931, then
dropped precipitately to 6½ per cent in 1932.

After the flurry over Starke's contract in 1923, the board raised his
salary to $12,000 in 1929, and to $15,000 the next year. His health
was not good by that time, and the board, showing much sympathy,
voted him three months' leave of absence. But the publisher's time
was running out. He died on July 31, 1931, being then nearly sixty-
three years old, for thirty-three of which he was a newspaper leader in
Norfolk. The directors said of him that:

> Col. Starke's publishing ideals were of the highest and
> reflected his own impatience with sham and cheapness in any
> guise, his distaste for ostentation, his abhorrence of vulgarity
> and sensationalism, his passion for truth, fairness, justice and
> decency. Those who came into the organization soon absorbed
> this viewpoint if it was not already their own, with the result
> that the Virginian-Pilot was written and edited by men and
> women sympathetic with Col. Starke's publishing aims. . . .

The directors delayed the election of a successor to Starke, perhaps
because of uncertainty, possibly because of disagreement. After two
months Turner died, October 2, 1931, and now the need for action was
acute. On October 16 the directors elected Wilkinson president. They
named W. J. Gwaltney of the advertising department secretary and
B. E. Twine, who was in the accounting department, treasurer.

This was a heavy burden to pile on Wilkinson. Filling the place
of a chief executive of nearly thirty years would have been difficult
for any man. Wilkinson was a careful and precise money manager and
was conscientious in all things. But his experience had been limited.
He had not known the broadening range of a publisher or exercised
command responsibilities. He was put in charge of a business when

throughout the country public confidence was deteriorating and earnings were drying up. In its news and editorial departments the *Virginian-Pilot* was in strong position. It was gaining on the *Ledger-Dispatch* in circulation. But the *Virginian-Pilot*'s leadership and new management faced grave problems, and the future caused concern.

Thus the two newspapers entered the black year of 1932. The *Ledger-Dispatch* was keyed up by its new ownership, which was seeking to prove itself, but was troubled by the national and local economy and was looking more anxiously over its shoulder at the gaining *Virginian-Pilot*. The *Virginian-Pilot* was jarred by the change in command and the reliance on untried executives just when it needed broad experience and sure leadership for hard times.

It is not surprising, in the light of these circumstances—and in the light of the whole history of newspapers in Norfolk from 1865 to 1932—that men responsible for both newspapers began to ask themselves if they could meet these unprecedented conditions by bolder and more imaginative action. In the end, acting not unlike their journalistic ancestors for most of a century, they did.

CITY MANAGER I. WALKE TRUXTON OPENED 1932 BY CUTTING THE PAY OF city employees 10 per cent and his own salary 20 per cent. By the spring of 1933 the cuts of most city employees had reached 20 per cent; of those in higher brackets, 22½ to 27½ per cent; of the city manager, 42 per cent.

In this January of 1932 uncollected real estate taxes in Norfolk rose above $3,680,000. Forty-five per cent was owed, in the words of City Treasurer B. Gray Tunstall, by people "who can't pay the butcher and the baker and the candlestick maker."

Two million railroad workers across the country took a 10 per cent cut in pay in February of 1932. The Norfolk Southern went into receivership in July. The Seaboard Air Line Railroad, with headquarters in Norfolk too, had gone into receivership in 1930, a victim of the Florida collapse; the Cavalier Hotel, pride of Virginia Beach, had been turned back by a national hotel management chain to local owners. The Monticello Hotel, largest in Norfolk, held out until mid-1933 before going into receivership. In mid-1932 the state auditor in Richmond reported that one-fourth of the treasurers of Virginia's hundred counties were short in their accounts. They, too, were having trouble collecting taxes.

The Norfolk Community Fund, born in 1923 and perennially in trouble in meeting its goals, sought $295,350 in 1932. It got $199,320. By December a Citizens Emergency Relief Committee was raising funds, with heavy support from newspapers and radio, for a commissary depot to provide shelter and food. A public welfare center was being organized.

This was the year when the Great Depression was tightening its grip on nearly every family in Norfolk, and in the whole land. Hunger around dining room tables was tearing at the hearts of parents.

Statistics and percentages in official reports were poor tools to measure the long-range effect on men when suddenly they found themselves out of work and unable to do much about it.

It was the year of Hoover's renomination without formal opposition, of Roosevelt's winning the Democratic nomination after a sharp convention fight, and of Roosevelt's smothering Hoover in November. It was simultaneously the year that ordained the death of the Eighteenth Amendment. Election and repeal were inextricably related. When Hoover favored repeal and state option, Bishop Cannon lamented that it was impossible "for the dry vote to be delivered effectively to either candidate." The country's mind was made up.

Both Norfolk newspapers strongly opposed Hoover, warmly endorsed Roosevelt. ("He is supported by Democrats as no other candidate since Woodrow Wilson has been," the *Virginian-Pilot* thought in July.) Both looked forward with satisfaction to the ending of the prohibition era. The campaign lacked the excitement of a neck-and-neck drive down the stretch, but interest was high enough in a city that gave 70 per cent of its vote to Roosevelt for the *Virginian-Pilot*'s presentation of the returns to fill the City Auditorium.

"A striking demonstration of good will," the *Virginian-Pilot* described the election results. It added, "May patience in reasonable measure follow" Roosevelt's election—"he will need it." It was sure Roosevelt was "definitely not of the left wing" and thought his attitude toward international debts was "cautious and conservative." The New Deal was unborn. People waited in hope but in deep uncertainty.

Such was the season when the newspapers went into action on their own account.

Both newspapers charged $7.00 then for a yearly subscription, fifteen cents a week by carrier. Single copies were three cents; the Sunday *Virginian-Pilot*, seven cents. In circulation the *Virginian-Pilot* was showing 44,812 for the six-day average and 45,264 on Sunday against the *Ledger-Dispatch*'s six-day average of 45,620. For the six days before Christmas of 1932 the *Ledger-Dispatch* published 144 pages, an average of 24; the *Virginian-Pilot*, 102 pages for six days, or an average of 17 pages, including 26 on Sunday.

The drop in advertising was universal and unavoidable. The *Ledger-Dispatch* command was more immediately disturbed by the possibility of the *Virginian-Pilot*'s going ahead in circulation. The new officers thought the Sunday *Virginian-Pilot* was hurting them. They considered establishing a Sunday edition of the *Ledger-Dispatch*—a costly remedy at the start and difficult to devise and maintain. But Slover had larger ideas. The wise step, he thought, was to merge the *Ledger-Dispatch* and the *Virginian-Pilot.*

This was familiar Slover doctrine. He had seen its effectiveness in Knoxville. He had put it into practice in Newport News with the *Times* and the *Herald*; in Norfolk with the *Public Ledger* and the *Dispatch*; in Petersburg with the *Progress* and the *Index*, and always with economic soundness and journalistic improvement. Newspaper mergers and consolidations had mounted to a national trend. He was not unaware of criticisms that could be raised against the trend, but the requirement of economic health in the newspaper publishing business was not only as strong as in other businesses but was the strongest and healthiest means of meeting the public responsibilities of newspapers and of resisting the special dangers, to which all newspapers are subjected, of being used by other interests for their own purposes.

A consolidation of the *Ledger-Dispatch* and the *Virginian-Pilot* would be a delicate and an extremely important operation, but unusual factors were in its favor. These included, first and most persuasive, the effect on both newspapers of financial difficulties which in 1932 were constantly growing worse and obscured the time and blurred the hope of improvement; the higher status of the *Ledger-Dispatch* in circulation, advertising, and earnings, and therefore its preferred position in bargaining; the generally good condition of the *Virginian-Pilot*, which was nowhere near distress but needed the strongest possible managerial leadership; and the respect and good feelings, despite the keen rivalry between the two newspapers, of the newspapers' owners and officers, and in some instances their personal friendship.

The two newspapers began a cautious examination of the merger idea. Once they had arrived at that stage, they moved ahead smoothly. By December the agreement was definite.

On the last day of 1932 the *Ledger-Dispatch*, with Huber as spokesman, announced the merger; on January 1, 1933, the *Virginian-Pilot* added its announcement. For the first time since ancient days, long before the Civil War, one ownership controlled all—that is, the two—daily newspapers of Norfolk.

Economic considerations received primary notice in the announcements, but something else seemed to both newspapers so important that they emphasized it heavily. The initial announcement by Huber said that "the consolidation will in no way affect the editorial or news policies of the Virginian-Pilot or the Ledger-Dispatch. They will pre-

Weather Forecast

Norfolk Virginian-Pilot

Sun and Tides

Vol. CXCIII. No. 4 — Norfolk, Virginia, Tuesday, October 4, 1949 — Price Five Cents

New Norfolk Out of Old: Program Outlined

Redevelopment Plans Go Far Beyond Initial Aim of Slum Attack

Major City Traffic Routes, Connections Projected

**U. S. N(...)
'Shot,' (...)
With E(...)**

Documents Release(...)
Secretly, Bear Boga(...)
Denfield Signatures(...)
Crommelin Bac(...)

Radford Quoted in La(...)
Incident of Naval-Air
Tug-of-War

Washington, Oct. 3.—(AP)—Documents secretly slipped to re-
today pictured United States
morale as shot up (...) in the
nation's security imperiled (...)
the present unified defense (...)

The documents, signed (...)
names of high naval officers
handed to reporters by a (...)
who ran a stairway corridor
downstairs office building (...)
taking that his name was (...)
be used and that the paper
not to be published until (...)
EST. tonight.

The documents, which (...)
of typed copies of letters (...)
official officers, included (...)

(...) a statement by Adm.
Denfeld, chief of naval oper-
that a "Navy stripped of its (...)
sive power means a setting (...)
of its offensive power." (...)

2. A warning by Vice Ad-
ral F. Bogan, commander (...)
First Task Fleet in the Pacif(...)
Navy morale has plumbet(...)
went to despondency becau(...)
widespread belief that the (...)
is being "sold a false bill of (...)

Crommelin Gets Happe(...)
3. A statement by Adm.(...)
Radford, commander in chie(...)
Pacific Fleet, that a main(...)
efficiency of that battle(...)
fleet's views and also in th(...)
pressed by Naval Capt. J.(...)
Crommelin. Crommelin con-
sensation recently for (...)
charging that the Navy's (...)
power is being "whittled to (...)
in the Pentagon, defense be-
lers.

Navy officials declined (...)
mediate comment on the re(...)
the documents.

The release was the late(...)
dent in a long tug-of-war (...)
the Navy and the Air Fo(...)
congressional appropriation(...)
the right to carry out str(...)
assignments.

The Navy planned a gi(...)
crash carrier capable of (...)
A-bomb planes, but come(...)
was cancelled by Secretary (...)
fense Johnson. Cedric H(...)
civilian naval aide now on(...)
pension, prepared a memo(...)
that the Air Force's (...)
bomber was a dubious (...)
foisted on the taxpayers b(...)
eal bumbocaine, Worth B(...)
named his charges.

Then came Captain Cro(...)
who said he was risking (...)
career by charging that the(...)
offensive power was being (...)
In one of the documents (...)
today, Vice Admiral Rad(...)

See Navy Morale, Page 14

**'U. S. Psychologica(...)
Russian Ge(...)
For Atom(...)**

This is the last of a (...)
Russia's development of (...)
gained from reliable sour(...)
chief of United States nav(...)

By Ric(...)
Unite(...)
Wartime Depa(...)
(Copyright, 1949,(...)

New York, Oct. 3.—N(...)
have the atomic bomb, th(...)
mysterious bomb itself.

Why did the Russian (...)
propaganda brag by being (...)
to announce the atomic (...)
to the public?

And why did they—whi(...)
historical feat on all (...)
fail to explain this part(...)
vention on which Stalin (...)
placed a premium amount(...)

The answer to this que(...)
gained through the inst(...)
of high-ranking Red Arm(...)
now refugees from Comm(...)
pression. According to (...)
the instructions of this (...)
to its administration of p(...)
and ultimate aim to play(...)
sion possession of the bor(...)
play up the socialized (...)
plan. This plan concern(...)
ification of an interustde(...)
item for the outlawing (...)

**Benefits Seen
For All of City
By Chairman**

Private Enterprise To Be
Given Inducements
In Redeveloping

Four Prime Areas

Public Housing Held Only
Answer for Replacement
Of Low-Income Shacks

By Frank Sullivan

Norfolk's multi-million dollar redevelopment and housing
program, the broad outlines of
which were revealed yesterday,
is geared to go far beyond its
initial objective of eradicating
slum conditions of a city that
has twice as much bad housing
as the national urban average.

The program, as it is now
constituted, sets forth a bold
plan to redevelop eight slum or

(See Key Maps, Page 38)

blighted areas, preferably with
the assistance and cooperation
of private enterprise, and to undertake, as soon as feasible, the
erection of 3,000 public housing units to accommodate eligible families to be uprooted from
their present habitats in the initial clearance work.

But it goes further in many
respects, as it integrates with the
long-range plans of various city
departments and the ideas immediately outlined of the Elizabeth
River Tunnel and Bridge Authors-
ity in designing the route it will
follow in connecting Norfolk and
Berkley with a new span.

It calls for major highway improvements which would make
possible the orderly flow of traffic
in and out of the city, and we all

(Other Maps, Pages 22 and 23)

sections therein, and designed to
correct problems which have been
the logjams of the central business
mobile age.

Envisaged also is the conversion
of considerable (...) craftmanli-
ship concerns in redevelopment
areas for industrial uses, and the
acquisition of specified sites for
schools, playgrounds, industry,
business and other purposes.

A 130-page report, augmented by
numerous maps and charts, was re-
leased last yesterday by the Norfolk Redevelopment and Housing
Authority, which will administer
the program, and drew an obser-
vation from Chairman Charles L.
Kaufman that "the future of Norfolk for the rest of its history will
be fixed by the extent to which
this program is followed during the
next 15 years."

In releasing the report, which
was prepared by the New York consulting firm of Harrison, Ballard
and Allen following a comprehensive nine-month physical study of
the city in collaboration with the
authority and numerous Federal,

See New Norfolk, Page 21, Col. 1

Home

...tion Speeded;
s Issue Delayed

...lation vastly expanding the govern-
a clearer today for quick House ac-
...a this month. Meanwhile, the Tre-
...bury the end of the 1949 session by

...number of workers covered by old
...age and survivors insurance, for a
...new total of 46,000,000.

2. Increase old age benefits by
an average of 70 to 80 per cent.

3. Create a new insurance system
...for persons who become totally and
...permanently disabled, and

4. Boost the payroll taxes by
...more than 300 per cent in the next
...15 years.

The House Ways and Means Com-
...mittee, in approving the bill, 22 to
...3, warned against "very costly and
...'liberalized' systems of noncon-
...tributory pensions. It said finance
...ing of such plans "may become
...impossible and their economic effect
...disastrous."

Meanwhile, Sterling Democratic
Leader Lucas said after a White
House conference that probably
the first issue to be tackled when
Congress returns in January will be
the highly controversial Taft
...anti-poll tax provisions measure.

This is a prime item on President
...Truman's legislative program.

See Congress, Page 14, Col. 8

The *Norfolk Virginian-Pilot*'s headlines announcing Norfolk's redevelopment proved prophetic indeed. The two inset photographs depict
the startling changes predicted in the October 4, 1949, headlines.

Ideal Spring Weather
Due Thursday, Friday
Weather Details on Page 6.
Wednesday, April 15, 1964

LEDGER-STAR
Norfolk, Portsmouth, Virginia Beach, Chesapeake, Va.

Final
Edition
88th Year, Five Cents

A 200 Million Dollar Dream Comes True

Dignitaries on Hand for Bridge-Tunnel Opening Ceremony
Left to Right.

As One Era Closes on the Bay, Another Opens

By Arthur P. Henders
Ledger-Star Business Edit

VIRGINIA BEACH — Virgin
17½ million dream—The 1
mile Chesapeake Bay Brid
Tunnel—became a reality tod
At a ceremony this after
the project was described as
engineering marvel, an exam
of efficient construction,
economic stimulus to the a

Evasion Indictm

Illinoi
Faces

CHICAGO (AP)—Illinoi
mer Republican governor
liam G. Stratton, was indi
today by a federal grand
which accused him of eva
$46,676 in income taxes ov
four years, 1957 through 1

A four-count indictment
returned by the August
grand jury before Judge
liam J. Campbell in U.S.
trict Court on Thursday bu
ordered suppressed until t
morning.

The amount of taxes alle
ly evaded over four years
$46,676 on income this the f
ernment said was averag
and totaled $82,542.02.

Edward V. Hanrahan,
district attorney, declined to
what the source of the m
was. Stratton left office at
ernie in 1960.

The indictment was return
by Vincent P. Russo, assist
attorney in the Department
Justice, Washington.

The alleged evasion occurred
in tax returns filed by Stratton
and his wife, Shirley. Although
Stratton and his wife filed join
returns, Mrs. Stratton was no
indicted.

A summons will be issued for
Stratton. His bond has been set
at $5,000.

Stratton was not immediate
ly available for comment. His
worked as a political commen
tator for a Chicago television
station Tuesday night.

Government investigators said
that Stratton paid only $22,311.81
in taxes for the four years
whereas he should have paid
$88,987.84, leaving an alleged
evasion of $46,676.03, on unre
ported income.

Hanrahan said Internal Rev
enue Service agents had followed
normal procedures in checking
Stratton's returns and had dis
cussed his taxes with him.

"He had an opportunity to
pay," Hanrahan said.

The government charged tha
Stratton understated amount from
amounts he had received in 1957,
$14,851; 1958, $14,350; 195...
371; 1960, $3,404. His unreported
income amounted to more than
$82,500, the indictment said.

If convicted of the charges,
Stratton could receive a maxi
mum penalty of 20 years in
prison and a $40,000 fine.

ers and two amphibious forc
ships will be overhauled at the
Naval Shipyard in Portsmouth
instead of at other shipyards
far from their home port here.

This is a change in the
original orders assigning these
ships to yards for overhaul work.

Second District Rep. Porter
Hardy Jr. said today he had
been notified by Rear Adm. W.
A. Brockett, chief of the Navy's
Bureau of Ships, that the ship
yard assignment changes have
been made.

In addition to the Randolph,
the destroyers DuPont and Mur
ray, the LST Talbot County
and the attack transport E. E.
Hall will undergo overhaul work
at the Portsmouth yard. All are
home-ported at Norfolk.

The Randolph and the de
stroyers had been scheduled for
overhaul at the Boston Naval
Shipyard. The other two ships
had been assigned to private
yards elsewhere.

Hardy had urged the Navy
to assign the ships to the Ports
mouth yard because the crews
would be in their home port
during the yard work.

In a letter to Hardy con
firming the Navy's decision to
assign the ships to Portsmouth,
Brockett said that in making the
changes, "the Navy was in
fluenced principally by fleet
home port requirements and the
feasibility of equalizing to the
extent practicable the distribution
of available work."

about the future of the Ports
mouth yard. A report now be
ing prepared is expected to
order the shutdown of some
naval shipyards.

Said Hardy, "I am still hope
ful that the reduction in force
(at Portsmouth) will be less
than originally anticipated."

Would Call Cassius

Draft Law Probe Predicted

WASHINGTON (AP) — A
congressman predicts the House
will soon launch a major inves
tigation of the draft law and
heavyweight champion
Cassius Clay as its star witness.

The prediction came from
Rep. William G. Bray, R-Ind.,
who told a newsman:

"I think the Selective Service
made a mistake in rejecting
Cassius Clay. I'm not sure what
the devil you could do with him.
But I think the Army could
have found a place for him."

The Army had said Clay was
rejected after he failed to pass
mental tests.

Bray, who is the ranking Re
publican member of the House
Armed Services subcommittee
on personnel, said he was not
sure just which congressman
would do the investigating.

He said he was hoping to
persuade his subcommittee to

do it. He said there also was
a possibility that a joint com
mittee, made up of members of
the Armed Services and Educa
tion and Labor committees,
would do the job.

In any case, Bray said, he was
confident that some subcommit
tee or committee would even a
investigation soon and call Clay
as a witness.

There was no official con
firmation, however, of any com
mittee plans. Rep. F. Edward
Hebert, D-La., chairman of
Bray's subcommittee, said "I
don't know anything about it."

Bray said there had been
much discussion among mem
bers of Congress for some time
about what they consider the
failings of the draft system.

"I'm not blaming Selectiv
men, one with a stocking over
his face and the other wearing
women's makeup, robbed a mo
tel of $10,000 early today, police

to reject a heavyweight boxing
champion."

Rep. Thomas B. Curtis,
R-Mo., recently told the House
that "the draft law has been
perverted from a system of
satisfying the emergency man
power needs of the military in
wartime into an inefficient,
wasteful program of universal
military training in peacetime."

Sen. Kenneth B. Keating, R-
N.Y. and several other senators,
both Democratic and Repub
lican, have proposed a presi
dential commission to study the
draft.

Masked Pair Rob
Motel of $10,000

WASHINGTON (AP) — Two

In Today's
LEDGER-STAR

No Shave, No Job — So
ODC Man Sheds Itchy
Growth—Page 21.
Russia: The Winds of
Change. Editorial. —
Page 18
Infield Aces Mean Win
ning Hand for Cards. —
Page 25.

	Page
Amusements	30
Classified Ads	35-41
Comics	12-13
Editorial	18
Financial	14
Obituaries	32
Society-Women's	6-7
Sports	25-29
Television and Radio	18

ning and travel facilities. Har
on continued.
"In many minds," the gover
r said, "its very scope would
re it among those public im
provements that only the feder
government was big enough
undertake.
"But there is no tax money on
bridge-tunnel. It stands as an
real monument to the propo

(Continued on Page 2)

ons

hnson

tion, leaving it to the execu
e branch to determine the
imum.

Budget Bureau officials indi
ted Tuesday that, particularly
ler to the recently enacted
neral upgrading of the Civil
rvice pay scale, agencies
ed the device of rapid promo
to achieve their aim of giv
their employes pay increases
te that in private indus
This, it was suggested, is
reason for the "speed
up" in average grade.

visions

Unnecessary—Byrd

WASHINGTON (AP) — Sen.
Harry F. Byrd, D-Va., argued
today that Presidential orders
and federal court decisions have
made unnecessary key parts of
the civil rights bill.

The Virginian, first speaker of
the day for the Southern forces
in the civil rights debate, held
forth for an hour and 12 minutes
in a voice so soft his words
could not be heard at all in
the galleries. It was his second
speech in the 21 days of debate.

The first two hours of the Sen
ate's session were taken up with
talks on extraneous subjects and
with quorum ca

Byrd attacked two major sec
tions of the bill—the one setting
up an equal employment oppor
tunity commission and the one
authorizing cutoff of federal
funds to programs in which dis
crimination is practiced.

He said actions of the Presi
dent's equal employment oppor
tunity committee dealing with
government contracts have made
the former provision entirely un
necessary.

As to the federal funds sec
tion, Byrd said decisions in
cases involving federal hospital
grants and other programs in an
effort to show that this matter
already has been settled in the
courts. The Virginian described
the provisions as "an effort to
make respectable what already

400 Official
Dead in Storm

DACCA, Pakistan (AP) — A
cyclone in the Eastern district
of East Pakistan last weekend
left with such savage force that
in some villages rescuers found
no signs of life, "No bodies, no
trees, no houses," Gov. Moneem
Khan said today.

Officially, 400 bodies have been
counted and 700 persons have
been listed as injured with 1,400
others missing. But unofficial es
timates put the death toll at
2,000.

Small Shops Strike

ROME (AP) — Italy's small
butchers, restaurants and pastry
shops were closed today by a
24-hour strike.

The *Ledger-Star*'s headline writer capsuled the truth about the opening of the Chesapeake Bay Bridge-Tunnel, April 15, 1964. Bridge-tunnel picture is superimposed.

serve their distinct personalities and characteristics unchanged, each independent of the other, and under the continued direction of the news and editorial executives who have guided them in the past."

The same idea was expressed in the *Virginian-Pilot*'s announcement on January 1:

> The union of the two Norfolk newspapers for more efficient operation will in no way alter their independent status otherwise. Each has in many years of independent publication achieved a personality distinct from the other. The complete separateness, one from the other, in news department and editorial opinion, is to be perpetuated. The consolidation is for operating and economic purposes alone and is not for the purpose of modifying in the slightest degree the characters and viewpoints of the two papers as they have become known to several generations of readers.

To emphasize the point, the *Ledger-Dispatch* of January 2 said editorially that "the merger or consolidation . . . departs from the customary combination in the radical respect that each maintains its complete identity, consolidating only their business and operating departments."

If this repeated stressing of news and editorial independence and competition was actuated by the desire to reassure all people against fears that the end of separate publication meant the end of competition and the death of independence, this was not the only reason. Both newspapers believed in the virtues of this kind of competition *per se*, both were determined to maintain it in the new situation, and both set about doing so. The third of a century that followed has built up a large body of evidence that the results have followed the design.

The merger plans—largely the work of a young lawyer, Charles L. Kaufman, who thereafter played an increasingly important role as counsel and member of the board of directors—called for a new corporation, Norfolk Newspapers, Inc. To it most assets of the two newspapers were assigned and from it stockholders received new stock in exchange. Included in these assets was the *Ledger-Dispatch*'s Radio Station WTAR. But because a primary purpose was to bring both publishing operations under one roof where machinery for one would do equally well at another time of day for the other, both newspaper plants were not needed, and the *Virginian-Pilot*'s plant on Tazewell Street was not included in the merger.

As many parts of the newspapers' operations as possible were squeezed into the *Ledger-Dispatch*'s Plume Street plant, but parts of the *Virginian-Pilot* operation had to be continued nearly five years in Tazewell Street quarters, for which Norfolk Newspapers, Inc., paid rent. Ultimately a new and much larger building was contemplated and was built for occupancy in 1937. The Virginian and Pilot Publishing Company continued in existence until 1939 while liquidating for the benefit of its own stockholders property not included in the merger.

Of the fifteen thousand shares of stock of Norfolk Newspapers, Inc., former *Ledger-Dispatch* stockholders received ten thousand shares and former *Virginian-Pilot* stockholders received five thousand shares. This two-to-one division rested largely on earnings over the past five years. It placed the *Ledger-Dispatch* stockholders in clear control and command. Officers and directors of Norfolk Newspapers, Inc., were: Slover, chairman of the board; Huber, president of the corporation; Frederick Lewis, vice president and treasurer; Wilkinson, vice president; Henry S. Lewis, secretary and assistant treasurer. Of these only Wilkinson came from the *Virginian-Pilot*. Additional directors were Gordon from the *Ledger-Dispatch*, and William S. Glennan, Sargent, and Jaffé from the *Virginian-Pilot*.

The Ledger-Dispatch Corporation continued its corporate existence for the organizational and financial convenience of its stockholders. Since it held two-thirds of the stock of Norfolk Newspapers, Inc. (the name of which was changed in 1957, after the purchase of the Portsmouth *Star*, to Norfolk-Portsmouth Newspapers, Inc.), the control of the Ledger-Dispatch Corporation represented, in practical effect, control of the overall corporation.

Gordon continued as editor of the *Ledger-Dispatch*. Lineweaver as associate editor divided his time between editorial writing and news writing, chiefly about political affairs. In 1934 he went to Washington to be secretary of the Federal Power Commission, and in September of that year Leslie, then the *Virginian-Pilot*'s chief political reporter, moved over to the *Ledger-Dispatch* with the title of associate editor.

Shortly after the consolidation Perkins stepped aside from the driving requirements of managing editor to calmer duties: writing editorial paragraphs, conducting a fifty-years-ago column, and filling in as needed. He held the title of associate editor. Keville Glennan, after several years away from newspaper work, came back as managing editor of the *Ledger-Dispatch*. Shank was city editor. Hanes was sports editor but was showing signs of broader interests.

Jaffé had long since matured into a nationally known and respected editor. Before the 1920's ran out he had lost Aiken to the Baltimore *Sun*. As replacement he had brought in Lenoir Chambers, associate editor of the Greensboro *Daily News*, who earlier had been a reporter and city editor in Greensboro. He began in December, 1929, thirty-two years of newspaper work in Norfolk that was to include the editorship of each newspaper.

Winder Harris was in full stride as managing editor and had grown active in civic affairs. After he had led two Community Fund campaigns the Cosmopolitan Club's selection committee chose him in 1934 for the club's distinguished service medal, the winner of which was commonly called Norfolk's First Citizen. Hanes had devised this annual distinction. In the following January, on behalf of the club, he made the formal presentation. "It is the first time in my life," he told the audience, "that I ever gave a *Virginian-Pilot* guy anything."

John Spencer and Frank Pace were night and day city editors; "Governor" Potts, a real veteran, had been succeeded as sports editor by W. N. Cox, who came in from the Greensboro *Daily News* and earlier the Durham *Herald* for a long career in sports writing and editing. In areas of work where manpower could be consolidated—advertising and circulation, for examples—*Ledger-Dispatch* men generally were in command.

In those depression years no one escaped salary reductions: normally, two cuts of 10 per cent each. In October of 1933 *Virginian-Pilot* charges went up: from seven cents to ten cents for the Sunday issue: from fifteen to twenty cents for a week, carrier-delivered: from $7.00 to $10.00 for a year's subscription. Efforts were made to offset circulation losses that followed these increases: Sunday comics spread out from four to eight pages, women's news expanded. A real innovation was plane delivery of newspapers, morning and afternoon, to the Eastern Shore of Virginia, an overwater jump of fourteen miles where ferry transportation was slow. It was the first distribution of newspapers by plane in Virginia. But it proved impractical and was not continued.

Deep differences in principles and politics between the two newspapers were rare. Traditionally, the *Ledger-Dispatch* was more restrained, the *Virginian-Pilot* more progressive. But the age of courtesy had matured, and there were few editorial duels. Differences in spirit, judgment, taste, style, and subject matter were frequent, as, for instance, when the General Assembly of 1940 was adopting a state song.

The *Ledger-Dispatch* cheered the legislators for changing the title of James A. Bland's *Carry Me Back to Ole Virginny* to *Carry Me Back to Old Virginia*. This was the way to spell the name of the Commonwealth and its accompanying modifier, it pointed out. The *Virginian-Pilot*, on the other hand, challenged the change on the ground that no one has a right to alter another's artistic production whether the issue is a colloquially spelled minstrel song or a geographically erroneous Shakespearian line. (The *Virginian-Pilot* left that field of honor unsatisfied: the version of the song as embedded in the *Acts of the General Assembly* still records the name of "Virginia" and not "Virginny," as Bland wrote it.)

In the news columns the *Ledger-Dispatch* continued to be a lively newspaper, going hard after the readable news, playing it up big, fighting for first place. The *Virginian-Pilot*, which cared strongly about good writing and had a morning newspaper's longer hours to prepare it, kept the competition at high speed. Soon after the consolidation it began to benefit from more effective top management. Its circulation increased, and its advertising volume rose. It had the advantages in regional and distant circulation that a morning newspaper generally has, and it grew. Once it had attained improved vigor in its new surroundings, it went to the top in circulation and stayed there.

In the months before the consolidation, news and editorial staffs of both newspapers were subjected to the contradictions and confusions of the Norfolk end of the search for kidnappers of the Lindbergh baby. The principal Norfolk figure was John Hughes Curtis, a boatyard industrialist of good social standing. He called on two Norfolk men to assist him in informing Lindbergh of contacts that Curtis said had been made with him by men who professed to have contacts with the kidnappers. One of the Norfolk men called in by Curtis was Rear Admiral Guy H. Burrage, a retired naval officer. He had been ordered by President Coolidge to bring Lindbergh home on the cruiser *Memphis* after the transatlantic flight of May, 1927, and thus knew the national hero. The other was Dean H. Dobson-Peacock, with an English background, who was rector of Christ Episcopal Church in Norfolk. He had known the Dwight W. Morrows and their daughter, later Mrs. Lindbergh, when the American ambassador and his family attended in Mexico City the Episcopal cathedral of which Dobson-Peacock was dean. Burrage and Dobson-Peacock had no information other than that which Curtis gave them.

The baby was kidnapped March 1, 1932. By March 9 Curtis was trying to reach Lindbergh. The three men did see and talk with Lindbergh. He did regard the Curtis reports as sufficient to justify his going to the Norfolk area several times, joining Curtis in long searches on yachts for go-betweens who were never found.

The searches were presumably for rum-running types of men in remote, hidden, and dangerous lairs or on mysterious vessels, and necessarily became known to the Coast Guard. The newspapers learned of them early, but it was a time of anxiety, of sympathy for the Lindberghs, and of strong feeling against the kidnappers. The newspapers respected pleas for secrecy.

But censorship could not last. By March 25 rumors were running wild, testing the judgment of newspaper men with half-truths, whole truths, or no truths at all. From eastern America reporters and photographers poured into town. Press conferences found forty men and women on hand, scrutinizing, questioning, and weighing answers. But to the big questions of where could something be learned, where could something be found, there were no answers in Norfolk.

There were no answers anywhere until May 12. On that day, when Curtis and Lindbergh once more were searching afloat, the word flashed out to the yacht. The dead body of the baby had been found in New Jersey near the Lindbergh home.

The shock in Norfolk was profound. "Find and kill the killers," the *Ledger-Dispatch* fairly shouted. "The baby was dead when [Al] Capone was making offers and promises. So, too, the people with whom Dr. [John F.] Condon dealt—through go-betweens—were all liars and thieves and double-crossing thugs. Let them be turned up, too. There need be no possible question of keeping faith with men who were false in the beginning, false in the end and false all the while."

To the national tragedy Norfolk had to add the shock of its sudden doubts about the role of its three citizens, especially Curtis. When he signed what the New Jersey state police superintendent, Col. H. Norman Schwarzkopf, called "a complete confession" saying that his contacts and negotiations were made-up, he was indicted on charge of obstructing justice. He pleaded not guilty. A police spokesman quoted him as saying that "at the present time I am sane, but I honestly believe that for the last seven or eight months I have not been myself, due to financial troubles." No charge was made against Burrage or Dobson-Peacock.

"Mr. Curtis is about to be tried, one suspects," the *Virginian-Pilot* commented, "not for obstructing justice in New Jersey, but for the duping of Lindbergh in Virginia." This was before Curtis repudiated the confession. In the trial in New Jersey the charge was changed from obstructing justice to refusal to give all his information to the police.

In July a jury convicted him, and a judge sentenced him to a year in prison and fined him $1,000. In November the case was reopened, the fine was confirmed, but the prison sentence was suspended. The *Virginian-Pilot* summed up again:

> Those who have believed that the trial and conviction of Curtis was dubious business, have at least the satisfaction of knowing that to an important extent their belief must be shared by the prosecution, which but lately was demanding punishment to the full extent of the law.
>
> The details of that trial . . . left the impression that the defendant had not received justice in the curious punishment. That was the opinion of the Virginian-Pilot at the time, and it has been the opinion of this newspaper ever since. . . .

These words were published in November, 1932. It was not until September of 1934 that Bruno Richard Hauptmann was arrested. Long before then the news story had moved away from Norfolk, not to return. But the futilities of the Norfolk angle remained a vivid memory to the newsrooms. They counted it the most unsatisfactory national story that Norfolk editors and reporters had ever been required to handle.

The Lindbergh case was an interlude. In the early 1930's the newspapers could never stay away from the depression. The city government found itself sinking deeper into a financial pit. Its operating deficits had been growing year by year. Tax collections sagged far below estimates. Councilmen feared new taxation. Retrenchment of the necessary scope seemed beyond their capacity.

City Manager Truxtun asked in January of 1933 to be relieved of the financial duties of his position, and the Council named a director of finance. Local bankers announced that they had not approved of the way the city was handling its finances. Sinking fund commissioners refused to lend more to the city until past-due loans had been paid.

In February, Mayor P. H. Mason resigned as a member of the Council because his business required him to live elsewhere. His absence left the four remaining councilmen split. They could not agree on a fifth councilman, yet they did not care to make important and embarrassing decisions without full membership. This was a situation made for old-time Democratic politicians. They demanded that the charter be rewritten to enlarge the number of councilmen, to elect them by wards, and to endow the mayor with the veto power—the very evils from which Norfolk had turned when it established council-manager government in 1918.

On March 14, 1933, the Council reached a climax. Councilman W. R. L. Taylor nominated a citizen for the vacancy. The vote was two for, two against. He nominated a second man. The vote was the same. He nominated a third. The vote did not change. He nominated a fourth—and immediately all four councilmen voted in his favor. The choice was Slover, chairman of the board of Norfolk Newspapers, Inc. Slover accepted.

This was a surprising development. "Council has by unanimous vote elected to its membership a man who has never in his life aspired to public office," the *Virginian-Pilot* pointed out. "It may be taken for granted," the editorial continued, that Slover "accepted the election not to gratify an ambition for place, but to lend a hand in the direction of the city's affairs at a time when it is sorely in need of the best business talent the city affords, and when his own broad experience might be usefully employed in the solution of some of the city's pressing problems."

A week later (March 21, 1933) the Council elected Slover its president and in effect mayor. As he assumed office Slover stated his position in these few words: "As I interpret the temper of this community, it wants assurance from us that we promise to live within our income under a balanced budget, and that such action as may be necessary to this end will be promptly taken. With this objective as our goal, as I have been assured before accepting your election, I have agreed to join you and gladly enlist in the service for that period and no longer."

Those who knew Slover knew—and soon the whole city would know—that this spare statement was packed with meaning. "Assurance" was a key word. "Live within our income under a balanced budget" was a certainty. "Such action as may be necessary will be promptly taken" might sound like a commonplace generality, but the words were precise and fully loaded. When Slover said he would remain a member of the Council "no longer" than the time required to carry out the plan of action ("for this term only," he said elsewhere), the city could count on his doing just that.

The decision must have caused Slover to think hard. He was still trying to reduce his own responsibilities, not enlarge them. He had never shown interest in governmental office. He did not have the mind or spirit of a politician. He never sought public acclaim. He knew that he could not lead in reestablishing the city's financial structure without hurting some people. He was surely aware of risks to the newspapers themselves. Their independence in commenting on city financial policies would be difficult to maintain. Yet at the moment the crisis seemed to him to tower above all.

The first test came a week after Slover's election. The Council had already directed City Manager Truxtun to cut the 1933 budget. On March 28 more than a thousand people, most of them city employees, jammed the Council chamber, packed the corridors, spread over the City Hall and surrounding streets—the largest public attendance at, and outside, a Council session on record. The session moved to the City Auditorium. But the Council moved in nothing else except to increase, not reject, cuts in the budget.

The display excited the neighbors. The nearby Suffolk *News-Herald* nominated Slover for governor (the election would be held that year). "A new deal in Virginia," it said, was possible only "with fresh leadership untainted by political ties and unfettered by obligations that make it a slave to a political caste. . . . Our choice falls upon S. L. Slover, lately drafted for the City Council of Norfolk and then called to the mayoralty."

The Portsmouth *Star* across the river reprinted that editorial and went further. "If Slover in two weeks could cut Norfolk's budget $500,000 as current municipal operations proceed," it said, "think of what he might be able to cut from Virginia's present appalling budget, grown in 25 years from $7,000,000 to $42,000,000 per annum."

Letters poured in to Slover telling him that he was needed in the Virginia Capitol and would have a good chance in 1933 to get there. Support came from important Virginians. They wrote like men in earnest. But however strong the pressure was, Slover put it aside. He had much to do in Norfolk.

City Manager Truxtun resigned in October of 1933 to become collector of customs in Norfolk, and Thomas P. Thompson, a local architect, whom Slover had worked with earlier and knew well, succeeded him. Thompson was a builder. He brought life to many of the dormant possibilities for recovery and renewed growth. But firm, careful, orderly, and skilled management of the governmental controls was the foundation of the new leadership and of the new assurance in Norfolk.

Slover held fast to his promise not to continue in public office. On December 27, 1933, nine months after his election, he resigned as president of the Council. The plans and policies to which he had been giving most attention would, he thought, be "brought to a successful conclusion in a short time." He reminded the Council that "it never was, is not and never will be my purpose to enter into political life." He would remain a councilman a short time longer, but he was going away for a few weeks. Absence would not involve any forfeiture of pay, as the charter required, "since I have drawn no salary and shall draw none."

On January 1, 1934, accordingly, Slover stepped down as mayor, and W. R. L. Taylor was elected in his place. Governmental costs in 1933 had been cut by 21 per cent. By the following June the floating debt was below $340,000 after being ten times as high. It would be entirely paid by August. Funded debt had been reduced in three years by $2,000,000. A small bond issue in June, 1934, to pay notes held by New York banks sold above par with interest at 5 per cent—down from recent demands for 6 per cent. On March 27, 1934, Slover pointed out that "matters have reached such an acceptable conclusion that my services are no longer required." He resigned as a councilman. It was twelve months since he had been elected.

His associates in government beat the drums. Mayor Taylor recalled that:

> Colonel Slover came into Council at a heavy personal sacrifice and at a critical time in its affairs. . . . With his keen analytical mind, he devoted himself unstintingly to a solution of the problems. His efforts have been appreciated fully only by those with whom he worked. . . . All internal dissension has gone. . . . We have gone far toward solution of our financial problems. . . . The people of Norfolk should be grateful to him.

Roosevelt's New Deal often startled the newspapers in Norfolk and on some issues aroused their opposition. But both the *Virginian-Pilot* and the *Ledger-Dispatch* thought, despite setbacks by court decisions, breakdowns in administration, and political measures (the *Virginian-Pilot* cited the silver purchase policy as one of these), that the Roosevelt leadership had innate merits and was strongly preferable to the visible alternatives. They supported the Roosevelt candidacy in 1940 because of economic improvement at home, the leadership he provided in the spreading war, and the confusion of the opposition. In 1944 they thought the war was going well and a change at the top was not justified and might have bad effects.

The Norfolk government went hard after federal aid, and the marks are all over the city to this day: streets, highways, bridges, and buildings of many kinds including schools, colleges, hospital, airport, museum, post office, and other Federal operations. New defense needs brought expansion of airfields and other facilities, modernization of old battleships and merchant ships long in storage, and construction of carriers, battleships, and destroyers.

The *Virginian-Pilot* set down 1935 "as the first year of recognizable recovery" (but this agony had begun in 1930!) and thought that 1936 had "carried the recovery movement so far and so fast that it closed on a note resembling a building boom." The *Ledger-Dispatch* was sure Norfolk was entering 1937 "in a state of genuine well being. The past year has witnessed the return of a large measure of material prosperity which was lost in the depression years."

Legal liquor had made life more cheerful and orderly. Illegal liquor had never been effectively dammed, to be sure, though obstacles were not negligible. The Coast Guard had increased its vessels and improved its techniques so much that by 1925 a *Virginian-Pilot* report said that "it is as difficult for a rum craft to get its cargo ashore as it would be for a first-line battleship to go to Richmond." Occasionally a scandal exploded, as when the naval transport, *Beaufort*, in from the West Indies, was discovered to have forty cases of liquor lined up row by row, exclusive of other cases believed to have been dumped when the alarm sounded. Many merchant ship captains did not like to have liquor aboard: the fine, in event of detection, would be equal to the value of the liquor itself. The wooded countryside in the Virginia and North Carolina counties around Norfolk and the fast cars for the midnight runs were more reliable even though the battles in the dark were costly and tragic.

When the 1932 election decided the issue, and the approval of the Twenty-first Amendment by December, 1933, sealed it, problems of organization still puzzled a state where antiliquor sentiment long had been fervent. In the referendum of October, 1933, that sentiment was expressed over the state by a third of the voters. Norfolk was different. Its vote was six to one for legal liquor.

A commission headed by State Senator John W. Eggleston of Norfolk (later of Virginia's Supreme Court of Appeals and long its chief justice) had the task of reconciling the decision of Virginia for liquor with the sentiment of most Virginians that sales of liquor (beer and wine were regarded in a different light) could not be trusted to private interests and ought not to yield private profits, and therefore should be sold by the state itself. The feeling was general that saloons of the old breed should have no place in the new day.

The *Ledger-Dispatch* and the *Virginian* championed these objectives with enthusiasm. In the legislative debate over the Eggleston plan they strongly supported the controls, insisted on, no politics in the system, and won most of these goals with Eggleston's firm hand and the selection of Norfolk's former Mayor S. Heth Tyler, a man of ability and character, to head the Virginia Alcoholic Beverage Control Board, which would preside over all. On May 28, 1934 (after an opening in Richmond on May 15), the first state store in Norfolk sold legal liquor. Newspaper reporters, knowing news when they saw it, recorded every detail. Thirty years later the system had not changed materially.

A certain symbolism seemed to attach to 1934. Boxing had been legal only in clubs, but it had grown so popular in the seaport and naval atmosphere of Norfolk that the *Virginian-Pilot*'s sports editor, Bill Cox, wrote: "There were more fights per square mile in Norfolk and vicinity last year [1931] than in any other district of the country except the large metropolitan areas." March of 1934 brought an act of the General Assembly to allow public prizefighting.

In 1927 Virginia's highest court had upheld fines levied on eighteen Portsmouth and Richmond professional baseball players for playing on a Sunday in 1926. But in May of 1934 a Norfolk jury acquitted the Norfolk Tars' Dan Hall (the selected guinea pig) of a charge of violating the law by playing in a Piedmont League game on Sunday.

So in December of 1934 the surprise was not great when Norfolk's Judge R. B. Spindle, Jr., held that Sunday movies were a work of necessity. No high-level maneuvers designed the succession of steps that marked 1934 as a year of release. The newspapers welcomed the steps; the town took them in stride. Perhaps everyone was growing up. But a year in which liquor sales, prizefighting, Sunday baseball, and Sunday movies all received the blessings of legality belongs to history.

In 1930 the city government deeded an old public school building for a Norfolk Division of the College of William and Mary (in Williamsburg). A modest junior college started with 160 students. Virginia Polytechnic Institute, bringing in engineering courses, became a second sponsor in a year. A junior college for Negroes that started in 1935 under the auspices of Virginia Union University of Richmond won city aid as Norfolk Polytechnic Institute in 1942, and grew into a branch of Virginia State College in 1944. Depression and war years made the going hard at first, but the tenacity of the two colleges was unyielding, and, once firmly established, they grew swiftly. The first attained independence as the full-scale Old Dominion College (state-supported) and had more than seven thousand students in the middle

1960's and a graduate school getting on its feet. The second, also state-supported, had more than five thousand students then and was growing in quality and recognition.

Both these institutions had strong and continuing newspaper support; both added a new tone and new ranges of interest to the community.

The struggle through most of the 1930's to provide by city action one Negro bathing beach out of all the scores of miles of beaches within easy reach of Norfolk had symbolic and historical meanings as well as obvious recreational obligations and opportunities. Respected citizens, white and colored, fought long for this project. It encountered the hard and prolonged opposition (as Jaffé wrote later in a review of these times) of "immemorial prejudice, inertia, distrust of the untried, political timidity and vested selfishness."

The *Virginian-Pilot's* editorial page was preeminently the voice of those who championed the fairness and communal justice of the enterprise. and the *Ledger-Dispatch* gave the cause strong support during the legal actions initiated by bitter resisters. In the end the beach won. It was a mere ten-acre stretch of sand, with a few facilities, on Chesapeake Bay. In the later age of desegregation it lost its significance. But for its era, and at the moment of its birth as a municipally established beach for the Negro population, it was a new and rare achievement.

The newspapers kept in mind growing space, traffic routes, and post office proximity when they selected as the site of their new building the hodgepodge of small real estate holdings, some of them slums, on Brambleton Avenue between Voss Street and National Lane, which in turn were between the more important Granby and Boush Streets. The building was designed to be larger than immediate needs called for. The top floor was rented to the Chesapeake & Potomac Telephone Company amid speculation about when the newspapers would need that floor for their own operations. They needed it in ten years. In less than another ten years they needed the first of the large additions to the main structures.

There were two main structures, extensively connected: the first, a four-floor squarish newspaper office building with clean lines and a limestone front; the second, a newspaper industrial building behind and to the north. The two measured 111 by 230 feet and cost $350,000 exclusive of site and equipment—it had been a good time to build. The two newspapers employed then 325 people and had a payroll of $22,000 a week and a production cost of $1,350,000 a year. They had additional (and much smaller) offices in Portsmouth, Suffolk, and Berkley. Independence and competition were stressed by exactly similar newsrooms and editorial offices on opposite sides of the building, looking a little like prizefighters facing each other and ready to exchange blows. It was the largest newspaper plant that Virginia had ever seen. In comparison with quarters that most of the 325 men and women in it had ever known before, it was luxurious. The *Virginian-Pilot* and the *Ledger-Dispatch* were first printed there on October 18, 1937.

The location was a striking change. All newspapers in Norfolk since the Civil War and long before had lived and published and died, or merged, downtown: the region of Main Street, Roanoke Avenue, Commercial Place (the earlier Market Square), Bank Street, Hill Street, Plume Street, City Hall Avenue, and, for a bold advance, Tazewell Street. Now the *Ledger-Dispatch* and the *Virginian-Pilot* had vaulted all the way to midtown, far from the waterfront on the south and the covered marshes of the original Norfolk. They had planted themselves near the northern edge of the principal business district that seemed then to have no way to expand except northward.

Later municipal planning, with its sweeping slum clearance and its civic center concept, would revive and reorganize older and worn areas, all of which the newspapers strongly supported. Norfolk was growing large enough to justify many regions of new and officially directed growth.

"It is fit and proper with a successful enterprise," Slover said in a radio address on the night (October 28, 1937) of the formal dedication of the new building, "that as we grow older and less active, the business grows younger and stronger." His intimation of age was unusual. Sixty-four years old then, clear of eye, straight of back, direct in speech, firm in decision, Slover had twenty-two more years to live. The young men were all around him. They were happy that night. But they were all facing collisions abroad and testings at home that few of them had ever experienced. For the world was changing fast.

The rise of Mussolini and Fascism in Italy and of Hitler and the Nazi Storm Troopers in Germany; Japan's conversion of Manchuria into a colony and its multiplying attacks on China; the revolt in Spain against the republican government and the war that for Germany and the Soviet Union was a proving ground; Italy's invasion of Ethiopia; the withdrawals from the League of Nations; the sanctions that did not restrain; the pacts, the deals, the border crossings, the partitions, the hand-wringing, the surrenders—all these were the overture for a curtain that everyone knew would disclose far more terrible drama when it rose.

The year 1938 was the year of the largest amount of peacetime building in Norfolk since the first World War, and 1939's total rose higher. Simultaneously 1938 was the year of Hitler's seizure of Austria, of British and French failure in Munich, of the carving of Czechoslovakia. It was a year when one battleship award ($70,000,000) went to the Navy Yard in Portsmouth, a second ($70,000,000) went to Newport News, and a third to Quincy in Massachusetts. Three months later a carrier award to Newport News followed.

The *Ledger-Dispatch* thought 1938 ended "amid a crescendo of verbal and actual conflict among the nations." To the *Virginian-Pilot* 1938 proved that "the appeasement policy is plainly leading nowhere, and its Munich inventors are, one and all, preparing for the day when it will go up in smoke. If and when that happens, the American nation will have something far more serious to worry about than the outlook for business."

International news commanded more front-page space, more inside-page analysis and interpretation, more editorial page judgment. This was less strange to Norfolk than to many other cities. Norfolk had always lived closer to foreign lands, psychologically as well as in sheer distance and familiarity. The rising possibilities of war on the great scale had a special meaning for a city that was a home of the Navy. It could never avoid intimate participation, in a thousand personal ways, with any war that involved the United States.

All through 1939 the tempo of preparation rose sharply in Norfolk. Invariably the newspapers' editors, regretting the necessity, approved and applauded the purpose. September of 1939, when Hitler unleashed his tightly trained armies against Poland, brought bigger and blacker headlines. The neutralism that was urged in some parts of America was recognized as a theory, but both Norfolk newspapers rejected the idea as unrealistic. They pinned no hope on isolationism. A Hitler world they could never contemplate.

By that time Italian and Danish ships were interned in Norfolk waters. On May 12, 1941, a British carrier, camouflaged in jagged, hard-edged, mottled colors, and carrying the marks of battle damage, slid slowly and silently up the Elizabeth River, past the Norfolk waterfront, plain for all to see, and settled in a Navy Yard dry dock in Portsmouth. She must be—she was—*Illustrious*, almost fatally battered by German planes near Malta though patched up well enough there to flee to Alexandria. But she needed thorough going over. Down the Suez she had limped, and around Good Hope, and up the long haul across the south Atlantic to the Navy Yard for major repairs and—it seemed to the two sympathetic and moved cities—for nursing and rest.

The whole town knew about *Illustrious*. But no word about her appeared in newspaper type until August when Captain Lord Louis Mountbatten came to take command.

Nor did Norfolk newspapers report any word of the battleship *Royal Sovereign* when she came in for months of repair and overhaul, or of other British fighting ships that found succor in the Navy Yard. The newspapers lived under a voluntary censorship desired by Washington and requested by the Navy. They had their perplexities. In March the *Virginian-Pilot* had criticized the New York *Herald Tribune* for reporting (with picture) the arrival of the British battleship *Malaya*, in New York waters for repairs, visible to anyone looking her way.

Then the British Ministry of Information itself announced that Mountbatten had arrived in the United States and would command *Illustrious*, now "in an American shipyard undergoing repairs." The *Virginian-Pilot* threw up its hands. Variations in voluntary censorship were "beyond our guessing."

Three days after the German invasion of Russian soil, the *Ledger-Dispatch* took a firm stand on a disputed issue (June 25, 1941):

> We must move these supplies to Britain. . . . We must move these supplies even if it becomes necessary to employ the American Navy to guarantee them a safe passage—and even if the employment of this force results in carrying us into the "shooting" phase of a war in which we have for all practical purposes been involved almost from its beginning. The time for convoy is here.

Before July ended the *Virginian-Pilot*, expressing itself "On a Hitherto Taboo Subject," faced up to the stern and approaching necessities. It declared that "if our safety and security require full-scale war, we shall fight it with whatever resources in manpower and weapons we can command and wherever military strategy calls for it to be fought. Any other course, and in particular any half-way course, would be very near the topmost peak of folly."

When 1939 ran out the Atlantic Squadron, based in Norfolk, included four battleships, five cruisers, thirty-five destroyers, and a single carrier—what lessons were still to be learned and put into practice!

The greater part of American naval force was in the Pacific, much of it transferred from Norfolk. But the Atlantic build-up, especially in the Norfolk region, was enormous. By the end of 1940 sixteen thousand civilians were working in the Navy Yard; in all naval installations in the Norfolk area there were more than twenty-six thousand. Long before then the housing shortage had forced the swift construction of living quarters, two hundred or three hundred units at a clip, five hundred units at Merrimack Park, more than one thousand units at Benmoreell—both of these for naval families.

The historic Sunday of December 7, 1941, touched off almost automatically the long series of steps that war itself demanded of the Navy and of the Army units at nearby Fort Story and Camp Pendleton and of the city too. A naval car driving above street speeds on the long Hampton Boulevard stretch to the Naval Base could start rumors now. The blackouts and the air raid warning systems showed a seriousness that befitted a region dotted with naval and military establishments. A new kind of censorship took hold. Strange small boats, bobbing in Norfolk waters—landing craft, people learned—told that it was going to be that kind of a war.

But in the first instance it was for Norfolk a submarine-merchant ship-tanker kind of war, fought out almost in the front yard of the Virginia and North Carolina coast and sometimes within view of civilians on the beaches. Where coastal traffic tends to congest off Cape Hatteras, and tankers loaded with Latin-American and Caribbean oil and headed northward to the big ports run close to land, the prizes were rich. Submarines manned by German officers and men with long Atlantic experience dived in for the kill.

In those early months before antisubmarine warfare was well organized, huge splotches on the surface of the ocean marked the deaths of many tankers and of many tanker men. Hollow-eyed survivors were brought into Norfolk week after week, even day after day, straining local facilities to care for them. A Fort Story officer considered a question as to whether it was all right to go in swimming. The *Virginian-Pilot* of that May of 1942 reported his answer: "If the bathers don't mind stepping in oil, and if they can stand seeing a body wash ashore now and then from some ship blown up by the Germans, it's all right with us."

Norfolk was overwhelmed now by construction of every kind, the shortage of nearly everything, and waves of new population that inundated the town. Older residents who remembered the collapse of the first World War's mushroom growth feared a worse collapse at the end of a war that was just beginning. But nothing could stop the torrents of wartime development, and not much that local efforts or Federal aid measures could do kept the developments neat or orderly or clean or pretty or pure.

In time the national writers discovered as much. From *Collier's Weekly* to the *Architectural Forum*, from *McCall's* to the *Survey Graphic*, from the *American Mercury* to the *Woman's Home Companion*, they investigated what some of them called "the worst war town." They described girlie trailer camps on the outskirts of Norfolk surrounded by red, white, and blue stockades, and carrying appropriate signs over the trailer doors: "It Happened One Night" and "All That Money Can Buy."

The red light district on East Main Street had been closed in a burst of municipal fervor (and after prolonged debate) before the war. When "the biggest morals raid ever conducted here"—as the *Virginian-Pilot* called it—went into action in the summer of 1942, it struck toward Southern Cabins, Shack's Cabins, Timkin's Cabins, and comparable conveniences. They were all out of bounds for Navy men, but half of the arrests were of women, and most of the men wore uniforms. Norfolk did not know what to do with these women—very young girls, most of them—and, as in the first World War, jammed them into already overcrowded jail quarters.

The *Ledger-Dispatch* cheered these forays. "Clamp down on the joints," it demanded. But the city police force was below strength in the war years, and the newspapers admitted that "young men who go on patrol duty only once in a while" were not very effective. It saw Norfolk as "something like an armed camp." A permanent shore patrol set up by the Navy and operated by it was hailed as a necessity. In time it developed into an elite corps.

A subcommittee of the House Naval Affairs Committee came to Norfolk for a hard look, and a commission headed by New York's ebullient Robert Moses included Norfolk in its studies of congested war centers. The judgments of the latter were not made public. The *Virginian-Pilot*, which could not understand this secrecy and did not like it, said that "the latest of these Federal diagnoses—the one made by the Moses investigators—is still guarded against vulgar eyes as if it were a chart of the Chesapeake mine fields." It let loose a bomb of its own: "Norfolk has never been able to find out why, after nearly two years of Federal planning, the 200 or 300-bed hospital plant to be erected on Granby Street is still nothing more than a hole in the ground."

The congressmen heard tales of food shortages, housing shortages, crowded street cars, and inadequate taxi service, which many thousands of civilians could have substantiated. A naval officer suggested more women drivers for more street cars, but he was told to his face that women would require rest rooms, and rest rooms would require priority orders from the War Production Board. City government and adjoining county governments disputed which carried more blame for dens of iniquity, with the Navy generally supporting the contentions of the city that it was more circumspect. Housing needs were never met in full. Recreation for young men was a perpetual issue.

Mathematics ran against easy solutions for such problems. The census of 1940 credited Norfolk with a population of 144,332; Portsmouth, with 50,745. Estimates of the civilian increase since the April of the census ranged from 50,000 upward for Norfolk alone. By June of 1941, before the United States was formally in the war, 10,000 recruits were in training at the Naval Base, 15,500 officers and men were stationed there, and 14,400 more officers and men were on ships based there. The Navy Yard in Portsmouth had increased its civilian workers by 11,000 since mid-1940 to 21,000 and was planning to add 13,000 and so reach 35,000 in that industrial plant—which at the height of the war the Yard exceeded.

On many a weekend 50,000 men in uniform—by some estimates, above 65,000—poured into Norfolk to see what they could see. On a comparative basis that would be about the same as if in a city of 3,000,000 as many as 1,000,000 men in uniform, or more, came into town over a Saturday and Sunday looking for recreation.

The Federal government produced much of large importance in those years, for the armed forces and the war workers, and ultimately for the whole community: the hospital (De Paul Hospital), which took a long time in coming; a theater-arena combination with many possibilities and wide use; a trailer camp said to be the largest in America; increased housing and recreation of many kinds. The dances in the new arena drew two thousand on the floor at a time, and the USO's were bursting with activity. Still, the restaurants, though they had multiplied, seemed never to have a seat, gasoline was hard to come by, and liquor rationing tightened to a quart a month, and there were long lines to get that quart too.

Newsprint grew more and more scarce until pages dwindled, advertising could not find a place to appear on those that were left, and half of the editorial pages were turned over to the news departments. Circulation at a distance that required much gasoline and punished delivery truck tires grew so difficult to maintain—notably, deep in North Carolina—that much of it was allowed to slip away. Regaining it later was costly. Editions were telescoped in ways that hurt circulation in Portsmouth, and for the long run that was costly too.

But income was up to such an extent that at the end of 1943 the newspapers gave to the Norfolk Museum of Arts and Sciences $25,000, the income of which was to be used for purchasing material relating to the Tidewater regions of Virginia and North Carolina. Huber's announcement in April, 1944, called the gift "a long cherished desire to make a material contribution to the development of a Norfolk cultural institution that we regard as of the highest importance and which, we feel, has a mission of public service and enlightenment not unrelated to that of the newspaper."

The armed forces drained young men from every department and created major manpower problems. Veteran newspaper men had to shoulder more of the load. They hired nearly anyone who floated within their vision, and they signed up more and more women, especially for the *Ledger-Dispatch*, where the hours were more attractive.

Women did what women had never done before. In late 1942 the *Ledger-Dispatch* ran out of sports editors. Looking around, Tom Hanes, the managing editor, saw Mary Hopkins, an all-round newspaper woman who had been begging for the police beat. "Take the sports desk first," he told her; she did, and she turned out a good job too.

The saving grace in these perplexing times was that the newspapers had superior men for command and staff and as department heads, and the changes there, though they came, were comparatively few. Slover's managerial skills, determination, and judgment were of great value. Huber had matured into a general manager of poise, steadiness, and strength. The advertising, circulation, mechanical, news, and editorial areas were in the hands of men of experience and capacity.

Hanes had come into the managing editorship of the *Ledger-Dispatch* in 1936, and Charles F. Reilly, Jr., had followed him as sports editor (though he went out with the Coast Guard, but eventually came back). Winder R. Harris left the *Virginian-Pilot* managing editorship in May of 1941 to go to Congress. A vacancy in the Second Virginia District appeared when Representative Colgate W. Darden, Jr., resigned in order to run for governor—the first governor from Norfolk since Littleton W. Tazewell in the 1830's.

Harris won his congressional election by beating Norman R. Hamilton, the Portsmouth publisher, among his opponents. He resigned during his second term to work for a shipbuilders' association. Spencer, the night city editor, succeeded Harris as managing editor, and Larson moved from the telegraph to the city desk. As a sideline Larson helped editorial writers produce the editorial paragraphs which the *Virginian-Pilot* published: four—never more, never less—at the head of the editorial columns. They were widely read and reprinted across the country, notably by the *Literary Digest*.

Gordon died in March of 1944, just under sixty-eight years old. He had come to the *Ledger-Dispatch* twenty-seven years earlier. His distinctive style, his personal interests as they appeared in lighter editorials, and his theatrical and musical reviews were Norfolk institutions. Chambers moved from the *Virginian-Pilot*, after fourteen years as associate editor there, to replace him. Leslie and Perkins were associate editors of the *Ledger-Dispatch*.

Alonzo T. Dill, a young North Carolinian with a sense of history, who had come up from the newsroom, continued to help with *Virginian-Pilot* editorials. Jaffé brought in as his main associate Jack W. Schaefer, then with the Baltimore *Sun*, earlier with the New Haven *Journal-Courier* and with theater and movie journals. It would not have been easy to guess that this intense and systematic editorial writer was also writing, in odd hours but persistently, the manuscript that became the Western classic, *Shane*. It led the way into a dozen novels and volumes of short stories that marked him as an authority in Western writing. He soon left Norfolk for the trans-Mississippi regions that were his spiritual home.

William S. Meacham succeeded Schaefer. Meacham knew the state well. He had long been interested in penology and the practical aspects of public welfare. Governor Darden appointed him the first state parole commissioner, and he laid important foundations. Throughout these Norfolk years he wrote occasional editorials for the New York *Times*, especially on Southern subjects.

In 1949, when Dill won the first Ogden Reid Fellowship for a year's study abroad, Harold G. Sugg, also from eastern North Carolina, then the *Virginian-Pilot*'s top reporter on city government and politics and state affairs, substituted for Dill.

Looking back over the years since they had consolidated, the *Virginian-Pilot* and the *Ledger-Dispatch* could have reflected that always they had been forced to wrestle with a furiously changing world. Their consolidation was a product of the great depression. Their struggles then brought them face to face with the age that Roosevelt ushered in. Their emergence from depression plunged them into the darkness of Mussolini and Hitler, of Japanese swords, and of the death of the League of Nations. They lived in the presence of the greatest threat to Western civilization in modern times. They fought, as best they could, four years of desperate war. They recorded the arrival of the atomic age.

The consolidated newspapers had rarely known normal times as they used to think of normal times. They were parts of a world in which, for these years, nothing was as it had been. On issue after issue they had to form their judgments and make their decisions less and less by the lamp of experience and more and more in the light of their own courage, their own intelligence and wisdom.

On what else could men rely? For in the end—come good, come bad, come the inexplicable, come the seemingly impossible—they must turn within to those sources of human spirit and strength that always have rescued mankind. This the men of the newspapers could do in good hope. For nothing is so certain in the long decades of newspaper history in Norfolk from the end of the American Civil War to the end of the second World War as the simple truth that it is a story of newspapers but a triumph of men.

24 · 1945-1965: YOUTH TAKES COMMAND

by Harold Sugg

MORE THAN MOST CITIES, NORFOLK COULD REJOICE AT THE END OF World War II, the *Ledger-Dispatch* said in a V-J Day editorial. "The expansion the war made necessary has literally pulled the city out of shape." At its peak, the city's population had been roughly doubled by the influx of war migrants, and on August 16, 1945, the city still was overcrowded. "It will be some time before Norfolk can bid farewell to crowds, queues, taut tempers, and shortages of everything from diapers to doctors," the *Ledger-Dispatch* predicted.

In successive days, the newspapers took inventory. Streets were dirty and broken. The mass transit system needed new buses it could not get, and the Norfolk municipal airport was "a shabby, rundown, dilapidated and makeshift station." The downtown slums were worse by four years of incredible crowding. The police force was 25 per cent below complement, and the *Virginian-Pilot* complained September 10 of "a particularly atrocious murder and an unusual sequence of burglaries, robberies and holdups."

The newspapers' situation was not unlike the city government's. Their building needed maintenance, their newsprint was rationed and their equipment badly beaten up; a new Scott press ordered in 1945 could not be delivered until 1948. Their future was linked with the ability of the area to pull itself together for a swift and wise rehabilitation. That prospect was marred by a quarrel between City Manager Charles B. Borland and the Norfolk City Council that erupted with Colonel Borland's abrupt resignation in December, 1945.

A reformation came the following June with the election of a businessmen's City Council ticket—Richard D. Cooke, Pretlow Darden and John Twohy II, who offered themselves, an advertisement said, "to serve only one term of four years as an effective means of driving politics out of the conduct of city affairs." They called themselves "The Peoples Ticket" (their opponents called them "The Silk Stocking Ticket"). Their real origins lay in the prewar success of getting top businessmen to take over the Community Fund. Oscar F. Smith, colorful fertilizer company founder, decided that if businessmen could run the Community Fund, they could also run the city government.

Judging by the support the *Virginian-Pilot* and *Ledger-Dispatch* gave the new administration, late returning servicemen could have assumed this was the newspapers' ticket. Actually, neither paper endorsed a slate, and the *Virginian-Pilot* said on election day: "We do not think anything truly fundamental is at stake in today's election." The comment was justifiable: incumbent Councilmen James W. Reed, C. E. Wright and Richard W. Ruffin had worked in an almost impossible wartime situation, and besides, they wore high quality socks, too. But the decisive vote in a record turnout suggested that the *Ledger-Dispatch* had come closer to measuring the public temper when it termed the campaign, the day before the election, "the healthiest and most valuable since Norfolk adopted the city manager form of government 28 years ago."

The day after the election, marveling at the huge turnout and manifest desire for a change, the *Ledger-Dispatch* said the voting was "a decision of great and perhaps historic influence." It was. In the remarkable twenty years to come, during which Norfolk was almost rebuilt, much of progressive significance had roots in the Cooke-Darden-Twohy regime—an era that also might be called the "C. A. Harrell regime" for the dynamic city manager the city councilmen brought in from Schenectady, N.Y.

What came through the news columns, besides solid achievement, was the style of Businessmen-Councilmen, who thought they could run a city without being politicians. Two holdover councilmen, George R. Abbott and J. Rives Worsham, knew better, but Messrs. Cooke, Darden and Twohy thought at first they could please everybody. Council meetings ran from five to six hours long. Political forces around the Courthouse, still smarting from what they considered unfair charges in the campaign, subtly encouraged opposition to the new councilmen.

Typical news of the era, although hardly the most important, was a picture that appeared in the *Virginian-Pilot* September 16, 1947. In it, the august members of the City Council (two of whom were then or later became First Citizens) were sniffing the pig pens and packing plants at Smithfield, Virginia, to see if any odors emanated therefrom. The reason for the trip was that Swift & Company proposed to build a packing plant near Ballentine Place in Norfolk and Ballentine Place residents objected. The councilmen took the day off to see if a packing plant *really* did smell. It did not, they reported—but Swift & Company changed its plans, anyway.

"Young man," said Jaffé to a marveling reporter in those days, "don't get the idea this is the way city government works. It works this way only once in about 25 years. The reformers get tired, the regulars take over—and things have to be pretty bad before the reformers come back again." For the newspapers, covering city hall had rarely been so exciting; in the end it was the openness and frankness of the amateurs and their professional city manager that saved the administration from deep controversy—and a serious police scandal that echoed old charges of "The Wickedest City."

Police Captain C. J. Staylor—"Bubba" Staylor, a clean-cut and popular Norfolk Tar baseball player before joining the force—gathered twelve policemen on a December, 1948, afternoon in High Rock ballpark. These policemen ordinarily did not make raids; no member of the vice squad was present; Chief of Police Claude M. Lindsay and Director of Public Safety Calvin H. Dalby were out of town. Taking their orders from Staylor, the twelve men bumped off two large numbers-writing establishments on Church Street, causing 114 arrests and, later, 11 convictions and fines totaling $11,700.

Not even Staylor had suspected what would turn up, he testified later. On December 15, the *Virginian-Pilot* reported the raiders were also handed a list of policemen reputedly paid off for protection; how many was speculative—ultimately twenty-two were tried and exonerated. The alleged numbers king was convicted once, but appealed and was found not guilty on his fourth trial.

Notwithstanding these results, drastic action followed a recommendation by a special grand jury that the police department "as presently staffed be completely reorganized." Police Chief Lindsay resigned angrily, protesting his innocence. Out of the affair emerged a remarkable new chief of police, Colonel Amor LeRoy Sims, USMC (Ret.), who retired at the Marine Barracks, Naval Base, as a brigadier general one day and reported as Norfolk's chief of police the next. A small, erect man with a swagger stick, Sims was a disciplinarian. He hounded prostitution, gambling and what were called "private clubs"—clubs so private the police had to negotiate several barriers before reaching the interior where, of course, they found nothing. Chief Sims even managed to jail (on whiskey charges) a madam who had flourished for twenty years.

But if wickedness was being sharply diminished in Norfolk, there were new opportunities across the boundary line, where police numbers were small in comparison to the square miles. The *Ledger-Dispatch* September 4, 1951, called upon Norfolk County to crack down on hoodlums, noting: "Norfolk police have been making war on the numbers writers and other racketeers and some of them have taken refuge in Norfolk and Princess Anne Counties."

In Princess Anne County, a big-time robbery at the Piney Point Boat Club in September, 1948, netted armed gunmen up to $100,000. Year after year, around the resort of Virginia Beach, there appeared to be a regular pattern of gambling activity broken by a late August raid and resumed thereafter. The *Ledger-Dispatch* commented sourly in August, 1955: "It has been common knowledge in this vicinity that beach and county clubs never really give up their unlawful operations, that they merely shut up shop while the heat is on."

What is "common knowledge," however, is not always easy to prove. In August, 1955, Frank Batten—who had not completed his first year as publisher—called upon one of his newspapers to prove gambling at Virginia Beach. By a flip of a coin, *Pilot* Managing Editor R. K. T. Larson won the assignment from the *Ledger*'s Tom Hanes, and on August 3 appeared this front-page headline:

ROULETTE, ANYONE
OR DICE? SPOTS OPEN

With the headline was a photograph (made by Neal Clark with a concealed camera) showing gambling activity in the Pine Room which appeared to be (but technically was not) part of the Surf Club. The story was written by Robert C. Smith and Ron May; their wives contributed sidebar stories on the excitement of visiting illegal nightclubs at company expense. The Smith-May story contained this interesting paragraph: "We passed two Princess Anne County policemen lounging by the main entrance to the swank Surf Club. They stood only yards from the door which led to the roulette room."

As in the case of the Staylor raid in Norfolk six years before, the editorial pages rumbled and Circuit Court Judge Floyd E. Kellam summoned a special grand jury. And as with the Norfolk grand jury in 1949, and an earlier Princess Anne grand jury in 1951, the mountain's labor produced a few convicted mice. But the final result in both cities was a trend towards better law enforcement. By the 1960's, Princess Anne had merged into Virginia Beach; Norfolk County into Chesapeake. Swift urbanization helped support a larger police force and create a different climate. Either crime did not pay or other activities became more profitable.

In the newspaper plant, the first postwar decade was almost as eventful as for the city government. Huber died in September, 1946, and the loss of his steady guidance brought Colonel Slover from semi-retirement into a more active role. Slover personally nominated Henry S. Lewis as publisher, advising the board that "Mr. Huber many times expressed to me his judgment that Mr. Henry S. Lewis was, among all the men in our organization, the best equipped to succeed him. I concur in that judgment." Huber's will made Colonel Slover and Henry Lewis trustees for his stock. Frederick Lewis resigned as vice president, to be succeeded by N. N. Hill.

The Henry Lewis era (1946-54) saw the consolidation of the retail advertising staffs under one advertising director (later a vice president), Ellis Loveless. It also saw the reorganization of the circulation department under T. Earl Roberts, circulation director and for two years president of the International Circulation Managers Association. Besides the Scott press in 1948, Lewis added a new Goss press in 1952. In these activities, Lewis' close associate was C. Ralph Beamon, who rose in thirty-three years from circulation carrier boy to become vice president, secretary and treasurer of the company.

In retrospect, the outstanding event of the 1946-54 era may have been a project of Campbell Arnoux, president of radio station WTAR. The station gained television channel 3—such a speculative venture at the time that no other group applied for it! WTAR-TV went on the air April 2, 1950, and soon became a major factor in area communications. As in radio, the news operation of WTAR-TV was completely separated from the newspapers'.

Lewis died unexpectedly in October, 1954, and left Colonel Slover an interesting problem in management. There were two heirs apparent in the plant, active in the business and obviously on the way up, but they were young. There was the Colonel's nephew (he had no children of his own): Frank Batten, age twenty-seven, a graduate of the University of Virginia and the Harvard Graduate School of Business Administration. There was Paul S. Huber, Jr., age thirty-three, son of the former president and publisher, educated at the University of North Carolina.

For a while Slover toyed with the idea of calling in an experienced general manager—for instance, John D. Wise, his old associate and general manager of the Richmond newspapers—to serve as interim publisher until Batten and Huber gained experience. He did not toy long. Rather swiftly he prevailed with the board to name Frank Batten publisher, to have charge of "news, circulation, advertising and public relations," and Paul Huber president to have charge of "business office, production, personnel and employee relations."

This was a novel arrangement; newspaper operation is an integral process, every department being linked to another. The young team had been in office less than six months when it underwent trial by fire—the purchase of the Portsmouth *Star* and subsequent competition in Portsmouth. In an afternoon at his residence on Fairfax Avenue, Slover bought back for $1,000,000 the newspaper he and his partners had sold thirty-one years before for $75,000.

The repurchase of the *Star* might have been accepted gracefully in Portsmouth; Hamilton's preoccupations with politics and the use of the *Star* as a political vehicle had left him some enemies. But a decision was made to publish the *Star* in the Norfolk plant as a special but component part of the *Ledger-Dispatch*; a $2,000,000 expansion program, underway, was revised to accomplish this. The decision produced community opposition.

Portsmouth citizens seemed to be angry that the *Star* should be printed across the river. Led by merchants and assisted by professional men, a stock company was organized to establish the Portsmouth *Times*. Many old *Star* employees moved to the new paper although others rallied around Richard F. Wood, who remained as Portsmouth general manager for the combined paper.

At the first Norfolk Newspapers board meeting following the organization of the *Times*, Batten took note of the support for the new Portsmouth paper. But, he said, the new company was undercapitalized and its management had purchased far more equipment than was needed. The assessment could have been used as the accurate postmortem for the *Times* which appeared first on May 6, 1956, and last on March 24, 1957. The *Ledger-Dispatch* and Portsmouth *Star* became the *Ledger-Star* in September, 1962.

A titan of the Old Guard passed with the death of Louis Jaffé, editor of the *Virginian-Pilot*, in March, 1950. His fingers crippled with arthritis but as keen of mind as ever, Jaffé was stricken with a heart attack when it seemed that an editorial goal of thirty years would be achieved: the abolition of the Virginia poll tax as a requirement for voting. Sponsored by Delegate Walter A. Page, of Norfolk, the repealer had passed the House of Delegates and came before the Senate. Had Jaffé stayed in his hospital bed as the doctors ordered, he might have survived this, his first, heart attack.

The master editor could no more stay out of this fight than a fire horse could sleep through an alarm; he was up and down, consulting with associate editor William S. Meacham, revising proofs (he was *never* satisfied) and making suggestions. Although the repealer might have passed a full Senate vote, it was channeled into the traditional execution chamber, the Senate Committee on Privileges and Elections. There it died. So did Jaffé—symbolically within the same hour that the Speaker of the House in Richmond pronounced the session adjourned.

To realign his editorial command, Slover transferred Chambers back to the *Virginian-Pilot* as editor. On the *Ledger-Dispatch*, Joseph A. Leslie, Jr., became editor. Thus were named two friends who were to disagree dramatically during the mid-1950 crisis begun with the Supreme Court decision outlawing segregation in public schools because of race.

Since Chambers and Jaffé had been intimately associated, professionally and personally, for more than a decade, their styles might have been assumed to be the same. Their policies, yes; styles, no. Jaffé could take an associate's editorial, rewrite it so completely that the next morning only one or two sentences would be recognized— and then congratulate the writer on his good work! Confronted with the same problem, Chambers would gently suggest that perhaps this sentence could be improved or that point be checked. Both were careful strategists; both emphasized judgment as the most important characteristic of an editorial: both were bears for accuracy. But their modus operandi was quite different and reporters, admiring both, will forever debate which is the best.

For four years, the Leslie group and the Chambers group carried on reasonably amicable competition, the *Ledger-Dispatch* being more conservative as a rule and the *Virginian-Pilot* being more liberal—if these limping adjectives will serve. Even after the May 17, 1954, decision of the Supreme Court against segregation in the public schools because of race, their reactions were not too far apart. The *Ledger-Dispatch* noted the lower ratio of Negro to white population in Virginia as compared to the Deep South and wrote: "The impact of the decision upon Virginia as a whole will be relatively light. The court's decision does violence to the right of the states to manage their own affairs. But with adequate time for preparation, it should be possible to handle the transition without too great violence to public education in the South."

The *Virginian-Pilot* was particularly impressed by the court's withholding of final decrees until it could hear from the states themselves how to make the transition. It said: "In this sense the court has set an example which the intelligent leadership of the South should follow. . . . Not in the memory of any but a handful of men and women now living in the South has the need for this intelligence and wisdom, this earnest and honest search for sound action, been so powerful an obligation on the entire region as it is now."

Even after the final decrees of May 31, 1955, the papers were not diametrically opposite. What began to move the papers apart—what, indeed, ultimately split the Tidewater area—were winds blowing from outside Tidewater Virginia. Southside Virginians, soon after Governor Thomas B. Stanley's apparently calm acceptance of the May, 1954, decision, had descended upon and effectively stifled his original impulse. From the Southside grew chapters of the Defenders of State Sovereignty and Individual Liberty—a more polite form, as suitable to Virginia, of the White Citizens Council organized in the Deep South. The political base of the dominant Byrd organization was in the Southside.

Not until October, 1954—five months after the Supreme Court decision—did Governor Stanley get around to appointing a legislative study commission. For months thereafter little reached the public as to what the commission, headed by State Senator Garland Gray, of Waverly, was doing. By May 17, 1955, the *Virginian-Pilot* warned: "The tasks ahead will not be examined—or even approached—by a policy of negation. Virginia has qualities of mind and heart that are not reflected in such a policy." In June it assailed the secrecy and apparent inactivity of the Gray Commission.

When the Gray Commission did report in November, 1955, it recommended a pupil assignment plan which used health, welfare and educational levels—but not race—as criteria for assigning pupils; in effect, this would minimize the transfer of Negro pupils into white schools. More essentially, it recommended a constitutional amendment that would enable the state government to provide, out of public funds, tuition grants for students attending private schools. This was presented as a "safety valve" for parents adamant against desegregation. To the *Ledger-Dispatch*, the recommendations represented "a more reasonable approach to a solution to this problem than do any of the visible alternatives." The Gray plan, it said December 2, "offers much less danger to the public school system than integration by force."

The *Virginian-Pilot* opposed the abandonment of Virginia's historic doctrine that public money should not be given to private groups; in addition, it asked some questions. Where would the teachers come from to fill the schools to be supported by tuition grants? What school buildings? Where? These were asked by the *Virginian-Pilot* in a series of editorials looking towards a popular vote on the amendment scheduled January 9, 1956. "The blunt fact is that the effect on the public school program . . . depends on too many unknowns to be measured," it said December 18. Throughout the debate the *Virginian-Pilot* questioned whether a plan adopted deliberately to frustrate a Supreme Court decision was constitutional.

The *Virginian-Pilot* seemed terribly alone in that debate; most of the state's newspapers and a sizeable number of public figures it admired were for the Gray plan. Norfolk's former Governor Colgate W. Darden, Jr., then president of the University of Virginia—and keenly aware of the fury of opposition to desegregation in the Southside—delivered a telling blow for the plan. His logic was similar to that expressed by the *Ledger-Dispatch* on January 3: "The point is that without some means of ameliorating the harshness of the court decision . . . many areas of Virginia are going to be without any school facilities."

The statewide referendum verdict was two to one for the plan; in Norfolk, the margin was six to five and in Portsmouth eight to five. Perhaps the closer margin in the Norfolk area represented some effectiveness of the *Virginian-Pilot*. But that was of poor comfort to Chambers' staff on the cold, rainy day the results were made known. The worst was yet to come. Hardly were they adjusted to a defeat before the state of Virginia—with U. S. Senator Harry F. Byrd, Sr., back from Europe and charting the course—embarked upon a new policy of total, or "massive," resistance. A thicket of obstructions was erected. The inner fort of what became known as the "Stanley plan" contained two redoubts: (a) once a Negro child was assigned to a white school, whether voluntarily or by court order, the governor would close the school, remove it from the school system and divest local authorities of all control; (b) all state school funds for that school would be cut off. The second line of defense provided for the possibility that a City Council might petition the governor and regain control of the school—but without any state funds.

To the *Virginian-Pilot*, the threat of the Stanley plan was "an appalling reality. Once the standards are gone, the work of a generation may be destroyed," it said. The *Ledger-Dispatch* said that "the Stanley plan would not be of any courtroom use." But, it said, "A fundamental purpose would be to deter Negro children from applying for admission to white schools in the first place." The *Virginian-Pilot* doubted—quite correctly, it turned out—that the NAACP would give up so easily the victories it had won in court.

The Stanley plan became law in September, 1956; three public high schools and three junior high schools in Norfolk closed September, 1958, along with schools in Charlottesville and Warren County, Va. In between were twenty-four months of phantasmagoria in which advocates of the plan said the schools would not really be closed and, if they were, would be shut only a few days because the governor would find some way to reopen them. A Committee for Public Schools was formed in Norfolk and advocated strenuously and skillfully. The Norfolk state legislators, hitherto a sturdy if outnumbered minority for local option, began to weaken in despair. The Norfolk wing of the Byrd Democratic Organization—which originally had been critical of the Stanley plan—began to yield to the hard-core segregationists. The Defenders captured the Norfolk Parent-Teachers Association Council and cowed many of the school PTA's.

The City Council, following the lead of Mayor W. Fred Duckworth, a vigorous figure, became sharply critical of the School Board. The School Board, under Chairman Paul T. Schweitzer, held fast for keeping the schools open, six to two—the latter two votes representing recent appointments of the Duckworth Council. Also holding fast were Superintendent of Schools J. J. Brewbaker and most of the public school teachers.

When Federal District Judge Walter E. Hoffman ordered the Norfolk School Board to assign seventeen Negro children to six white secondary public schools, the Stanley plan was triggered into operation. Governor J. Lindsay Almond, Jr., who had succeeded Stanley on a strong segregationist platform, turned on the machinery which closed Norfolk school doors to ten thousand students; three thousand more were to be locked out in Charlottesville and Warren County. Facing the grim prospect, the *Virginian-Pilot* commented August 30, 1958: "There is no moral justification for the harsh punishment of the state's largest city. . . . Surely there is greater wisdom in Virginia than this would imply."

The *Ledger-Dispatch* said, however, that the responsibility would not be upon the governor, the legislature or the people: "It will rest squarely on the federal machinery and those who have set the court machinery in motion."

Of all the dramatic events of the fall, the most important may have been the decision of Norfolk public school teachers not to flirt with the idea of working for private, segregated schools set up as a substitute for public education. Instead they taught private, makeshift classes arranged by parents to obtain some kind of interim education. Their professional organization, the Norfolk Education Association, in early October voted 487 to 89 urging a reopening of the schools. The Norfolk District of the Virginia Education Association ratified that position October 13. On October 14, the *Ledger-Dispatch* decided: "Virginia's program of massive resistance to public school integration, as presently constituted, is facing a dead end."

The state, however, could not find soon, or was not willing to look for, a way out of the dead end. Continued resistance was encouraged in November by an advisory referendum sought by and phrased by the City Council, which by now had completely disregarded the School Board. In the referendum twenty-one thousand persons voted three to two against petitioning the governor to reopen the schools on an integrated basis. Printed on the ballot was a warning that should the six schools be reopened, parents would have to pay "a substantial tuition for each child" to replace the withdrawn state funds. To the *Ledger-Dispatch* the referendum issue was clear; to the *Virginian-Pilot* it was a fraud. Politically, the results were a victory for Mayor Duckworth and the Defenders.

On January 1 of the new year, the *Virginian-Pilot* said somberly: "We cannot continue this way. The state is bound by every obligation of governmental principle and human dignity and decency, and its own self interest, to find a better policy than the one we live under." To the *Ledger-Dispatch* on New Year's Day it had become "clear, in any event, that school closings as carried out so far are not the answer to the integration dilemma."

In the end, the Stanley plan was demolished January 19, 1959, by a State Supreme Court decision, written by Chief Justice John W. Eggleston, of Norfolk, and by a three-judge federal court decision—the blows coming one right after the other. In the meantime, two events helped prepare public opinion, one of them a backfire. Encouraged by the November referendum, the City Council took action which would have added thirty-six more schools to the closed list; only one councilman, Roy B. Martin, Jr. (who was to succeed Duckworth as mayor), dissented from this action. So far as popular support was concerned, this move pushed some on-the-fence opinion towards reopening public schools.

Following this threat, one hundred leading business and professional men signed a public statement urging the reopening of schools even at the price of some desegregation. Carefully timed to appear after the court decisions, the statement was published January 20. Although late coming into the open, the Establishment's support of public schools was a decisive factor in stabilizing support for reopening schools and integrating them peacefully.

The demolished Stanley plan was left in the hands of Governor Almond. He summoned a special session of the General Assembly. By a narrow margin, the General Assembly passed a "freedom of choice" plan which was remarkably similar to the old Gray plan the Virginia Byrd organization had once won and then dumped in favor of massive resistance. The six closed Norfolk schools were peacefully reopened February 2, 1959.

To tell the complete story of the school closing is beyond the scope of a newspaper history. The event was a local epic and possibly a watershed in Virginia political history. It encompasses a fiery Governor Almond, who breathed indignation almost to the end but ultimately accepted the realities. It includes breaks in long friendships, utter astonishment, insults and occasionally unexpected praise. It put Norfolk on nationwide television. None who lived through those days will ever forget them.

In all of this the *Virginian-Pilot* and *Ledger-Dispatch* were vital. Accurate news coverage and editing were never more important. Editorials were never more read, praised and damned. Letters to the editor flowed like rivers. The news editors possibly leaned over backward. Kenneth Harris, popular artist and a key spokesman for the Committee for Public Schools, once complained that his committee got better treatment in the *Ledger* (which editorially supported the Stanley plan) than in the *Pilot* (which opposed it).

The day after two courts knocked down massive resistance, the *Virginian-Pilot* commented: "Together the two decisions not only knock down—that is now the first necessity. They also clear away the rubbish. For the rest, a historic opportunity now opens for Virginians. The great of heart and mind will rise to it."

To the *Ledger-Dispatch,* the massive resistance program had not been without "its beneficial result. It threw up a bulwark that held fast against integration for three years. And this struggle served the highly important purpose . . . of demonstrating how serious is the issue of the encroachment of federal powers upon state sovereignty."

To both editors came honors. When Leslie retired the following June, he was summoned before the City Council and presented a Citation for Outstanding Service. Later he became a hard working and valuable member of the Norfolk City School Board.

For Chambers the reward was a Pulitzer Prize for distinguished editorial writing for his work the year the schools reopened—1959, the same year William Morrow and Company published his two-volume distinctive biography of Confederate General Stonewall Jackson. A remarkable aspect of Chambers' achievement was that after a heavy day's work as editor, he wrote a biography of Jackson at night. The book's publication was specially helpful to newsroom personnel called upon to answer telephone calls from irate segregationists about their "Yankee liberal editor." For years they had taken delight in advising that Chambers was a native of North Carolina. Now they could say he was the biographer of a Confederate general, Robert E. Lee's right arm.

Colonel Slover died in 1959 at age eighty-six, two years after he had left the office for the last time—still an erect, commanding figure. Batten purchased his stock—at that time 17 per cent of the Ledger-Dispatch Corporation, the major owner of Norfolk Newspapers, Inc. Mrs. Slover sold the Colonel's stock in Richmond Newspapers, Inc., to the heirs of Frederick Lewis and in return purchased the Lewis stock in the Ledger-Dispatch Corporation, which had become 34 per cent. Mrs. Slover and Batten together then held 51 per cent of the controlling corporation.

Though the ownership was solidified, Batten and Huber had discovered the business to be under a strain. Production methods had not changed essentially since the turn of the century—production was a mystery which managements had largely left to the craft unions. The cost of newsprint had tripled in twenty years; the advent of television had cut sharply into the newspapers' most profitable advertising revenue—national accounts. The end of the Korean war boom spelled also the end of a period in Norfolk when newspapers could succeed without really trying new methods.

The story of internal change in a newspaper is rarely as interesting as the front page, but to those involved the period from 1955-65 was exciting. The new management's first move—one that affected every other move—was to reach down into the newsrooms, pull out L. Cameron Gregory, and make him personnel director. Higher standards of recruiting and a more even administration of employee benefits were among the immediate results. Of longer-range consequence was an educational policy that sent scores of executives and managers to college and university courses, more than fifty reporters and editors to Columbia University seminars, and offered all employees free tuition for work-related courses at Old Dominion College.

Arthur T. Gormley, Jr., was brought in from Dallas (New Orleans and Des Moines) to become vice president for production and industrial relations; Harry E. Eisenbeiss, retired from the Internal Revenue Service, had earlier been brought in to be the company's controller and establish what is routine for most businesses but was unusual for a newspaper company at that time: a budget. From the Harvard Business School, J. W. Diederich became research director and was promoted to vice president and treasurer following Beamon's death. Harold Sugg, associate editor of the *Virginian-Pilot*, became Batten's assistant and later senior vice president.

Retirement dates brought salutes to the Old Guard—members of the Slover team. Perry Morgan, a Nieman Fellow and Charlotte *News* writer, succeeded Leslie as editor of the *Ledger-Star* for a year before returning to Charlotte. William H. Fitzpatrick took over the direction of the *Ledger-Star*, arriving by way of the *Wall Street Journal* and New Orleans *States*, where he had won a Pulitzer Prize for editorial writing. Robert H. Mason, an old newsroom hand who was held in high esteem by associates, was prevailed upon to give up part-ownership of the Sanford, N. C., *Herald* and become successively associate editor, managing editor and editor of the *Virginian-Pilot*, succeeding Chambers.

With the new realignment both newspapers returned to the earlier principle that the editor is responsible for the entire content. In the *Virginian-Pilot* editorial department, Meacham became editorial page editor to be succeeded, upon retirement, by Guy Friddell, colorful political writer for the Richmond *News Leader*. On the *Ledger-Star* associate editor George J. Hebert similarly assumed responsibility as editorial page editor.

In the *Virginian-Pilot* newsroom, John Spencer had been succeeded by R. K. T. Larson, who was to become associate editor for public service for both newspapers. Under the new alignment, Sidney L. Griffin and Joseph R. Bobbitt split the job of managing editor into day and night shifts until Bobbitt became associate editor. In the *Ledger-Star* newsroom, Charles F. Reilly, Jr., took over for his old boss, Tom Hanes, who had doubled in brass as managing editor, one-time production manager, founder and director of the newspapers' Christmas Joy Fund.

New methods inevitably followed the change from respected old-line management to younger direction. This was nowhere more true than in the advertising departments. Ellis Loveless retired as vice president and advertising director and was succeeded by Peter B. Bush, who placed more emphasis on retail advertising. John T. Grant, a veteran of competitive wars in Washington, D. C., and Indianapolis, Indiana, took over from William S. Davis, completely revised the classified advertising format and established national records for classified advertising gains.

Many of these changes were followed by a realignment of responsibility. But the most important realignment came not from within but from without—from the political struggles of Princess Anne County and Norfolk County, targets of annexation by Norfolk and Portsmouth.

On January 1, 1963, Princess Anne County merged with the resort city of Virginia Beach and became a new Virginia Beach, embracing 86,000 people and 222 square miles. On the same date, Norfolk County and South Norfolk merged into the brand new city of Chesapeake, including 73,647 people and 344 square miles. Both these mergers were preceded by hot political campaigns, humor concerning the number of farms and bears to be found in a "city," and elections which were decisive. But for the *Ledger-Star* and the *Virginian-Pilot*, the upheaval proved a fact of life: no longer were they *Norfolk* or *Norfolk-Portsmouth* newspapers. They were the hometown newspapers of four cities, of the metropolitan area. On the effective date of the merger, beneath the masthead, both papers began naming their address as "Norfolk, Portsmouth, Virginia Beach and Chesapeake." The *Virginian-Pilot* published an advertising salute to Virginia Beach and Chesapeake; the *Ledger-Star* editorially concluded: "What old Ben Franklin said of the colonies is equally true of Tidewater's people. We can either hang together or, economically, we will surely hang separately." Both editorial pages foresaw eventually some form of metropolitan cooperation.

Name changes, of course, were not enough. The *Ledger-Star* staff had begun producing a special tabloid in 1962, the *Beacon*, containing local news and advertising of Virginia Beach. Distributed with both newspapers, the *Beacon* was an instant success as a weekly; four years later it added a Sunday edition. The Portsmouth editions of both newspapers were revamped to become Portsmouth-Chesapeake editions. Each newsroom named a "metropolitan editor" to supervise all city editors—to become, in effect, the super city editor for four cities.

Earlier both papers had taken the gamble that the Chesapeake Bay Bridge-Tunnel would be completed and increased their circulation on the Eastern Shore of Virginia by 38 per cent. A special *Virginian-Pilot* campaign increased its circulation in thirteen counties of Eastern North Carolina by 37 per cent—regaining what had been lost during the wartime newsprint shortages. The Suffolk edition of the *Virginian-Pilot* similarly expanded its circulation.

Internally, editors Fitzpatrick and Mason overhauled newsgathering and display techniques. Series of articles to present interpretations in depth became a consistent technique. To cover a school board meeting was not enough—reporters had to learn and report what four different school systems were doing with the same subject. Military reporting at long last was given the status it deserved in four communities supported to a large degree by the United States Navy. More white space, better typography, better pictures, detailed advance planning—these were characteristic of both newspapers. Supplementary news services were added for depth. Bureaus were established in Richmond and Washington.

There was much to celebrate in 1965 as the *Virginian-Pilot* neared November 21, its hundredth anniversary. But both newspapers had to interrupt their self-congratulation with a frank admission they had been wrong on a basic issue and pay a salute to Mayor Roy B. Martin, who had succeeded Mr. Duckworth in 1962, and especially to City Manager Thomas F. Maxwell, who had succeeded City Managers Harrell and Sherwood Reeder in 1956. The issue was a local sales tax for Norfolk only, to support an expansion of municipal services, especially in public education.

Both newspapers looked favorably upon a state sales tax. They went hammer and tongs against a proposal they feared would make Norfolk a "sales tax island." So did the influential members of the Norfolk Redevelopment and Housing Authority, who were trying to get a new department store for the redeveloped downtown; so did the retail merchants and so—apparently—most bankers, business and professional men. Mayor Martin, Mr. Maxwell and the City Council stood fast. As soon as Norfolk adopted a sales tax, each neighboring city—one after another—adopted an almost identical tax. The move spread rapidly across Virginia. When the rurally dominated Virginia General Assembly adopted a state sales tax in 1966, the cities were in a much better position to bargain for their fair share because they had followed Norfolk's 1965 lead: Mr. Maxwell's and Mr. Martin's lead.

This was financial statesmanship of great perception and the newspapers admitted it. The *Ledger-Star* congratulated Mr. Maxwell and the Council for calculating "correctly, as it turned out, that in Norfolk's taking the lead, others would be tempted to follow." The *Virginian-Pilot* noted that Charles L. Kaufman, chairman of the Norfolk Redevelopment and Housing Authority, had dined on crow at a Rotary Club meeting in which he, too, saluted the Council. "Move over, Mr. Kaufman," the *Pilot* said, adding "And never did crow taste more like turkey."

Editorially, the *Virginian-Pilot* and *Ledger-Star* had been wrong; but their news columns and letters to the editor columns had made a full discussion possible. And if some editorial ribbons were necessary for a one hundredth anniversary, plenty were available. Lawrence M. Cox, executive director of the redevelopment authority, told an international group in Geneva, Switzerland, that Norfolk's magnificent redevelopment program could not have been undertaken without newspaper support. R. L. Sheetz, executive director of the United Communities Fund, told a meeting in Kansas City that the newspapers were essential to Norfolk's remarkable record of twenty-four straight successful Community Fund campaigns.

Since the creation and infancy of a slum clearance and redevelopment program, the *Virginian-Pilot* and *Ledger-Star* had given sturdy support to the Norfolk Redevelopment and Housing Authority. Their general counsel, Mr. Kaufman, had been the authority's chairman and guiding spirit since its early years. By 1965 the newspapers could look back on a program that cleared 1,061 acres of slum property, created 5,296 public housing apartments, and made land available for such community assets as the rapidly expanding Medical Center, Old Dominion College and Virginia State College, the Kirn Memorial Public Library, the Golden Triangle Hotel, the $15,000,000 civic center, and the cultural and convention center that was in the preconstruction stage. Tall, new buildings were under way for the Virginia National Bank and Seaboard Citizens National Bank in a redeveloped downtown. A new Brambleton Avenue linked the city's eastern and western sides, while the long-planned Waterfront Drive was soon to enter the construction phase. The face of one of the nation's oldest cities had been radically changed—and was still being changed—by the redevelopment program.

Delayed by a few years of political opposition, Portsmouth came along with a similar redevelopment program, transforming a dilapidated waterfront into an attractive area containing a new federal building and Coast Guard headquarters, a new Citizens Trust Company bank building, a navy yard museum, a motel and marina, and a high-rise apartment. At the end of 1965, another dramatic redevelopment program downtown was beginning in Portsmouth.

Any chronicler of the times could prove the newspapers' contribution to the transformation of Norfolk Division, College of William and Mary into an independent Old Dominion College (of which Frank Batten became the first rector) and to the growth of Norfolk Division, Virginia State College. The newspapers had consistently sponsored the creation of the Norfolk and Virginia ports authorities, with a consequent expansion of port facilities; two Norfolk-Portsmouth tunnels, a Hampton Roads Bridge-Tunnel, and the great 17.5-mile Chesapeake Bay Bridge-Tunnel to the Eastern Shore. The Kirn Memorial Library in Norfolk—keystone of an expanding Norfolk Public Library; a new main library in Portsmouth and new library systems in Chesapeake and Virginia Beach—these had long been urged, and were attained. Hospital and school expansions in four cities could be claimed. Perhaps some day even the long newspaper advocacy of better Tidewater highways would succeed.

On the corporate level, the new vigor spilled over into a diversification program. The newspaper company purchased the Greensboro, North Carolina, *Daily News and Record* and an associated television station, effective January, 1965. Bush went to Greensboro as the newspapers' vice president and general manager. The company established a new division—a CATV division which could provide one community antenna and deliver up to thirteen perfect television signals by cable to individual subscribers. At the end of the anniversary year programming or installation was underway in Roanoke Rapids, North Carolina, Beckley, West Virginia, and Princeton, West Virginia.

The rate of change for the tenth decade of a hundredth anniversary was faster than for the first ninety years. In 1965 was completed the second major building expansion in less than ten years—a $2,000,000 project which added a second press building and a Goss press which could produce seventy thousand sixty-four-page newspapers per hour. On November 21, 1965—the hundredth anniversary of the *Virginian*—computers were helping set type, and most display advertising was being set by a photographic (or photocomposition) technique. In twenty years, aided by the merger with the *Star*, the combined daily circulation had grown from 143,278 to 230,392—a gain of 60 per cent. Sunday circulation had gone up even more spectacularly, from 87,558 to 166,539—a gain of 90 per cent. In twenty years, the total working complement had gone from 580 in 1946 to 979 at the end of 1965. Significantly, the greater increase for the last ten years was in the number of news reporters, editors and allied personnel. From a single-man photographic staff—veterans Borjes of the *Pilot* and Vollmer of the *Ledger*—the newspapers grew to a merged photographic staff of twelve craftsmen serving both newspapers.

The new reporters, old hands were willing to concede, were not only more numerous than in early days, they were, as a group, all college-educated. As individuals, none might challenge H. Warner Twyford, George M. Kelley, Jr., and Frank Sullivan, of the *Virginian-Pilot*, or Charlton Harrell, Tom Reilly and Lloyd Lewis, Jr., of the *Ledger-Star*. As a group they began to dominate the Slover Awards, established by Batten in 1960 for consistent excellence and named for his uncle. *Virginian-Pilot* winners in this period were Luther J. Carter, William L. Tazewell, James E. Mays, William K. Stevens, and Donald G. Hill. Runners-up included Glenn A. Scott, Margaret R. Wilkins, Raymond L. Bancroft, Joseph B. Phillips, Russell E. Borjes, James M. Harper, III, and Staige D. Blackford. *Ledger* staff winners were Jack Kestner, Wayne Woodlief and Lawrence W. Bonko. Runners-up included Lewis, Chester J. Paschang, William R. Sauder, Gene A. Owens, James R. Stiff, and Robert Willis. Among the photographers, winners were Orby G. Kelley, Jr., Clifton Guthrie, Noah "Mike" Williams, and James A. Walker, Jr., with the runners-up including Neal V. Clark, Jr., Robert L. Yingling and Charles Meads. These staffs together won more awards in Virginia Press Association competition than the staffs of any other two newspapers from 1955 through 1965. The *Ledger-Star* became the first (and in 1965 the only) newspaper to win three times the VPA's Copeland Award for distinguished service to Virginia.

Often more important than prizes in the newspaper business is the day-by-day bread and butter writing; often more vital are the silent, never bylined news editors who run the shop, correct the reporters' mistakes, lay out the pages and write the headlines. And behind the news editors is a complex of advertising, production, circulation and business staffs equally without bylines but critical to the enterprise. Perhaps the chief characteristic of the *Virginian-Pilot* and *Ledger-Star* staffs from 1945 through 1965 is that they rapidly grew too large to permit, in one brief chapter, the mention of all who made its history. The significance of the prize winning is its mark of grow-

ing competence and size to meet the needs of a new era and a growing population.

News of the world and nation was prominent on the front page of
the *Virginian-Pilot* and *Ledger-Star* in these twenty years and distant
critics frequently asked "why?" The answer was simply that in Tidewater Virginia salt water mixed with printer's ink. The United States
Navy and the merchant marine had given a cosmopolitan touch to
the area even when it was occupied by small towns; the establishment
in 1952 of the Supreme Allied Command Atlantic (SACLANT), the
seagoing part of the North Atlantic Treaty Organization, in Norfolk
gave the area a formal international character. In 1965, amid great
change and expanding horizons, the *Virginian-Pilot* and *Ledger-Star*
could still anchor themselves in the prospectus of the group's first ancestor which advertised in the grim November of 1865 that it "shall
be especially devoted to the advancement of Norfolk and Portsmouth,
and the large sections of Virginia whose interests are common with
theirs." The cities and the sea were inseparable.

BIBLIOGRAPHY

THE BIBLIOGRAPHY OF THIS NEWSPAPER HISTORY MUST START WITH THE newspapers themselves. The files have a few blanks, chiefly among the earlier newspapers, extending in a few instances over a month. But by far the greater part of the files exists today, chiefly in Norfolk with the newspapers and in the Norfolk Public Library. Scattered copies of the newspapers, and occasionally nearly all copies of a newspaper, can be found in other libraries in Virginia and elsewhere. Lester J. Cappon's invaluable *Virginia Newspapers, 1821-1935: A Bibliography with Historical Introduction and Notes,* lists the location of most of these. His "Historical Introduction" contains excellent information.

Joseph E. Shank's reduction of the files to approximately a million words has been recorded in the Preface. The book rests principally on these. In so far as it is a history of Norfolk, Lower Tidewater Virginia, and Virginia, it is the record—or part of it—that the newspapers published. Standard American histories and biographical material, such as the *Dictionary of American Biography,* are necessary adjuncts.

Other books, and in several instances articles from historical journals, that proved useful are listed below:

Bailey, James H. "Anthony M. Keiley and 'The Keiley Incident',"
    Virginia Magazine of History and Biography, Vol. 67 (January,
    1959).
Blake, H. M. *William Mahone of Virginia, Soldier and Political In-
    surgent.* Richmond: Garrett & Massie, 1935.
Borum, Samuel R. *Norfolk, Port and City: Facts and Figures of Its
    Trade, Commerce and Transportation.* Norfolk: Norfolk Cham-
    ber of Commerce, 1896.
Bruce, Philip Alexander. *Virginia: Rebirth of the Old Dominion.*
    Virginia biography by special staff of writers. 5 Vols. Chicago and
    New York: Lewis Publishing Co., 1929.
——. *History of the University of Virginia, 1819-1919: The Length-
    ened Shadow of One Man.* 5 vols. New York: Macmillan, 1920-
    1922.
——, Lyon G. Tyler, Richard L. Morton. *History of Virginia.* 6 vols.
    Vol. 3, "Virginia Since 1861," by Morton; Vols. 4, 5, and 6, biog-

raphies of Virginians by special staff of writers. Chicago and New York: The American Historical Society, 1924.

Burton, H. W. ("Harry Scratch"). *The History of Norfolk, Virginia.* Norfolk: The Norfolk Virginian Job Print, 1877.

Butler, Benjamin F. *Butler's Book: Autobiography and Personal Reminiscences.* Boston: A. M. Thayer & Co., 1892.

——. *Private and Official Correspondence of Major-General Benjamin F. Butler During the Period of the Civil War.* 5 vols. Norwood, Mass.: Plimpton Press, 1917.

Cappon, Lester J. "The Yankee Press in Virginia, 1861-1865," *William and Mary Quarterly*, Vol. 15, Series 2 (January, 1935).

——. *Virginia Newspapers, 1821-1935: A Bibliography with Historical Introduction and Notes.* New York: D. Appleton-Century Co., 1936.

Dabney, Virginius. *Dry Messiah: The Life of Bishop Cannon.* New York: Knopf, 1949.

Davis, Curtis Carroll. "Very Well Rounded Republican: The Several Lives of John S. Wise," *Virginia Magazine of History and Biography*, Vol. 71 (October, 1963).

Eckenrode, H. J. *The Political History of Virginia During the Reconstruction.* Baltimore: The Johns Hopkins Press, 1904.

Forrest, William S. *Historical and Descriptive Sketches of Norfolk and Vicinity.* Philadelphia: Lindsay & Blakiston, 1853.

Holzman, Robert S. *Stormy Ben Butler.* New York: Macmillan, 1954.

Hope, James Barron. *A Wreath of Virginia Bay Leaves.* Poems of James Barron Hope, selected and edited by his daughter, Janey Hope Marr, with introduction and biographical details. Richmond: West, Johnston & Co., 1895.

Johnson, Gerald W., Frank R. Kent, H. L. Mencken, Hamilton Owens. *The Sunpapers of Baltimore.* New York: Knopf, 1937.

Keiley, Charles Russel. *The Official Blue Book of the Jamestown Tercentennial Exposition.* Norfolk: Colonial Publishing Company, 1909.

Kelly, F. C. *The Wright Brothers: A Biography Authorized by Orville Wright.* New York: Harcourt, Brace, 1943.

Lamb, Robert W. *Our Twin Cities of the Nineteenth Century (Norfolk and Portsmouth): Their Past, Present and Future.* Norfolk: Barcroft, 1887.

Mott, Frank Luther. *A History of American Journalism, 1690-1960.* New York: Macmillan, 1963.

Nowitzky, George I. *Norfolk: The Marine Metropolis of Virginia and the Sound and River Cities of North Carolina.* Norfolk: Nowitzky, 1888.

Pearson, Charles Chilton. *The Readjuster Movement in Virginia.* New Haven: Yale University Press, 1917.

Reid, Whitelaw. *After the War: A Southern Tour, May, 1865, to May, 1866.* New York: Moore, Wilstach & Baldwin, 1866.

Sheldon, William DuBose. *Populism in the Old Dominion: Virginia Farm Politics, 1885-1900.* Princeton: Princeton University Press, 1935.

Squires, W. H. T. *The Days of Yester-Year in Colony and Commonwealth: A Sketch Book of Virginia.* Portsmouth: Printcraft Press, 1928.

——. *Through Centuries Three: A Short History of the People of Virginia.* Portsmouth: Portsmouth Press, 1939.

——. *Through the Years in Norfolk.* Norfolk: Norfolk Advertising Board, 1936.

——. *Unleashed at Long Last: Reconstruction in Virginia, April 9, 1865-January 26, 1870.* Portsmouth: Printcraft Press, 1939.

——. Scrapbooks in Sargeant Room, Kirn Memorial Library, Norfolk Public Library, containing articles published in Norfolk *Ledger-Dispatch*, 1935-1948.

Stewart, William H. *History of Norfolk County, Virginia, and Representative Citizens.* Chicago: Biographical Publishing Co., 1902.

Stover, John F. *The Railroads of the South, 1865-1900: A Study in Finance and Control.* Chapel Hill: University of North Carolina Press, 1935.

Tyler, Lyon G., ed. *Encyclopedia of Virginia Biography.* New York: Lewis Historical Publishing Co., 1915.

Wertenbaker, Thomas J. *Norfolk: Historic Southern Port.* Durham: Duke University Press, 1931. Second Edition, edited by Marvin W. Schlegel, 1962.

Whichard, Rogers Dey. *History of Lower Tidewater Virginia.* New York: Lewis Historical Publishing Co., 1959.

Woodward, C. Vann. *The Strange Career of Jim Crow.* New York: Oxford University Press, 1955.

INDEX